LOOKING FOR FORMS OR APPLICATIONS?
DOWNLOAD THE MOST RECENT VERSIONS AT
USPA.ORG/DOWNLOADS

2023-2024 SKYDIVER'S INFORMATION MANUAL

©2022 United States Parachute Association®. All rights reserved. May not be reproduced without the express permission of USPA.

United States Parachute Association
5401 Southpoint Centre Blvd.,
Fredericksburg, VA 22407

(540) 604-9740 (phone)
(540) 604-9741 (Fax)
uspa.org

Cover photo by Bartley Carlson | C-41463
Pete Collies flies through a hoop held by Jack Schafer and Diana Kruchten at Skydive Milwaukee/Sky Knights Sport Parachute Club in East Troy, Wisconsin.

uspa.org/downloads
- ✓ forms
- ✓ most current electronic version
- ✓ mid-cycle change documents

INTRODUCTION

A. PURPOSE AND SCOPE OF THE USPA SKYDIVER'S INFORMATION MANUAL

The Skydiver's Information Manual (SIM) provides basic skydiving standards (the Basic Safety Requirements) and recommendations agreed upon by USPA members for the conduct of safe and enjoyable skydiving. It also describes the programs USPA administers to recognize individuals for their expertise, ability to train others, and proficiency or tenure in the sport.

Although the SIM provides much basic information for skydivers, each jumper should research further and consult USPA and industry officials, documents, and other produced media, as well as other reliable individuals for clarification and additional information.

B. THE SIM AND SKYDIVING'S SELF-POLICING PRINCIPLE OF REGULATION

Although USPA is a voluntary membership association with no regulatory power, USPA can suspend or revoke any USPA license, rating, award, appointment, or membership it issues, according to terms and conditions stated in the USPA Governance Manual. Compliance with the Basic Safety Requirements (BSRs) contained herein is mandatory for participation in USPA programs. The BSRs represent the commonly accepted standards for a reasonable level of safety.

However, the recommendations contained herein, unless otherwise stated (such as in the case of compliance with a Federal Aviation Regulation), are put forth as guidance and are not mandatory. Moreover, a deviation from these recommendations does not necessarily imply negligence and is not to be used in a court of law to demonstrate negligence.

Voluntary compliance with rules, recommendations, and standards within the SIM demonstrates that jumpers and drop zone operators are exercising self-regulation.

C. HOW TO OBTAIN OR RECOMMEND CHANGES TO THIS MANUAL

The SIM from time to time requires updating. It is the responsibility of SIM holders to keep their version current. New copies may be downloaded free of charge from the USPA website, www.uspa.org, or purchased from the USPA Store: (540) 604-9740; 604-9741 (fax), or email membership@uspa.org.

Readers are encouraged to submit comments or recommended changes in writing to USPA, 5401 Southpoint Centre Blvd., Fredericksburg, VA 22407; by phone to (540) 604-9740; by fax to 604-9741; or by email to uspa@uspa.org.

> **This manual provides procedure to address many foreseeable situations, but each situation is different. Deviations from these recommendations does not imply negligence.**

WARNING

IMPORTANT NOTICE

SPORT PARACHUTING OR SKYDIVING IS A POTENTIALLY DANGEROUS ACTIVITY THAT CAN RESULT IN INJURY OR DEATH. EACH INDIVIDUAL PARTICIPANT, REGARDLESS OF EXPERIENCE, HAS FINAL RESPONSIBILITY FOR HIS OR HER OWN SAFETY.

THE FOLLOWING INFORMATION IS PRESENTED AS A MEMBERSHIP SERVICE BY THE UNITED STATES PARACHUTE ASSOCIATION (USPA). USPA MAKES NO WARRANTIES OR REPRESENTATIONS AND ASSUMES NO LIABILITY CONCERNING THE VALIDITY OF ANY ADVICE, OPINION OR RECOMMENDATION EXPRESSED IN THIS MATERIAL. ALL INDIVIDUALS RELYING ON THIS MATERIAL DO SO AT THEIR OWN RISK.

An individual's safety can be enhanced by exercising proper precautions and procedures. This manual contains some of the knowledge and practices that, in the opinion of USPA, will promote the safe enjoyment of skydiving. The UNITED STATES PARACHUTE ASSOCIATION is a nonprofit, voluntary membership organization of the participants and supporters of the sport of parachuting. The sport is also referred to as skydiving. USPA has no involvement in the conduct or operations of any skydiving center, parachute center, or drop zone. **USPA, AS A PRIVATE, NON-REGULATORY ORGANIZATION WHICH HAS NO LEGAL AUTHORITY TO REGULATE OR CONTROL INDIVIDUALS OR CORPORATIONS, CANNOT BE HELD LIABLE FOR ANY JUMP OR TRAINING OPERATIONS THAT RESULT IN INJURY OR DEATH TO ANY PARTY.** Regardless of any statements made in any USPA publications, USPA has neither been given nor has it assumed any duty to anyone. USPA has no obligation to anyone concerning his or her skydiving activities. All references by USPA to self-regulation refer to each individual person regulating or being responsible for him or herself. USPA issues various licenses, ratings, awards, and appointments and provides various types of information, advice, and training but does not authorize anyone in any capacity to act for USPA as an agent or representative in connection with the regulation or control of skydiving operations.

It is the responsibility of each student to ask whatever questions are necessary for him or her to have a thorough understanding of the actions and procedures that he or she must perform in order to make a safe jump. Each skydiver has the responsibility to exercise certain practices and perform certain actions to maintain safety for himself or herself and for other people.

USPA MAKES NO WARRANTIES, EXPRESSED OR IMPLIED, AS TO THE INFORMATION SET FORTH IN THIS MANUAL. PEOPLE RELYING THEREON DO SO AT THEIR OWN RISK.

CONTENTS

i	**Introduction**
ii	**Warning**
iv	**USPA Values Statement**
1	**Section 1: The United States Parachute Association**
2	The United States Parachute Association (Overview)
3	**Section 2: Basic Safety Requirements and Waivers**
4	Basic Safety Requirements and Waivers (Overview)
5	2-1: Basic Safety Requirements
9	2-2: Waivers to the Basic Safety Requirements
11	**Section 3: Classification of Skydivers**
12	3-1: USPA Licenses
14	3-2: License Exam and Application Procedures
16	3-3: Ratings
17	**Section 4: USPA Integrated Student Program**
19	4-2: Categories A-H Objectives Overview
20	4-3: USPA Integrated Student Program: An Introduction
23	4-A: Category A
37	4-B: Category B
45	4-C: Category C
55	4-D: Category D
63	4-E: Category E
71	4-F: Category F
79	4-G: Category G
87	4-H: Category H
93	**Section 5: General Recommendations**
94	5-1: Skydiving Emergencies
99	5-2: Currency Training
100	5-3: Equipment
104	5-4: Pre-Jump Safety Checks and Briefings
106	5-5: Weather
107	5-6: Aircraft
108	5-7: Spotting
109	5-8 Incident Reports

111	**Section 6: Advanced Progression**
112	6-1: Group Freefall (Relative Work)
113	6-2: Freeflying, Freestyle and Skysurfing
115	6-3: Freefall Rate of Descent and Time Table
116	6-4: Night Jumps
118	6-5: Water Landings
120	6-6: Canopy Formations
123	6-7: High Altitude and Oxygen Use
128	6-8: Camera Flying Recommendations
131	6-9: Wingsuit First Flight Course (FFC) Syllabus
137	6-10: Canopy Flight Fundamentals
140	6-11: Advanced Canopy Piloting Topics
146	6-12: Movement Jumps
149	**Section 7: Exhibition Jumping and Rating**
150	7-1: Exhibition Jumping
153	7-2: Professional Exhibition Rating
156	7-3: Instructions for completing FAA Form 7711-2
157	**Section 8: Membership Awards Programs**
158	8-1: Service Awards
168	8-2: Achievement Awards
169	8-3: Performance awards
170	8-4: Membership Tenure Certificates
171	8-5: Sportsmanship Award
173	**Section 9: FAA Documents**
174	9-1: Federal Aviation Regulations
192	9-2: Advisory Circulars
211	9-3: FAA Air Traffic Bulletins
213	**Glossary**
221	**Appendix A: Freefall Hand Signals**
223	**Appendix B: USPA Category Quiz Answers**
227	**Appendix C: USPA License Study Guide**

USPA VALUES STATEMENT

USPA is committed to promoting an atmosphere that allows our sport to be safe, inclusive and fun. We advocate for the dignity and well-being of all individuals and respect diverse traditions, heritages and experiences. We value inclusivity and reject discrimination based on race, ethnicity, gender, sexual orientation, religious belief or any other attribute not related to performance or merit. USPA affirms its vision of a safe and healthy skydiving environment free of violence and any form of discrimination, including sexual or racial harassment.

For additional information, refer to the USPA Policy Regarding Discrimination and Harassment in Governance Manual Section 1-9.

Section 1

THE UNITED STATES PARACHUTE ASSOCIATION

SECTION SUMMARY:

The United States Parachute Association is a membership organization, incorporated as a not-for-profit association, such that each regular member has an equal vote and an equal voice in establishing the policies of the Association.

In its sporting role, USPA is the official U.S. skydiving representative recognized by the National Aeronautic Association (NAA) and the official skydiving representative of the Fédération Aéronautique Internationale (FAI) in the USA.

In its governing role, USPA is officially recognized by the Federal Aviation Administration (FAA) as the representative of skydivers in the United States.

USPA is an organization of skydivers, run by skydivers for skydivers, and it is your voice in skydiving. USPA keeps skydivers skydiving.

WHO NEEDS THIS SECTION?

- anyone first getting acquainted with USPA

1 THE UNITED STATES PARACHUTE ASSOCIATION

THE UNITED STATES PARACHUTE ASSOCIATION (OVERVIEW)

A. YOUR USPA REPRESENTATIVES

USPA Regional Directors are jumpers from your region of the country and are elected by you (and the other members within your region) to the USPA Board every three years. There are 14 USPA Regions and, therefore, 14 USPA Regional Directors. The USPA Board also includes eight National Directors, elected by the USPA membership at large.

Nearly all drop zones have at least one USPA S&TA who is appointed by and serves as your direct link to your USPA Regional Director. The S&TA is a local jumper who is available on your drop zone to provide you with administrative services and information.

B. USPA LEADERSHIP

The members of the USPA Board elect officers, including a president, vice president, secretary, treasurer, and chair of the board. The officers, together with an additional member-at-large, also elected from among the USPA Board members, make up the USPA Executive Committee. The Executive Committee is responsible for making decisions and taking care of important matters that arise between the USPA Board meetings.

C. USPA POLICY MAKING

The USPA Board of Directors establishes USPA policies and procedures during meetings held twice a year. The board operates through a committee system comprised of USPA Board members with special qualifications and interests. Each of the committees provide guidance and advice in major areas of activity within the sport.

The actions of each working committee must be approved by the full USPA Board before becoming USPA policy. Each USPA Director has one vote at USPA Board meetings. Voting responsibility includes not only making business decisions and setting policy, but also the establishment and modification of the Basic Safety Requirements and official USPA Recommendations. USPA Board members cast their votes based on the input they receive from their constituency (the membership) and their own judgment.

D. THE USPA HEADQUARTERS STAFF

Between the meetings of the USPA Board, held twice each year, USPA's administrative staff conducts the day-to-day business of the organization. The USPA Board hires the Executive Director, who assumes all the various responsibilities and duties assigned by the USPA Board. The Executive Director, in turn, hires the staff, which operates from USPA Headquarters, in Fredericksburg, Virginia.

In summary, USPA Headquarters, led by the Executive Director, serves the USPA membership and carries out the instructions and policies set by the Board of Directors.

E. USPA CONSTITUTION AND BY-LAWS

USPA operates under a constitution and by-laws that define the organization's purpose. They are contained in the USPA Governance Manual, available on USPA's website or from USPA Headquarters.

United States Parachute Association
5401 Southpoint Centre Blvd.
Fredericksburg, Virginia 22407
(540) 604-9740 (phone)
(540) 604-9741 (fax)
uspa@uspa.org
www.uspa.org

Section 2

BASIC SAFETY REQUIREMENTS AND WAIVERS

SECTION SUMMARY:

Skydiving is based on the Basic Safety Requirements (BSRs) that have been established as the cornerstone of a self-policing principle. The BSRs represent the industry standard generally agreed upon as necessary for an adequate level of safety. Research can be conducted to develop and document new methods and procedures within the BSRs and, when necessary, under waivers to the BSRs, to establish a justifiable basis to modify these standards. This section includes two fundamental, interrelated USPA publications: the Basic Safety Requirements and Waivers to the Basic Safety Requirements.

WHO NEEDS THIS SECTION?

- jumpers studying for license tests
- USPA instructional rating candidates
- drop zone staff responsible for setting policies
- USPA officials

2 BASIC SAFETY REQUIREMENTS AND WAIVERS

BASIC SAFETY REQUIREMENTS AND WAIVERS (OVERVIEW)

A. HOW THE BSRS AFFECT SAFETY

1. The BSRs promote practices aimed at eliminating incidents in skydiving and, by doing so, make skydiving safer and more enjoyable.
2. The BSRs are established by evaluating incidents and identifying their root causes.
3. Safety is accomplished by reducing the risk factors, which requires everyone involved in skydiving to:
   a. acquire knowledge and make a continuing effort to increase and improve that knowledge
   b. practice and prepare for both the expected and the unexpected
   c. evaluate the risk factors
   d. accurately evaluate personal capabilities and limitations
   e. stay alert and aware of surroundings
   f. keep options open
   g. exercise good judgment
4. Failure to follow the BSRs may not always result in an incident, but many incidents are the result of not following these risk-reduction procedures.

B. WAIVERS AND CHANGES TO THE BSRS

1. Also included in this section, "Waivers to the Basic Safety Requirements" describes procedures for approving and documenting exceptions to the BSRs.
   a. Waivers provide for the responsible development of new techniques and methods.
   b. The BSRs are designed to establish safety standards for common situations; however, local circumstances may allow for greater tolerance in some cases.
   c. The purpose for filing a waiver is to document that the particular BSR has been evaluated in the individual case and that the prescribed deviation and conditions do not represent an unacceptable compromise of safety.
   d. Waiverability
      (1) Each BSR is categorized for the level of authority necessary for the approval of the waiver.
      (2) Each BSR requires full board approval of a waiver, except for those designated with an [S] (S&TA or Examiner), or an [E] (Executive Committee).
2. The BSRs are changed from time to time by the USPA Board of Directors as equipment and practices develop and evolve.

2-1: BASIC SAFETY REQUIREMENTS

Note: Every BSR requires full board approval if a waiver is requested, unless the BSR has a marginal notation of [S] or [E], which identifies its waiverability by others as indicated in Section 2-2.

A. APPLICABILITY

1. The Basic Safety Requirements apply to all jumps except those made under military orders, or those training personnel under military orders, and those made because of in-flight emergencies. USPA members must comply with the Basic Safety Requirements, protecting the best interests of both the participants and the general public.
2. A "skydive" is defined as the descent of a person to the surface from an aircraft in flight when he or she uses or intends to use a parachute during all or part of that descent.
3. All persons participating in skydiving should be familiar with the Skydiver's Information Manual and all federal, state, and local regulations and rules pertaining to skydiving.

B. COMPLIANCE WITH FEDERAL REGULATIONS

1. For skydives made within the U.S. and its territories and possessions, no skydive may be made in violation of Federal Aviation Administration (FAA) regulations.
2. FAA regulations include the use of restraint systems in the aircraft by all skydivers during movement on the surface, takeoff, and landing. [FAR 91.107]

C. MEDICAL REQUIREMENTS

1. All persons engaging in skydiving must:
   a. Possess at least a current FAA Third-Class Medical Certificate; or
   b. Carry a certificate of physical and mental fitness for skydiving from a registered physician; or
   c. Agree with the USPA recommended medical statement in Section 4-3.
2. Any skydiver acting as tandem parachutist in command must possess a current FAA Third-Class Medical or military flight or diver physicals that are required by their position or duty status by their military command authority. Alternatively, if acting as tandem parachutist in command outside the United States, its territories or possessions, a current medical certificate recognized by the civil aviation authority of the country where they will be exercising their tandem rating privileges may be substituted.
   a. A tandem parachutist in command with a medical condition that would not allow the use of their FAA medical certificate to act as a pilot in command of an aircraft may not act as a tandem parachutist in command.
   b. A tandem parachutist in command with a medical condition that would not allow the use of the privileges of their USPA accepted equivalent medical certificate may not act as a tandem parachutist in command.
3. Any foreign national in the United States, its territories or possessions for the purpose of qualifying as a tandem parachutist in command, or to fulfill rating renewal or currency requirements, must be under the direct supervision of a tandem examiner and must possess a current FAA Third-Class Medical Certificate or a current medical certificate recognized by the civil aviation authority of the country where they will be exercising their tandem rating privileges.

D. AGE REQUIREMENTS

1. For skydives made within the U.S. and its territories and possessions, skydivers are to be at least 18 years of age. [E, during interim]
2. For skydives made outside the U.S. and its territories and possessions, the minimum age is specified by the country's (or its national air sport control's) requirements. Such skydivers who are under 16 years of age will not be issued a USPA license.
3. A waiver for tandem jumps may be issued to terminally ill persons under the age of 18 with manufacturer approval. The organizer of such jumps must submit a USPA Waiver Request form to the director of safety and training and the chairman of safety and training committee for approval prior to such jumps.

E. MEMBERSHIP

USPA membership is required of any skydiver cleared for self-supervision at a USPA Group Member drop zone, except for non-resident foreign nationals that are a member of their own national aero club.

F. ALCOHOL AND DRUGS

1. No person may make a parachute jump, or attempt to make a jump, if that person is or appears to be under the influence of either;
   a. alcohol.
   b. any drug that affects that person's faculties in any way contrary to safety.
2. No person may make a parachute jump, or attempt to make a jump, within 8 hours after the consumption of any alcoholic beverage.

G. STUDENT SKYDIVERS

Note: All references to USPA instructional rating holders apply to higher rating holders in that training discipline.

1. General [E]
   a. All student training programs must be conducted under the supervision as required by an appropriately rated USPA Instructor until the student is issued a USPA A license.
   b. A person conducting, training, or supervising student jumps must hold a USPA instructional rating according to the requirements that follow.
   c. On any student jump, the supervising instructor or both instructors if a two-instructor jump, must submit a completed incident report to USPA within 48 hours if any AAD was activated on the jump. No disciplinary action will result from this self-report
   d. Each Instructor or Coach must ensure that all gear used on a student jump has received a complete gear check and is ready to jump before boarding the aircraft.
2. First-jump course [E]
   a. All first-jump non-method-specific training must be conducted by a USPA Instructor or a USPA Coach under the supervision of a USPA Instructor.
   b. All method-specific training must be conducted by a USPA Instructor rated in the method for which the student is being trained.
3. All students must receive training in the following areas, sufficient to jump safely [E]
   a. equipment
   b. aircraft and exit procedures
   c. freefall procedures (except IAD and static-line jumps)

2-1 BASIC SAFETY REQUIREMENTS

   d. deployment procedures and parachute emergencies
   e. canopy flight procedures
   f. landing procedures and emergencies
4. Advancement criteria
   a. IAD and static line [E]
      (1) All jumps must be conducted by a USPA Instructor in that student's training method.
      (2) Before being cleared for freefall, all students must perform three successive jumps with practice deployments while demonstrating the ability to maintain stability and control from exit to opening.
      (3) All students must be under the direct supervision of an appropriately rated instructor until completing one successful clear-and-pull.
      (4) Following a successful clear-and-pull, each student must be supervised in the aircraft and in freefall by a USPA Coach or Instructor until demonstrating stability and heading control prior to and within five seconds after initiating two intentional disorienting maneuvers involving a back-to-earth presentation.
      (5) All ground training must be conducted by an instructor in that student's training method, until demonstrating stability and heading control prior to and within five seconds after initiating two intentional disorienting maneuvers involving a back-to-earth presentation.
   b. Harness-hold program
      (1) All students must jump with two USPA AFF rating holders until demonstrating the ability to reliably deploy in the belly to-earth orientation at the correct altitude without assistance, except:
         (i) Students who have been trained in a wind tunnel may jump with one AFF rating holder after demonstrating the following in the wind tunnel:
            - basic stability (neutral body position)
            - heading control
            - controlled forward and backward motion
            - controlled turns
            - proper response to hand signals
            - simulated altimeter checks and time awareness
            - wave-offs
            - simulated main parachute activation
         (ii) The wind tunnel training and tunnel flight sessions must be conducted by an AFF rating holder, or a tunnel instructor who is under the direct supervision of an AFF rating holder. All training must be documented.
      (2) All students must jump with one USPA AFF rating holder, exit safely, maintain stability, and deploy at the planned altitude without assistance prior to attempting disorienting maneuvers.
      (3) All students must jump under the direct supervision of an appropriately rated USPA Instructor until demonstrating stability and heading control prior to and within five seconds after initiating two intentional disorienting maneuvers involving a back-to-earth presentation.
   c. Tandem training jumps [E]
      (1) Any USPA member conducting a tandem jump must have successfully completed a tandem instructor course conducted by the manufacturer of the tandem parachute system used in the parachute operation, been certified by the appropriate parachute manufacturer or tandem course provider as being properly trained on the use of the specific tandem parachute system to be used, and must hold a current USPA Tandem instructor rating.
      (2) For progressive training requirements following tandem jumps, refer to "Crossover training."
      (3) Intentional back-to-earth or vertical orientations that cause tandem freefall speeds exceeding that of droguefall are prohibited.
      (4) Tandem equipment instruction must be conducted by an individual approved by the tandem equipment manufacturer of that system.
      (5) All student tandem skydives must be conducted in accordance with the specific manufacturer's age requirements for the tandem system used for that jump.
      (6) Use of any extendable or fixed pole camera mounts, attached or hand-held by the tandem instructor or student, is prohibited.
      (7) Any person acting as parachutist in command on a tandem skydive is required to conduct system-handles checks as defined by the manufacturer of the specified tandem equipment being used immediately after deploying the drogue.
      (8) Any person making a tandem skydive may not perform a turn of more than 90 degrees below 500 feet AGL.
      (9) Tandem instructors must have at least 200 tandem skydives before any camera device may be used, held or attached to the tandem instructor or tandem student.
5. Crossover training [E]
   a. Students may transfer after the first or subsequent jumps to another training method after demonstrating sufficient knowledge and skill in the areas of equipment, aircraft, exits, freefall maneuvers, deployment, emergency procedures, canopy control, and rules and recommendations to enter into that program at a comparable level of proficiency and training.
   b. Students previously trained in a tandem program may continue in a harness-hold program or must demonstrate a solo exit and practice deployment with stability in the IAD or static-line program prior to advancing to freefall.
   c. Students who have completed at least two tandem jumps and demonstrated the ability to reliably pull the drogue release at the correct altitude, maintain heading and a stable body position, without requiring any control or altitude prompts from the

tandem instructor, may progress to single instructor AFF jumps after completion of solo ground training.

d. Students previously trained in a harness-hold program must have exited stable without assistance or performed a stable IAD or static-line jump with a practice deployment supervised by a USPA IAD or Static-Line Instructor prior to performing freefall jumps with any non-AFF-rated USPA Instructor.

e. Students previously trained in Categories A-C in SL, IAD and tandem programs may jump with one AFF instructor after demonstrating the AFF wind tunnel requirements.

6. Students training for group freefall [S]

a. Student freefall training for group freefall jumps must be conducted by either a USPA Coach or a D-license holder approved to make coach jumps by their S&TA, under the supervision of a USPA Instructor, and;

b. The maximum group size allowed for any group skydive is four if that group includes any solo students cleared for self-supervision. The solo student must have successfully demonstrated the skills of ISP Category G. There must be at least one instructor, coach or D-license holder (that has been approved by an S&TA) for each student involved.

7. Instruction of foreign students [E]

a. Foreign non-resident instructional rating holders appropriately and currently rated by their national aero club may train students from that nation in the U.S., provided the instruction is conducted in accordance with the USPA Basic Safety Requirements.

b. Appropriately and currently rated USPA instructional rating holders may assist in this training.

8. No skydiver will simultaneously perform the duties of a USPA instructional rating holder and pilot-in-command of an aircraft in flight.

9. All student jumps, including tandems, must be completed between official sunrise and sunset.

H. WINDS [S]

Maximum ground winds

1. For all solo students

a. 14 mph for ram-air canopies

b. 10 mph for round reserves

2. For licensed skydivers are unlimited

I. MINIMUM OPENING ALTITUDES

Minimum container opening altitudes above the ground for skydivers are:

1. Tandem jumps–5,000 feet AGL [E]

2. All students and A-license holders–3,000 feet AGL [E]

3. B-license holders–2,500 feet AGL [E]

4. C- and D-license holders–2,500 feet AGL [S] (waiverable to no lower than 2,000 feet AGL)

J. DROP ZONE REQUIREMENTS

1. Areas used for skydiving should be unobstructed, with the following minimum radial distances to the nearest hazard: [S]

a. solo students and A-license holders—330 feet

b. B- and C-license holders and all tandem skydives—165 feet

c. D-license holders—40 feet

2. Hazards are defined as telephone and power lines, towers, buildings, bodies of water, highways, vehicles, and trees covering more than 32,292 square feet. However, clusters of trees must not be greater than 10% of the designated landing area.

3. Manned ground-to-air communications (e.g., radios, panels, smoke, lights) are to be present on the drop zone during skydiving operations.

K. PRE-JUMP REQUIREMENTS

The appropriate altitude and surface winds are to be determined prior to conducting any skydive.

L. EXTRAORDINARY SKYDIVES

1. Night, water, and demonstration jumps are to be performed only with the advice of the appropriate USPA S&TA, Examiner, or Regional Director.

2. Pre-planned breakaway jumps are to be made by only class C- and D-license holders using FAA TSO'ed equipment. [E]

3. Demonstration jumps into Level 2 areas require a D license with a USPA PRO Rating for all jumpers, including both tandem jump participants. [E]

4. Contact canopy formation activity is prohibited on tandem jumps. [E]

5. Tandem jumps into stadiums are prohibited. [E]

6. Any person performing a wingsuit jump must have at least 200 skydives, and hold a current skydiving license. [E]

7. Freefall within 500 feet vertically or horizontally of any student under parachute, including tandem students, is prohibited. (This requirement excludes scenarios where—during a training jump—a student's instructor(s) and videographer may be within this distance.) Freefall within 500 feet vertically or horizontally of any licensed skydiver under canopy requires prior planning and agreement between the canopy pilot and the skydiver in freefall.

M. PARACHUTE EQUIPMENT

1. FAA regulations [FAR 105.19] require that when performing night jumps, each skydiver must display a light that is visible for at least three statute miles from the time the jumper is under an open parachute until landing.

2. All students are to be equipped with the following equipment until they have obtained a USPA A license:

a. a rigid helmet (except tandem students)

b. a piggyback harness-and-container system that includes a single-point riser release and a reserve static line

c. a visually accessible altimeter (except tandem students)

d. a functional automatic activation device that meets the manufacturer's recommended service schedule

e. a ram-air main canopy suitable for student use

f. a steerable reserve canopy appropriate to the student's weight

g. for freefall, a ripcord-activated, spring-loaded, pilot-chute-equipped main parachute or a bottom-of-container (BOC) throw-out pilot chute

3. Students must receive additional ground instruction in emergency procedures and deployment-specific information before jumping any unfamiliar system.

4. All instructional rating holders must have a visibly accessible altimeter when conducting student jumps.

5. All skydivers wearing a round main or reserve canopy and all solo students must wear flotation gear when the intended exit, opening, or landing point is within one mile of an open body of

water (an open body of water is defined as one in which a skydiver could drown). [S]

N. SPECIAL ALTITUDE EQUIPMENT AND SUPPLEMENTARY OXYGEN

Supplementary oxygen available on the aircraft is mandatory on skydives made from higher than 15,000 feet (MSL).

2-2: WAIVERS TO THE BASIC SAFETY REQUIREMENTS

A. WHY BSRS MAY NEED TO BE WAIVED

1. The Basic Safety Requirements represent commonly accepted standards necessary to promote safety in average conditions.
2. Since these standards may be an unnecessary burden in some individual circumstances, USPA provides procedures to document exceptions, known as waivers to the BSRs.
3. These waivers also provide for the responsible research and development of improved techniques and methods.

B. CLASSIFICATION OF WAIVERS

1. Waivers to the Basic Safety Requirements are filed at three levels:
   a. the USPA S&TA or USPA Examiner
   b. the Executive Committee of USPA
   c. full Board of Directors of USPA
2. Neither USPA Headquarters nor any other person or group of persons except those here stated has the authorization to file a waiver to any BSR.
3. Each BSR is waiverable only by the full board, except for those BSRs designated as being waiverable by:
   a. S&TA or Examiner only [S]
   b. Executive Committee of the USPA Board only [E]

C. PROCEDURES FOR FILING WAIVERS

1. Waivers are to be filed only when the person(s) filing the waiver is assured that there will be no compromise of safety.
2. Inspections
   a. The person(s) filing the waiver should make periodic inspections to ensure that safety is not being compromised and to determine if the waiver should be rescinded.
   b. In the case of waivers by the Executive Committee, the Regional Director will perform these inspections and make recommendations to the Board.
3. Form of waiver
   a. Any waiver filed by an S&TA or Examiner except for the deployment altitude exception in 2-1.I.4 will be in writing on the waiver form available for download at uspa.org.
   b. A copy of the waiver will be sent to both the USPA Regional Director and USPA Headquarters.
   c. The S&TA may waive the minimum deployment altitude for C and D license holders from 2,500 feet down to 2,000 feet for a jump or a series of jumps if necessary.
   d. The deployment altitude waiver does not require any written notification to USPA Headquarters or the Regional Director, however the S&TA should make a note of the waiver for his own records.
4. S&TAs are not to file waivers for skydiving activities outside their assigned area.
5. If there is a conflict between an S&TA and an Examiner as to whether a waiver should be filed, the decision of the S&TA will be final.
6. The Executive Committee or full Board of Directors will not approve a waiver without consulting and notifying the local S&TA or USPA Regional Director.
7. Any waivers filed by S&TAs or Examiners must specify a location with a copy to USPA Headquarters and the USPA Regional Director for that location.
8. The waiver will remain in place permanently unless the drop zone changes ownership or location, or the S&TA or Regional Director rescinds the waiver.

D. FILING OF WAIVERS

1. Persons filing waivers will maintain permanent records of all waivers filed by themselves.
   a. The S&TA and Regional Director will maintain permanent records of all waivers filed for skydiving activities within their area.
   b. The records will be kept in such a manner as to indicate those waivers currently in effect and those that have been rescinded.
2. USPA Headquarters will maintain a permanent record of all waivers.

2-2 WAIVERS TO THE BASIC SAFETY REQUIREMENTS

Section 3

CLASSIFICATION OF SKYDIVERS

SECTION SUMMARY:

Skydivers can qualify for and receive a variety of licenses and ratings according to their experience, skill, and knowledge level.

USPA Licenses are essentially documents of proficiency and are divided into four classes from the lowest to highest levels: A, B, C, and D.

Many skydivers also pursue ratings, which require qualifications in addition to those required for licenses. Three separate types of ratings can be obtained as an individual develops expertise in a specific area, such as student instruction, professional demonstration jumping, and competition judging. The FAA issues certificates for riggers, pilots, and aircraft mechanics, which may be of interest to skydivers.

This section of the SIM describes the requirements and privileges of USPA licenses. For more details on the USPA instructional ratings, see the USPA Instructional Rating Manual. For the USPA PRO Exhibition rating, see SIM Section 7, "Exhibition Jumping." For information on competition judging, see the USPA Skydiver's Competition Manual. And for FAA ratings, refer to the FAA documents included in this manual.

IMPORTANT REFERENCE NUMBERS
- license requirements and privileges—3-1.E
- license exam instructions—3-2.A
- application checklist—3-2.C

WHO NEEDS THIS SECTION?
- jumpers seeking licenses
- USPA officials certifying license applications and administering license exams

3-1: USPA LICENSES

A. BACKGROUND

1. License requirements are intended to encourage the development of the knowledge and skills that should be acquired by each skydiver as experience is gained.
2. USPA licenses, recognized in all FAI member countries, serve as official documentation that the stated experience and skills have been attained.
3. Licenses are a valuable instructional tool in that they serve both as goals to be accomplished and as a guideline to acquire the skills and knowledge necessary to provide a reasonable level of safety and enjoyment.
4. USPA license authority
   a. The United States Parachute Association is authorized by the National Aeronautic Association and the Fédération Aéronautique Internationale to issue internationally recognized sporting licenses.
   b. Licenses are issued based upon demonstration of skill, knowledge, and experience and are ranked according to the level of accomplishment.

B. GENERAL CONDITIONS FOR LICENSES

1. USPA licenses are valid only while the holder is a current regular USPA member or a current temporary USPA member; there is no other renewal requirement.
2. USPA ratings are only valid while the holder is a current regular USPA member.
3. USPA licenses are valid in all FAI member countries and, while valid, entitle the holder to participate in open skydiving events organized in FAI member countries.
4. USPA issues licenses only to USPA members who meet the conditions set forth for that license.
5. License qualifications made during military training jumps and all the dive flows and ground training requirements outlined in the USPA ISP must be properly recorded on the USPA A license progression card or higher license application for that USPA license and verified by the appropriate USPA official.
6. Total freefall time is defined to include both freefall and droguefall time.
7. Static line and IAD jumps count towards jump numbers needed for licenses and ratings.
8. USPA licenses may be refused, suspended, or revoked only when authorized by the USPA Board of Directors or in compliance with existing USPA Board directives.

C. LOGGING JUMPS FOR LICENSES AND RATINGS

1. Skydives offered as evidence of qualification must have been:
   a. made in accordance with the USPA requirements in effect at the time of the jump
   b. legibly recorded in chronological order in an appropriate log that contains the following information:
      (1) jump number
      (2) date
      (3) location
      (4) exit altitude
      (5) freefall length (time)
      (6) type of jump (formation skydiving, freeflying, canopy formation, style, etc.)
      (7) landing distance from the target
      (8) equipment used
      (9) verifying signature to include a legible USPA membership number, skydiving license number, or pilot certificate number
2. Jumps to meet the number of jumps requirements for USPA licenses and ratings must be signed by a witness of the jump who may be another licensed skydiver, pilot, Instructor, Examiner, S&TA, or board member.
3. Jumps to meet skill requirements must be signed by a Coach, Instructor, Examiner, S&TA, or Board member. Special requirements and additional qualifying items needed for Examiner ratings such as air evaluations, ground evaluations, and teaching requirements must be logged and signed by an Examiner.
4. Use of digital devices for logging skydives
   a. Many skydivers use digital devices to log skydives, instead of traditional paper logbooks.
   b. Any jump logged in a digital device must contain the required information, including a signature verification from a licensed skydiver, the pilot, or a USPA National or FAI Judge who witnessed the skydive.
   c. Each instructor, S&TA or Examiner who verifies license requirements for a USPA license must review and verify the jumps logged in a digital device.
   d. For skydivers who are pursuing licenses and ratings, it is especially critical that the first 500 jumps are clearly logged and easily verifiable by the officials who must verify the jumps for licenses and ratings.

D. VERIFICATION OF APPLICATION

1. Experience verification: The certifying official should verify that the number of jumps and total freefall time are correct and meet the listed requirements for the license sought.
2. Skill verification: Jump numbers, scores, or date(s) of completion require the initials of a current USPA Instructor, S&TA, Examiner, or USPA Board member.
3. Except for jumps to meet the number of jump requirements; all jumps needed to meet requirements for licenses or ratings must be signed by an Instructor, Examiner, S&TA, or board member. Special requirements and additional qualifying items needed for an Examiner ratings such as FJCs, air evaluations, ground evaluations, and teaching requirements must be logged and signed by the S&TA, Examiner, or board member.
4. Signature Verification: Applications for all licenses must be signed by an appropriate official (as listed in this Section) before the application is forwarded to USPA Headquarters.
   a. USPA Instructors may verify A, B, and C licenses.
   b. S&TAs, Examiners, and USPA Board members may verify any license application.
5. Every USPA B license must also include a completed and signed copy of the Canopy Piloting Proficiency Card.
6. The completed Canopy Proficiency Card must be signed by a current USPA S&TA, Examiner, or board member.
   a. The S&TA must ensure that a qualified course director conducts the training in this section.
   b. In some situations, the best candidate to teach this material may

not hold any USPA ratings, but may have extensive knowledge about canopy control and landings.

c. The signature of the S&TA on the proficiency card is to verify that the training has been satisfactorily completed by the candidate.

7. You may not sign for your own license application or initial any of the verification blocks of your own license application.

8. USPA will charge a separate license fee for each license number issued.

E. LICENSE PRIVILEGES AND REQUIREMENTS

A LICENSE

Note: USPA Headquarters will accept either completed card signed by a USPA Instructor without the official stamp. The registration fee must be included.

1. Persons holding a USPA A license may jump without supervision, pack their own main parachute, engage in basic group jumps, perform water jumps, and must have—

   a. completed 25 freefall skydives

   b. completed all requirements listed on the USPA A License Proficiency Card

   c. completed five group freefall skydives involving at least two participants

   d. received the signature and official stamp on the USPA A License Proficiency Card or USPA A License Progression Card (ISP) which validates the A license for a 60-day time limit following the completion of the card

   e. The completed and signed USPA A License Proficiency Card or USPA A License Progression Card must be validated within 60-days of completion by sending the card to USPA Headquarters. Once validated, USPA will issue a license number that becomes a permanent record of the member.

   f. passed the USPA-developed written and oral USPA A-license exams conducted by a current USPA I, Examiner, S&TA, Judge or board member

B LICENSE

1. Persons holding a USPA B license are able to exercise all privileges of an A-license holder, perform night jumps, with 100 jumps are eligible for the USPA Coach Rating, and must have—

   a. met all current requirements for, or hold, a USPA A license

   b. completed 50 jumps including:

      (1) accumulated at least 30 minutes of controlled freefall time

      (2) landed within 33 feet of target center on ten jumps

   c. successful completion of the planned formation(s) on ten formation skydives, or ten formation freefly skydives, at least five of which, in either discipline, must involve at least three participants

   d. documentation of live water landing training with full equipment in accordance with the procedures in the Skydiver's Information Manual

   e. complete all of the requirements listed on the USPA Canopy Piloting Proficiency Card

   f. passed the written USPA B-license exam conducted by a current USPA I, Examiner, S&TA, Judge or board member.

C LICENSE

1. Persons holding a USPA C license are able to exercise all privileges of a B-license holder, are eligible for the USPA Instructor rating (except USPA Tandem Instructor), participate in certain demonstration jumps, may ride as passenger on USPA Tandem Instructor training and rating renewal jumps, and must have—

   a. met all current requirements for or hold a USPA B license

   b. completed 200 jumps, including accumulating at least 60 minutes of controlled freefall time

   c. landed within seven feet of target center on 25 jumps

   d. Successful completion of fifty formation skydives, or fifty formation freefly skydives, at least ten of which, in either discipline, must involve at least four participants

   e. Passed the USPA written C-license exam conducted by a current USPA I, Examiner, S&TA, Judge or board member.

D LICENSE

1. Persons holding a USPA D license are able to exercise all privileges of a C-license holder, are eligible for all USPA ratings, and must have—

   a. met all current requirements for or hold a USPA C license

   b. completed 500 jumps including accumulating at least three hours of controlled freefall time

   c. completed at least two of the following skills requirements (a requirement may be repeated):

      (1) night jump (following the SIM recommendations)

      (2) landed within seven feet of the target center on 100 jumps

      (3) participated in a canopy formation of a 3-stack or larger, completing a full rotation

      (4) completed an intentional water jump

      (5) successful completion of 100 formation skydives, at least 25 of which must involve at least eight participants

   d. Passed the written USPA D-license exam conducted by a current USPA Examiner, S&TA, Judge Examiner or board member.

F. RESTRICTED USPA LICENSES

1. Under extreme circumstances, such as physical handicaps, a USPA Restricted license may be issued to applicants who are unable to meet all of the specific license requirements.

2. A person may be qualified for a Restricted license if the applicant has (all of the following):

   a. submitted a petition to the Safety & Training Committee, containing:

      (1) type of license requested

      (2) specific license requirement(s) which cannot be met

      (3) circumstances which prevent compliance with license requirements

      (4) license application completed, except for the restricted activities

   b. met all requirements for the license desired except for those listed in the petition

3. Each application will be considered individually on its own merit, totally without precedent.

4. If the waiver is approved by the board of directors, the license will be issued with the word "restricted."

3-2: LICENSE EXAM AND APPLICATION PROCEDURES

A. LICENSE EXAM INSTRUCTIONS

1. A license:

    a. The examining USPA Instructor conducts a 40-question written USPA A-license exam and an oral quiz of at least 20 questions taken from the USPA Integrated Student Program syllabus, with emphasis on the following:

        (1) cloud clearance and visibility requirements

        (2) equipment operation and maintenance

            (i) wing loading and its effects

            (ii) closing loop

            (iii) velcro and tuck flaps

            (iv) packing and authorization to pack

        (3) canopy flight

            (i) traffic patterns and collision avoidance

            (ii) braked turns and obstacle avoidance

            (iii) low turn avoidance and recovery

            (iv) downwind landing procedures

            (v) obstacle landing emergency and recovery procedures

        (4) aircraft procedures

            (i) during jump run and exit to observe balance limits

            (ii) distance between groups to maintain separation

            (iii) aircraft emergency procedures

        (5) group breakoff recommendations

        (6) parachute emergency procedures

            (i) deployment malfunctions

            (ii) cutaway decide-and-act altitude

            (iii) two-canopies-deployed scenarios

        (7) accountability for FAR compliance

    b. The examining USPA Instructor conducts or arranges the review training required for the student to answer all questions correctly.

    c. The examining USPA Instructor conducts a skydive with the applicant to verify practical knowledge in the following areas:

        (1) choosing the spot and selecting and guiding the pilot to the correct exit and opening point in routine conditions

        (2) pre-jump equipment checks for self and others

        (3) planning an effective group break-off

        (4) right 360, left 360, and a back loop (back loop to be completed within 60 degrees of the original heading)

        (5) docking from 20 feet (evaluator flies into position)

        (6) breakoff altitude recognition and tracking for a minimum of 100 feet

        (7) signal before deployment and overall awareness during and after deployment

        (8) planning and flying a logical landing pattern that promotes a smooth traffic flow and avoids other jumpers

        (9) packing and preparing equipment for the next jump

    d. Once the student has successfully completed the A-license check dive and answered all questions correctly on the oral exam and passed the written exam with a score of at least 75%, the certifying USPA Instructor may sign the student's A License Proficiency Card or the USPA A License Progression Card and apply the official USPA A-license stamp as proof of license qualification.

    e. The card is then considered a valid USPA A license for a 60-day time period.

    f. The completed card must be submitted to USPA Headquarters for processing to be considered a valid license beyond the 60-day time period.

2. For B, C, and D licenses, the examining USPA official:

    a. gives the applicant an answer sheet and the questions to the exam

        (1) No references or other assistance are permitted during the exam.

        (2) After the test, the examining official collects the materials and grades the exam.

        (3) A score of 75% is required to pass.

    b. The score is recorded on the license application and in the applicant's logbook.

        (1) The applicant not passing will be eligible to retake this exam after seven days.

        (2) Applicants who have not passed the USPA online license testing program may retest using the same method immediately for a total of three attempts per day.

        (3) To qualify for a higher license, the applicant must possess a USPA license, meet all qualifications for lower licenses, and have passed all lower-class license exams.

B. PRESENTING A COMPLETED LICENSE APPLICATION

1. A license

    a. The completed A license Proficiency Card or USPA A-License Progression Card signed by the certifying USPA Instructor and bearing the official A-license stamp, is proof of a USPA A license for a 60-day period from the completion date.

    b. To receive an A license, the holder must submit a completed A-License card to USPA with the appropriate license registration fee:

        (1) Fax both sides of the completed license application to USPA with a credit card authorization.

        (2) Photocopy both sides of the completed license application and mail it with payment.

        (3) Scan and email a copy of the card to membership@uspa.org

        (4) A completed and signed A-License application need not be stamped to be registered with USPA (USPA keeps a copy of all USPA Instructor signatures on file); however, an A License Proficiency Card is not considered official until the card is submitted to USPA for verification and a license number is issued.

2. B, C, and D license applicants may email, mail or fax their completed application with the appropriate fee to USPA Headquarters.

3. Once any new license has been registered with USPA, the applicant will receive a new membership card with the license number, which is also published in *Parachutist*.

C. LICENSE APPLICATION CHECKLIST

1. The verifying official signing the license application should check that each of these items has been completed:
   a. applicant's personal information
   b. experience verification
      (1) number of jumps
      (2) freefall time, if applicable
   c. skill verification

2. The official verifies (by initialing) either that:
   a. The jump number, date, or score for each requirement is correct and can be found in the applicant's logbook.
   b. If applicable, the applicant's appropriate license number is included with the application.

3. Official verifying B, C, and D licenses should check that the written exam answer sheet is complete with a passing score.

4. For the B License, include a copy of the completed Canopy Piloting Proficiency Card with the license application.

5. Sign and print name, title, and date in the space provided on the application.

3-3: RATINGS

A. USPA INSTRUCTIONAL RATINGS

USPA issues instructional ratings to each skydiver who qualifies by fulfilling all requirements for the rating being sought. These ratings attest that the holder has not only achieved skydiving skills but has also demonstrated the techniques needed to teach these skills to others.

1. Ratings are issued at the following levels (from lowest to highest):
   a. Coach
   b. Instructor
   c. Examiner
2. USPA Instructors may be qualified to conduct initial skydiving training in one or more disciplines:
   a. harness hold (USPA Accelerated Freefall or AFF)
   b. instructor-assisted deployment
   c. static line
   d. tandem

The USPA Coach may act as a supervised assistant to the USPA Instructor to teach specified portions of the first-jump course. Any USPA instructional rating holder may perform the duties of the USPA Coach or of any lower rating holder in his or her discipline.

USPA Examiners appoint qualified instructional rating holders as course evaluators in accordance with the requirements outlined in the USPA Instructional Rating Manual. All policies, procedures, new rating and renewal requirements, and the rating course outlines, support materials and examinations are found in the USPA Instructional Rating Manual.

B. NEWLY RATED INSTRUCTORS

Instructors who have just completed a certification course should be paired with more seasoned staff as they begin to work with students in any new discipline. The Instructional Rating Manual includes recommendations for new rating holders in Section 1 of each of the rating course sections.

C. USPA PRO PROFESSIONAL EXHIBITION RATING

The Federal Aviation Administration and USPA cooperate on an alternative means for skydivers to demonstrate competence to perform skydiving shows before the public via a USPA PRO Exhibition rating. The program is described in the Exhibition Jumping Section of the SIM. The FAA may ask jumpers who do not hold a USPA PRO rating to demonstrate competence prior to issuing a Certificate of Authorization to conduct a parachute exhibition jump.

D. USPA JUDGE RATING

To assist in the administration of skydiving competitions at various levels from local and regional to World Championships, USPA conducts the USPA Judges program. Judges are rated as Regional, National, and International. Details on the USPA Judge rating program and the National Judge Training Course are detailed in the USPA Skydiver's Competition Manual.

E. FAA RATINGS

The Federal Aviation Administration administers the programs that certify parachute riggers, aircraft mechanics, and pilots. The rules for these drop zone staff members are found in the Federal Aviation Regulations, many pertinent parts of which are included in the SIM Section 9, FAA Documents.

Skydiving students study the role of the rigger and supervised packers in detail while preparing for the USPA A license using the Integrated Student Program in the SIM. In addition, they overview pilot rating requirements and the role of the FAA mechanic.

Section 4

USPA INTEGRATED STUDENT PROGRAM

SECTION SUMMARY:

Regardless of discipline, the USPA Integrated Student Program advances students through eight categories of proficiency (A-H) to qualify them for their USPA A license.

Each student completes a series of required skills and knowledge sets while making the prescribed training jumps in each category. At the end of each category, a student in any training discipline has achieved similar skills and knowledge. The number of jumps to complete each category depends on the training discipline and the student's performance.

When a student completes the requirements for each category, the USPA Instructor records it on the student's USPA A-License Proficiency Card and Application and administers an oral quiz. Especially in Categories A-D, the student should complete all the objectives of one category before making any jumps in the next.

An appropriately rated USPA Instructor must directly supervise each student jump until the student is cleared to self supervise during Category E. A USPA Coach may conduct freefall training and supervise jumps for those students in Categories E through H. A USPA Coach may also supervise static-line and IAD students following a successful clear-and-pull in Category C. Until the USPA A license, all student training remains the responsibility of the USPA Instructor.

Once meeting all the requirements listed on the USPA A-License Application, the student will make a check jump with a USPA Instructor to be issued the USPA A license. The check jump consists of an overall review of the training and includes a final quiz with questions taken from the quizzes at the end of each category.

The USPA Integrated Student Program provides one effective and detailed progression for training students for their A license. It is not a required program or the only good training outline. However, students should ensure that the training program at their school meets the USPA standards outlined in the Basic Safety Requirements.

WHO NEEDS THIS SECTION?

- skydiving students
- instructional rating holders
- drop zone staff developing student training programs

4-1: STUDENT SKILL AND KNOWLEDGE SETS

	Jump Numbers and Supervision	Exit and Freefall	Canopy Flight	Equipment	In-Depth Emergency Review*	Rules and Recommendations	Spotting and Aircraft
A	AFF: 1 (Two AFFIs) SL/IAD: 1-2 (SLI/IADI) Tan: 1 (TI)	Adaptation to skydiving environment; principles of deployment	Steering; intro pattern; wind line; landing procedures	Altimeter and operation handle orientation; instructor gear checks	Passive aircraft emergencies (instructor leads)	FAR 91.107 (seat belts); SIM 2-1 (first-jump course topics)	Propeller avoidance; movement in aircraft
B	AFF: 2 (Two AFFIs) SL/IAD: 3-5 (SLI/IADI) Tan: 2-3 (TI)	Relaxed body position; leg awareness; unassisted stable deployment (simulated for SL/IAD)	Assisted pattern; assisted flare; written flight plan; review PLF	Handle operation and protection	Training harness: deployment problems; partial and total malfunctions; stability recovery; and altitude awareness	SIM 2-1 (students), 5-1 (malfunctions); FAA AC-90-66A (illustration of aircraft traffic patterns)	Airport orientation and recognition; runway and approach incursions; aircraft patterns
C	AFF: 3-4 (Two AFFIs, then one) SL/IAD: 6-8 (SLI/IADI) Former Tan: 4-5 (AFFI)	Solo controlled and relaxed fall; heading maintenance; wave-off	Solo pattern and flare; wing loading; turbulence; downwind landings	Complete orientation (main closed); observe pre-flight	Open parachute in aircraft, off-airport landings; obstacle recognition and avoidance; turbulence; collapsing the canopy on landing	SIM 2-1 (student equipment); FAR 105.43.b.1 (equipment); local laws; canopy owner's manual	Pattern selection
D	AFF: 5-6 (AFFI) SL/IAD: 9-12 (SLI/IADI, Coach) Former Tan: 6-7 (AFFI)	Solo exit (AFF); heading control; freefall speeds and times	Back-riser control with and without brakes; stand-up; 165 feet assisted	Assisted pre-flight; AAD operation; AAD owner's manual	Training harness: routine opening problems; instant recognition and response; building landings	SIM 5-1 (buildings), 5-3 (AADs); FAR 105.17 (clouds)	Jump run observation; looking below for aircraft
E	AFF: 7-9 (AFFI) until cleared from AFF, then Coach SL/IAD: 13-15 (SLI/IADI, Coach) (Merge tandem)	Door exit; aerobatics; unsupervised freefall	Stalls; traffic avoidance; 165 feet unassisted; the "sweet spot;" rectangular v. elliptical	Complete orientation (open canopy); component identification; unassisted pre-flight; comprehensive RSL	Training harness: two canopies out; high-wind landings; independent aircraft emergencies	SIM 2-1 (winds), 2-1.M (oxygen), 5-1 (dual deployments), 5-3 (RSLs); 5-3 (altimeters); FAR 91 (pilot responsibilities); FAR 105.43.a and b (packing authorization and interval)	Aircraft orientation; airspeed; weight and balance; winds aloft; intro spot selection; assist with jump run
F	AFF: 10-13 SL/IAD: 16-17 Coach	Tracking; two clear and pulls for former AFF students	Braked turns, approach, and landing; maximum glide; 82 feet on two jumps	Assisted packing; pin check (others), parachute system and canopy owner's manuals	Power line landings	SIM 2-1 (all), 3-1 (all), 5-1 (power lines), 5-2 (currency recommendations), 5-7 (group separation); parachute system and reserve owner's manuals	Group separation; assisted jump run; calculating exit point from winds aloft
G	AFF: 14-17 SL/IAD: 18-21 Coach	Group exits; forward motion; rate of descent; docking; break-off and separation	Collision avoidance review; reverse turns; 65 feet on two jumps	Solo packing; rigger's responsibilities; maintenance orientation; AAD review	Canopy collision response; tree landings	SIM 5-1 (trees), 5-1 (collisions), 5-5 (weather), 6-1 (group freefall); FAR 105.43.c (AAD maintenance)	Unassisted jump run; weather
H	AFF: 18-21 SL/IAD: 22-25 Coach	Diver exit; diving; traffic awareness during diving, tracking and deployment	Front riser control; 65 feet on three jumps	Owner maintenance (three-ring, closing loop)	Water landings; low-turn recovery	SIM 5-1. (water), 5-1 (low turns), 6-2 (breakoff); FAR 105.13 (aircraft radio); 105.15 (notification); AC 105-2C App. (aircraft)	Notification to FAA of jump activity; review STC, 337, etc.

*After training recommended in the USPA Integrated Student Program for solo students coming from tandem.

4-2: CATEGORIES A-H OBJECTIVES OVERVIEW

CATEGORY A

all—
- canopy control
- landing approach
- landing principles
- exit
- stable fall
- deployment
- aircraft emergencies

solo students—
- equipment emergencies
- landing emergencies

CATEGORY B
- relaxing in the skydiving environment
- heading awareness
- parachute deployment
- more on the landing pattern
- airport orientation
- protecting handles
- equipment emergency review

CATEGORY C
- unassisted freefall with heading maintenance
- hover control
- solo deployment
- landing patterns for higher winds
- downwind landings
- wing loading
- accidental opening review
- turbulence
- landing off
- obstacle recognition
- the FAA rigger
- the closed parachute system

CATEGORY D
- solo, unassisted exit (AFF students)
- freefall turns
- freefall speeds and times review
- back-riser control
- building landing review
- AAD (owner's manual)
- pre-jump equipment check
- introduction to three-ring release operation
- cloud clearance and visibility
- observe jump run

CATEGORY E
- door (unpoised) exit
- recovering stability and awareness
- aerobatics
- stalls
- the canopy's "sweet spot"
- two canopies deployed (review)
- high-wind landings
- reserve static line
- open parachute orientation
- parachute packing and supervision
- wind limits
- aircraft briefing
- aircraft emergency procedures
- selecting the opening point

CATEGORY F
- introduction to tracking
- two clear and pulls (former AFF students)
- braked turns, approaches, and landings
- extending the glide
- acting as jumpmaster or jump leader
- power-line landing review
- packing with assistance
- checking others' equipment
- procedures following inactivity
- winds aloft and the exit point
- separating groups during exit

CATEGORY G
- group exits
- floater position
- forward and backward movement
- adjusting fall rate
- start and stop
- docking
- maximum-performance canopy turns
- collision avoidance and response review
- tree landing review
- equipment maintenance inspection
- weather for skydivers

CATEGORY H
- diver exit
- diving
- breakoff
- front riser control
- water landing review
- owner maintenance of gear
- aircraft radio requirements
- FAA notification requirements for jumping
- FAA approvals for jump planes

4-3: USPA ISP: AN INTRODUCTION

4-3: USPA INTEGRATED STUDENT PROGRAM: AN INTRODUCTION

A. RECOMMENDATION

USPA recommends that skydivers complete training in the Integrated Student Program (ISP), an effective means of preparing a student for the USPA A license.

B. WHAT IS THE ISP?

1. USPA developed the ISP as a comprehensive training outline that meets the USPA Basic Safety Requirements (BSRs) for student training in all training methods.
   a. Some schools have developed equivalent programs that train the student to meet all the qualifications of the USPA A license.
   b. A prospective student should be able to ask a school to compare its program against this industry standard program.
2. USPA recognizes the following training methods, or disciplines:
   a. USPA Accelerated Freefall (AFF or harness hold), where the student exits with two instructors who hold the student by the parachute harness for guidance and observation.
   b. Instructor-Assisted Deployment (IAD) and Static Line, the same method using different equipment during the initial jumps
      (1) pilot chute deployed by the instructor as the student exits (instructor-assisted deployment)
      (2) deployment via a static attachment to the aircraft that separates once the parachute deploys (static line)
   c. Tandem, where the student's harness is attached to the front of the instructor's harness as part of a specially designed and built parachute system for tandem skydiving
   d. vertical wind tunnel training, where a student receives instruction and practices basic freefall control and maneuvering
3. As ISP students progress, those training in one method demonstrate an equivalent level of knowledge and skill as ISP students trained in other methods.

C. CHOOSING A SCHOOL

1. Many regions are served by more than one skydiving center, so shop around.
2. Ask questions (personal observation is even better) about the types of training offered, the type of equipment used, staff qualifications, etc.
3. Skydiving schools are often listed in the local yellow pages under "parachute" or "skydiving."
4. USPA maintains a list of current Group Member drop zones on the USPA website, uspa.org.

D. WHAT TO EXPECT

1. Registration
   a. Upon arrival at the jump center, register with the skydiving school.
   b. All jumpers will be required to fill out a registration form which will usually ask for name, address, age, height, weight, occupation and the name, address, phone number, and relationship of someone to contact in case of emergency.
2. Liability release
   a. Each participant will also be required to agree to and sign a liability release.
   b. This release will verify that the person understands that there is risk involved in skydiving and that the participant freely agrees to accept that risk.
   c. The legal release will usually contain a contract or covenant by which the participant agrees not to sue the skydiving school or anyone else if the participant is injured.
3. All participants in skydiving must meet the USPA BSRs for medical fitness.
   a. A person should be in good health and physical condition to skydive and should not be on medication; however, some conditions can be properly managed if the instructor knows about them.
   b. An FAA flight physical or a doctor's statement of fitness for skydiving may be required in some cases.
   c. The instructor also needs to know about any recent donations of blood.
   d. People who participate in SCUBA diving should not fly for at least 24 hours afterward.
   e. Refer to faa.gov/pilots/medical/ for more information on medical fitness for flight.

> **USPA STATEMENT OF MEDICAL FITNESS**
>
> "I represent and warrant that I have no known physical or mental infirmities that would impair my ability to participate in skydiving, or if I do have any such infirmities, that they have been or are being successfully treated so that they do not represent any foreseeable risk while skydiving."
>
> "I also represent and warrant that I am not taking any medications or substances, prescription, or otherwise, that would impair my ability to participate in skydiving."

4. All participants in skydiving must meet the BSRs for age.
5. Upon completion of ground school and before the first jump, students should be required to pass written, oral, and practical tests.

E. STUDENT EQUIPMENT

1. Students are provided with additional safety devices not usually found on equipment used by non-students.
2. Special requirements for student parachute systems are listed in the BSRs.
   a. From the start, a student should be taught to be self-reliant and to respond quickly to emergency situations.
   b. Safety devices and features should be designed as emergency overrides or backups only, in the event that the student does not properly perform emergency procedures.
   c. Students should never use these features as a substitute for proper training and supervision
   d. Emergency back-ups give confidence to the student and peace of mind to the instructor.
3. Student equipment should be well maintained.

4. Standardization
   a. Changes in type of equipment and procedures should be avoided or minimized whenever possible during student training.
   b. When changes are made, adequate transition training must be provided in compliance with the BSRs.
   c. Foresight should be used to minimize the need to change emergency procedures as a student progresses.
5. Canopies used for students should be large, docile, and appropriate for the student's weight.

F. TRAINING PRIORITIES

1. The most important skill a skydiver must develop is the ability to cope with and respond to emergency situations. A student should review emergency procedures at the beginning of every jump day. The review must cover emergency procedures for these areas:
   a. equipment
   b. aircraft
   c. freefall
   d. deployment
   e. canopy
   f. landing
2. Development of these skills should start with the first jump rather than at a point where supervision of jumping activities is reduced.
3. Initial training, even if the student intends to make only one jump, should be designed to establish a foundation for the continuing growth and development of skills.

4-3 USPA ISP: AN INTRODUCTION

Category A

USPA ISP: CATEGORY A | 4-A

INTRODUCTION

This first category of the ISP includes the first-jump course, presented according to your training discipline.

A USPA Coach may teach the solo general section, which contains topics and procedures common to all solo first jumpers in the AFF, IAD, or static-line programs. A USPA Instructor in that student's training discipline is required to teach any sections unique to the student's training method.

Depending on school policy, tandem skydivers may train for only the minimum information required to make a tandem jump safely, or they may train to meet the Category A advancement criteria. Only a USPA Tandem Instructor may conduct skydiving training in the tandem method, but a USPA Coach may assist.

All ISP categories include recommended minimum deployment altitudes and the number of skydives it takes on the average to complete that category of training (column on right). They vary within a category, according to your training discipline.

Following each category introduction is a category overview called "Category at a Glance." It lists the advancement criteria you should meet before progressing to the next category of training. The school should provide you a USPA A-License Card and begin checking off training sessions and advancement criteria early in the training program.

At the end of each category, the supervising USPA Instructor conducts an oral quiz based on topics from the training outline and the recommended readings ("book stuff") listed with the "Category at a Glance."

Recommended plans (dive flows) for freefall and under canopy follow each outline. Notes for the supervising USPA Instructor are also found there.

Naturally, Category A includes the longest training outline, because there is a lot you must learn prior to making a first skydive. To improve retention, the school introduces only what you might need to know to make a first jump safely. Other important information can be presented as it becomes relevant and as you make a firmer commitment to learning more about the sport.

AFF AND TANDEM
- one jump

IAD/STATIC-LINE
- two jumps

RECOMMENDED MINIMUM DEPLOYMENT
- AFF: 4,500 feet
- IAD and static line: 3,500 feet
- Tandem: 5,500 feet

4-A USPA ISP: CATEGORY A

Category at a Glance

ADVANCEMENT CRITERIA

EXIT AND FREEFALL

AFF AND TANDEM STUDENTS

- reasonable arch and stability within ten seconds prior to planned deployment altitude
- reasonable altitude awareness
- initiate deployment procedures within 1,000 feet of the assigned altitude

IAD AND STATIC-LINE STUDENTS

- establish an arch and reasonable control after exit

CANOPY

- plan and execute canopy descent and landing pattern with assistance
- assisted flare for a safe landing within 60 degrees of correct landing direction
- land within 330 feet of the planned landing area, spot permitting

*Note: For reasons of safety, AFF, IAD, or static-line students who do not complete the flaring and landing advancement criteria on the first jump should be recommended for tandem or other comprehensive canopy training. If all other Category A advancement criteria have been met, the student may satisfy Category A canopy skills in another discipline and then advance to Category B in the preferred discipline.

ORAL QUIZ

BOOK STUFF

- FAR 91.107.a on seat belt use and responsibilities
- SIM Section 2-1 G.3 on the topics to be covered in the first-jump course

CATEGORY A: FIRST-JUMP COURSE OUTLINE

I. SOLO: GENERAL SECTION

Note: The needs of the operation will determine the order of presentation of the topics taught in the first-jump course. This section may be taught by a USPA Coach under the supervision of any USPA Instructor.

A. SOLO EQUIPMENT ORIENTATION

1. Location of all operation handles
2. Equipment responsibilities
   a. In Category A, the USPA Instructor takes responsibility for putting your equipment on, adjusting it correctly, and checking it as follows:
      (1) before you put it on
      (2) before boarding
      (3) in the aircraft shortly before exit
   b. IAD and static-line students check their deployment devices before climbing out of the aircraft.
   c. With the instructor's assistance, the student protects all operation handles while in and around the aircraft.
3. The altimeter indicates altitude in thousands of feet from the ground.
   a. Handle with care
   b. Reads only approximate altitudes
   c. Sometimes fails
   d. Use of the altimeter in freefall:
      (1) Skydivers freefall about 1,000 feet in the first ten seconds and 1,000 feet every 5.5 seconds thereafter.
      (2) The altimeter needle moves backwards at approximately the same speed as the second hand of a clock.
      (3) Freefall students should check the altitude—
         (i) after every task
         (ii) whenever encountering difficulty in completing the current task
         (iii) whenever uncertain of the altitude
         (iv) continually every few seconds
      (4) If you don't know the altitude, open the parachute.
   e. Static-line and IAD students count to keep track of the seconds after exit.
   f. All students use the altimeter under canopy.
   g. Altitude awareness is the skydiver's most important task until the parachute opens.
4. Parachute opening occurs in three stages:
   a. Activation—Deployment of the parachute begins once the container is opened (activated) in one of three ways:
      (1) pulling the ripcord
      (2) throwing the pilot chute
      (3) static line
   b. Deployment—The parachute comes out of the backpack.
   c. Inflation—The canopy fills with air.
5. Within three seconds after activation, determine whether or not the canopy has deployed, inflated properly, and is controllable.
6. The open parachute canopy
   a. To land safely, the parachute canopy must be regular in shape and controllable, and you must be able to reliably steer and flare the canopy for landing.
      (1) rectangular (may be slightly tapered) canopy overhead with untangled lines
      (2) lines connecting to four straps above the jumper's harness, called risers
      (3) slider: a rectangular piece of fabric at the top of the risers
         (i) moves down the lines during inflation.
         (ii) slows and organizes the opening.
      (4) steering handles, called "toggles" or "brakes," one on the back of each rear riser.
   b. Following a visual inspection, a canopy control check is completed after releasing the brakes (explained in the canopy piloting skills section).

B. FREEFALL POSITION

1. Skydivers first learn to fall belly first into the wind.
   a. Falling belly first results in a more reliable deployment of the parachute, worn on the back.
   b. The airflow when exiting the aircraft comes from ahead.
2. Arching and extending the legs slightly results in better belly-first control; and relaxing the rest of the body results in smooth, on-heading fall.
   a. hips forward with back arched
   b. knees at shoulder width
   c. legs extended slightly, knees bent 45 degrees, toes pointed
   d. upper arms positioned 90 degrees or less from the torso and relaxed
   e. elbows bent 90-120 degrees, up, and relaxed
   f. head up
   g. practice until natural
3. Consciously breathing will help you relax.
4. Communications
   a. Using hand signals (some examples are shown in SIM Appendix A), the instructor may coach you for a better body position and to improve awareness.
   b. Your method-specific instructor will introduce you to the signals he or she may use.
   c. You should respond to all adjustments smoothly and slowly and maintain the new position.

C. MAIN DEPLOYMENT

FREEFALL

1. Establish belly-to-wind (arched) body position.
2. Maintain the arch and locate the deployment handle.
   a. If the deployment handle is mounted on the bottom of the container, look up while reaching for the handle.
   b. Ripcords mounted more forward may allow you to look at the ripcord before reaching.
   c. Regardless of location or technique, accentuate the arch while reaching for the activation handle.
3. For equal deflection of air (balance), stretch your left hand overhead and across as the right hand reaches for the deployment handle.

4-A | USPA ISP: CATEGORY A

4. Activate (pull or throw) the handle vigorously, returning to the original position.
5. Verbalize each action, e.g., "Arch! Reach! Pull!"
6. Pull Priorities
   a. Pull—You must deploy the parachute
   b. Pull at the proper altitude—You should maintain altitude awareness and pull at the assigned altitude.
   c. Pull at the proper altitude while stable—The priority is to deploy the parachute at the assigned altitude. Deploying in a stable body position will help to reduce the chances of experiencing a parachute malfunction, but never sacrifice altitude for stability.
7. After activation:
   a. Remain flat, stable, and shoulders-level through deployment, counting to three by thousands.
   b. After the count of three, visually check for pilot chute deployment.

IAD AND STATIC LINE

1. As you exit the plane, remain arched, stable, and shoulders-level through deployment, counting to five by thousands.
2. Look over your shoulder for the pilot chute (if used) and main canopy deployment.

D. CANOPY PILOTING SKILLS

1. Basic canopy aerodynamics
   a. A ram-air canopy is an inflatable wing that performs like the wing of an airplane.
      (1) Once it is open and inflated, the canopy will start gliding forward and down through the air.
      (2) The forward movement creates a flow of relative wind around the canopy.
   b. The airflow around the canopy creates lift.
2. Steering the canopy
   a. With both toggles all the way up, the canopy should glide straight ahead at full speed.
   b. The canopy turns right when you pull the right toggle (steering control line handle) down and turns left when you pull the left toggle down.
   c. To prevent a collision with another jumper, always look first in the direction of the intended turn.
   d. The canopy will turn as long as one toggle is held down and stops turning when it is let up.
   e. Pulling one toggle down a small amount produces a slow turn with a relatively small amount of dive.
   f. Small toggle inputs can be used to make minor heading corrections at any point in the canopy flight.
   g. Pulling one toggle down farther will produce a faster turn and causes the canopy to dive, which can have serious consequences near the ground.
   h. Pulling both toggles down decreases the rate of descent and forward speed of the canopy.
3. Post-deployment canopy check
   a. Check the canopy for proper inflation after the deployment.
      (1) The canopy should be large and fully inflated.
      (2) The canopy should have four well-defined edges forming a rectangular shape.
      (3) The suspension lines should cascade down in four neat line groups to each riser, the slider should be down to the tops of the risers, and the canopy should be flying wing-level toward the horizon, without spinning or turning. (Stable)
   b. Grab the steering toggles and perform a control check to ensure the canopy will steer and flare.
      (1) Release the brakes by pulling both toggles down smoothly to the belly and raise back up to full flight.
      (2) Look to the right to ensure clear airspace and pull the right toggle smoothly down toward the belly to initiate a right-hand turn and continue the turn for at least 90 degrees before returning the toggle all the way up to resume straight and level flight.
      (3) Look to the left to ensure clear airspace and pull the left toggle smoothly down toward the belly to initiate a left turn and continue the turn for at least 90-degrees before returning the toggle all the way up to resume straight and level flight..
      (4) Pull both toggles down smoothly all the way to full arm extension to flare the parachute, then smoothly return the toggles back to the full up position for a full glide, straight and level flight.
      (5) To be considered a good main canopy, it should turn and flare correctly and fly in a straight direction with the toggles in the full up position.
4. Canopy speed and wind
   a. When facing into the wind or "holding," the canopy will fly more slowly across the ground.
   b. When flying in the same direction as the wind, or "running," the canopy will move more quickly across the ground.
   c. When facing perpendicular to the wind or "crabbing," the canopy will move forward and also drift sideways across the ground.
   d. These effects become more pronounced in stronger winds.
5. Landing patterns
   a. Each jumper is responsible for landing safely in a clear area.
   b. Prior to boarding the aircraft before each jump, you should plan your landing pattern using an aerial photograph, diagram, map, or model of the drop zone.
   c. Determine the current speed and direction of the wind.
   d. Locate the intended target and determine the wind line, which is an imaginary line going through the target indicating the direction of the wind.
      (1) If the canopy is upwind of the target, the wind will tend to push the canopy toward the target.
      (2) if the canopy is downwind of the target, the wind will tend to push the canopy away from the target.
   e. In no-wind conditions or light and variable winds, the instructor and student should choose a predetermined landing direction and base the landing pattern on that plan.

f. Choose a point on the ground downwind of the landing target and on the wind line where you will start your final approach at 300 feet.
g. Choose the point where you will start your base leg at 600 feet.
h. Choose the point where you will start your downwind leg at 1,000 feet.
i. The location of each point and shape of the pattern will vary depending on the strength of the wind.
   (1) In light winds, the pattern will resemble a square, with the downwind leg, base leg, and final approach being the same length.
   (2) In light winds it is important to have plenty of clear space past the target in case you overshoot.
   (3) As the winds become stronger, the final approach and base legs become shorter, and the downwind leg becomes longer.
   (4) In strong winds, it is important to make the base leg and final approach turns over a clear area, in case you land short of the target.
j. Determine the shape and location of the holding area; this is ideally where you should be when the canopy opens, and where you should remain for most of the canopy flight.

   Note: The USPA Instructor may need to adjust the shape of the pattern or the checkpoint altitudes to account for various circumstances.

6. Normal canopy flight procedures
   a. After checking for a good canopy, check your altitude then look directly below your feet and observe your position over the ground.
   b. Locate your holding area, target, and the "check points" where you will start each leg of your pattern, and establish a line to your preplanned 1,000-foot pattern entry point.
   c. Divide the line logically according to the remaining altitude (halfway down, halfway back); for example, if open at 4,000 feet—
      (1) Divide the line in half and remain over the first half of the line until 2,000 feet.
      (2) Fly over the remaining half of the line until reaching the pre-planned pattern entry point at 1,000 feet.
   d. Remain inside the holding area until 1,000 feet.
   e. As long as you are in the holding area and above 1,000 feet, you may practice turns and flares.
   f. Watch for other canopies, check your altitude, and check your position over the ground

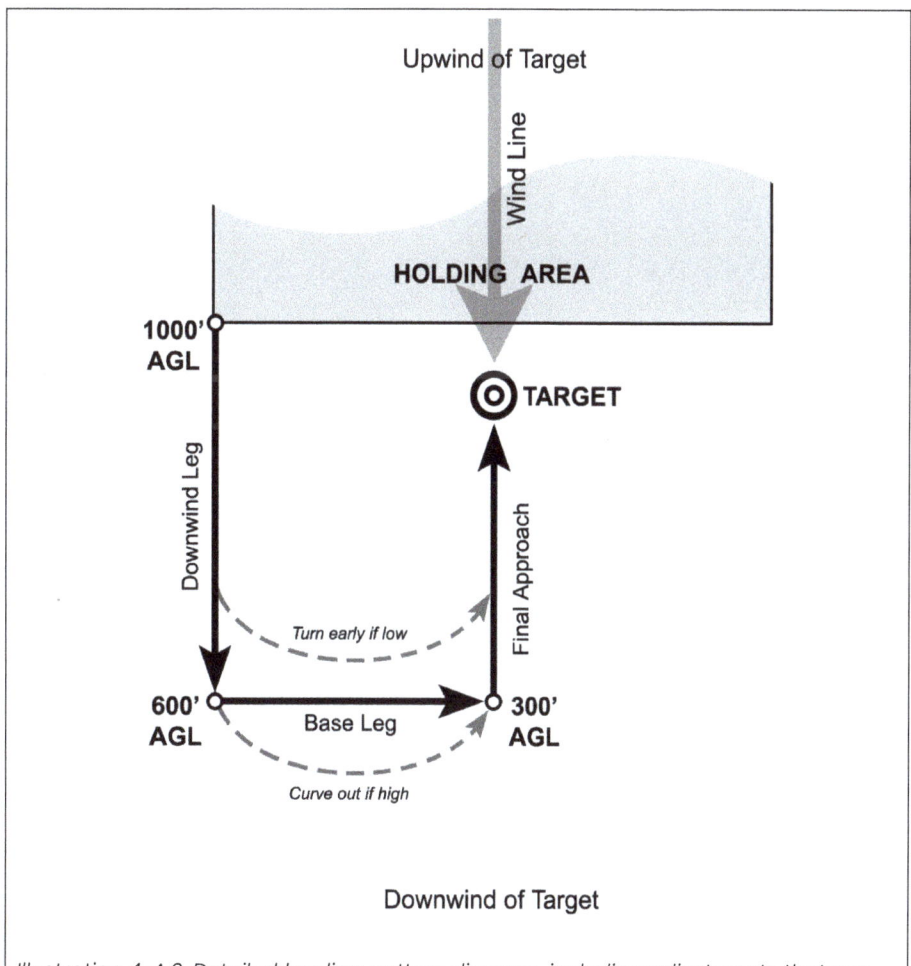

Illustration 4-A.1. Examples of calm wind and strong wind landing patterns.

Illustration 4-A.2. Detailed landing pattern diagram, including adjustments that can be made to base leg if too high or low.

4-A — USPA ISP: CATEGORY A

periodically, especially after each turn or practice flare.

g. Begin your pattern at 1,000 feet, flying to each of the checkpoints you picked on the ground.
   (1) You may need to begin your base leg turn at 600 feet even if you have not arrived at the planned checkpoint.
   (2) If arriving too high at the planned 600-foot checkpoint, correct by looping out during the base leg on the way to the 300-foot point.

7. Final approach and landing
   a. Once you have begun your final approach, your main priority is to keep the canopy flying straight toward a clear, open area.
      (1) Small toggle inputs may be used to avoid on the ground.
      (2) If the canopy begins to drift, use the appropriate input to stop the turn and keep the canopy flying straight toward a clear area.
      (3) The best way to avoid obstacles is to always look towards a clear area and guide the canopy towards a clear landing spot, rather than focusing on an obstacle.
   b. If the canopy is flying straight, keeping the toggles all the way up in the full glide position will help the canopy produce more lift when you flare.
   c. It is easier to judge the flare height by looking mid-way towards the horizon rather than straight down below your feet.
   d. During the last part of the final approach, put your feet and knees together in a PLF position.
   e. Just before landing, convert the forward speed of the parachute to lift by flaring.
      (1) When your feet are approximately twice your height above the ground, flare to half brakes.
      (2) Flare the remainder of the way just before touching down.
      (3) Your instructor may vary the exact flare technique based on the type of canopy you will be using or other factors.
   f. If you start the flare too high, stop flaring and hold the toggles where they are.
      (1) Letting the toggles up abruptly causes a steep dive.
      (2) Keep looking ahead and keep the canopy flying straight.
      (3) Push the toggles the rest of the way down before touching down.

   Note: Beginners should jump large, docile canopies that allow for errors. These canopies should be resistant to stalling and should simply maintain a low airspeed and rate of descent if flared too high.

   g. You should be prepared to perform a parachute landing fall (see Illustration 4-A.3) every time you land.
   h. A stand-up landing should only be attempted if you touch down softly and are confident that you can comfortably remain on your feet.

8. Perception of speed
   a. The canopy may seem to fly very slowly until you get lower on final approach.
   b. You may notice the speed for the first time at this point, which may trick you into flaring early.
   c. The canopy needs speed for an effective flare.
   d. Wait until the correct altitude to flare.

9. Changing winds
   a. Landing into (against) the wind is desirable, but not absolutely necessary.
   b. Use available wind indicators to check the wind direction during your canopy flight.
      (1) On days when the winds are light and variable, it may be best to maintain your original, planned pattern and landing direction even if the wind indicators change direction.
      (2) If it is necessary to land in a different direction than planned, rotate your original pattern around the target so it lines up in the desired direction.
   c. Once you have begun your final approach, keeping the canopy flying straight toward a clear area is more important than landing directly into the wind.
   d. Landing downwind or crosswind in a clear area is far less risky than making an aggressive turn near the ground.

10. Alternate landing areas
    a. Whether you land in the intended landing area or an alternate one, you should be prepared to make your own correct decisions and land safely without assistance.
    b. If you are not in your holding area or close to it when the canopy opens be prepared to pick an alternate landing area.
    c. Maintain altitude awareness while flying back towards your 1,000-foot point.
    d. At or above 2,000 feet you should decide whether or not you will be able to reach your 1,000-foot point.
    e. If it is obvious that the 1,000-foot point is unreachable:
       (1) Look for your 600-foot and 300-foot points.
       (2) If you are sure that you will be able to reach one of those points, fly toward it and remain over that point until you reach the correct altitude to begin that leg of your pattern.
       (3) If it is obvious that you will not reach any point in your pattern by the correct altitude, then plan to land in a nearby open area, free of obstacles.
       (4) Visually transfer the intended landing pattern to the new landing area.
       (5) Fly the new landing pattern.
    f. Any time you must land in an alternate area off of the airport property:
       (1) Look carefully for obstacles and avoid them by looking and steering the canopy towards a clear and open area.
       (2) Perform a parachute landing fall (PLF).
       (3) Wait for assistance or further instructions.
       (4) Be polite to property owners.

11. Priorities for all landings
    a. Land with the wing level and flying in a straight line.

b. Land in a clear and open area, avoiding obstacles.

c. Flare to at least the half-brake position.

d. Always be prepared to make a PLF.

E. BASIC LANDING TRAINING– PARACHUTE LANDING FALL

1. Parachutists absorb the shock of a hard landing with a Parachute Landing Fall (PLF).

    a. To prepare for a PLF, press your feet and knees together with your knees slightly bent.

    b. Flare the canopy completely with both hands together and close to the front of your body to help prevent wrist and hand injuries.

    c. Chin to the chest to help prevent neck injuries.

    d. Allow your feet to make contact with the ground first.

    e. Maintain the PLF position throughout the entire landing roll.

    f. As your feet touch the ground:

        (1) Lean into the direction of the landing to roll down one side of the body.

        (2) Lay over to the side of one calf.

        (3) Continue to roll to the thigh on the same side.

        (4) Continue rolling on to that hip (side of the butt).

        (5) Roll diagonally across your back to the opposite shoulder.

        (6) Allow your body to continue rolling and absorb the energy of the fall.

2. The PLF position is also the proper way to prepare for a stand-up landing.

    a. The PLF position keeps your weight balanced in the harness and helps avoid the tendency to reach for the ground.

    b. If you touch down softly you can step out of the PLF position and remain on your feet.

F. LANDING HAZARDS (AT TRAINING HARNESS)

1. Landing hazards include water, trees, buildings, power lines, and any similar hazards.

2. These hazards can usually be avoided by:

    a. Properly preparing for the canopy flight by observing the winds and planning an appropriate landing pattern before boarding the aircraft.

    b. Choosing the correct exit and opening points and spotting the aircraft correctly before exiting.

    c. Following the procedures described above under "Alternate landing areas."

WATER

1. Refer to the USPA BSRs for equipment requirements on jumps near water, but many drop zones have waivers on file.

2. Procedure for an unintentional water landing:

    a. If possible, land close to shore or to a boat, buoy, or other floating object.

    b. Inflate the flotation device (if available).

    c. Loosen the chest strap (keep your hands in the steering toggles to maintain control if possible; however, this may require taking your hands out of the steering toggles first).

    d. Enter the water with lungs full of air.

    e. Releasing the main canopy and attempting to fall away into the water is not recommended.

        (1) Altitude above water can be difficult to judge.

        (2) Falling from a significant height into water can result in fatal injuries

        (3) The water may be shallow or there may be unseen objects below the surface.

    f. Prepare for a PLF.

    g. Flare the parachute to half brakes at ten feet above the water (may be difficult to judge) and enter the water feet-first in a PLF position.

    h. If the canopy lands on top of you:

        (1) dive down and swim out from under the canopy, or

        (2) pull the canopy off of your head, remaining clear of the lines.

    i. Take a deep, full breath of air at every opportunity.

    j. Release or slide off the leg straps and swim carefully away to avoid entangling in the suspension lines.

    k. Even if you are in shallow water or are a strong swimmer, leave the parachute system behind.

TREES

1. Most tree landings are survivable, but accidents may also occur during the recovery.

2. Continue steering to avoid trees but avoid sharp turns near the ground.

3. Procedures for landing in a tree:

    a. Flare to half brakes.

    b. Keep your legs tight together in a PLF position, but not crossed.

    c. Protect your face with both hands and forearms, with both elbows tightly together and close to your stomach.

    d. Try for the middle of the tree, then hold on to the trunk or main branch to avoid falling.

    e. Prepare for a hard landing on the ground if falling through the tree.

    f. Stay in the tree and wait for help; do not attempt to climb down.

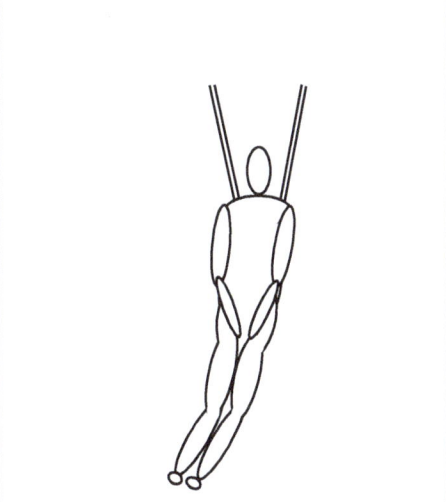

Illustration 4-A.3. The PLF position at touchdown.

4-A — USPA ISP: CATEGORY A

BUILDINGS

1. A jumper could land into the side of a building or on top of it.
2. Make slight steering corrections to avoid the building or object, but stop any turns in time to prepare to land.
3. Procedures for landing in or on a building:
    a. When landing on top of a building, prepare for a hard landing utilizing a Parachute Landing Fall (PLF) position.
    b. Flare at ten feet above the building.
    c. Strike the object feet first.
    d. After landing on top of a building in windy conditions, pull the cutaway handle to prevent being dragged off the building.
    e. When striking the side of a building, try to strike it in a PLF position feet first, then the side of your body with a glancing blow, if possible.
        (1) Make slight steering corrections or turn your body to the side in your harness.
        (2) Flare to half brakes.
        (3) Protect your face and vital organs while keeping a proper PLF position in anticipation of a secondary impact.

POWER LINES

1. Power lines typically appear along roads, between buildings, and along straight-line paths through wooded areas.
2. They may be invisible, except for their poles.
3. Power lines can be extremely dangerous: if there is no other alternative, landing in trees, in water, or on a small obstacle may be preferable to landing in power lines.
4. Sharp turns close to the ground can be equally dangerous, so it is important to identify power lines and steer clear of them while enough altitude remains to do so safely.
5. Procedure for landing in a power line:
    a. Drop any ripcords.
    b. Pull both toggles to the halfway position, prepare for a hard landing, and turn your head to one side. (With a round reserve canopy, place your hands between the front and rear risers on each side.)
    c. Touch no more than one wire at a time.
    d. If suspended in the wires: the parachute can conduct electricity, so the power needs to be off before making contact with anyone or anything on the ground.

ANY OBSTACLE LANDING

1. Remain still and keep your helmet on.
2. Prepare to drop the rest of the way to the ground at any moment.
3. Wait for competent, knowledgeable help (drop zone staff) for help in getting down.

LANDING OFF FIELD

1. Steer for a clear area
2. Transfer the planned landing pattern to the new, clear area.
3. Look for and avoid obstacles.
4. Perform a PLF.
5. Wait for assistance or further instructions.
6. Be polite to property owners.

RECOVERING THE CANOPY IN HIGHER WINDS

1. Land using a PLF.
2. Get up quickly and attempt to run toward the canopy until it collapses.
3. Pull in one toggle and steering line to assist in collapsing the canopy (especially if being dragged).
4. Cut away the canopy as a last resort or if injured, but wait for assistance before walking anywhere.

ROUND CANOPY (RESERVE USE ONLY)

1. Round canopies have vents in the rear to enable forward speed (less than ten mph).
2. Steer the canopy using the back risers or, if rigged on two risers only, the steering lines.
3. Steer across or with the direction of the wind toward a clear area.
4. Steer into the wind at 200-300 feet before landing and continue steering to avoid obstacles.
5. Prepare to land using the PLF.

G. EQUIPMENT PROBLEMS (AT TRAINING HARNESS)

1. For a parachute to be safe to land it must be:
    a. "There," meaning deployment has occurred and something is overhead.
    b. "Square," meaning that the parachute is inflated, rectangular (or slightly tapered), and regular in shape.
    c. "Steerable," meaning that you can turn left and right and flare.
    d. In the event of a toggle malfunction, the rear risers may be used for steering and flaring the canopy.
        (1) Landing by flaring with rear risers should be practiced at sufficient altitude before attempting an actual landing with rear risers.
        (2) (2) Flaring with rear risers will require more strength than flaring with just the toggles.
2. If the parachute fails any of the above tests, you must initiate reserve parachute procedures.
3. Decide if the parachute is controllable and ready to land by 2,500 feet; otherwise, execute the planned emergency procedures.
4. Routine problems in order of correction:
    a. To find a missing deployment handle, first find its location on the system (two additional tries).
        (1) For bottom of container location, feel across the bottom of the back pack to the corner; then down the side to the corner, then go to reserve.
        (2) For ripcord handle mounting on the harness, locate that part of the harness or harness intersection; if that fails after two tries, go to reserve.
    b. For a stuck main deployment handle, try again twice with both hands, if possible, then deploy the reserve.
    c. To clear a pilot chute hesitation (burble), twist at the waist and look over your shoulder to change the airflow.
    d. To untwist the lines, spread the risers and kick, but release the brakes only after clearing the twist.

e. To bring down a stuck slider, depress the toggles to the flare position and pump them.

f. To open the end cells, depress the toggles to the flare position and hold them.

g. If the canopy has opened normally but turns on its own, be sure both brakes are released.

h. Broken lines, rips, other canopy damage, or pilot chute entangled in the lines: Determine by 2,500 feet whether the canopy is steerable and flares without problems.

H. EQUIPMENT EMERGENCY PROCEDURES

TOTAL MALFUNCTION

Note: Some schools teach partial malfunction procedures as an alternative to the following procedures for when the parachute has been activated but has failed to deploy.

1. Return to the arch position.
2. Ripcord systems: Discard the main ripcord if extracted.
3. Look for and locate the reserve ripcord handle.
4. Pull it all the way out to activate the reserve parachute.
5. Arch and check over the right shoulder for reserve pilot chute deployment.

PARTIAL MALFUNCTION

Note: On single-operation systems, pulling the reserve ripcord releases the main canopy first before deploying the reserve. Partial malfunction procedures for a single-operation system (SOS) are the same as for a total malfunction.

1. Check altitude.
2. Return to the arch position.
3. Ripcord systems only: Discard the main ripcord.
4. Locate and grasp the cutaway handle.
5. Locate the reserve ripcord handle.
6. Pull the cutaway handle until no lower than 1,000 feet.
7. Pull the reserve ripcord handle immediately after cutting away or by at least 1,000 feet, regardless of stability, to initiate reserve deployment.

8. Arch and check over the right shoulder for reserve pilot chute deployment.
9. Cut away above 1,000 feet.

    a. If a malfunction procedure has not resolved the problem by then, deploy the reserve (requires a cutaway with an SOS system).

    b. In the event of any malfunction and regardless of the planned procedure or equipment, the reserve ripcord must be pulled by no lower than 1,000 feet.

OTHER UNUSUAL SITUATIONS

1. Premature container opening in freefall (hand deployment only):

    a. Attempt to locate and deploy the pilot chute first (no more than two attempts or two seconds, whichever comes first).

    b. If the pilot chute can't be located after two tries or if deploying the pilot chute results in a partial malfunction, cut away and deploy the reserve.

2. Both parachutes deployed:

    a. Biplane

        (1) Do not cut away.

        (2) Steer the front canopy gently using toggles or leave the brakes stowed and steer by pulling on the rear risers.

        (3) Leave the brakes stowed on the back canopy.

        (4) Make a parachute landing fall on landing.

    b. Side-by-side (two alternatives)

        (1) side-by-side alternative one

            (i) If the two canopies are not tangled, cut away and fly the reserve to a safe landing.

        (2) side-by-side alternative two

            (i) Steer the dominant (larger) canopy gently using toggles or leave the brakes stowed and steer by pulling on the rear risers.

            (ii) Leave the brakes stowed on the other canopy.

            (iii) Make a parachute landing fall on landing.

    c. Downplane: Cut away the main canopy.

3. Canopy collision:

    a. Jumpers must avoid collisions with other jumpers under open parachutes.

    b. If a collision is imminent, in most cases both jumpers should steer to the right.

    c. If two jumpers collide and entangle, they must communicate their intentions before taking further action.

    d. If it is too low for a safe cutaway (below 1,000 feet) and the canopies are uncontrollable, both jumpers should deploy their reserves.

    Note: Deploying the reserve on a single-operation system necessitates a cutaway.

PREMATURE DEPLOYMENT IN AIRCRAFT

1. The student should attempt to contain the open parachute and inform the instructor.

2. If the parachute goes out the door, the student must follow immediately before being extracted.

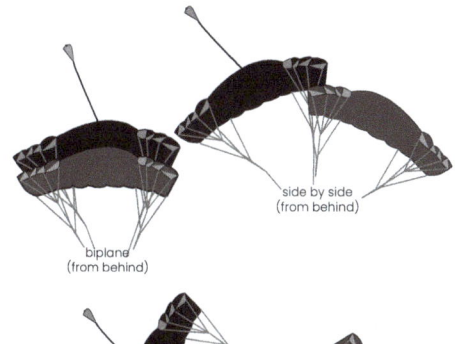

Illustration 4-A.4. When both canopies deploy, they tend to stabilize into one of three configurations, as shown.

4-A USPA ISP: CATEGORY A

II. SOLO: METHOD-SPECIFIC SECTION

Note: This section must be taught by either a USPA Instructor or Examiner rated for the method-specific discipline in which the student is being trained.

A. AIRCRAFT PROCEDURES

1. Approach, enter, and move about the aircraft, engine running or not, only when accompanied by your instructor.
2. To avoid contact with the propeller, always approach fixed-wing aircraft from the rear.
3. Be mindful of the size of the parachute equipment when climbing into and moving about the aircraft.
4. The pilot and the jumper are jointly responsible that seat belts are worn during taxi, takeoff, and landing (see the FARs on seat belt use).
5. Climbout and exit procedures prepare you to meet the relative wind in a stable, belly-first freefall body position.
   a. Into position or climbout: Move into position using practiced steps for efficient placement in the door (larger plane) or on the wing strut (Cessna, etc.).
   b. Set-up: The pre-launch position should place your belly (pelvis) into the relative wind as part of the launch from the plane.
6. Count or "go" command
   a. AFF students: Verify that the instructors are ready.
      (1) Call "Check in!" to the inside instructor, who responds, "OK!"
      (2) Call "Check out!" to the outside instructor, who responds, "OK!"
      (3) Take a breath to relax and then begin a verbal and physical cadence of three ("Up, down, arch!" or "Out, in, arch!" etc.) to help the instructors leave simultaneously with you.
   b. Static-line or IAD students: Climb into position and wait for the instructor's command.
      (1) Look for corrective signals from your instructor (examples in SIM Appendix A).
      (2) On "Go!" take a breath to relax and look up.
      (3) Release from the plane, count out loud by thousands to five-thousand, then check the parachute.
   c. You must exit soon after climbout to ensure that you open the parachute over the correct place on the ground.

B. EXIT PRESENTATION

1. Upon release from the plane, move efficiently into the flying position to reduce unwanted momentum.
2. Present the correct belly-to-wind position: hips to the wind, head back, legs extended, and hold.
3. Head-high presentation to the relative wind helps you remain oriented; however, you might also exit sideways or head down in relation to the horizon while remaining stable, belly first, on the relative wind.

C. EXIT PROBLEMS

1. Special considerations for AFF exits:
   a. In case of instability, (in order)—
      (1) arch until the horizon comes flat into view
      (2) read the altimeter
      (3) establish communication with the instructors (examples of signals in SIM Appendix A)
   b. Continue as usual in the event of the loss of one instructor.
   c. If both instructors become unavailable at any time during the freefall, open the parachute immediately.
2. Special considerations for static-line exits:
   a. Arch to regain lost stability on exit.
   b. If the static line fails to disconnect from the parachute system and you are being towed behind the aircraft, (in order)—
      (1) Remain arched and use a predetermined signal to communicate recognition of the problem.
      (2) Wait for the instructor to cut the static line.
      (3) After falling free, deploy the reserve.

D. AIRCRAFT EMERGENCIES

1. In the event of an aircraft emergency:
   a. Sit still, with helmet on and seat belt fastened
   b. Wait for a command from your instructor
2. In the event of a problem during flight, the instructor will help prepare you for one of four actions:
   a. All land with the aircraft.
   b. Exit and deploy the reserve parachute.
   c. Exit and deploy the main parachute (passive deployment for IAD and static-line).
   d. Perform a routine exit with or without instructor assistance.
3. Rough landing procedures:
   a. Helmet and seat belt on
   b. Knees to chest
   c. Hands clasped behind head to reinforce neck
   d. Immediate but orderly exit from the aircraft on landing
   e. Jumpers exiting a wrecked aircraft should go immediately to the nearest exit, touch nothing on the aircraft, and walk at least 100 feet away from the plane.
4. After an emergency exit and once under an open canopy:
   a. Look for the instructor's parachute and follow it to a clear, open landing area.
   b. Select any clear area if an instructor can't be found.

III. AFF PROCEDURES

Note: This section must be taught by either a USPA AFF Instructor or Examiner.

A. FREEFALL PROCEDURES

1. After exit, take a breath and relax into the correct freefall position.
2. Perform a "circle-of-awareness" check:
   a. Look at the ground about 45 degrees ahead and below.
   b. Read the altimeter.
   c. Look first to the reserve-side instructor and then to the main-side instructor for an acknowledgment or any communication (corrective signals, see SIM Appendix A).
3. Perform three practice deployments.
   a. Practice slowly and deliberately.
   b. Verbalize each action, e.g., "Arch, reach, touch!"
   c. Pause to feel the deployment handle each time.

d. Reinforce the correct body position before, during, and after each practice deployment.

4. Perform a second circle-of-awareness check.

5. Monitor altitude and body position for the remainder of the freefall.
   a. altitude (most important)
   b. arch (hips forward)
   c. legs (check leg position and probably extend them slightly)
   d. relax (breathe)

6. Video camera flyer
   a. You must pay attention to the altitude, not the camera flyer.
   b. The benefit of video is recognized for all training jumps.

7. At 5,500 feet, initiate deployment procedures:
   a. Signal deployment to instructors by waving both arms overhead.
   b. Deploy the parachute as practiced.
   c. The instructor may assist with activation and deployment.

B. AFTER DEPLOYMENT

1. Look for traffic (other canopies).
2. Follow "normal canopy flight procedure" practiced in first jump course.
3. If unable to locate primary landing area, follow the instructors to a safe landing area or steer to the nearest clear area for landing.

IV. TANDEM PROCEDURES

Note: This section must be taught by either a USPA Tandem Instructor or Examiner. FAA-approved tandem parachutists in command may jump with passenger parachutists but are not USPA-rated skydiving instructors.

A. TANDEM TRAINING STRATEGIES

1. Not all schools train students to complete Category A on the first tandem jump, and not all students desire it.
2. Much of the instruction on the Tandem first jump may take place during the jump itself.

B. MINIMUM TANDEM COURSE

1. Before boarding the aircraft, you should be briefed on how to do the following:
   a. check the four points of attachment to the instructor's harness
   b. place both hands in the safety position
   c. establish an arch on exit
   d. maintain a stable freefall position
   e. read the altimeter
   f. operate the drogue release handle by 5,000 feet
   g. prepare for landing

2. Refer to FAR 105.45.a.2.i in Section 9 of the SIM.

C. CATEGORY A VIA TANDEM JUMPING

1. Category A freefall position, main deployment, canopy skills, training and advancement criteria are the same as for solo students.

2. PLF landing training, solo equipment orientation, equipment malfunction training, and all method-specific training are to be completed during Category B.

3. Since the minimum drogue release altitude for tandem jumps is 5,000 feet (BSRs), Tandem students should begin deployment procedures by at least 6,000 feet.

4. Most of the Category A training can be conducted as the jump progresses.

5. Special training notes:
   a. freefall position: On at least the first Tandem jump, your hands should remain in the safety position on the front of the harness at all times, unless otherwise directed by the tandem instructor.
   b. deployment: in terms of a solo rig.
   c. climbout and exit:
      (1) The instructor will teach you the exit that best presents you face-first into to the relative wind.
      (2) The instructor verifies that you are ready, and then begins a cadence of three ("Ready, set, go!" "Up, down arch!" etc.) to help you anticipate the exit.
   d. equipment:
      (1) In Category A, the Tandem instructor takes responsibility for correctly putting on and adjusting your equipment and protecting the operation handles during pre-jump operations.
      (2) Before moving into exit position at the jump door, you must verify the harness attachment in two places at the shoulders and two places near the hips.
   e. freefall procedures
      (1) After exit, take a breath and relax into the correct freefall position.
      (2) Look for signals from the instructor (SIM Appendix A) or listen for verbal corrections.
      (3) If you exited with both hands in the safety position, the instructor may signal to move them into the freefall position.
      (4) Once in freefall, perform according to the Category A dive flow for tandem students.
   f. Canopy flight procedures are the same as the canopy dive flow for solo students.
   g. landing
      (1) You'll prepare for routine landings with a technique specific to tandem jumping for that day's conditions.
      (2) A severe situation requires a parachute landing fall (PLF), which the instructor can teach on the ground or while under canopy in the event of a problem.
      (3) Ordinarily, you'll learn the PLF during transition training to solo freefall (first-jump course).
   h. The instructor may need to provide additional training to prepare you for landing a tandem parachute in higher winds.

4-A | USPA ISP: CATEGORY A

dive flows

CATEGORY A FREEFALL DIVE FLOWS

AFF
- Exit in a relaxed arch
- Instructors release arm grips
- Circle of Awareness
- Three practice deployments
- Circle of Awareness
- Altitude, arch, legs, relax
- Begin wave off at 5,500 feet
- Pull by 4,500 feet

IAD AND STATIC LINE
- Check deployment device prior to climb-out
- Climb out
- Exit on command with legs extended
- Count aloud to five by thousands
- Check canopy

TANDEM : CATEGORY A TRAINING
- Exit with arms in safety position
- On instructor's signal, relax into neutral arch
- Check altitude
- Three practice deployments
- Altitude, arch, legs, relax
- Begin wave off by 6,000 feet
- Pull by 5,500 feet

CATEGORY A CANOPY DIVE FLOW
- (also used for tandem students training to meet Category A objectives)
- Release brakes and fix routine opening problems
- Look left, turn left
- Look right, turn right
- Flare
- Check altitude, position, and traffic
- Locate holding area, pattern "checkpoints," and target
- Remain in holding area until 1,000 feet
- Follow preassigned pattern over landing area
- Flare to land and PLF (solo students)

CATEGORY A INSTRUCTOR NOTES
- Budget training time to cover only the most important topics.
- To reduce student workload and training effort, employ staff support as much as possible, including assistance after landing.
- The instructor is responsible for putting the student's equipment on, adjusting it, and performing all equipment checks; students make sure checks are performed.
- The instructor closely supervises the student when approaching, boarding, and being seated in the aircraft, including providing instruction on seat belt use during seating.
- The instructor directs the student on the correct action in the event of any aircraft emergency (except in the event of the student's parachute deploying out the door).

category a quiz

ADMINISTERED PRIOR TO CONDUCTING JUMPS IN THE NEXT CATEGORY

Quiz answers are listed in Appendix B.

1. Describe how to avoid the propeller(s) when approaching an aircraft.

2. Who is responsible for seat belt use in the aircraft?

3. When must seat belts be fastened?

4. From whom do you take directions in the event of an aircraft problem?

5. Why is it important to exit on "Go!" (or "Arch!")?

6. Where does the wind come from initially upon exit from the aircraft?

7. Why do skydivers first learn to fall stable face to earth (think in terms of the equipment)?

8. What changes during a turn that makes low turns so dangerous?

9. What are the landing priorities?

10. What is the purpose of the landing flare?

11. Describe the procedure for a hard landing (parachute landing fall or PLF).

Mental Relaxation: The Key to Body Flight

In the early categories, like a magic mantra, you'll hear over and over again from your instructors: "Altitude, arch, legs, relax." Managing all four points at once is the key to controlled freefall.

After altitude awareness, relaxing is your key goal. It takes only a little push from the hips to get an effective arch, and you usually need to extend your legs only a little to get use of them in the wind. But you need to relax your other muscles a lot.

So how can a brand-new skydiver relax in such an adrenaline-charged, exciting, and new environment?

Sports psychologists all recognize the value of staying loose and mentally relaxed for peak performance. Many describe ways to achieve a state of prepared relaxation. Each athlete learns to develop one technique and uses it to gain that state before and maintain it during every performance.

There are many other relaxation techniques you can borrow or develop, but choose one and practice it until you perfect it, even when you're not skydiving.

Almost all the techniques begin with slower, deeper, controlled breathing. Learn to breathe from deep in your lungs, using the muscles of your diaphragm. Practice breathing in slowly until your lungs are full and then emptying your lungs completely when you breathe out.

While you practice controlled breathing, you can use one of several suggested devices to relax your mind and your body:

- Imagine yourself in a familiar, comfortable place, trying to visualize every sensual experience that you can associate with it: sight, sound, odor, taste, and touch. Picture the colors of the background and the details, try to smell the air as it would be, imagine you hear the sounds, and feel the air on your face. Imagine you just took a sip of your favorite drink.
- Relax your body part by part, starting with your toes, then your ankles, calves, thighs, hips, abdomen, etc., spending five to ten seconds in each place while continuing your controlled breathing.
- Count up to ten with each breath and then backward to zero.

There are many other relaxation techniques you can borrow or develop, but choose one and practice it until you perfect it, even when you're not skydiving. That way, you can relax yourself quickly and effectively whenever the need arises—such as just before a skydive.

You should continue controlling your breathing as you're getting ready to jump. Move slowly and deliberately in the aircraft as you approach the door and get into position, not only for safety but to help you maintain your relaxed, prepared state for the jump. Take another breath just before you actually launch from the aircraft and again to help you settle into freefall as soon as you let go. Make breathing part of every sequence, especially as you go through your "altitude, arch, legs, relax" sequence.

While skydiving is inherently a high-speed sport, you'll notice that the best skydivers never do anything in a hurry.

Category B

USPA ISP: CATEGORY B | 4-B

INTRODUCTION

In Category B, you learn to become more comfortable in the skydiving environment.

• AFF and tandem students perform leg awareness exercises to improve control and also may perform assisted turns (if trained) in preparation for heading maintenance in Category C and controlled turns in Category D.

• Static-line and IAD students get introduced to the self-deployment device and practice mock deployments after exit.

• Tandem students take a more active role in the exit, leading the count and presenting their bodies correctly to the wind. Each tandem student should hold a correct body position until establishing stability and then maintain it throughout the freefall.

Training in this category reviews and expands your understanding of the canopy landing pattern and the airport environment, with attention to avoiding aircraft on or approaching the runways. You help with pre-flight planning and the use of the written flight plan, including opening point, the projected wind line, and the landing pattern. Also, you learn to use the runway as a reference for direction and distance when observing the drop zone from the aircraft or under canopy.

For AFF, IAD, and static-line students, emergency review emphasizes topics from the first-jump course on parachute malfunctions. Tandem students will also learn and practice parachute malfunction procedures before advancing from this category to solo freefall.

In Category B, you become more responsible for your equipment, particularly while moving around and inside the aircraft. Study topics introduce USPA Basic Safety Requirements for student jumps.

To advance, AFF and tandem students should monitor altitude and deploy at the correct altitude without prompting from the instructor. IAD and static-line students must complete three successive, stable practice deployments.

AFF
- one jump

IAD/STATIC-LINE
- three jumps

TANDEM
- two jumps

RECOMMENDED MINIMUM DEPLOYMENT
- AFF: 4,500 feet
- IAD and static line: 3,500 feet
- Tandem: 5,500 feet

INSTRUCTOR: TRANSITION PROTOCOL

Crossover students to harness hold who have completed Category A in the tandem program must complete the harness-hold first-jump course before making AFF jumps in Category B.

Crossover students to AFF who have completed Category A in the IAD or static-line program will need additional training on the climbout, set-up, and count; AFF freefall communications; use of the altimeter in freefall; and use of the main parachute deployment device, including deployment device malfunctions and premature container opening.

Crossover students to tandem who have completed Category A in the solo jumping programs will need to complete any additional required paperwork and understand their responsibility to check the tandem system hook-ups before exit, as well as any special landing procedures.

Crossover students to IAD or static line who have completed Category A in another solo training method will need training in their main deployment system and its specific emergency procedures.

Category A students crossing over to IAD or static line from the tandem program will need to complete the solo first-jump course before making IAD or static-line jumps in Category B.

4-B | USPA ISP: CATEGORY B

Category at a Glance

ADVANCEMENT CRITERIA

EXIT AND FREEFALL

AFF AND TANDEM STUDENTS
- stability within ten seconds of exiting the aircraft
- maintain correct body position for stability throughout, including leg awareness and control
- assisted deployment within 500 feet of the assigned altitude
- in addition, tandem students complete the solo first-jump course

IAD AND STATIC-LINE STUDENTS
- three successive exits with stable practice deployments within five seconds of exit

CANOPY
- understanding and planning descent strategy from opening to pattern entry and pattern principles
- steering including clearing airspace (looking before turning) without prompting (self-evaluated)
- assisted flare for a safe landing within 30 degrees of heading into the wind

EQUIPMENT
- understanding routine canopy problems and the correct responses

ORAL QUIZ

Note: For reasons of safety, AFF, static line, or IAD students who do not complete the flaring and landing advancement criteria in Category B should be recommended for tandem or other comprehensive canopy training. If all other Category B advancement criteria have been met, the student may satisfy Category B canopy skills in another discipline and then advance to Category C in the preferred discipline.

BOOK STUFF

- read and discuss SIM Section 2-1.G for student training, jumps and supervision requirements
- read and discuss the USPA recommendations on parachute malfunctions and procedures, SIM Section 5-1.A – E
- study the illustration in FAA Advisory Circular 90-66, Appendix 3, in SIM Section 9-2

CATEGORY B: LEARNING AND PERFORMANCE OBJECTIVES

USPA ISP: CATEGORY B | 4-B

- relaxing in the skydiving environment
- heading awareness
- parachute deployment
- more on the landing pattern
- written flight plan
- airport orientation
- protecting handles
- equipment emergency review

A. EXIT AND FREEFALL

1. Student-led exit (all students)
   a. Review the exit set-up from Category A.
   b. IAD and static-line students perform the climbout with little or no assistance from the instructor and exit promptly on the "Go!" command.
   c. Tandem students climb into position after the instructor's OK, check with the instructor once in position, and initiate the exit count.
2. Altitude awareness to recognize and act at the assigned pull altitude is the most important task in freefall.
3. "Altitude, arch, legs, relax:" Repeat to establish and maintain awareness, stability, and control.
   a. Know your altitude (static line students know their exit altitude and count to keep track of time after release from the aircraft).
   b. Check your arch (hips forward a little).
   c. Check your legs (most beginners need to extend their legs a little and point their toes).
   d. Relax
      (1) Breathe consciously to release tension.
      (2) Use this technique just before and after releasing from the aircraft.
4. Deployment
   a. AFF and tandem students
      (1) Practice deployment in freefall until smooth and comfortable with locating the deployment handle.
      (2) Wave-off to signal deployment.
      (3) Pull at the correct altitude without prompting from the instructor.
   b. IAD and static-line students practice deployment within five seconds of exit (three successful jumps in a row required before solo freefall).
5. Leg awareness
   a. AFF and tandem students practice leg awareness by extending legs while arms remain in a neutral position.
      (1) Extending the legs from the neutral position adds more drag in the back, lifting your lower body.
      (2) The off-level attitude causes you to slide forward on the deflected air (less noticeable in tandem droguefall).
      (3) Hold the position for three seconds and return to neutral to cancel the effect.
      (4) Finish all maneuvers 1,000 feet above wave-off altitude or 6,000 feet, whichever comes first.
   b. IAD and static-line students increase leg awareness during the exit set-up and after release from the plane.
6. Maintaining a heading
   a. First, relax into a comfortable, relaxed, neutral body position.
   b. Find a point ahead on the horizon as a heading reference.
   c. If turns are trained and performed (AFF and tandem):
      Note: Although not required, team turns—like relaxation—may aid a student in preventing turns on later jumps.
      (1) The student turns 90-degrees in one direction.
      (2) The student turns back to the original heading.
      (3) Check the altitude.
      (4) Repeat in the opposite direction if time permits.
      (5) If the student does not initiate the turn, the instructor(s) may turn the student.

B. CANOPY

1. Clearing airspace: both before and during any turn, look in the direction of the turn.
2. Using a DZ photo or taking a walk in the field, you'll preview with an instructor the expected opening point and prepare a written flight plan together.
3. Review the descent strategy:
   a. Determine position and altitude upon opening.
   b. Locate the target and establish a line to the pre-planned 1,000-foot pattern entry point.
   c. Divide the line logically according to the remaining altitude (halfway down, halfway back); for example, if open at 4,000 feet—
      (1) Divide the line in half and remain over the first half of the line until 2,000 feet.
      (2) Fly over the remaining half of the line until reaching the pre-planned pattern entry point at 1,000 feet.
4. Fly to the instructor-assigned pattern entry at 1,000 feet, as identified on the written flight plan.
5. Fly the pre-planned pattern using downwind, base, and final approach legs, with specific points to overfly at specified altitudes.
6. Fly a straight-in final approach without S-turns (S-turns present a hazard to other traffic).
7. Flare at ten feet, based on Category A experience.

Note: Flaring is covered in more detail in Categories C and F.

8. Review the PLF and its value to protect against a hard landing.

4-B USPA ISP: CATEGORY B

C. EMERGENCY PROCEDURE REVIEW

Note: After completing the solo first-jump course, tandem students should review this section each day before making any jump in Category C. This section also serves as a review outline for any jumper undergoing general review following a period of inactivity.

1. Deploy at the correct altitude, regardless of stability.
2. Review common problems at the training harness (tandem students may review while under canopy):
   a. correct response to line twist:
      (1) Spread the risers and kick to untwist, but release the brakes only after clearing the twist.
      (2) If spinning, twist the risers to untwist the lines and stabilize canopy, then kick to untwist the risers.
      (3) By 2,500 feet, be sure line twist can be corrected at a safe altitude, or initiate emergency procedures.
   b. slider up:
      (1) Bring both toggles to the bottom of the stroke to slow the canopy and pump at the bottom of the control range.
      (2) Alternatively, pump the back risers.
      (3) The slider needs to be at least halfway down for landing.
      (4) Repeat remedial procedures twice or until reaching the decide-and-act altitude of 2,500 feet.
   c. end-cell closure:
      (1) Pull both toggles to the bottom of the stroke and hold them until the end cells open, then release them smoothly.
      (2) Alternatively, hold down both back risers.
      (3) If the end cells can't be cleared, evaluate controllability and flare before reaching the decide-and-act altitude of 2,500 feet.
   d. If the canopy has opened normally but turns on its own, be sure both brakes are released.
   e. Evaluate controllability and flare before reaching the decide-and-act altitude of 2,500 feet for:
      (1) Broken steering line: Use back risers.
      (2) Broken suspension line(s)
      (3) Pilot chute entangles with canopy or lines.
      (4) Damage: Canopy rips or tears.
3. Review deployment problems for manual activation (introduction for IAD and static-line students).
   a. Make only two attempts to correct the problem before initiating reserve procedures.
   b. lost deployment handle:
      (1) Hip or chest handle location: Follow harness webbing for two seconds only.
      (2) Bottom of container location: Sweep bottom of container, then side of container to corner for two seconds only.
   c. hard pull:
      (1) Hip or chest handle location: Try again with two hands.
      (2) Bottom of container: Place elbow against container for leverage.
   d. pilot chute hesitation:
      (1) Twist while looking over the right shoulder to modify the airflow.
      (2) Repeat over the left shoulder.
4. Practice for deployment handle problems and pilot chute hesitation.
5. Review premature container opening in freefall for hand deployment:
   a. Attempt to locate and deploy the pilot chute first.
   b. If the pilot chute can't be located after two tries or if deploying the pilot chute results in a partial malfunction, cut away and deploy the reserve.
6. Review student-in-tow procedures for static-line: Signal to the instructor readiness to deploy the reserve once the static line is cut.
7. Practice for recognizing and responding to total and partial malfunctions (from Category A procedures).
8. Review minimum cutaway altitude and reserve deployment without cutaway if necessary.
   a. Decide to cut away by 2,500 feet and act.
   b. If below 1,000 feet without a functioning canopy, deploy the reserve (will result in a cutaway on an SOS system).
   c. If in a canopy entanglement with another jumper below 1,000 feet and it appears the canopies cannot be separated in time for a safe landing, deploy the reserve (will result in a cutaway with the SOS system, so may not be an option).
   d. Both parachutes deployed:
      (1) Biplane—do not cut away, steer the front canopy gently using toggles or leave the brakes stowed and steer by pulling on the rear risers; leave brakes stowed on the back canopy; PLF.
   e. Side-by-side (two alternatives)
      (1) side-by-side alternative one
         (i) If the two canopies are not tangled, cut away and fly the reserve to a safe landing.
      (2) side-by-side alternative two
         (i) Steer the dominant (larger) canopy gently using toggles or leave the brakes stowed and steer by pulling on the rear risers.
         (ii) Leave the brakes stowed on the other canopy.
         (iii) Make a parachute landing fall on landing.
   f. Downplane—cut away the main canopy.
   g. Premature deployment in aircraft:
      (1) Attempt to contain the open parachute and inform the instructor.
      (2) If your parachute goes out the door, follow it immediately, before being extracted.

D. EQUIPMENT

1. Parachute deployment with opportunities for malfunctions explained (actual deployment on the ground recommended)—
   a. lost or unrecoverable deployment handle
   b. impossible deployment handle extraction
   c. pack closure
   d. pilot chute hesitation

USPA ISP: CATEGORY B | 4-B

    e. pilot chute in tow

    f. premature deployment (hand deploy)

    g. pilot chute entanglement

    h. horseshoe

    i. bag lock

    j. streamer

    k. line-over

    l. fabric or line failure sufficient to interfere with control and flare

    m. slider hang-up

    n. control-line entanglement

2. Review parachute retrieval after landing.

E. RULES AND RECOMMENDATIONS

1. Review the USPA Basic Safety Requirements (BSRs) on supervision and progression requirements for students.
2. Review the BSRs on wind limits for students (waiverable by a USPA S&TA).
3. Review the BSRs on minimum required deployment altitudes for students and USPA A license holders.
4. Review the BSRs on drop zone requirements for students (waiverable by an S&TA) and what is considered a landing hazard.

F. SPOTTING AND AIRCRAFT

1. Minimum, careful movement in the aircraft helps prevent premature activation.
2. Runway lengths and headings (use of a compass)

    a. The runway heading provides a reference for direction (north, south, east, and west).

    b. The runway length provides a reference for judging distance from the air (in tenths of a mile for GPS and Loran).

3. Winds are described by their direction of origin, said as a compass heading (for example, "The winds are two-seventy," means the winds are blowing from the west).
4. Avoid runways and approaches, including getting clear of a runway after landing on or near one.
5. Discuss local aircraft traffic approach altitudes and landing patterns and their relationship to canopy approach and landing patterns. (See the illustration below, and also refer to the illustration in FAA Advisory Circular 90-66, Appendix 3, in SIM Section 9-2.)
6. Crossing the runway

    a. Know the airport and drop zone rules about crossing a runway.

    b. If allowed, look both ways and minimize the time spent on the runway.

Illustration 4-B.1. Normal flight practices separate aircraft and parachutes at airports, but jumpers need to respect the runways and approaches.

2,500 ft. AGL — minimum parachute opening altitude

1,000 ft. AGL — aircraft pattern altitude

surface

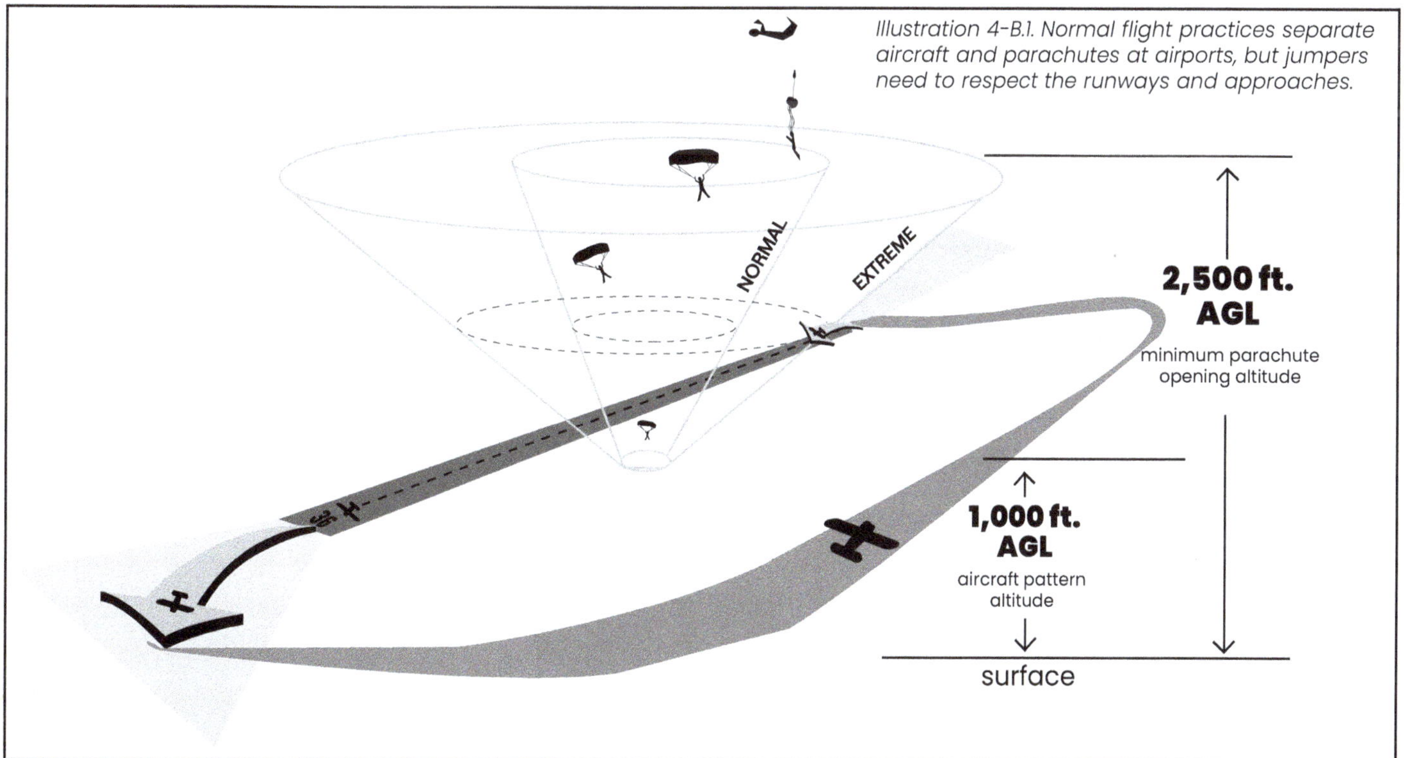

4-B USPA ISP: CATEGORY B

dive flows

CATEGORY B FREEFALL DIVE FLOWS

AFF
- Exit in a relaxed arch.
- Instructors release arm grips.
- Circle of Awareness.
- Practice deployments until comfortable.
- Altitude, arch, legs, relax.
- Extend legs for three seconds and hold.
- Altitude, arch, legs, relax.
- Repeat as altitude permits.
- Team turns (if trained).
- Begin wave off at 5,500 feet.
- Pull by 4,500 feet.

IAD AND STATIC LINE
- Check deployment device prior to climbout.
- Climb out.
- Exit on command with legs extended.
- Practice deployment with count to track time.
- Check canopy.

TANDEM
- Initiate count after instructor's OK.
- Exit in a relaxed arch.
- Altitude, arch, legs, relax.
- Practice deployment until smooth and comfortable.
- Altitude, arch, legs, relax.
- Extend legs and hold for three seconds.
- Altitude, arch, legs, relax.
- Repeat as altitude permits or turns (if trained).
- Begin wave-off by 6,000 feet.
- Pull by 5,500 feet.

CATEGORY B CANOPY DIVE FLOW
- Release brakes and correct routine problems.
- Look left, turn left.
- Look right, turn right.
- Flare.
- Check altitude, position, and traffic.
- Find landing area and pattern entry point.
- Divide flight path by thousands of feet.
- Instructor explains minor canopy problems and remedies (tandem only).
- Look at runway and determine compass heading.
- Steer over correct portion of flight path until 1,000 feet.
- Look for obstacles around landing area.
- Follow preassigned pattern over landing area or alternate.
- Flare to land and PLF if necessary.

CATEGORY B INSTRUCTOR NOTES
- The instructor must consider carefully before advancing students more quickly than the recommended progression during the rudimentary skills training in Categories A-C. Repetition of fewer skills during the initial categories improves success in later categories and leads to higher overall satisfaction for the student.

Have you joined USPA?

The United States Parachute Association represents and works for skydivers like you. USPA maintains FAA-recognized skydiving training, licensing, and rating programs, sanctions competitions and much more.

As a USPA member, you receive third-party personal liability and property damage skydiving insurance coverage.

Maintaining a strong association of skydivers requires your participation. Please join at your local drop zone, on line at uspa.org, or call (540) 604-9740.

USPA ISP: CATEGORY B | 4-B

category b quiz

ADMINISTERED PRIOR TO CONDUCTING JUMPS IN THE NEXT CATEGORY

Quiz answers are listed in Appendix B.

1. Who must directly supervise your student training jumps?

2. What is your most important task when in freefall?

3. What are the maximum winds in which any student may jump?

4. How would you clear a pilot chute hesitation?

5. In the event of a canopy problem, students should decide and act about executing emergency procedures by what altitude?

6. How would you address the following routine opening problems: line twist, slider up, end cell closure?

7. What is the appropriate action if below 1,000 feet without a landable parachute?

8. If the pilot chute goes over the front of the canopy after it has opened, how can you tell if it's a malfunction?

9. What is the correct response to an open container in freefall using a hand-deployed system?

10. If part of the deployed parachute is caught on the jumper or the equipment (horseshoe), what is the correct response?

11. If the pilot chute extracts the deployment bag from the parachute container (backpack) but the deployment bag fails to release the parachute canopy for inflation, what is the correct response?

12. What are the compass headings of the runway nearest the DZ at your airport?

13. What compass directions do the runway heading numbers represent (northeast-southwest; north-south, etc.)?

14. How long is the longest runway at your airport?

15. Describe the three legs of the canopy landing pattern with relation to the wind direction.

16. At what altitude over the ground do aircraft enter the traffic pattern at your airport?

17. Why is it undesirable to land off the end of a runway?

4-B | USPA ISP: CATEGORY B

Category C

USPA ISP: CATEGORY C | 4-C

INTRODUCTION

By this time, you have had several opportunities to learn controlled, stable fall. Freefall students (AFF and tandem) have a head start on the point of the next lesson's freefall skills: relaxed control using the procedure, "altitude, arch, legs, relax."

Tandem and AFF students usually begin this category with two AFF Instructors but should jump with only one before advancing.

IAD and static-line students perform the first jump in this category identically to the last jump in Category B, preferably on the same day. On subsequent jumps, they practice controlled freefall for ten seconds before deployment on at least two jumps to become accustomed to the shift in direction of the relative wind from ahead to below. It also introduces them to the speed of a near-terminal-velocity freefall.

You need to establish confidence and relaxed freefall control. A controlled freefall in Category C may include some random heading drift, which you learn to lessen by relaxing and focusing on the basics: altitude, arch, legs, and relax.

The instructor shows you more about how to plan a canopy pattern for various wind speeds and directions to improve traffic flow and avoid conflicts with obstacles and other jumpers. You learn to predict, avoid, and react to turbulence induced by wind over obstacles and heated areas.

You'll learn ways to approach an off-field landing, and the drop zone manager explains how off-field landings may affect neighbor relations.

You'll meet the FAA-rated parachute rigger, who packs and maintains the reserve parachute. He or she will familiarize you with the closed parachute system, and you'll observe the pre-flight equipment check.

Emergency review includes discussion on an inadvertently opened parachute in and around the aircraft and how to avoid and respond to it. Also, your instructor provides more details on recognizing and avoiding landing obstacles and how to approach off-field landings.

AFF
- two jumps

IAD/STATIC-LINE
- three jumps

RECOMMENDED MINIMUM DEPLOYMENT
- 4,000 feet

INSTRUCTOR: TRANSITION PROTOCOL

The USPA Tandem program terminates after Category B. All former tandem students may continue in the AFF program, or the remainder of the USPA IAD or static-line progression.

Crossover students to AFF who have completed Category B in the IAD and static-line program will need additional training on the AFF climbout, set-up, and count; AFF freefall communications; use of the altimeter in freefall; and the main parachute deployment device, including deployment device malfunctions. IAD and static-line students may make the first jump in this category with one AFF Instructor on the recommendation of the USPA IAD or Static-Line Instructor and with the concurrence of the USPA AFF Instructor.

Crossover students to IAD or static line who have completed Category B in another training method will need additional training on the IAD or static-line climbout, set-up, and exit commands and use and malfunctions of the IAD or static-line deployment system. AFF and tandem students who have completed Category B must demonstrate a stable practice deployment on an IAD or static-line jump before proceeding to a clear and pull.

4-C USPA ISP: CATEGORY C

Category at a Glance

ADVANCEMENT CRITERIA

EXIT AND FREEFALL

AFF STUDENTS
- demonstrate the ability to freefall safely with one AFF Instructor
- stable solo deployment at assigned altitude

IAD AND STATIC-LINE STUDENTS
- one stable clear and pull
- two stable ten-second freefalls

ALL STUDENTS
- control within five seconds of exit
- stable, relaxed fall
- ability to dampen turns and heading drift using "altitude, arch, legs, relax"
- wave-off and pull at the assigned altitude

CANOPY
- fly a recognizable pattern with minimal assistance
- flare with minimal assistance

SPOTTING AND AIRCRAFT
- understanding of how to plan and adjust the landing pattern for wind speed and direction

ORAL QUIZ

BOOK STUFF
- review BSRs on equipment required for student jumps, SIM Section 2-1.M.2 – 5
- study FAR 105.43.b.1 (SIM Section 9-1) regarding the requirements for periodic inspection and repacking of reserve parachute systems
- discuss with the drop zone owner the ramifications of off-field landings, both legal and from a neighbor and public relations perspective
- read the canopy owner's manual

CATEGORY C: LEARNING AND PERFORMANCE OBJECTIVES

USPA ISP: CATEGORY C | 4-C

- unassisted freefall with heading maintenance
- hover control
- solo deployment
- landing patterns for higher winds
- downwind landings
- wing loading
- accidental opening review
- turbulence
- landing off
- obstacle recognition
- the FAA rigger
- the closed parachute system

A. EXIT AND FREEFALL

1. Pull priorities:
   a. Jumpers must deploy at the planned altitude, regardless of stability.
   b. Priorities are in the following order of importance (top down):
      (1) Pull
      (2) Pull at the correct altitude
      (3) Pull while stable

2. Review of smooth climbout and exit (minimal assistance)
   a. exact hand and foot placement
   b. smooth launch to reduce momentum
   c. correct presentation of hips and chest to the relative wind
   d. legs out for a few seconds to add control

3. Single-instructor exit (AFF, when applicable)
   a. Revise the climbout procedure for one instructor.
   b. Prepare for slightly different results after launch with one instructor (typically more vertical).

4. Review of stability recovery and maintenance "altitude, arch, legs, relax" (IAD and static-line students only after successful clear and pull)—
   a. A.I.R. Provided you are Altitude aware, In control, and Relaxed (AIR), you may continue in freefall and deploy at the assigned altitude.
   b. If you are above your assigned deployment altitude but cannot control your freefall (spinning rapidly or tumbling) employ the stability recovery and maintenance procedure. If unsuccessful after 5 seconds deploy your main canopy immediately. Deploy your main canopy at the assigned deployment altitude regardless of stability.
   c. If you are above your assigned deployment altitude and falling in a back-to-earth orientation, roll to one side to recover to a stable, belly-to-earth body position. Check altitude, arch, look towards the ground to the right, bring the right arm in across your chest, as your body rolls to the right and you are facing the ground bring your right arm back to the freefall position. Check altitude. This is commonly referred to as the "roll out of bed" technique.
   d. know the altitude by reading the altimeter or counting from exit (depending on exit altitude)
   e. arch at the hips to improve belly-to-wind stability
   f. check your leg position and adjust as needed (probably extend to 45 degrees).
   g. relax by taking a breath and letting go of unwanted body tension.
   h. recognize heading (actively correct only if turn training was introduced in Category B).

5. Alternate freefall altitude references
   a. Judge altitude by keeping track of time (average ten seconds for the first 1,000 feet, 5.5 seconds for every additional 1,000 feet).
   b. Look at the ground during the climb to altitude and cross check against the altimeter.
   c. Observe the cloud bases on the ride to altitude to use later as an altitude reference.
   d. Look at the ground after initiating deployment and while waiting for inflation; check what you observed against the altimeter after opening.

6. IAD and static-line students (after first successful clear and pull):
   a. exposure to continuous freefall (two stable ten-second delays recommended to complete Category C)
   b. transition of the relative wind from opposite the aircraft heading to below
   c. altitude, arch, legs, relax
   d. wave-off to signal other jumpers prior to deployment

B. CANOPY

1. Wing loading and canopy size
   a. The wing-loading ratio is the jumper's exit weight (geared up) divided by the square footage of the canopy.

WING LOADING EXAMPLES

jumper's exit weight	215
divided by canopy size (sq. ft.)	280
wing loading	.77:1
jumper's exit weight	215
divided by canopy size (sq. ft.)	195
wing loading	1.1:1

   b. The canopy manufacturer publishes wing loading or load recommendations for each model of canopy.
      (1) in the canopy owner's manual
      (2) on the manufacturer's website
   c. Canopy performance changes with wing loading.
      (1) With a higher wing loading, expect:
         (i) faster forward speed
         (ii) faster descent rate
         (iii) quicker turns
         (iv) steeper and longer dive from a turn
         (v) more violent malfunctions
         (vi) more skill to flare correctly

4-C USPA ISP: CATEGORY C

(2) With a lighter wing loading, expect
  (i) less drive against a strong wind
  (ii) slower turns
  (iii) more forgiveness of landing errors
  (iv) less predictable in turbulence

d. Use the example to calculate the wing loading for the canopy the student is about to jump (one of the Category C advancement criteria).

e. Canopies may appear easier to land with more weight, to a point.
  (1) A good landing in ideal conditions does not mean a smaller canopy is safe to jump in all conditions.
  (2) A more highly loaded canopy will stall at a higher airspeed.

f. With the same wing loading a smaller canopy of the same model will exhibit more lively performance characteristics.
  (1) faster turns and turn response
  (2) quicker dynamic stall response

2. Converting forward speed to lift:
  a. Flaring the canopy quickly to half brakes causes the canopy to slow down abruptly.
  b. Your momentum causes you to swing forward briefly, raising the front of the canopy and flattening the glide.
  c. Continue to flare, braking the canopy more and holding the high nose angle to maintain your lift while reducing the forward speed.
  d. Time your flare so your feet touch the ground before you begin to swing back under the canopy (dynamic stall) or begin to fly backwards (full stall).

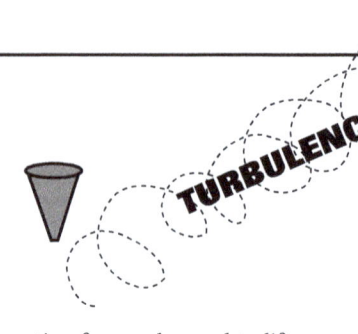

Illustration 4-C.2. Airplane propellers create turbulence.

3. Turbulence sometimes occurs in the landing area.
  a. Anticipate turbulence 10-20 times the height of an obstacle on the downwind side.
  b. The effects and likelihood of turbulence increase with wind speed.
  c. Turbulence often occurs—
    (1) near runways
    (2) alongside roads
    (3) where two areas of different colors or textures meet
    (4) behind other canopies (wake turbulence)
    (5) over irregular terrain
    (6) downwind of the propeller wash of a taxiing aircraft

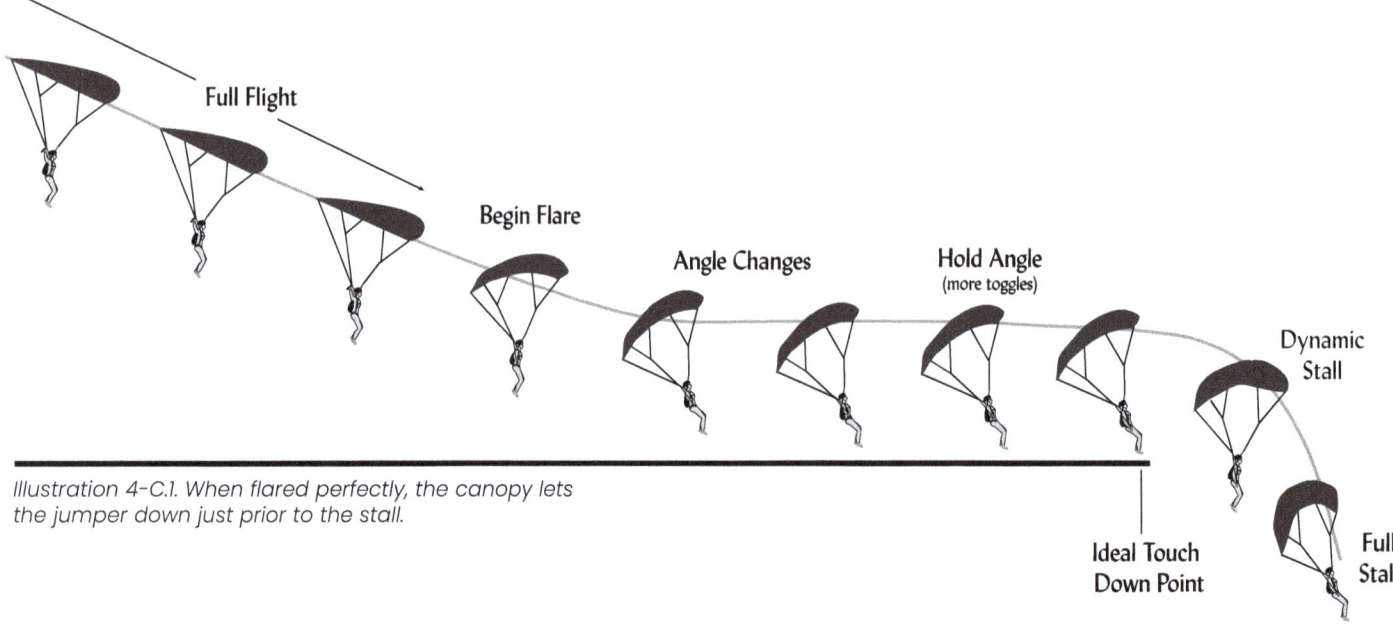

Illustration 4-C.1. When flared perfectly, the canopy lets the jumper down just prior to the stall.

4. When flying in turbulence—
   a. Maintain the desired heading using smooth but effective toggle input.
   b. Fly full speed or as directed in canopy owner's manual.
   c. Prepare for a hard landing.
5. Recognition of a clear field
   a. Power lines run along roads and between buildings, as well as randomly in open fields.
   b. A row of vegetation often hides a fence.
   c. Rocks, hills, and other terrain irregularities often remain invisible until just prior to touchdown.
   d. Inspect an unfamiliar landing area more closely at every 500-foot interval during descent and continuously below 500 feet.
6. Planning a landing pattern (intended landing area or alternate) for smooth flow and separation of traffic:
   a. Jumpers on left-hand (left-turning) approaches should land on the left side of the landing area; jumpers on right-hand approaches should land on the right side of the landing area to prevent conflicts.
   b. The turn from base leg to final is the most hazardous because of opposite approaching traffic
   c. See and avoid.
7. Downwind landings are better than low turns.
   a. On calm days, unexpected wind shifts sometimes require jumpers to land with a light wind, instead of against it.
   b. On windy days, jumpers sometimes fly downwind too long and run out of time to complete a turn into the wind, also requiring them to land with the wind.
   c. When faced with deciding between a low turn or a downwind landing, the downwind landing is the correct decision.
   d. When making a downwind landing—
      (1) Flare at the normal altitude, regardless of ground speed.
      (2) Roll on landing, using the PLF hard-landing procedure.
      (3) Tripping when trying to run out a high-speed landing can result in serious neck injury or death.
8. When to attempt a stand-up landing:
   a. when you're in control of all the variables
   b. after a good flare at the appropriate altitude

C. EMERGENCY PROCEDURE REVIEW

Note: Tandem students should additionally review all Category B emergency procedures on the same day before making any jump in Category C. IAD and static-line students should additionally review procedures for deployment handle problems, premature container opening in freefall (hand deployment), and pilot-chute hesitations before making any jump in Category C.

1. Open parachute in aircraft
   a. extreme care required when leaning back against anything in aircraft
   b. importance of a pre-jump equipment check before leaving the aircraft
   c. importance of careful movement near or outside the door, especially with an AAD
   d. If a parachute opens in the plane:
      (1) If door is closed, secure the parachute and land with the plane.
      (2) If the door is open, contain the parachute, close the door, and land with the plane.
      (3) If the parachute goes out the door, so must the jumper.
2. Importance of deployment at the correct altitude, regardless of stability

USPA ISP: CATEGORY C | 4-C

3. If an off-DZ landing is unavoidable—
   a. Look for an open, clear, accessible field.
   b. Decide on an alternate landing area by 2,000 feet.
   c. Fly a predictable landing pattern.
   d. Transpose the planned landing pattern from the intended field onto the alternate field.
   e. Land well clear of turbulence and obstacles.
   f. Prepare for a hard landing in any unfamiliar landing area.
   g. Be considerate of the property owner when leaving the landing area.
      (1) Cross only at gates or reinforced areas.
      (2) Leave all gates as they are found.
      (3) Do not disturb cattle.
      (4) Walk parallel to (between) any rows of crops until reaching the end of the field.
      (5) Repair or replace any damaged property.
4. Review of landing priorities
   a. Land with the wing level and flying in a straight line.
   b. Land in a clear and open area, avoiding obstacles.
   c. Flare to at least the half-brake position.
   d. Perform a parachute landing fall
5. Collapse an inflated canopy on landing by pulling in one toggle and running toward it.

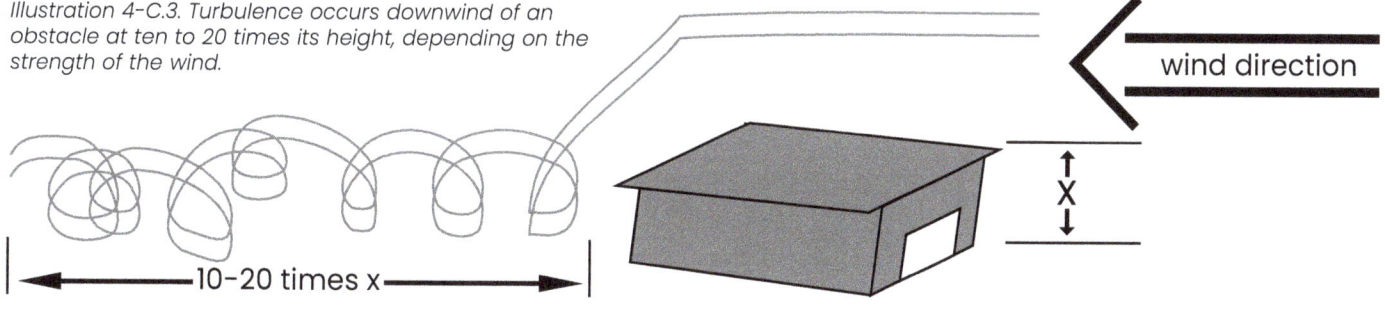

Illustration 4-C.3. Turbulence occurs downwind of an obstacle at ten to 20 times its height, depending on the strength of the wind.

4-C USPA ISP: CATEGORY C

D. EQUIPMENT

1. The automatic activation device:
   a. activates the main or reserve parachute
   b. is worn only as a back-up

   Note: Detailed AAD operation is explained in Category D.

2. Observe the instructor performing the pre-flight check:
   a. top to bottom, back—
      (1) reserve pin in place and straight.
      (2) reserve closing loop must have no visible wear.
      (3) reserve ripcord cable movement in housing.
      (4) reserve packing data card and seal (especially on an unfamiliar or rental rig).
      (5) AAD turned on and/or calibrated.
      (6) main activation cable or pin in place, free of nicks or kinks.
      (7) main closing loop worn no more than ten percent.
      (8) pilot chute bridle routing or ripcord cable movement.
      (9) main activation handle in place.
   b. top to bottom, front—
      (1) overview operation of three-ring release—pulling the cable releases the rings

      Note: Pre-flight details for the three-ring release are covered in Category D. Disassembly and maintenance are explained in Category H.)

      (2) RSL connection, routing, and basic function to back up the jumper in pulling the reserve following a cutaway

      Note: Comprehensive RSL operation is explained in Category E.

      (3) chest strap and hardware intact
      (4) cutaway handle in position
      (5) reserve handle in position
      (6) leg straps and hardware operational and correctly threaded

E. RULES AND RECOMMENDATIONS

1. The BSRs list gear requirements for student jumps in Section 2-1.M.2 through 5.
2. The FAA also regulates the training and certification of the FAA rigger, according to FAR 65.
3. Some skydiving centers are subject to state and local rules or restrictions concerning landing off the DZ.
4. The student should discuss with the drop-zone staff how an off-field landing may affect the jumper and the DZ.

F. SPOTTING AND AIRCRAFT

1. The landing pattern is square on a calm day, with each leg based on the canopy's projected glide distance from 300 feet of altitude (see illustration).
   a. Each jumper must know his or her own canopy's glide distance from 300 feet in no wind to plan a pattern.
   b. The instructor estimates the 300-foot no-wind glide distance for beginning students.
2. The planned final approach must be shortened from the known zero-wind square pattern as the wind increases; for example, cut the final approach approximately in half for ten mph.
3. The base leg also shortens as the wind increases; for example, also cut the base leg approximately in half for a ten-mph wind.
4. Plan the 1,000-foot pattern entry point farther upwind as winds increase; for example, double the length of the downwind leg used for calm conditions, ending at the new projected 600-foot point for ten-mph winds.

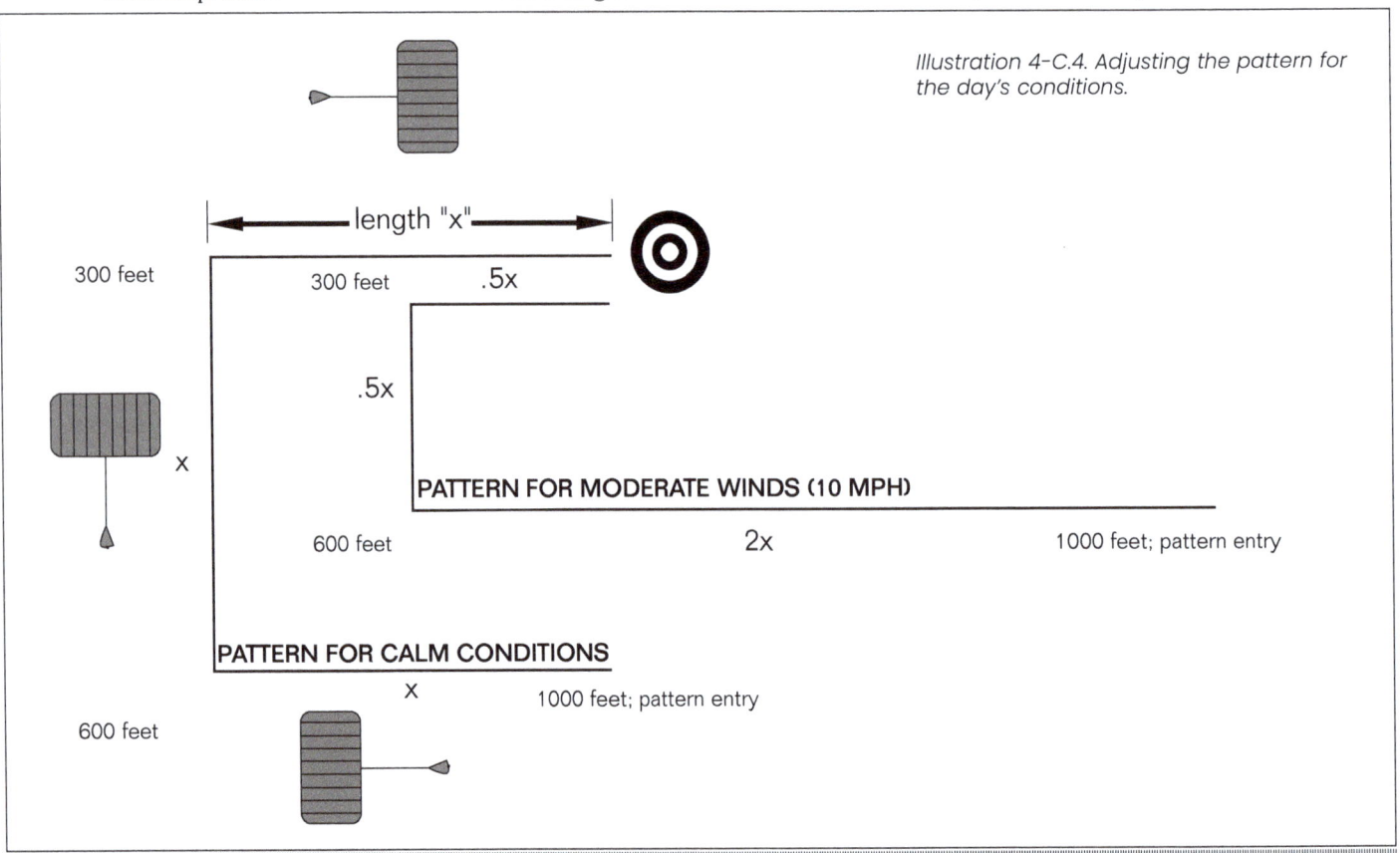

Illustration 4-C.4. Adjusting the pattern for the day's conditions.

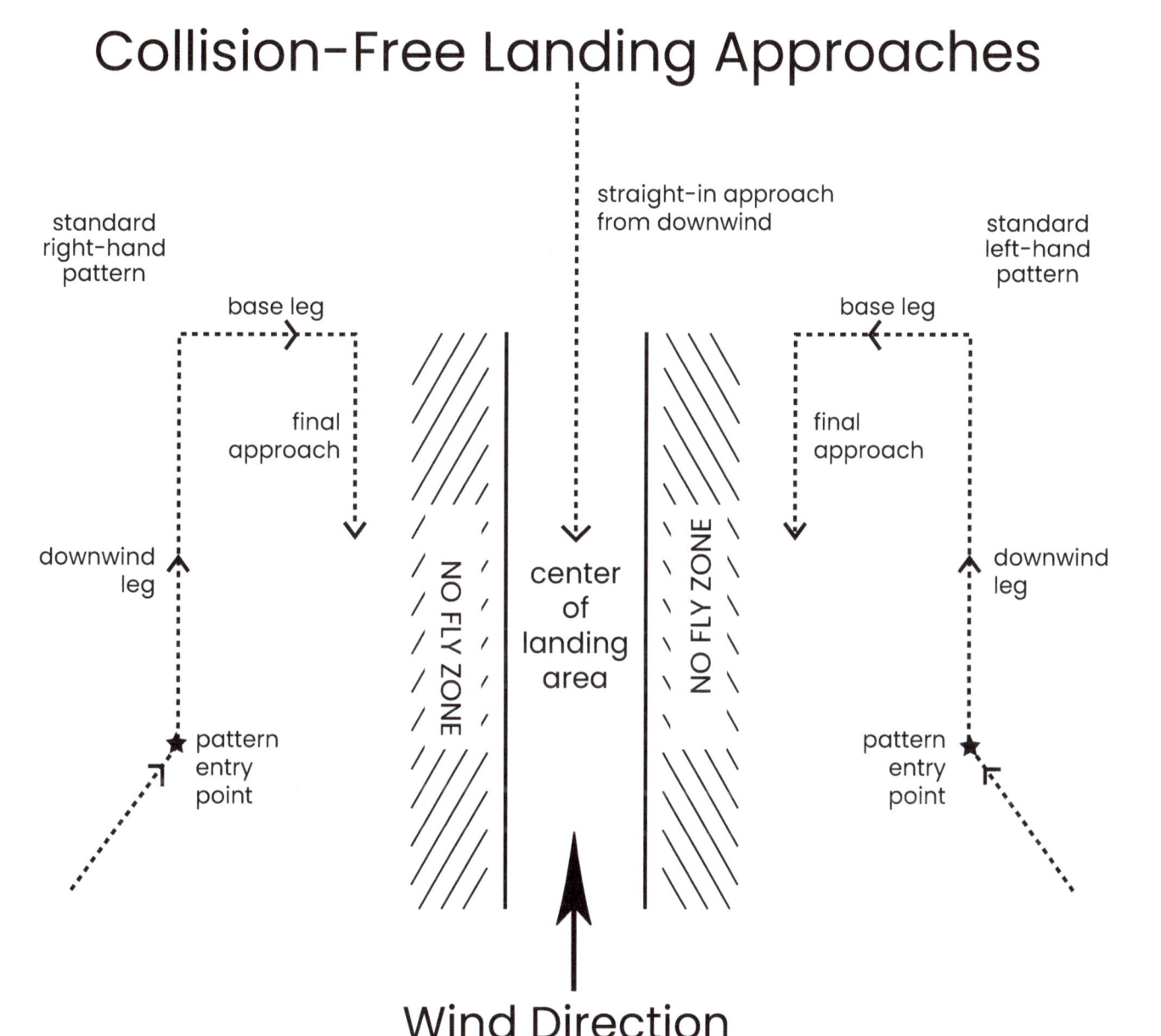

Illustration 4-C.5. Jumpers flying a right-hand pattern should land on the right side of the field; jumpers flying a left-hand pattern should land on the left side of the field.

4-C USPA ISP: CATEGORY C

dive flows

CATEGORY C FREEFALL DIVE FLOWS

AFF

- Exit in a relaxed arch.
- Circle of Awareness.
- Practice deployment(s) until smooth and without assistance.
- Circle of Awareness.
- Instructor(s) release grips as situation allows.
- Altitude, arch, legs, relax.
- Instructor(s) make sure of student control by 6,000 feet or re-grip through deployment.
- Wave-off at 5,500 feet and deploy by 4,000 feet.

IAD AND STATIC-LINE DIVE PLAN #1: CLEAR AND PULL

- Exit on command with legs extended.
- Initiate deployment sequence as practiced on prior jumps, regardless of stability.
- Check canopy.

IAD AND STATIC-LINE DIVE PLAN #2: TEN-SECOND FREEFALL (TWO JUMPS)

- Exit with legs extended.
- Relax into neutral.
- Maintain count to ten by thousands while checking altimeter.
- Wave-off at seven seconds or 4,500 feet and initiate deployment by ten seconds or 4,000 feet, regardless of stability.

CATEGORY C CANOPY DIVE FLOW

- Release brakes and address any routine opening problems.
- Look left, turn left.
- Look right, turn right.
- Flare.
- Check altitude, position, and traffic.
- Find the landing area and pattern entry point.
- Divide the flight path by thousands of feet.
- Identify suspect areas of turbulence.
- Verify landing pattern and adjust as necessary.
- Steer over correct portion of flight path until 1,000 feet.
- Follow planned pattern over landing area or alternate.
- Flare to land and PLF.

CATEGORY C INSTRUCTOR NOTES

- Following release by their AFF Instructors, AFF students who have not received turn training in Category B may encounter heading drift. These students should be taught to recognize a heading change, consider it acceptable, and to correct it using the "altitude, arch, legs, relax" procedure.
- Students who were taught turn technique in Category B may add "correct turn" at the end of that sequence, placing emphasis on the other four, more important points. Relaxed stability must first be established for proper, relaxed control.
- The instructor should advance students only according to the recommended progression during the rudimentary skills training in Categories A-D. Repetition of fewer basic skills improves success later.

category c quiz

ADMINISTERED PRIOR TO CONDUCTING JUMPS IN THE NEXT CATEGORY

Quiz answers are listed in Appendix B.

1. In flat and stable freefall at terminal velocity, how long does it take an average jumper to fall 1,000 feet?

2. What is the correct procedure for recovering from instability to the belly-to-earth position?

3. Which is better, to pull at the planned altitude or to fall lower to get stable before pulling?

4. What is the purpose of the wave-off before deployment?

5. What is the purpose of the parachute landing fall (PLF), and why is it important for skydivers?

6. What part of the landing pattern is most dangerous to skydivers?

7. How do higher wind speeds affect the planned landing pattern as compared to the pattern plan for a calm day?

8. In moderately strong winds, how far downwind of an obstacle would you expect to find turbulence?

9. What is the best procedure to use when flying your canopy in turbulent conditions?

10. What weather conditions and wind direction(s) are most likely to cause turbulence at your drop zone?

11. Why is it important to protect your parachute system operation handles when in and around the aircraft?

12. Describe the equipment pre-flight strategy to use before putting on your gear.

13. How does the three-ring main canopy release system disconnect the main parachute from the harness?

14. How do you know if a reserve parachute has been packed by an FAA rigger within the last 180 days?

15. How do you know the reserve container has not been opened since the FAA rigger last closed it?

16. If the surface winds are blowing from west to east, which direction will you face to fly the downwind leg of the landing pattern (instructor's illustration)?

17. What is the wing loading of the parachute you will use on your next jump?

18. Which canopy size (same model design) will exhibit quicker control response?

    a. 210-square feet with a 210-pound jumper (geared up)

    b. 170 square feet with a 170-pound jumper (geared up)

19. When is it OK to attempt a stand-up landing?

Visualization: Mind Over Body

Did you know that done properly, visualizing what you're about to do can be as effective as practicing it for real? Studies show that the only part of an athlete's performance that visualization won't help is gaining the strength necessary to perform the task.

Exercise is hard, and skydiving is expensive, but visualization is cheap and easy. To begin, go where you can relax and where distractions won't affect you. (Potential distractions may be all around, but you can train your mind to tune them out.) Breathe rhythmically and slowly and recall or imagine a pleasant experience or moment where you are calm and very comfortable.

Then, imagine your upcoming performance exactly as you want it to occur. Start from the beginning, which includes moving to the door of the aircraft, and imagine your actions through to the end. You should even visualize your descent under canopy.

Visualize every detail: where you will place your hands and feet in the door, the cold air rushing in, the noise of the plane, the clean smell of the air, the feel of the aircraft metal on your hands, and everything you can associate with the upcoming experience.

Imagine how you will move every part of your body during the count and exit and how you will feel as you fly away from the plane. Think of where you will position your hands, feet, head, and torso, particularly as you explore techniques for maneuvering in freefall. Visualize every move, including looking at the ground, checking your altimeter, and seeing your instructors.

At this stage of your training, your performance requires as much of your attention as any skydiver training for competition.

Some athletes visualize the upcoming performance from their point of view, while others visualize as if they were watching themselves on TV from above or alongside.

Visualize in slow motion or real time, but no faster. See your performance as one continuous flowing action, rather than as snapshots. As you visualize your actions, associate the motions by feigning the small movements with your hands or your legs with each action ("twitch") as you mentally rehearse the performance.

Leave yourself a few minutes to take in the sights and sounds on the way to altitude, but keep your performance first on your mind. The jumpers who succeed best all practice their routines on the climb to altitude, so you shouldn't feel out of place. Just look around at the others doing the same thing!

At this stage of your training, your performance requires as much of your attention as any skydiver training for competition. Use these same visualization tips that help top athletes in skydiving and other sports to help you improve your performance and increase your overall satisfaction from each jump.

Category D

INTRODUCTION

By now, you have learned to safely control freefall by keeping track of your altitude, focusing on a neutral body position—especially your hips and legs—and relaxing. In Category D, you'll learn to control heading by modifying the neutral position using your upper body to deflect air. You will want to demonstrate relatively effortless control of 90-, 180-, and 360-degree freefall turns before moving on to aerobatics, introduced in Category E.

IAD and static-line students start this category with a 15-second freefall, using the altimeter. IAD and static-line students jump from progressively higher altitudes as they demonstrate control and awareness. On delays of 15 seconds or more, a USPA Instructor should accompany the student in freefall for observation and coaching.

Under canopy, you'll explore rear-riser control, which opens new safety options and adds fun to the canopy ride. Before advancing, you should demonstrate the ability to return to the drop zone and steer a planned, recognizable landing pattern without assistance. To progress to Category E, you should also by now be able to flare and land with minimal assistance. And each student should have been able to stand up on landing by the end of this category.

In Category C, you observed your instructor prepare and inspect your gear for the jump. Now, it's your turn. In Category D, you'll begin studying skydiving equipment in earnest to become responsible for your own pre-flight equipment checks. You'll read the owner's manual for the automatic activation device and learn how to operate one.

The USPA Instructor introduces some of the elements of spotting, which means choosing the correct exit point and guiding the pilot to it. You'll observe jump-run operations from the door.

Study assignments include the FAA requirements for cloud clearance and visibility, which you will need to memorize.

AFF
- two jumps

IAD/STATIC-LINE
- four jumps

RECOMMENDED MINIMUM DEPLOYMENT
- 4,000 feet

INSTRUCTOR: TRANSITION PROTOCOL

AFF students transferring to the remainder of the IAD or static-line progression must first exit stable on an AFF jump without instructor contact or make a stable IAD or static-line jump with a practice deployment (BSRs).

AFF students transferring to the remainder of the IAD or static-line progression must first exit stable on an AFF jump without instructor contact or make a stable IAD or static-line jump with a practice deployment (BSRs).

4-D USPA ISP: CATEGORY D

Category at a Glance

ADVANCEMENT CRITERIA

EXIT AND FREEFALL

AFF STUDENTS
- stability within five seconds after an unassisted poised exit

ALL STUDENTS
- cumulative four 90-degree turns, 20-degree tolerance
- cumulative two 180-degree and two 360-degree turns, 45-degree tolerance

CANOPY
- cumulative two 90-degree rear riser turns with brakes set
- cumulative two 90-degree rear riser turns with brakes released
- one 180-degree rear riser turn, and one 360-degree rear riser turn with brakes released
- two rear riser flares above 2,000 feet
- landing within 165 feet of the target with minimal assistance

EQUIPMENT
- operate the AAD

SPOTTING AND AIRCRAFT
- recognize and observe the airport and the spot from the aircraft door during jump run

ORAL QUIZ

BOOK STUFF

- read and memorize the table on cloud clearance and visibility requirements in FAR 105.17 (SIM Section 9-1)
- review SIM Section 2-1.G.9 (BSRs) on daylight requirements for student jumps
- study SIM Section 5-1.F to review building landing procedures
- study SIM Section 5-1.E on equipment malfunctions
- read the AAD owner's manual
- study SIM Section 5-3.G on AADs

CATEGORY D: LEARNING AND PERFORMANCE OBJECTIVES

USPA ISP: CATEGORY D | 4-D

- solo, unassisted exit (AFF students)
- freefall turns
- freefall speeds and times (review)
- rear riser control
- building landing review
- AAD (owner's manual)
- pre-jump equipment check
- introduction to three-ring release operation
- cloud clearance and visibility
- observe jump run

A. EXIT AND FREEFALL

1. AFF students: poised exit without assistance

   Note: Instructor grips are optional, based on previous performance.

   a. Use the same climbout, set-up, launch, and flyaway procedure as on previous exits.
   b. Prepare for slightly different results without an instructor gripping the harness on exit.
   c. Altitude, arch, legs, relax.
   d. Review Category C freefall stability recovery and maintenance procedures (AIR, ROB, Five-Second rule, etc.)
   e. Exit without assistance and establish control within five seconds before advancing from Category D.

2. Initiating freefall turns

   a. First establish a comfortable, relaxed, neutral body position.
   b. Find a point ahead on the horizon as a primary heading reference (and also use the instructor).
   c. Initiate a turn by changing the level of your upper arms to deflect air to one side; the forearms should follow.
   d. Assist the turn's effectiveness by extending both legs slightly to counter the effects of tension in the upper body.
   e. Any deviation from the neutral position (as when initiating a turn) demands more effort to maintain the rest of the body in neutral.
   f. Maintain leg pressure and arch for a smooth turn.
   g. Stop small turns (90 degrees or less) by returning to the neutral body position.
   h. Stop larger turns (180 and 360 degrees) using the "start-coast-stop" principle.

      (1) Start the turn using the turn position for the first half to three quarters of the turn.
      (2) Return to neutral (to coast) when the desired heading comes into view.
      (3) Counter the turn if necessary to stop on heading.

   i. To regain lost control: altitude, arch, legs, relax (neutral position), then pick a new heading to maintain.
   j. Stop all maneuvers at 5,000 feet and maintain a stable arch on heading with positive leg pressure through wave-off and deployment.

3. Calculating freefall time according to exit altitude based on average terminal velocity of 120 mph:

   a. ten seconds for the first 1,000 feet
   b. 5.5 seconds for each additional thousand feet (round down to five seconds for an added safety margin)
   c. example: jump from 5,000 feet with a planned deployment altitude of 3,000 feet—

      (1) Allow ten seconds from 5,000 to 4,000 feet.
      (2) Add five seconds from 4,000 to 3,000 feet.
      (3) Plan a total of 15 seconds for freefall.

B. CANOPY

1. Rear riser steering

   a. Steer using the rear risers with the brakes still set to change heading quickly after opening.

      (1) With the brakes set, the canopy has less forward momentum to overcome for a turn.
      (2) The rear risers operate more than the entire back quarter of canopy.

   b. Using risers to steer in case of a malfunctioned toggle (discussion):

      (1) Release both brakes.
      (2) You need to conserve enough strength to complete all turns with rear risers until landing and still be able to flare.
      (3) Especially on a smaller canopy, you should practice riser flares many times above 2,000 feet on a routine jump before committing to a riser landing (important).
      (4) Your plan to land or cut away your canopy in the event of a malfunctioned toggle should be made before you ever encounter the problem.
      (5) One locked brake with the other released may necessitate a cutaway; decide and act by 2,500 feet.

   c. Practice all riser maneuvers above 2,000 feet and focus on the canopy pattern and traffic from 1,000 feet down, using a standard pattern for landing.
   d. Before making any turns, look in the direction of the turn to prevent collisions and entanglements.

2. With minimal assistance, land within 165 feet of the target before advancing from Category D.

C. EMERGENCY PROCEDURE REVIEW

1. Training harness review (study Section 5-1.E of this manual):

   a. quicker recognition and decision-making ability for good or bad canopy (lower pull altitude)

      (1) Review sample problems not requiring a cutaway and practice the procedures.
      (2) Review premature deployment.
      (3) Review sample malfunctions requiring a cutaway and practice the procedures.

   b. procedures for testing a questionable canopy above cutaway altitude

4-D USPA ISP: CATEGORY D

   (1) Make two tries to clear the problem with toggles or back risers if altitude permits.
   (2) The canopy must fly straight, turn, and flare reliably to be able to land safely.
   (3) Decide to cut away or land the canopy by 2,500 feet and act.
2. Procedures for landing on a building: Refer to the procedures in Section 5-1.F of this manual.

D. EQUIPMENT

1. Automatic activation device operation
   a. The instructor or a rigger explains the basics of how to operate the AAD.
   b. More AAD information is contained in the owner's manual, which every jumper should read.
   c. Refer to Section 5-3.G of this manual for more information on AADs.
2. Checking assembly of the three-ring release system:

   Note: Disassembly and maintenance of the three-ring release is covered in Category H.

   a. Each ring passes through only one other ring.
   b. The white retaining loop passes through only the topmost, smallest ring.
   c. The white retaining loop passes through the cable housing terminal end.
   d. The release cable passes through the loop.
   e. The retaining loop is undamaged.
   f. The release cable is free of nicks, kinks, and burrs (especially on the end).
3. Pre-jump equipment checks

   Note: The instructor should guide you through a complete pre-flight equipment check using a written checklist.

   a. Before each jump, check your equipment before putting it on.
   b. With the help of another jumper, get a complete equipment check with all your gear on before boarding
   c. Get your equipment checked once again before exiting the aircraft.
      (1) "check of threes" (jumper self-check)
         (i) three-ring assembly (and reserve static line)
         (ii) three points of harness attachment for snap assembly and correct routing and adjustment
         (iii) three operation handles—main activation, cutaway, reserve
      (2) pin check back of system (by another jumper) top to bottom
         (i) reserve pin in place (and automatic activation device on and set)
         (ii) main pin in place
         (iii) ripcord cable movement or correct bridle routing
         (iv) activation handle in place
      (3) personal equipment check ("SHAGG")
         Shoes—tied, no hooks
         Helmet—fit and adjustment
         Altimeter—set for zero
         Goggles—tight and clean
         Gloves—lightweight and proper size
4. Jumpsuit or clothes
   a. access to handles—shirt tails, jackets, and sweatshirts tucked in, pockets zipped closed
   b. protection on landing
   c. provide correct fall rate

E. RULES AND RECOMMENDATIONS

1. Cloud clearance and visibility requirements for skydivers (FAR 105.17)
   a. Memorize the cloud clearance and visibility table in FAR 105.17 (or see illustration 4-D.1).
   b. The FAA places the joint responsibility for cloud clearance and visibility on the jumper and the pilot.
2. USPA requires that all student jump operations be completed prior to sunset (BSRs).

F. SPOTTING AND AIRCRAFT

1. Instructor-assisted planning with the landing pattern for the day's conditions
2. Overview of aircraft spotting and jump-run procedures (what "spotting" means):

   Note: It is recommended that a jump pilot explain spotting procedures in Category E.

   a. determining the best opening point
      (1) calculations from wind forecasts
      (2) observation and discussion of previous jumpers' canopy descents
   b. pre-flight briefing with the pilot to discuss the correct jump run and exit points
   c. guiding the pilot on jump run
   d. verifying that the area below is clear of clouds and other aircraft before jumping
3. During jump run, observe spotting procedures and demonstrate the technique for looking straight down from the aircraft.
   a. Sight from the horizon looking forward.
   b. Sight from the horizon looking abreast.
   c. The junction of the two perpendicular lines from the horizon marks the point straight below the aircraft.
4. You must get your head completely outside the aircraft to effectively look below for other aircraft and clouds.

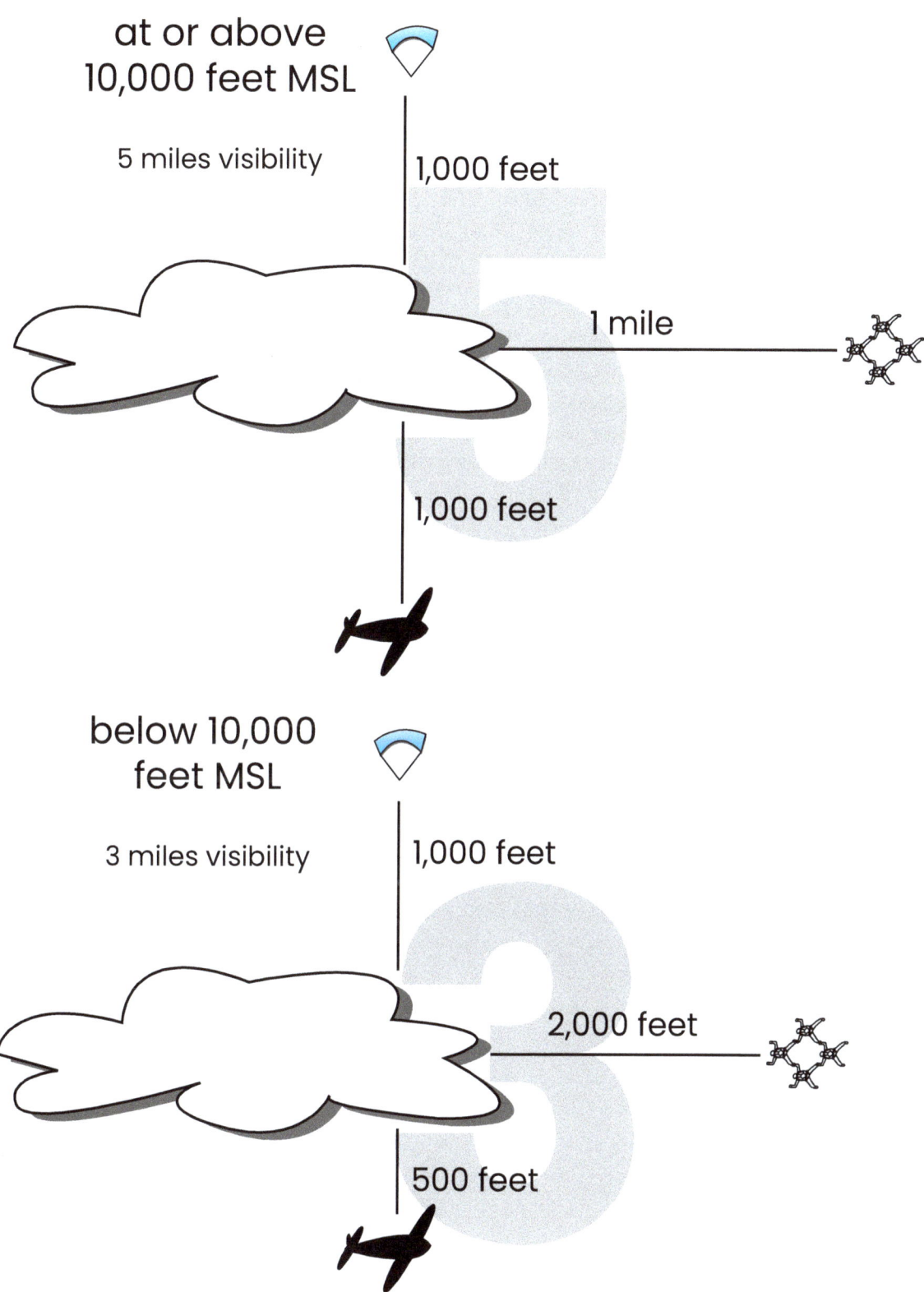

Illustration 4-D.1: Jumpers must observe the FAA requirements for visibility and clearance from clouds to avoid other aircraft flying over the drop zone.

4-D | USPA ISP: CATEGORY D

dive flows

CATEGORY D FREEFALL DIVE FLOWS

AFF DIVE PLAN #1: 90-DEGREE TURNS

- Observe spotting from the door.
- Exit in a relaxed arch (grip optional).
- Circle of Awareness.
- Practice pull(s) (optional).
- Altitude, arch, legs, relax.
- Find a reference point on the horizon and determine the position of the instructor.
- Ask permission to turn (head nod).
- Receive reply from instructor (head nod).
- Start a turn and stop at 90 degrees.
- Altitude, arch, legs, relax.
- Perform (with instructor's permission each time) alternating 90-degree turns until 5,000 feet; initiate no turns below 6,000 feet.
- Altitude, arch, legs, relax.
- Wave-off at 5,000 feet.
- Pull by 4,000 feet.

AFF DIVE PLAN #2: 180- AND 360-DEGREE TURNS

- Observe spotting from the door.
- Solo poised exit in a relaxed arch.
- Circle of Awareness.
- Practice pull(s) (optional).
- Altitude, arch, legs, relax.
- Find a reference point on the horizon and determine the position of the instructor.
- Ask permission to turn (head nod).
- Receive reply from instructor (head nod).
- Start a turn and stop at 180 degrees.
- Altitude, arch, legs, relax.
- If altitude permits, turn 180 degrees back to instructor.
- Perform (with instructor's permission each time) alternating 360-degree turns until 5,000 feet; initiate no turns below 6,000 feet.
- Altitude, arch, legs, relax.
- Wave-off at 5,000 feet.
- Pull by 4,000 feet.

IAD AND STATIC LINE:

90-, 180- and 360-Degree Turns

Note: Recommended are two 15-second delays, two 30-second delays, and then longer delays until the cumulative four 90-degree, two 180-degree and two 360-degree turns required have been accomplished.

- Observe spotting from the door.
- Exit in a relaxed arch.
- Awareness check (ground and altimeter).
- Practice pull (optional).
- Altitude, arch, legs, relax.
- Find a point on ground 45-degrees ahead and below.
- Start and stop a turn on a planned heading,
- 90 degrees (4)
- 180-degrees (2)
- 360-degrees (2)
- Between each turn: Altitude, arch, legs, relax.
- Repeat turns in alternating directions until 5,000 feet.
- Altitude, arch, legs, relax.
- Wave-off at 4,500 feet.
- Pull by 4,000 feet.

CATEGORY D CANOPY DIVE FLOWS

DIVE PLAN #1

- Correct minor canopy problems (line twist, slider, end cells) using rear risers with brakes set.
- Look right, turn right 90 degrees using right rear riser.
- Check altitude, position, and traffic.
- Repeat to the left.
- Check altitude, position, and traffic.
- Release brakes, conduct control check and move to the holding area
- Look right, turn right 90 degrees using rear risers.
- Check altitude, position, and traffic.
- Repeat to the left.
- Look right, turn right 180 degrees using rear risers.
- Check altitude, position, and traffic.
- Repeat to the left.
- Check altitude, position, and traffic.
- Practice rear riser flares.
- Return to normal controls for landing by 2,000 feet.

DIVE PLAN #2

- Correct minor canopy problems (line twist, slider, end cells) using rear risers with brakes set.
- Look right, turn right 90 degrees using right rear riser.
- Check altitude, position, and traffic.
- Repeat to the left.
- Check altitude, position, and traffic.
- Release brakes, conduct control check and move to the holding area
- Look right, turn right 360 degrees using right rear riser.
- Check altitude, position, and traffic.
- Repeat to the left.
- Check altitude, position, and traffic.
- Practice rear riser flares.
- Return to normal controls for landing by 2,000 feet.

category d quiz

ADMINISTERED PRIOR TO CONDUCTING JUMPS IN THE NEXT CATEGORY

Quiz answers are listed in Appendix B.

1. For planned deployment initiation at 3,000 feet, approximately how long should an average-sized jumper fall after exiting at 5,000 feet?

2. What is the most appropriate response to loss of heading control in freefall?

3. What is the best way to avoid a canopy collision when turning?

4. What is the quickest and safest way to change heading immediately after opening?

5. How would you steer a parachute that has a broken brake line?

6. How would you prepare to land a canopy using the rear risers to flare?

7. Describe your procedure for landing on a building

8. What is the purpose of the automatic activation device?

9. Describe the "check of threes."

10. What must the spotter do to determine what is directly underneath the aircraft while on jump run?

11. How far horizontally must jumpers be from any cloud?
    a. below 10,000 feet MSL?
    b. 10,000 feet MSL and above?

12. What are the minimum visibility requirements?
    a. below 10,000 feet MSL?
    b. 10,000 feet MSL and above?

13. Who is responsible for a jumper observing cloud clearance requirements?

14. According to the BSRs, what is the latest a student may jump?

15. Describe the technique for determining the point straight below the aircraft during jump run.

16. What must the jumper look for below before exiting the aircraft?

Learning Spotting One Jump at a Time

Before earning a USPA A license, you are expected to learn to spot in routine conditions. "Spotting" simply means choosing the opening point and guiding the pilot to the correct position over the ground for exit. You can calculate the spot from a winds-aloft report. FAA Flight Service provides these reports, which you can get from the pilot.

When you're in the door before exit, spotting starts with determining exactly what's straight down and how the plane is moving across the ground. A good spotter's training never ends.

Here are some tips for beginners:

1. Be familiar with the DZ and surrounding area, including the correct exit and opening points for the day's conditions. The USPA Instructor will simply tell you at first and then show you how to figure it for yourself later.
2. Look out of the aircraft, obviously done best with the door open and your head all the way outside. Small aircraft give you more opportunities to practice spotting. In larger aircraft, your instructor will arrange some door time. First, just get comfortable looking out. Put your head all the way out into the windstream.
3. Identify the DZ, the climbout point, and exit point from the open door of the aircraft. Point them out to your instructor or coach.
4. Look straight down, using horizon reference points. Avoid using the aircraft as a reference. On jump run, the plane is often climbing, banking, skidding, or crabbing.
5. Determine the track of the aircraft. Once you can identify two points straight below the plane on jump run, you know the actual path of the aircraft across the ground. If you see that it will take you too far to the left or right, suggest a correction to the one supervising your jump, who will relay your corrections to the pilot.
6. Allow enough time (distance) for your climbout and set-up to separate you from other jumpers. Learn when to climb out.

Soon, you'll give directions to the pilot under supervision. After a while, the USPA Instructor or Coach won't interfere unless your spotting appears unsafe.

Your spotting training will require several jumps, and the staff will log your progress. Spot as often as you can during your training as a student so you'll feel confident later when you're on your own.

When you're in the door before exit, spotting starts with determining exactly what's straight down and how the plane is moving across the ground.

Category E

USPA ISP: CATEGORY E | 4-E

INTRODUCTION

This is the last category that distinguishes between students of different disciplines. Once you have demonstrated the ability to regain stability and control within five seconds after initiating a disorienting maneuver, a USPA Instructor in your discipline may clear you to jump without instructor supervision in freefall. At that point, any USPA Instructor may perform gripped exits with you, as well.

From Category E on, a USPA Instructor makes sure you are properly trained and supervised on each jump.

In Category E, you practice unpoised (door) exits and aerobatics to increase your confidence, awareness, and control in freefall. You should by now be jumping from the highest altitude available at your drop zone.

Under canopy, you'll practice for softer landings by looking for the "sweet spot" in the flare—the flaring stroke that provides the best lift for that canopy with that jumper's weight. The goal is to flare your canopy to fly as flat as possible until you begin to touch down. The USPA Instructor will also remind you of your responsibility (and every jumper's responsibility) to observe and steer clear of other canopies.

By the end of Category D, you should have been able to land within 165 feet of the target with minimal assistance. In Category E, you should be able to do it on your own.

Part of the emergency procedure review includes a detailed discussion on preventing premature openings in freefall and more detailed procedures for two open canopies.

A rigger or instructor will introduce you to the open parachute system to identify its key components, along with the FAA's rules for packing parachutes. Supervised packing begins in Category F.

You'll discuss weight, balance, airspeed, jump run procedures, and aircraft emergency procedures, usually with a jump pilot. A jump pilot or USPA Instructor also shows you how to read a winds-aloft report. From that information, you'll learn to calculate the best opening point over the ground.

In Categories E through H, you're expected to select and prepare your equipment for jumping (with the supervising USPA Instructor's advice), including obtaining all recommended pre-jump equipment checks. You're also learning to spot, where to sit in the aircraft, and to allow enough distance between the jumpers exiting before you. You should know the surface winds and plan the appropriate landing pattern.

In order to be cleared to student self-supervision by a USPA Instructor, you must have obtained the following skills and knowledge:

1. Demonstrated the ability to regain stability and control in freefall within five seconds after initiating a disorienting maneuver.
2. Demonstrated sufficient canopy control skills to land safely in all expected conditions.
3. Demonstrated the knowledge required to select and inspect gear before use.
4. Shown knowledge of spotting required to make reasonable judgment about suggested exit points,
5. Shown knowledge of both normal and emergency aircraft procedures for all aircraft types in common use for skydiving.

ALL STUDENTS
- three jumps

RECOMMENDED MINIMUM DEPLOYMENT
- 4,000 feet

4-E USPA ISP: CATEGORY E

Category at a Glance

ADVANCEMENT CRITERIA

EXIT AND FREEFALL

- cumulative two successive disorienting maneuvers with stability and altitude awareness recovered within five seconds

Note: Once this requirement is met and you have received the endorsement of a USPA Instructor in your training discipline, your training may be supervised by any USPA Instructor. You may then self-supervise in freefall, but remain under USPA Instructor supervision. A USPA instructional rating holder should accompany you in the aircraft to verify the correct spot, clearance from clouds and aircraft, exit separation, and your position in the line-up.

- cumulative one barrel roll, one back loop, and one front loop
- one self-supervised freefall

CANOPY

- unassisted landing within 165 feet

EQUIPMENT

- complete open parachute system orientation
- RSL orientation

SPOTTING AND AIRCRAFT

- correct calculation of the opening point given simple wind conditions
- active participation with spotting procedures on jump run

ORAL QUIZ

BOOK STUFF

- review BSRs on wind restrictions for students, SIM Section 2-1.H
- read BSRs on oxygen requirements for jumps above 15,000 feet MSL, SIM Section 2-1.N; also FAR 91.211.A.3
- read and discuss USPA recommendations on dual ram-air deployments, SIM Section 5-1.E
- read and discuss USPA recommendations on reserve static lines in SIM Section 5-3.F
- read and discuss USPA recommendations on altimeters in SIM Section 5-3.J
- read and understand FAA Part 91 sections contained in SIM Section 9-1
- read and discuss with an FAA rigger FAR 105.43.a and .b (SIM Section 9-1) on parachute packing and supervision requirements for packers

CATEGORY E: LEARNING AND PERFORMANCE OBJECTIVES

USPA ISP: CATEGORY E | 4-E

- door (unpoised) exit
- recovering stability and awareness
- freefall aerobatics
- canopy stalls
- the canopy's "sweet spot"
- two canopies deployed (review)
- high-wind landings
- reserve static line
- open parachute orientation
- parachute packing and supervision
- wind limits for students
- aircraft briefing
- aircraft emergency procedures
- selecting the opening point

A. EXIT AND FREEFALL

1. Stable door (unpoised) exit—
   a. Position for the best launch.
   b. Present the front of your hips to the relative wind.
   c. Exit in a neutral position with your legs slightly extended (better stability).
   d. Maintain your arch as the relative wind changes from ahead to below after exit.

2. Recovering from exit and freefall instability—
   a. Altitude, arch, legs, relax (review).
   b. If falling stable back-to-earth although arching, briefly retract one arm and look over that shoulder at the ground to return face-to-earth (half barrel roll).

3. Barrel rolls, back loops, and front loops (instructor's preferred technique)
   a. Try barrel rolls first, because they have a built-in recovery component from back-to-earth.
   b. Any two disorienting maneuvers with recovery and reorientation within five seconds qualify you for self-supervision in freefall (the same one may be used twice).

4. Rolls, loops and other freeflying maneuvers result in faster and erratic fall rates; check altitude often.

5. Visual altimeters, especially when chest-mounted, may be unreliable during inverted positions (see SIM Section 5-3.J.4).

B. CANOPY

1. Types of stalls
   a. An aerodynamic stall is a stable, steady-state stall, or sink, with decreased glide and increased rate of descent.
      (1) associated with older designs and specialized accuracy canopies
      (2) may not be achievable with newer, flatter-gliding canopies, which often fly flatter almost until a full stall
   b. A dynamic stall occurs at the end of a flare when the jumper begins to rock back under the canopy and the canopy begins to nose forward.
      (1) associated with a sharp dive
      (2) may signal a full stall
   c. A full stall occurs when the trailing edge (tail) is pulled below the leading edge (nose) and the canopy begins to fly backwards.
      (1) collapses the canopy
      (2) may result in unrecoverable line twist in smaller, more highly loaded wings stalled with the toggles (a back-riser stall may be more controllable)
      (3) may be contrary to the manufacturer's recommendations
      (4) may result in entanglement with the jumper if released too abruptly
      (5) may result in injury if done too low

2. Raise the controls smoothly after any stall to avoid diving and partial collapse.

3. Proper flare technique:
   a. Keep your feet and knees together to maintain heading during the landing flare (level harness).
   b. Flare with the hands in front to provide visual feedback for level control.

4. Discovering the best landing flare ("sweet spot") for the canopy being jumped (nine practice flares):

Note: Complete all maneuvers above 1,000 feet.

   a. From full glide, flare to a mid-point in the toggle range.
      (1) approximately the bottom of the rib cage
      (2) at a medium rate of flare
   b. Feel the amount and duration of lift before the stall.
   c. Return gently to full flight for at least ten seconds.
   d. Repeat to the same depth.
      (1) once at a faster rate
      (2) once at a slower rate
   e. Compare the strength and duration of the lift before the stall.
   f. Flare at three different speeds to a point deeper in the toggle stroke, approximately at the hips.
   g. Flares at three different speeds to a higher point in the toggle stroke, approximately at the shoulders.
   h. Compare the flares to determine the stroke rate and depth that produces the maximum combined strength and duration of lift for that canopy.

5. Best flare height above the ground
   a. Use the best flare procedure (discovered during the nine practice flares) upon landing, beginning one body height above ground.
   b. Flare to minimum descent (or flat) and hold that toggle position when the glide begins to flatten.
   c. Smoothly continue the toggle stroke to maintain the flat glide.
   d. If the canopy begins to stall and drops several feet, begin the flare that much lower on the next jump.
   e. If you don't achieve the flattest glide before landing, begin to flare slightly higher on the next jump.

4-E USPA ISP: CATEGORY E

6. Review of traffic avoidance procedures:
   a. Watch for other traffic, especially upon entering the landing pattern.
   b. The most dangerous point of the pattern occurs when two jumpers on opposite base-leg approaches turn to final approach.
   c. The lower canopy has the right of way, but one jumper should not maneuver to assert right of way over another.
   d. It takes two people to have a collision, but only one to avoid it.

C. EMERGENCY PROCEDURE REVIEW

1. Preventive measures for two open canopies
   a. Deploy the main parachute at the correct altitude to avoid AAD activation.
   b. Initiate malfunction procedures high enough to cut away safely and avoid AAD activation.
   c. Maintain and correctly operate hand-deployed pilot chutes, especially collapsibles.
   d. Protect your equipment before exit to prevent pins or handles being knocked loose.
   e. Some AADs, particularly those used for student jumping, will activate under a fully open parachute when controlled too aggressively at lower altitudes.
2. Review detailed procedures for two canopies out as they pertain to experienced jumpers, found in SIM Section 5-1.
3. Procedures for high-wind landings
   a. Before landing, disconnect the RSL as a precaution in case a cutaway becomes necessary to prevent being dragged.
   b. Choose a point to the side or well downwind of any obstacle that may generate turbulence.
   c. Land using a PLF and pull one toggle in as quickly as possible until the canopy collapses.
   d. After landing, cut away if necessary (with an SOS, cutting away may open the reserve container, but only the reserve pilot chute will likely deploy).

D. EQUIPMENT

1. Attend the Category E Open Parachute Orientation (inset) to prepare for packing lessons.
2. Typical characteristics of elliptical canopies, compared to rectangular canopies of the same size and material:
   a. flatter glide for same airspeed
   b. faster turns
   c. greater loss of altitude in a turn
   d. may continue to dive after stopping control input following a turn
   e. slower, less predictable opening (some models)
   f. shorter toggle stroke for flare (some models)
   g. quicker, more abrupt stall (some models)
3. The stall speed of any wing increases with higher wing loading.
   a. more suspended weight
   b. sudden maneuvers, such as flaring hard after a dive
   c. Use and limitations of the reserve static line, or RSL (SIM 5-3).

E. RULES AND RECOMMENDATIONS

1. Winds
   a. Students are limited to 14 mph (ten mph for round reserves).
   b. A USPA S&TA may file a waiver for students to jump in higher winds (see Section 2-2 on waivers to the BSRs, for the procedure).
   c. Licensed jumpers must exercise judgment.
2. The FAA publishes rules for the periodic inspection and repacking of the main and reserve parachute system, found in FAR 105.43.a and b (SIM 9-1).

F. SPOTTING AND AIRCRAFT

1. Attend the Aircraft Briefing (inset).
2. Spotting (pilot or instructor)
   a. how to read a winds-aloft report
   b. true v. magnetic heading
   c. jump-run procedures
   d. spotting corrections
      (1) manual (hand signals, shoulder taps)
      (2) electronic (spotting buttons and lights)
      (3) verbal
3. The effect of winds during canopy descent
   a. A canopy descends at approximately 1,000 feet per minute.
   b. Divide the opening altitude by 1,000 feet to determine time of descent, e.g., 3,000 feet = three minutes of descent.
   c. Estimate in miles per minute the amount of drift during descent, as in Table 4-E.1:
4. Calculate the drift under canopy from

MPH	MILES PER MINUTE	DRIFT FROM 3,000 FEET
60	1	N/A
30	1/2	N/A
20	1/3	1 MILE
15	1/4	3/4 MILE
10	1/6	1/2 MILE
5	1/12	1/4 MILE

Table 4-E.1. Convert miles per hour to miles per minute and multiply times three minutes (approximately 1,000 feet of descent per minute) to estimate drift under canopy.

3,000 feet, based on the average of the known winds and a canopy descent rate of 1,000 feet per minute, to choose the correct opening point—example (Table 4-E.2):

   a. canopy descent time from 3,000 feet (at 1,000 feet per minute): three minutes
   b. total (uncontrolled) drift at 1/4 mile per minute: 3/4 mile
   c. ideal opening point: 3/4 mile due west

WINDS (FORECAST AND OBSERVED)		
Altitude	Direction	Speed
3,000 AGL*	280	20
Surface	260	10
Average	270	15

Use Table 4-E.1 above to estimate the canopy's drift during a three-minute descent in winds averaging 15 mph. under canopy.
*above ground level

DRIFT			
Open	Time	Distance	Direction
3,000 ft	3 min (x 1/4)	3/4 mi.	from 270

Table 4-E.2. Average the wind direction and velocity to estimate drift after opening at 3,000 feet above the ground.

USPA ISP: CATEGORY E — 4-E

5. Observe and ask jumpers on a previous load about the wind conditions and spot.
6. Jumper procedures during jump run
   a. The pilot determines when the door may be opened and may prefer to operate the door.
   b. Look below to—
      (1) check for clouds
      (2) check for aircraft
      (3) verify the jump run is correct
   c. When the pilot gives the OK to jump, verify that the aircraft is the desired distance from the drop zone and begin exit procedures.
7. Be sure to establish communications for spotting corrections with the pilot prior to flight.

AIRCRAFT BRIEFING

The following briefing for Category E students covers the interaction between the jumpers, the aircraft, and the pilots:

1. Sufficient airspeed is necessary for flight; without it, the aircraft wing stalls.

ALTERNATE METHOD FOR CALCULATING FREEFALL AND CANOPY DRIFT

EXAMPLE FOR CALCULATING FREEFALL DRIFT

Altitude	Heading	Speed (mph)
3,000 ft	250	15 mph
6,000 ft	260	18 mph
9,000 ft	280	22 mph
12,000 ft	290	25 mph
Average	270	20 mph

To simplify the process, convert mph to mile per minute (mpm).

*Assuming a one minute freefall, 20 divided by 60 equals .33 miles.

Freefall drift is equal to .33 miles at 270 degrees.

EXAMPLE FOR CALCULATING CANOPY DRIFT

Altitude	Heading	Speed (mph)
Surface	180	12 mph
3,000 ft	200	18 mph
Average	190	15 mph

To simplify the process, convert mph to mile per minute (mpm).

*Assuming a four-minute canopy flight, 15 divided by 60 is equal to .25 miles.

Canopy drift is equal to .25 miles multiplied by four minutes which is equal to one mile at 190 degrees.

2. Weight
   a. Aircraft weight limits are specified in the aircraft owner's manual and other documentation and, by law, may not be exceeded.
   b. Weight includes:
      (1) fuel
      (2) occupants
      (3) skydiving equipment
      (4) other (jump seats, oxygen systems, etc.)
   c. The weight must be calculated for each load.
3. Weight distribution (center of gravity)
   a. The load in an aircraft must be distributed within center of gravity limits to fly.
   b. Limits are published in the owner's manual and other documentation.
   c. The pilot must calculate and monitor weight distribution for each flight.
   d. Jumpers moving around the aircraft can place the load out of limits.
      (1) In aircraft with a door in the rear, some jumpers must remain forward as groups congregate near the door.
      (2) Large groups planning to exit together should inform the pilot.
4. Seat belts—
   a. prevent injuries in an emergency
   b. maintain the load within the center-of-gravity limits
5. Jumpers outside the aircraft—
   a. can block air flow to the control surfaces
   b. add drag that makes it harder to maintain the necessary airspeed
   c. When floaters (outside the aircraft) are out, jumpers must exit quickly to reduce the effect of drag.
6. Apply the concept of weight, balance, and drag to aircraft at the DZ.
7. Aircraft emergency procedures
8. Discussion on the sections of FAR 91 provided in this manual (Section 9-1); only the sections pertinent to skydiving are included there.

OPEN PARACHUTE ORIENTATION

A rigger or instructor introduces you to the parachute system when it is unpacked. You will learn the common points of parachute wear and maintenance requirements during Category G. Assembly and maintenance of the three-ring release is covered in Category H.

1. Packing is a function of identifying and organizing the parachute.
2. Identify:
   a. pilot chute, bridle, and collapsing system
   b. deployment bag or other device
   c. pilot chute attachment
   d. top skin and discuss the different characteristics of F-111 (0-3 cfm) and zero-P fabric
   e. packing tabs
   f. bottom skin
   g. leading edge (nose)
   h. trailing edge (tail)
   i. center of tail (warning label or tab)
   j. stabilizers
   k. manufacturer's label or logo (to identify end cell)
   l. slider stops
   m. loaded and unloaded ribs
   n. crossports
   o. A, B, C, D, and brake lines
   p. line cascades, including brake lines
   q. slider and slider grommets
   r. connector links and link protectors
   s. risers and brake system
3. Review and discuss (preferably with an FAA rigger) FAR Part 105.43.a and b (Section 9-1 of this manual).
   a. who may pack a main parachute
   b. how often it needs to be packed
   c. rigger supervision of non-rated packers

4-E USPA ISP: CATEGORY E

dive flows

CATEGORY E FREEFALL DIVE FLOWS

DIVE PLAN #1: BARREL ROLL AND RECOVERY

- Assist with spot.
- Solo, ungripped exit.
- Altitude, arch, legs, relax.
- Barrel roll.
- Altitude, arch, legs, relax.
- Barrel roll (or other disorienting maneuver).
- Altitude, arch, legs, relax.
- Continue aerobatics until 6,000 feet.
- Altitude, arch, legs, relax between each maneuver.
- Wave-off at 4,500 feet.
- Pull by 4,000 feet.

DIVE PLAN #2: FRONT LOOPS AND BACK LOOPS

- Assist with spot.
- Optional exit.
- Altitude, arch, legs, relax.
- Perform required aerobatics to standards until 6,000 feet.
- Altitude check between each maneuver.
- Wave-off at 4,500 feet.
- Pull by 4,000 feet.

CATEGORY E CANOPY DIVE FLOW

- Check altitude, position, and traffic.
- Flare to chest at a medium speed and hold.
- Recover to full flight for ten seconds.
- Check altitude, position, and traffic.
- Flare to chest at a quicker speed and hold.
- Recover to full flight for ten seconds.
- Check altitude, position, and traffic.
- Flare to chest at a slower speed and hold.
- Recover to full flight for ten seconds.
- Check altitude, position, and traffic.
- Flare to hips at a medium speed and hold.
- Recover to full flight for ten seconds.
- Check altitude, position, and traffic.
- Flare to hips at a quicker speed and hold.
- Recover to full flight for ten seconds.
- Check altitude, position, and traffic.
- Flare to hips at a slower speed and hold.
- Recover to full flight for ten seconds.
- Check altitude, position, and traffic.
- Flare to shoulders at a medium speed and hold.
- Recover to full flight for ten seconds.
- Check altitude, position, and traffic.
- Flare to shoulders at a quicker speed and hold.
- Recover to full flight for ten seconds.
- Check altitude, position, and traffic.
- Flare to shoulders at a slower speed and hold.
- Recover to full flight for ten seconds.
- Evaluate the most effective flare according to the strongest sustainable lift ("sweet spot").
- Initiate the best flare at head height above the ground.
- Continue to flare to maintain a flat glide until landing.
- Evaluate the flare height according to the landing results.

CATEGORY E EQUIPMENT

- Open Parachute Orientation

CATEGORY E SPOTTING AND AIRCRAFT

- Aircraft Briefing

CATEGORY E INSTRUCTOR NOTES:

- Each student should complete the equipment, spotting, and aircraft procedures training before advancing to Category F.
- When possible, an FAA rigger should conduct the Open Parachute Orientation and review of the FARs on packing.
- When possible, a jump pilot should conduct the Aircraft Briefing and overview of the pertinent sections of FAR 91.

category e quiz

USPA ISP: CATEGORY E — 4-E

ADMINISTERED PRIOR TO CONDUCTING JUMPS IN THE NEXT CATEGORY

Quiz answers are listed in Appendix B.

1. What happens to a jumper's fall rate when performing rolls, loops, or other freeflying maneuvers?

2. What happens to a visual altimeter when it's in the jumper's burble?

3. What is the best way to recover from a stall to full glide?

4. Describe an aerodynamic stall as it applies to a ram-air canopy.

5. When does a dynamic stall occur?

6. What happens after a dynamic stall if the tail is held lower than the nose?

7. What is the best way to determine a canopy's optimum flare speed and depth for landing?

8. Describe your procedure for landing in high winds.

9. How many A-lines does a nine-cell canopy have?

10. To what part of the canopy do the steering lines (brake lines) connect?

11. What lines go through the rear slider grommets?

12. Where does the main pilot chute bridle attach to the canopy?

13. Who may pack a main parachute?

14. How often do the main and reserve parachute need to be packed?

15. Who is in command of the aircraft?

16. Name two purposes for wearing seat belts in an aircraft.

17. Who is responsible that the aircraft is in condition for safe flight?

18. Above what altitude MSL is the pilot of an unpressurized aircraft required to breathe supplemental oxygen?

19. Above what altitude MSL are all occupants of an unpressurized aircraft required to be provided with supplemental oxygen?

20. In an aircraft with the exit door near the back, what must jumpers do to maintain the balance during exit procedures?

21. What is the biggest danger to a jumper when flying the canopy pattern?

22. What is the best way to avoid a canopy collision?

23. How does the RSL work?

24. What would happen if the main riser attached to the RSL breaks?

25. What is the best way to prevent risers from breaking?

26. Name one way to prevent a dual deployment.

27. What is generally the best action to take in the following two-canopy-out scenarios?
    a. Biplane
    b. Side by side
    c. Downplane

Categories F-H
Group Skydiving Skills

Skydiving is a sport for individualists who like to do things together. In the first portion of the USPA Integrated Student Program, Categories A-E, you focused on the skills required to survive independent freefall: stability control, deployment at the correct altitude, landing in a clear area, and how to use the equipment.

The remaining three categories, F-H, prepare you for more advanced freefall control. More importantly, you get ready for skydiving in groups—in freefall and under canopy.

Your education continues in canopy flight, equipment, and aircraft skills essential for safety. Soon, you'll graduate and become independent of supervision. Detailed review also continues on the emergency procedures introduced in the first-jump course.

With the direct assistance of other qualified staff members, such as the USPA Coach, the USPA Instructor continues to supervise your training and monitor your progress during all remaining student jumps until you obtain your USPA A license.

The freefall portions of Categories F through H address group flying techniques and skills. Under the supervision of a USPA Instructor, a USPA Coach may train you for the freefall skills in these last three categories and accompany you in freefall.

After completing all training and jumps at the end of Category H, you may sign up for a USPA A-license check dive with a USPA Instructor.

Categories F-H prepare you for more advanced freefall control. More importantly, you get ready for skydiving in groups—in freefall and under canopy.

Category F

INTRODUCTION

Tracking is a basic group skydiving skill that enables jumpers to gain sufficient freefall separation for a safe opening. It is such an important skill that the freefall training in this category is devoted entirely to tracking techniques.

To begin, while supervising yourself in freefall, you practice the basics of the delta position, the first step toward a flat track. The USPA Coach will evaluate and refine your tracking skills as part of the jumps in Categories G and H. Tracking evaluation is also part of the A-license check dive with the USPA Instructor.

Flying the canopy slowly and performing flat, altitude-conserving turns is an important skill that can help you out of a difficult landing approach in a tight area.

You'll learn more about how to handle aircraft emergency exit procedures independently. Emergency review includes power line recognition, avoidance, and landing procedures. During this category, former AFF students should make a practice clear and pull from 5,500 feet, followed by a clear-and-pull jump from 3,500 feet, as required for the A license.

By now, you're ready to learn how to pack and should begin working with a packing instructor.

The staff continues to build your understanding of aircraft procedures on jump run with emphasis on separation between groups exiting on the same pass. You also learn the specific procedures for coordinating with the pilot or jumpmaster in the event of an aircraft emergency.

ALL STUDENTS
- two tracking jumps

FORMER AFF STUDENTS
- two clear-and-pulls

RECOMMENDED MINIMUM DEPLOYMENT
- 4,000 feet

4-F USPA ISP: CATEGORY F

Category at a Glance

ADVANCEMENT CRITERIA

EXIT AND FREEFALL
- • cumulative three tracking sequences: track for five seconds within 30 degrees of the planned heading, turn 180 degrees, and track back for five seconds
- two clear and pulls (already accomplished by former IAD and static-line students)

CANOPY
- cumulative four 180-degree turns under canopy while flying in deep brakes
- braked approach and landing on a canopy that allows for a safe braked landing
- cumulative two unassisted landings within 82 feet of the planned target (jumps from previous categories count toward accuracy requirements)

EQUIPMENT
- one complete pack job with assistance
- perform a pre-jump equipment check on another jumper fully rigged and ready to jump

AIRCRAFT AND SPOTTING
- spot the aircraft, including all procedures, with minimum assistance

ORAL QUIZ

BOOK STUFF
- study USPA Basic Safety Requirements for A license holders (SIM Sections 2-1.B; G.3; H.2; J.1.a; J.2-3; M.5; and N)
- study USPA conditions, requirements, and privileges for A-license holders (SIM Section 3-1)
- study USPA recommendations on recurrent training (SIM Section 5-2)
- study SIM Section 5-1.F to review power-line landing procedures
- study USPA recommendations on group separation during jump run (SIM Section 5-7)
- read the owner's manuals for the main and reserve canopies and the harness and container system in use for jumps in this category

CATEGORY F: LEARNING AND PERFORMANCE OBJECTIVES

- introduction to tracking
- two clear and pulls (former AFF students)
- braked turns, approaches, and landings
- extending the glide
- power-line landing review
- packing with assistance
- checking others' equipment
- procedures following inactivity
- winds aloft and the exit point
- separating groups during exit

A. EXIT AND FREEFALL

1. Initiating track
   a. First locate a point on the horizon.
   b. Smoothly extend both legs fully to initiate forward motion.
   c. Control in the delta and track positions:
      (1) Dip one shoulder slightly in the direction of the turn to make heading corrections (instructor technique may differ).
      (2) Make only small corrections.
   d. Slowly extend your torso by stretching your shoulders toward your ears and flatten your arch.
   e. Fully extend your arms to the side 90 degrees to your spine and level with your hips (instructor technique may vary).

2. Refining the track
   a. Once establishing a heading in a positive forward dive, fully extend both legs with your knees locked and toes pointed.
   b. Stiffen your body slowly into a slight reverse arch, pushing down and forward slightly with your shoulders, while keeping your hands level with your hips.
   c. Continually adjust your body position to effectively meet the relative wind.

3. Tracking practice procedure
   a. Experienced jumpers often allow only five to ten seconds to obtain adequate separation.
   b. Practice entering and refining an on-heading track for five seconds, reversing direction, and repeating.

4. Tracking jump safety
   a. Fly exactly perpendicular to the jump run to avoid others up and down the line of flight.
   b. Always plan tracking dives with other groups in mind.
   c. Learn to control a track on heading first, then develop techniques for pitch and speed.

5. Clear and pull (AFF students only—IAD and static-line students have already met the clear-and-pull requirement in Category C.)
   a. A clear and pull is used for emergency exits and pre-planned low-altitude jumps.
   b. Use a familiar, stable exit technique.
   c. Present your hips to the relative wind and execute normal pull procedures (without wave-off) to deploy within five seconds of exit.
   d. Expect the parachute to open in relation to the relative wind, not overhead as usual.
   e. The sequence consists of a clear and pull from two altitudes:
      (1) first from 5,500 feet
      (2) once successful, from 3,500 feet

B. CANOPY

1. Braked turns:
   a. Performed correctly, braked turns provide the quickest heading change with the least altitude lost.
   b. A braked turn may be the best choice when a quick heading change is needed.
      (1) when suddenly encountering another jumper under canopy or someone in the landing area
      (2) recognizing an obstacle
      (3) too low to recover from a full-flight turn
   c. Practice braked turns.
      (1) From the slowest speed at which the canopy will fly, raise one toggle slightly to initiate a heading change in the opposite direction.
      (2) Try to change heading as quickly as possible without banking or stalling.

2. Using brakes to attain the maximum glide and minimum descent:
   a. On lower-glide designs, the minimum descent may begin nearer the half-braked position.
   b. On higher-glide designs, the minimum descent may be nearer the three-quarter braked position or just prior to a full stall (reverse flight).
   c. Some canopies achieve minimum descent using the back risers instead of the toggles.
   d. Minimum sustainable descent (float):
      (1) allows the jumper to remain above other jumpers on descent
      (2) allows the canopy to cover a greater distance

3. Recognizing and adjusting for minimum descent and maximum glide path
   a. Look ahead to the point on the ground that appears not to rise or sink in your field of vision.
      (1) Everything before that point appears to fall.
      (2) Everything beyond it appears to rise.
      (3) That point is the projected landing point on the canopy's current glide path.
   b. Pull the toggles down slightly to see if the stationary point moves farther away.
      (1) If so, the glide path has flattened.
      (2) The canopy will cover more distance.
   c. Repeat until the point begins to move closer, then return to the maximum glide position that you have just determined.

4-F USPA ISP: CATEGORY F

4. When flying downwind in maximum glide:
   a. As the winds decrease at lower altitudes, your glide path will become steeper.
   b. The actual landing area will be closer than you initially anticipated.
5. Increasing the glide when flying against the wind:
   a. in lighter winds, may improve distance
   b. in stronger winds, may slow the canopy too much and reduce its upwind range
6. Braked pattern and landing approach
   a. Fly one entire landing pattern in at least half brakes, to determine the effect on glide path.
   b. Plan for a change in glide path.
      (1) A lower-glide design may require a smaller pattern when flown in brakes.
      (2) A higher-glide design may require a bigger pattern when flown in brakes; extend the final approach to avoid overshooting the target.
   c. Fly final approach in quarter to half brakes.
   d. Flare carefully from the braked position:
      (1) Practice high to avoid a stall.
      (2) To get the best flare may require a shorter, quicker stroke initiated lower to the ground.
      (3) The stall may occur more abruptly.
      (4) Plan for a PLF.
   e. A smaller canopy may descend too quickly in deep brakes for a safe braked landing.
7. Accumulate two unassisted landings within 82 feet of the planned target.

C. EMERGENCY PROCEDURE REVIEW

1. Recognizing and avoiding power lines
   a. Expect power lines along roads, between buildings, in paths in the forest, and in random places.
   b. Scan every 500 feet of descent into an unfamiliar landing area and continually scan below 500 feet.
2. Power-line landing emergency procedures (training harness): Refer to Section 5-1 of this manual.

D. EQUIPMENT

1. Pack at least one parachute with the assistance of a knowledgeable packer.
2. Discuss the most important points of packing:

Note: An FAA rigger is your best resource for this discussion.

   a. lines straight and in place in the center of the completed pack job
   b. slider up
   c. tight line stows to prevent premature line deployment
3. Perform a pre-jump equipment check on another jumper who is in full gear.
   a. "check of threes" in the front
      (1) three-ring assembly (and reserve static line)
      (2) three points of harness attachment for snap assembly and correct routing, adjustment, and no twists
      (3) three operation handles—main activation, cutaway, reserve
   b. pin check back of system, top to bottom
      (1) reserve pin at least halfway seated (and automatic activation device on)
      (2) main pin fully seated
      (3) ripcord cable movement or correct bridle routing
      (4) if collapsible pilot chute, check the indicator window
      (5) activation handle in place
   c. check personal equipment ("SHAGG")
      Shoes—tied, no hooks
      Helmet—fit and adjustment
      Altimeter—set for zero
      Goggles—tight and clean
      Gloves—lightweight and proper size

E. RULES AND RECOMMENDATIONS

1. Study USPA BSRs applicable to USPA A-license holders, including Sections 2-1.B; G.2; H.2; I.1.a, 2, and 3; L.5; and M.
2. Study USPA recommendations on training following periods of inactivity, SIM 5-2.

F. SPOTTING AND AIRCRAFT

Note: This section should be conducted by a jump pilot or USPA Instructor.

1. Acting without a rated USPA instructor during routine jump operations and aircraft emergencies
   a. The person spotting the load usually serves as the jumpmaster.
   b. In larger aircraft, the jumpmaster should establish an exclusive chain of communication with the pilot.
      (1) A communication assistant should be able to communicate directly with the pilot and the jumpmaster simultaneously.
      (2) Other jumpers should not get involved in communication among the pilot, communications assistant, and the jumpmaster.
2. Review of low-altitude exit procedures
   a. The jumpmaster must determine if jumpers are over a safe landing area and communicate this information to the pilot.
   b. Establish firm altitudes at which certain aircraft emergency decisions would be made (DZ policy):
      (1) altitude below which all jumpers will land with the aircraft
      (2) altitude below which all jumpers will jump using their reserves
      (3) altitude below which all jumpers will jump and immediately use their main parachutes
   c. Jumpers must maintain correct weight distribution in the aircraft, especially during emergency exit procedures.
3. The effect of the winds aloft on the exit point
   a. Subtract the speed of the headwind on jump run (if flown into the wind) from the true airspeed of the aircraft to determine the ground speed.
   b. Jumpers first get thrown forward on exit (approximately 0.2 miles in calm winds, less with headwind) from residual aircraft speed and then fall straight down or blow toward the target.
   c. The winds aloft will cause freefalling jumpers to drift according to the wind's strength and direction.
   d. Winds generally diminish at lower altitudes.

e. Average the speed and the direction of the winds from exit altitude to 3,000 feet AGL to estimate freefall drift. See the example in Table 4-F.1 for a sea-level drop zone:

   (1) If flying jump run upwind, use the average heading of 270 degrees.

   (2) Aircraft forward throw is approximately 1/8-1/4 mile upwind in the light-to-moderate headwind.

   (3) Jumpers fall for one minute, drifting at 1/4 mile per minute for 1/4 mile of drift downwind.

   (4) Since the forward throw and the freefall drift approximately cancel each other, the ideal exit point is almost straight over the ideal opening point in this example.

CALCULATING FREEFALL DRIFT

EXAMPLE FOR CALCULATING FREEFALL DRIFT

Altitude	Heading	Speed (mph)
3,000 ft	250	7 mph
6,000 ft	260	14 mph
9,000 ft	280	16 mph
12,000 ft	290	23 mph
Average	270	15 mph

Table 4-F.1. Averaging the winds aloft. Note: Averaging wind force and direction works sufficiently in common jump conditions. A vector analysis provides more accurate results.

4. Group separation on jump run (SIM 5-7).

5. Perform all duties on jump run with minimum assistance, including—

   a. operating the door (if the pilot allows)

   b. monitoring progress during jump run

   c. directing the pilot to the correct spot

   d. choosing the correct exit point

4-F | USPA ISP: CATEGORY F

dive flows

CATEGORY F FREEFALL DIVE FLOWS

DIVE PLAN #1: TRACKING
- Spot with minimal assistance.
- Choice of exit position.
- Track for five seconds, turn 180 degrees, return.
- Altitude check.
- Repeat until 6,000 feet.
- Wave off and pull by 4,000 feet.

DIVE PLAN #2: CLEAR AND PULL FROM 5,000 FEET (FORMER AFF STUDENTS ONLY)
- Spot with minimal assistance.
- Poised exit.
- Initiate deployment within five seconds.

DIVE PLAN #3: CLEAR AND PULL FROM 3,500 FEET (FORMER AFF STUDENTS ONLY)
- Spot with minimal assistance.
- Poised exit.
- Initiate deployment within five seconds.

CATEGORY F CANOPY DIVE FLOWS

DIVE PLAN #1: BRAKED TURNS
- Check altitude, position, and traffic.
- Pull toggles smoothly and evenly to deep brakes.
- Perform a 180-degree-braked turn then return to full flight.
- Check altitude, position and traffic.
- Pull toggles smoothly and evenly to deep brakes.
- Perform a 180-degree-braked turn in the other direction then return to full flight.
- Check altitude, position and traffic.
- Repeat to no lower than 2,500 feet.
- The coach measures the student's landing distance from the planned target.

DIVE PLAN #2: BRAKED MANEUVERS AND LANDING (FROM 5,000 FEET)
- Check altitude, position, and traffic.
- Pull toggles smoothly and evenly to half-brakes hold for 3 seconds and finish the flare at a normal speed.
- Return to full flight for 10 seconds.
- check altitude, position, and traffic.
- Pull toggles smoothly and evenly to a half-brake position hold for 3 seconds and finish the flare at a quicker than normal speed.
- Return to full flight for 10 seconds.
- check altitude, position, and traffic.
- Pull toggles smoothly and evenly to a half-brake position while facing into the wind and observe glide path change.
- Return to full flight.
- check altitude, position, and traffic.
- Turn 180 degrees.
- Pull toggles smoothly and evenly to a half-brake position while going with the wind and observe glide path change.
- Return to full flight.
- check altitude, position, and traffic.
- Fly landing pattern in half-brake position, if winds permit.
- Flare from the braked position, if winds and canopy permit.
- The coach measures the student's landing distance from the planned target.
- Discovery of flattest glide; lowest descent.
- Practice flaring from deep brakes.
- Identify all the power lines in the area during descent.
- Fly the pattern in brakes.
- Landing flare from brakes (with suitable canopy).

CATEGORY F EQUIPMENT
- Pack with assistance.

category f quiz

ADMINISTERED PRIOR TO CONDUCTING JUMPS IN THE NEXT CATEGORY

Quiz answers are listed in Appendix B.

1. What is the best way to change the direction of canopy flight while conserving the most altitude?

2. What happens if a canopy is controlled too deeply in the brakes?

3. Describe the difference between flaring from half brakes and full glide.

4. How does the half-braked position affect the canopy's flight?

5. What is a glide path?

6. How do you determine your glide path?

7. How does wind affect the glide path?

8. How is heading corrected during a track?

9. When making tracking jumps from a large plane, why is it important to track perpendicular to the jump run?

10. What is the ground speed of a jump aircraft with a true airspeed of 90 knots when flying against a 50-knot headwind on jump run?

11. How can jumpers assure adequate separation between groups exiting the aircraft?

12. What are the three most important aspects of packing the main canopy?

13. How can you tell if the RSL is routed correctly?

14. What is the make and model of parachute system you are jumping?
    a. Main canopy?
    b. Harness and container system?
    c. Automatic activation device?

15. What is the minimum pull altitude allowed for student skydivers and A license holders?

16. What are the maximum winds allowed for student skydivers?

17. If a jumper falls for one minute through upper winds averaging 30 mph from the west:
    a. How far will the jumper drift? Note: 60 mph = 1 mile per minute; therefore, 30 mph = 1/2 mile per minute.
    b. In which direction?

18. Describe your procedure for landing in power lines.

19. In the event of an aircraft emergency with no students or instructors aboard, who should coordinate procedures between the pilot and the other jumpers on the load?

20. At your drop zone, what is the lowest altitude the pilot would likely ask jumpers to leave the plane during a routine engine-out emergency?

21. In an aircraft emergency, what is the lowest exit altitude that you would deploy your main parachute before choosing the reserve instead?

22. How many jumps are required for the USPA A license?

23. What does a USPA A license permit a skydiver to do?

24. What should an A-licensed jumper do to regain currency after a ten-week period of inactivity?

25. What should an A-licensed jumper do to regain currency after a four-month period of inactivity?

Category G

INTRODUCTION

Freefall skills in Category G address group skydiving maneuvers. They are outlined here for the discipline of formation skydiving (flat, or belly flying) but can be performed in other orientations with a USPA Coach knowledgeable in those techniques. The same performance and advancement criteria for maneuvering, docking, breakoff, and gaining separation for a safe opening apply, however.

In Category G, you'll review more in depth the procedures for avoiding and responding to canopy collisions, always more of a risk in group jumping. By now, you should be looking for traffic and steering with rear risers before releasing your brakes.

After opening, you'll explore the performance envelope of the ram-air canopy to prevent surprises near the ground. Practice includes maximum-performance turns, reverse turns, and keeping the wing in balance during performance maneuvers to avoid a line twist. You'll learn to feel the turn.

You'll take another look at avoiding tree landings and what to do in case one is inevitable.

By now, you should be packing with minimal assistance, but USPA recommends supervision until your A license. Along with practicing packing, you'll learn how to inspect the equipment for wear and how to prevent it. Before advancing, you should understand the responsibilities of the FAA rigger, who maintains most items.

All skydivers need to respect the power of various kinds of weather, which begins with understanding basic weather patterns and reading the danger signals. A pilot or instructor advises you on practical ways to predict the kind of weather that could compromise your safety.

ALL STUDENTS
- four jumps

RECOMMENDED MINIMUM DEPLOYMENT
- 3,500 feet

4-G | USPA ISP: CATEGORY G

Category at a Glance

ADVANCEMENT CRITERIA

EXIT AND FREEFALL
- two redocks from ten feet without assistance
- two redocks requiring an adjustment in fall rate
- break off at the planned altitude without prompting
- track 50 feet within ten degrees of the planned heading

CANOPY
- four maximum-performance reverse canopy turns
- two unassisted landings within 65 feet of the target (jumps from previous categories count toward accuracy requirements)

EQUIPMENT
- one complete pack job without assistance

AIRCRAFT AND SPOTTING
- spot the aircraft, including all procedures, without assistance

ORAL QUIZ

BOOK STUFF

- read and discuss USPA recommendations for tree landings (SIM Section 5-1.F)
- read and discuss USPA recommendations to experienced jumpers for automatic activation devices and reserve static lines (SIM Sections 5-3.F and G.)
- read and discuss USPA recommendations for canopy collisions (SIM Section 5-1.H)
- read and discuss USPA recommendations regarding weather (SIM Section 5-5)
- read and discuss USPA recommendations on group freefall skydiving, SIM Section 6-1
- read and discuss additional USPA recommendations on breakoffs for freeflying groups in SIM Section 6-2.E.5
- read and discuss FAR 65.125 through .133 (performance standards for parachute rigger privileges, record keeping, and seal requirements)
- read and discuss FAA regulations for packing main and reserve parachutes (FAR 105.43.a and .b)
- read and discuss FAA regulations for maintaining automatic activation devices (FAR 105.43.c)

CATEGORY G: LEARNING AND PERFORMANCE OBJECTIVES

USPA ISP: CATEGORY G | 4-G

- group exits
- floater position
- forward and backward movement
- adjusting fall rate
- start and stop
- docking
- maximum-performance canopy turns
- collision avoidance and response review
- tree landing review
- equipment maintenance inspection
- weather for skydivers

A. EXIT AND FREEFALL

1. Group exits
   a. Practice for an efficient climbout and launch.
      (1) Each jumper in a group has an assigned exit position and should know that position before climbout.
      (2) The exit position should include specific, exact foot and hand placement for the best launch position and presentation of hips and limbs into the relative wind.
      (3) The jumpers count together with body movement, where possible, for a simultaneous or near-simultaneous launch.
   b. Exit into a neutral body position and hold aircraft heading.
   c. Relax and confirm stability prior to turning toward your coach.
   d. exit grips:
      (1) If taken, grips should allow all jumpers to leave in a natural flying position.
      (2) Main lift web and chest strap grips are counterproductive for most belly-to-earth group exits.

2. Forward and backward movement (belly to earth)
   a. Use legs only for forward movement and steering.
      (1) Extending both legs tilts the jumper head-low and begins a slide in that direction.
      (2) Extending one leg more than the other causes a turn in the opposite direction.
         (i) Extending the right leg causes a left turn.
         (ii) Extending the left leg causes a right turn.
   b. Maintain both arms in neutral during forward movement and docking.
   c. Extend both arms and push down for backward movement.
   d. Extending the arms slightly to take a grip will counter forward movement but cause backsliding if initiated too soon or for too long.

3. Adjusting fall rate (belly to earth)
   a. Increase vertical freefall speed by streamlining.
      (1) hips forward
      (2) shoulders back
      (3) relax abdominal muscles
   b. Slow freefall speed by creating maximum turbulence.
      (1) cupping the shoulders around the sternum
      (2) rounding the spine (cupping the abdomen)
      (3) extending arms or legs to counterbalance and maintain a level attitude
   c. When recovering altitude from below the level of a formation:
      (1) Turn 90 degrees relative to the formation to keep it in view.
      (2) To avoid a collision, remain clear of the area immediately below and above any group.
   d. Recognize the visual cues for level approach (on exit, regardless of the horizon):
      (1) backpack in sight—come down
      (2) front of the leg straps in sight—come up
   e. Maintain altitude awareness.

4. Docking
   a. Dock using a level approach.
   b. Once docked, arch across the shoulders to maintain the fall rate (elbows up) and stay level with your partner or the formation.
   c. Extend both legs to counter any tension created in the formation when holding grips.
   d. Maintain altitude awareness.

5. Break-off
   a. Check altitude every four or five seconds and after each maneuver.
   b. Break off without prompting.
   c. Plan the break-off altitude to allow enough time to track 50 feet.
   d. The most positive way to signal break-off is to turn and track.
      (1) As a safety back-up in Categories G and H—
         (i) If the coach waves his or her arms, immediately turn and track to the planned deployment altitude.
         (ii) If the coach deploys, deploy immediately without tracking.
         (iii) Deploy at planned altitude whether or not you have turned or tracked.
         (iv) Never rely on the USPA Coach for breakoff or deployment cues.
      (2) You are always responsible to break off and open at the planned altitude on jumps with the USPA Coach and with others after you get your license.
   e. When tracking, establish and maintain the correct heading radially from the formation.
   f. For beginners, tracking moderately in a straight line in the right direction is more effective than going fast in a curve or in the wrong direction. Break off high enough to gain separation.

6. For additional requirements for break-offs from freeflying jumps, see SIM 6-2.

4-G USPA ISP: CATEGORY G

7. To avoid hard openings, slow to minimum freefall velocity before deploying.

B. CANOPY

1. Performance turn entry and exit with balance
   a. Enter a turn only as quickly as the canopy can maintain balance (center of lift over the center of load) during the turn.
   b. Surging, lurching, or line twist indicate a turn entered too quickly.
   c. A canopy is more susceptible to collapse from turbulence during entry and exit from a turn.
   d. The canopy dives sharply after a maximum-performance turn.
2. Reverse turns
   a. You must know the maximum safe rate of turn entry for each canopy you jump.
   b. Practicing reverse turns helps you determine the maximum safe toggle turn rate before inducing a line twist.
   c. Make a smooth but deep turn at least 90-degrees to the right, return to level flight for a split second, then reverse toggle positions smoothly but quickly for a 180-degree turn to the left (four sets recommended to complete Category G).
   d. Line twist can occur if the toggle is pulled down too quickly when starting a turn, or raised too quickly to stop a turn.
   e. The goal of this exercise is to learn the limits of the toggle input for your canopy, not to actually induce a line twist.
   f. A line twist at landing pattern altitudes may be unrecoverable in time for a safe landing, particularly with a higher wing loading.
   g. In case you induce a line twist, you should complete all maximum-performance turns above the 2,500-foot decide-and-act altitude for a cutaway.
3. The potential for collision with other jumpers increases when making performance maneuvers in traffic or near the ground (review).
   a. Other jumpers may be focused more on the target than on traffic.
   b. The lower jumper has the right of way.
   c. It takes only one jumper to avoid a collision.
   d. Jumping a faster canopy requires more attention to traffic.
4. Accumulate two unassisted landings within 65 feet of a planned target (five total required for A license).

C. EMERGENCY PROCEDURE REVIEW

Note: A USPA Instructor should teach this section. A canopy formation specialist is also a good source.

1. Canopy collision avoidance (review)
   a. Know where other nearby jumpers are during opening and steer with the back risers to avoid them.
   b. If a head-on collision is pending, both jumpers should turn right.
2. Collision response: Study the USPA recommended procedures in SIM 5-1.
3. Tree landing avoidance
   a. Spot clear of large areas of trees or other obstacles, and open high enough to clear them in the event of a bad spot.
   b. Fly in maximum glide to reach a clear area.
4. Tree landing procedure review (training harness): Refer to skydiving emergency procedures in SIM 5-1.

D. EQUIPMENT

Note: An FAA rigger should conduct this session.

1. Detailed identification and inspection of high-wear items requiring rigger maintenance
   a. pilot chute and deployment handle
      (1) Look for broken stitching around the apex and the seam where the pilot chute canopy fabric and mesh meet.
      (2) Check for security at the bridle attachment point.
      (3) The fabric and mesh should be in good condition; both eventually wear out.
   b. bridle velcro
      (1) Velcro anywhere degrades with use and needs to be replaced every 100-250 uses.
      (2) Bridle velcro is particularly important, because if it comes loose, it can cause a premature deployment.
      (3) Velcro should be clean, dry, and free of debris.
   c. deployment bag
      (1) Look for distortion in the grommets, especially at the bridle, and fabric damage around their edges.
      (2) Check the loops that hold the line stow bands.
      (3) If velcro is used, replace it as necessary.
   d. closing pin
      (1) Check that the loop holding the closing pin to the bridle is secure and not being cut by the eye of the pin.
      (2) Check for nicks or corrosion on the pin and replace it if any appear.
   e. pilot chute attachment
      (1) Look for wear where the bridle attaches to the canopy.
      (2) Look for broken stitching on the canopy itself where it is reinforced for the bridle attachment loop or ring.
   f. likely areas of damage on the top center skin, end cells, and stabilizers
      (1) Check for small holes on the top skin from where the bridle attachment stop ring has caught fabric in the bag's top grommet (avoidable with good packing technique).
      (2) Look for wear on the top skin and end cells caused by contact with sharp objects or stickers.
      (3) Look for wear in and around the reinforcements in the stabilizers that contain the slider stops.
      (4) Look for broken or missing stitching along the seams.
   g. slider
      (1) Inspect for distortion in the slider grommets and wear around their inside edges.
      (2) Sliders are important, high stress components and should be maintained to the highest standard.
   h. lines
      (1) Look for wear anywhere along the lines, but especially where the slider grommets contact metal connector links.

(2) Line damage at the links calls for line replacement, but the rigger can also advise the jumper about link choices, protection and habits that minimize damage.

(3) Lines sometimes shrink unevenly over time.

(4) All lines eventually require replacement; refer to the manufacturer's recommendations.

i. slider bumpers (metal connector links)

(1) Slider bumpers protect the slider grommets and lines from damage by taking it themselves; most require periodic replacement.

(2) Slider bumpers need to be tight on the link or secured to prevent them from sliding up the lines and stopping the slider.

j. brake system

(1) When Velcro is used, placing the toggles on the risers immediately after landing prevents Velcro damage and tangles.

(2) Velcro needs to be replaced when worn.

(3) Velcro and general use wears the lower brake lines, which a rigger can easily replace.

(4) Examine the brake lock eye for damage and wear.

(5) Look at the attachment point for the keeper ring, including the attachment ring stitching on the opposite surface of the riser.

(6) Inspect tuck-tab toggle keepers for security.

k. riser release system

Note: You will learn three-ring disassembly and maintenance in Category H.

(1) Look for wear in the loops holding the rings and the white retaining loop, especially if you drag your rig when stowing the lines (not advised).

(2) Be sure that any service bulletins on risers for that system have been accomplished.

(3) Check the fittings on both ends of the cable housings for security.

(4) Look for kinks in the release cable where it contacts the white retaining loop, which may indicate a problem with hard openings or the design and construction of the three-ring assembly.

(5) Check the front and back of the riser webbing for fraying or strains around the edges of the grommets.

(6) Look for broken or loose tackings on the cable housings.

(7) Check riser inserts (for cutaway cable ends) if installed.

l. riser covers

(1) Replace any retaining Velcro when it loses tackiness.

(2) Replace distorted tuck flaps when they become ineffective (happens with use).

m. main container closing grommets

(1) Inspect for distortion and fabric damage around the edges.

(2) Feel for severe distortion or breakage of the plastic stiffener inside the fabric where the grommet is set.

n. main and reserve pin covers

(1) Replace Velcro when it fails to stay firmly attached.

(2) Replace plastic stiffeners when distortion from use renders them ineffective.

2. Store the parachute in a cool, dry, dark place.

a. Heat weakens AAD batteries; cars are too hot for safe prolonged storage in the summer.

b. The ultraviolet rays of the sun degrade nylon.

c. moisture

(1) corrodes hardware (very dangerous, since rust degrades nylon)

(2) promotes mildew (undesirable but harmless to nylon)

d. Many chemicals and acids damage parachute materials.

e. Heat may weaken elastic stow bands.

3. Premature deployments near the door.

a. Handles

(1) Check your handles before moving to an open door.

(2) Be cognizant of your handles when you are near an open door and during climb out.

b. Remain clear of the area directly above and below another jumper, in case his or her parachute activates prematurely from the AAD or other unplanned event.

4. Pack one main parachute without assistance.

E. RULES AND RECOMMENDATIONS

Note: An FAA rigger should teach this section.

1. It requires at least an FAA senior rigger to maintain and repair the parachute system (FAR 65.125 through .133, Section 9-1 of this manual).

2. AADs, if installed, must be maintained according to the manufacturer's instructions (FAR 105.43.c, Section 9-1 of this manual).

F. SPOTTING AND AIRCRAFT

Note: A pilot or instructor should teach this section.

1. Refer to the information on weather in Section 5-7 of this manual and discuss:

a. weather conditions hazardous to skydivers

b. practical methods to observe weather and obtain forecasts

2. Select the spot and guide the pilot to the correct position without assistance in routine weather conditions.

4-G | USPA ISP: CATEGORY G

dive flows

CATEGORY G FREEFALL DIVE FLOWS

DIVE PLAN #1: FORWARD MOVEMENT TO DOCK

- Coach observes spot.
- Front floater exit position (outside strut) until successful.
- Initiate count after coach OK.
- Face the direction of flight until stable (two to three seconds).
- Coach moves into position and docks.
- Check altitude and nod.
- Coach backs up five feet and adjusts levels as necessary.
- Move forward and take grips.
- Altitude check every five seconds or after each maneuver, whichever comes first.
- Coach backs up ten feet; move forward and take grips.
- Altitude check every five seconds or after each maneuver, whichever comes first.
- Repeat until breakoff.
- Initiate break-off at 5,500 feet and turn to track.
- Coach remains in place and evaluates track.
- Wave off and pull by 3,500 feet.

DIVE PLAN #2: DOWN AND UP

- Coach observes spot.
- Rear floater exit position (inside strut) until successful.
- Initiate count after coach OK.
- Face direction of flight until stable.
- Turn to face coach.
- Coach moves into position and docks.
- Check altitude and nod.
- Coach backs up five feet and increases fall rate.
- Remain in position and match coach's fall rate.
- Altitude check every five seconds or after each maneuver, whichever comes first.
- Coach slows fall rate.
- Remain in position and match coach.
- Repeat until response is quick and accurate.
- Break off at 5,500 feet.
- Coach remains in place and evaluates track.
- Wave off and pull by 3,500 feet.

DIVE PLAN #3: DOCKING WITH PROBLEMS

- Coach observes spot.
- Review either floater position.
- Initiate count after coach OK.
- Face direction of flight until stable.
- Turn to face coach.
- Coach moves into position and docks.
- Check altitude and nod.
- Coach backs up ten feet and changes fall rate.
- Match coach's fall rate to level and dock.
- Altitude check every five seconds or after each maneuver, whichever comes first.
- Repeat until response is quick and accurate.
- Break off at 5,500 feet.
- Coach remains in place and evaluates track.
- Wave off and pull by 3,500 feet.

CATEGORY G CANOPY DIVE FLOWS

- Check altitude, position, and traffic.
- Make a sharp, balanced 90-degree turn.
- Reverse the toggle position aggressively and make a balanced 180-degree turn.
- Check altitude, position, and traffic.
- Repeat to no lower than 2,500 feet, in case of line twist.
- Coach measures the student's landing distance from a planned target.

CATEGORY G EQUIPMENT

- Owner inspection-of-equipment briefing by FAA rigger
- Pack without assistance

category g quiz

ADMINISTERED PRIOR TO CONDUCTING JUMPS IN THE NEXT CATEGORY

Quiz answers are listed in Appendix B.

1. What is the primary directional control when moving forward to dock in freefall?

2. What is the minimum break-off altitude for freefall in groups of five or fewer?

3. What is the danger of entering a toggle turn too quickly?

4. What does a canopy do after completing a maximum input toggle turn?

5. What are the three biggest dangers of a hard toggle turn near the ground?

6. What are the first things to do in the event of a collision and entanglement with another jumper?

7. What is the most critical aspect of closing the main container equipped with a hand-deployed pilot chute?

8. Why is it a bad idea to drag the harness and container system when stowing the lines?

9. When velcro is used on the brake system, why is it a good idea to place your toggles back on the velcro after you land?

10. Who may maintain a main parachute system?

11. Why is it bad to leave a parachute in the sun?

12. What damage could occur from storing a parachute for prolonged periods in a car during the summer?

13. What happens to velcro touch fastener when it is used frequently?

14. What happens to stiffened tuck flaps that are frequently used?

15. Who publishes and enforces rules regarding parachute packing and parachute maintenance?

16. What may result if recovering altitude (floating up) under a freefall formation?

17. What extra consideration is required when sitting or moving towards an opened door?

18. Why is it important to remain clear of the area directly above and below other jumpers in freefall?

19. Why is it important to maintain an automatic activation device to the manufacturer's standards?

20. What is the correct response to a canopy entanglement with another jumper below 1,000 feet if it appears the two canopies cannot be separated in time for a safe landing?

21. Describe your procedure for landing in trees.

22. What does a tall cumulus cloud indicate?

23. What is the most dangerous part of an incoming front for aircraft and skydivers?

24. How does a canopy's air speed, ground speed, and descent rate change with an increase in density altitude?

Category H

INTRODUCTION

The last category of the ISP finishes preparing you for the USPA A-license so you can supervise yourself as an independent skydiver. These are the last jumps where you require USPA Instructor supervision. Next you take your test.

Freefall skills combine gross movements using the start and stop principle to dive toward a position in the sky relative to another jumper, followed by the fine movements to safely dock that you learned in Category G. The freefall briefing includes a discussion on safety and the importance of recognizing and controlling formation approach speeds. You'll also learn to look around while tracking, signaling for pull, and during deployment.

Under canopy, students with sufficient upper body strength explore the use of the front risers. The instructor explains the benefits and dangers of front-riser maneuvers. The discussion includes how to best recover from a turn made too low, one of the sport's biggest killers.

Emergency procedure review covers unintentional water landings.

You should be able to demonstrate how to maintain the three-ring release system and replace a main container closing loop, two common owner operations.

Although A-license holders are not qualified for demonstration jumps, you will be authorized to jump off the regular DZ into landing areas meeting the BSRs for students and A-license holders. In this last category as a formal skydiving student, you'll study the FAA requirements for jumps into the airspace over a private field, including what additional approvals may be necessary for the jump aircraft. This discussion should be with a jump pilot who can discuss those sections of FAR 105.

ALL STUDENTS
- four jumps

RECOMMENDED MINIMUM DEPLOYMENT
- 3,000 feet

4-H USPA ISP: CATEGORY H

Category at a Glance

ADVANCEMENT CRITERIA

EXIT AND FREEFALL
- two dives and docks with minimum assistance
- break off at the planned altitude without prompting
- track 100 feet within ten degrees of the planned heading

CANOPY
- two cumulative 90-degree front-riser turns
- two cumulative 180-degree front-riser turns
- total of five unassisted landings within 65 feet of the target (A-license requirement)

EQUIPMENT
- disassemble, perform owner maintenance, and reassemble three-ring release system
- remove and replace or adjust a main container closing loop

ORAL QUIZ

A-LICENSE CHECK DIVE

BOOK STUFF
- study USPA recommendations on unintentional water landings (SIM Section 5-1.F)
- study USPA recommendations on recovery from low turns (SIM Section 5-1.I)
- study USPA recommendations on incident reporting (SIM Section 5-8.A and B)
- review the breakoff recommendations for groups (SIM Section 6-1)
- skim FAR 105.13 to overview radio requirements for jump operations
- study FAR 105.15 and AC 105.2, Appendix 1 (prior notice requirements before jumping)
- skim AC 105.2, Appendix 2 (aircraft approved for flight with door removed)

CATEGORY H: LEARNING AND PERFORMANCE OBJECTIVES

USPA ISP: CATEGORY H | 4-H

- diver exit
- diving
- breakoff
- front riser control
- water landing review
- owner maintenance of gear
- aircraft radio requirements
- FAA notification requirements for jumping
- FAA approvals for jump planes

A. EXIT AND FREEFALL

1. Diver exit
   a. Twist out the door to place your hips and chest into the air coming from ahead of the aircraft, with your body oriented side-to-earth.
   b. Exit in a slow-fall position to arrest your forward throw from the aircraft, which is moving you away from your coach.
   c. Before starting to dive, hold the slow-fall position for two to three seconds while slowly turning toward your coach.
   d. Use a delta position to begin diving toward your coach.

2. Using your spine to adjust dive angle
   a. Initiate the dive with your legs fully extended.
   b. Follow the person ahead closely, but be prepared to slow rapidly.
   c. Pitch up or down by curving your spine to increase or flatten the angle of the dive.
   d. Use fast- and slow-fall technique to adjust vertical position relative to the diver ahead.
   e. For safety and to prevent a collision, dive with an escape path in mind.

3. Traffic on approach to the formation
   a. Dive in a straight line.
   b. Prevent collisions by watching for other jumpers while on approach to the formation.

4. Start, coast and stop
   a. Once you are about halfway to the target, return to a more neutral position.
   b. You can increase your speed to the target if you find you have slowed too soon.
   c. Use a flare position (arms forward) to slow and stop at a position level and 10-20 feet away from the target; visual cues:
      (1) back pack in view: approaching too high
      (2) front of harness in view: approaching too low
   d. Begin a level approach using legs only.
   e. Remain aware of traffic to each side and for errant jumpers below the approach path.

5. Rapidly arresting forward movement (very effective):
   a. Extend both arms forward.
   b. Use slow-fall technique (cup sternum and abdomen).
   c. Drop both knees.

6. Breaking off and tracking
   a. Plan break-off altitude high enough for the jumper with the least experience to track to a safe distance from the formation, at least 100 feet for groups of five or fewer (minimum distance required for A-license check dive).
   b. breakoff
      (1) The minimum breakoff altitude recommendations contained in the section on Group Freefall in this manual apply to very experienced formation skydivers jumping at a familiar location, using familiar equipment, and jumping with familiar people.
      (2) If any of these conditions are not met, add 500-1,000 feet to your planned breakoff.
   c. Develop techniques to scan and steer clear of other jumpers ahead and below.
   d. Look sideways and above for other jumpers in the immediate area during wave-off and deployment so you can steer clear under canopy as soon as you open.

B. CANOPY

1. Using front risers
   a. Front risers may be used to dive the canopy:
      (1) Applying half brakes for several seconds immediately before starting these maneuvers will reduce riser pressure
      (2) to lose altitude rapidly
      (3) to maintain position over ground in strong winds
   b. Heading control with front risers depends on
      (1) airspeed
      (2) the rate of turn
      (3) the speed of turn entry
   c. Heading control with front risers takes practice to become predictable.
   d. Practice heading control with front-risers.
      (1) Pull both front risers down to dive straight ahead.
      (2) Pull one front riser to complete two 90-degree and two 180-degree turns.
   e. Initiate a sharp, deep front-riser turn, raise the riser slightly to decrease the turn rate, and then pull the riser fully down again to attempt to increase the rate of the turn.
      (1) The rate of turn may not increase.
      (2) The resistance on the riser may make it too difficult to pull the riser down farther after raising it.
      (3) This exercise demonstrates the different nature of front-riser heading control.
   f. Complete all front-riser maneuvers by 2,000 feet.

2. Front-riser safety

4-H USPA ISP: CATEGORY H

a. Watch for traffic below and to the sides prior to initiating a front-riser dive.
b. Front riser maneuvers can be very dangerous near the ground:
   (1) Turbulence may affect canopy heading or descent rate.
   (2) A mishandled front-riser turn can lead to an undesirable heading, e.g., towards an obstacle, without time to complete the turn safely before landing.
   (3) A crowded landing pattern is never the place for high-speed maneuvers.
c. Keep both steering toggles in hand when performing front-riser maneuvers to make heading changes more reliably and quickly if necessary.
3. Accuracy: perform the remaining unassisted landings within 65 feet of the planned target to meet the USPA A-license requirements (five total required).

C. EMERGENCY PROCEDURE REVIEW

1. Flotation devices for water landings
   a. water is an obstacle as defined in the BSRs (section 2-1 in this manual)
   b. are required for some jumpers; refer to the BSRs on Parachute Equipment
   c. are recommended for jumpers using ram-airs when jumping within a mile of water
2. Adjust the planned spot to avoid bodies of water.
3. Procedures for an unintentional water landing (see Section 5-1 in this manual)
4. Recovery from a turn made too low over or to avoid water (see Section 5-1 in this manual)

D. EQUIPMENT

Note: An FAA rigger or instructor should teach this section.

1. Owner maintenance of three-ring release system:
   a. Disassemble the system every month to clean the cable and massage the ends of the risers.
      (1) Nylon riser webbing develops a memory, especially when dirty.
      (2) When disassembled, twist and massage the nylon webbing around the two riser rings.
   b. Clean the cables.
      (1) Most three-ring release cables develop a sludge-like coating that causes them to bind, increasing the required pull force.
      (2) Refer to the manufacturer's instructions for cleaning.
2. Use the correct bands for each type of lines:
   a. Smaller lines require the smaller bands.
   b. Larger bands may be required for larger lines.
   c. Line stow bands should grasp the line stow bights tightly, resulting in six to 11 pounds of force to extract.
   d. Replace each stow band as it stretches, wears, or breaks.
3. Main closing loop
   a. Damage greater than ten percent warrants replacement.
   b. tension
      (1) Tension must be sufficient to keep the container closed in freefall.
      (2) The closing pin should require eight to 11 pounds to extract (or check owner's manual).
      (3) A loose closing loop could result in a premature deployment.
      (4) Freeflying maneuvers increase the importance of closing system security.
      (5) Adjust the closing loop tension by moving the overhand knot or replacing the loop with the knot tied in the correct place.
   c. Use only closing loop material approved by the harness and container manufacturer.

E. RULES AND RECOMMENDATIONS

1. Refer to "Book Stuff" at the beginning of this category for independent study passages.
2. Review all "Book Stuff" from other categories to study for the oral exam given with the A-license check dive.

F. SPOTTING AND AIRCRAFT

Note: An FAA-rated pilot or instructor should teach this section.

1. Overview of aircraft radio use requirements
   a. The jump aircraft must have an operating radio for jumping to take place.
   b. The pilot must be in contact with air traffic control prior to jumping.
   c. Skim the FAA's requirements for radio use in FAR 105.
2. FAA notification required before a jump
   a. A jumper or the pilot must notify the appropriate air traffic control facility at least one hour prior to jumping (no more than 24 hours prior) in most airspace.
   b. Some drop zones have a written notification renewed annually for that location only.
   c. Skim FAR 105.25 for rules on notifications and authorizations prior to jumping.
   d. Study the overview of notification and authorization requirements contained in AC 105-2, Appendix 1.
3. Aircraft approved for flight with door removed
   a. Some aircraft are unsafe for flight with the door open or removed.
   b. Aircraft approved for flight with the door removed may require additional modifications and usually require additional FAA field approval.
   c. Other modifications to a jump aircraft, e.g., in-flight doors, hand holds, or steps, require additional field approval or a supplementary type certificate.
   d. Review with the pilot the certificates of approval for modifications on the jump aircraft.

USPA ISP: CATEGORY H | 4-H

dive flows

CATEGORY H FREEFALL DIVE FLOW

DIVE PLAN: DIVING

- Exit from the door one second after the coach.
- Present belly to wind in the slow fall position and maintain it for two seconds.
- Coach establishes fall rate and holds heading.
- Turn toward coach.
- Dive and stop level ten to 20 feet out.
- Altitude check every five seconds.
- Approach and take grips.
- Altitude permitting, coach dives to a point 50 to 100 feet laterally and 20 to 40 feet below.
- Follow and repeat docking procedure.
- Break off at 5,000 feet.
- Coach remains in place and evaluates track.
- Wave off and deploy by 3,000 feet.

CATEGORY H CANOPY DIVE FLOW

- Check altitude, position, and traffic.
- Perform an on-heading front riser dive (keep toggles in hand).
- Check altitude, position, and traffic.
- Perform a 90-degree front riser turn (keep toggles in hand).
- Check altitude, position, and traffic.
- Perform a 180-degree front riser turn (keep toggles in hand).
- Check position and altitude.
- Enter a front riser turn, let up halfway and begin the turn again (keep toggles in hand).
- Complete all front riser maneuvers by 2,000 feet.
- Coach measures your landing distance from a planned target.

CATEGORY H EQUIPMENT

- Disassemble, clean, and reassemble a three-ring riser release system.
- Replace or adjust a main closing loop.

USPA A-LICENSE CHECK DIVE FLOW

INSTRUCTOR: Refer to SIM Section 3-2 for complete instructions on conducting the USPA A-license examination and check dive. This jump must be evaluated by a USPA Instructor or Examiner.

- Spot.
- Choose a comfortable exit.
- Perform a 360-degree turn to the right and left, and back loop.
- The evaluator moves 20 feet from the candidate and level.
- Dock on the evaluator.
- Initiate breakoff and track a minimum of 100 feet.
- Wave off and pull by 3,000 feet.
- Follow your preselected landing pattern.

category h quiz

ADMINISTERED PRIOR TO CONDUCTING JUMPS IN THE NEXT CATEGORY

Quiz answers are listed in Appendix B.

1. Why is it important to look ahead during a dive toward other jumpers in freefall?

2. What is the fastest way to slow down from a freefall dive approach?

3. What is the danger of a loose or worn main container closing loop?

4. Why must three-ring release cables be cleaned periodically?

5. If you see that you have begun to turn too low to the ground for a safe landing, what should be your first response?

6. What effect does pulling on the front risers have on the canopy?

7. When performing front riser maneuvers, what should you do with the toggles?

8. What are the two biggest dangers of front-riser maneuvers near the ground?

9. What are some of the possible results of a turn made too low to the ground?

10. Describe your procedure for landing in water.

11. What is the maximum percentage of visible wear allowable on a main closing loop?

12. Can a jump be legally made from an aircraft without an operating radio?

13. What is the least notification the FAA requires before any jump or series of jumps may be made?

14. Where can a pilot look to determine if a plane is approved for flight with the door removed?

15. Whose name will the FAA require when filing a notification for parachute jumping?

Section 5

GENERAL RECOMMENDATIONS

SECTION SUMMARY:

This section of the SIM provides USPA recommendations for skydiving that apply to all jumpers, regardless of discipline or experience. USPA updates them as equipment and techniques change.

Experience shows that proficiency in any skill depends on how often the skill is exercised, especially with skills that require presence of mind, coordination, sharpness of reflexes, and control of emotions.

IMPORTANT REFERENCE NUMBERS

- skydiving emergencies—5-1
- currency training (according to experience)—5-2
- RSLs and AADs—5-3.F and G
- pre-jump checklist—5-4.C
- hazardous weather for jumpers—5-5.B
- aircraft—5-6
- spotting—5-7

WHO NEEDS THIS SECTION?

- all active skydivers
- instructors preparing to conduct currency training (Section 5-2)
- all jumpers studying for USPA license examinations

5-1: SKYDIVING EMERGENCIES

A. PRACTICE EMERGENCY PROCEDURES

1. Regular, periodic review, analysis, and practice of emergency procedures prepares you to act correctly in response to problems that arise while skydiving.
2. Annually review all parachute emergency procedures in a training harness.
3. Long lay-offs between jumps not only dull skills but heighten apprehensions.
4. Before each jump, review the procedures to avoid emergency situations and the procedures to respond to emergencies if they occur.
5. Practice your reserve emergency procedures on the ground at every reserve repack.
    a. Simulate some type of main malfunction on the ground, then cut away and deploy the reserve.
    b. This practice will provide you first-hand knowledge about the potential pull forces and direction of pull on your gear.

B. PREVENTION AND PREPARATION

1. Proper preparation and responsible judgment greatly reduce the probability of encountering an emergency situation, but even with the most careful precautions emergencies may still occur from time to time.
2. Skydiving is made safer by always anticipating and being prepared to respond to the types of emergencies that may arise.
3. Failure to effectively deal with an emergency situation is one of the greatest causes of fatal incidents in skydiving.
4. Safety results from reducing risk by doing the following:
    a. Acquiring accurate knowledge.
    b. Jumping only in suitable conditions.
    c. Evaluating the risk factors.
    d. Knowing your personal limitations.
    e. Keeping your options open.

C. TAKE ACTION

1. Deploy the parachute.
    a. Open the parachute at the correct altitude.
    b. A stable, face-to-earth body position improves opening reliability but is secondary to opening at the correct altitude.
2. Promptly determine if the canopy has properly opened.
3. Perform the appropriate emergency procedures and open the reserve parachute if there is any doubt whether the main canopy is open properly and controllable.
4. Land in a clear area—a long walk is better than landing in a hazardous area.
5. Land safely—land with your feet and knees together in preparation for performing a PLF (parachute landing fall) to avoid injury.

D. AIRCRAFT EMERGENCIES

1. Each skydiving center should establish and review procedures for all possible aircraft emergencies.
2. Every pilot and non-student jumper should thoroughly understand these procedures.
3. All students should take direction from their instructor(s).

E. EQUIPMENT EMERGENCIES

PARACHUTE MALFUNCTIONS (GENERAL)

1. The majority of all malfunctions can be traced to three primary causes:
    a. poor or unstable body position during parachute deployment
    b. faulty equipment
    c. improper or careless packing
2. Malfunction procedures
    a. Refer to Category A of the Integrated Student Program for specific, basic procedures for dealing with parachute malfunctions.
    b. In addition, other procedures are discussed in this section for licensed jumpers who may need to adjust procedures to accommodate different techniques, equipment, and personal preferences.
3. All malfunctions can be classified as one of two types:
    a. total malfunction (parachute not activated, or activated but not deploying)
    b. partial malfunction (parachute deployed but not landable):
4. You should decide upon and take the appropriate actions by a predetermined altitude that should be no lower than:
    a. Students and A-license holders: 2,500 feet.
    b. B-D license holders: 1,800 feet.
5. Reserve activation
    a. Reserve pilot chutes are manufactured with a metal spring in the center, which adds weight to the reserve pilot chute.
    b. During a stable, belly-to-earth reserve deployment, the reserve pilot chute can remain in the jumper's burble for several seconds, delaying the reserve deployment.
    c. Immediately after pulling the reserve ripcord, look over your right shoulder while twisting your upper body upwards to the right, or sit up in a slightly head-high orientation, in order to change the airflow behind your container to help the reserve pilot chute launch into clean air.
    d. Most harness and container manufacturers secure the steering toggles to reserve risers using Velcro, which will firmly hold the toggle in place. Be sure to peel the Velcro before attempting to pull the toggles free from the risers to release the brakes.

TOTAL MALFUNCTION

1. Identification
    a. A total malfunction includes deployment handle problems (unable to locate or extract the main parachute deployment handle), pack closure, and a pilot chute in tow.
    b. If altitude permits, the jumper should make no more than two attempts to solve the problem (or a total of no more than two additional seconds).
2. Procedures:
    a. In the case of no main pilot chute deployment (e.g., missing or stuck handle, ripcord system container lock), deploy the reserve.
    b. hand-deployed pilot chute in tow malfunction procedures (choose one):

SKYDIVING EMERGENCIES 5-1

(1) For a pilot-chute-in-tow malfunction, there are currently two common and acceptable procedures, both of which have pros and cons.

(2) An instructor should be consulted prior to gearing up, and each skydiver should have a predetermined course of action.

PILOT CHUTE IN TOW PROCEDURE 1:

Pull the reserve immediately. A pilot-chute-in-tow malfunction is associated with a high descent rate and requires immediate action. The chance of a main-reserve entanglement is slim, and valuable time and altitude could be lost by initiating a cutaway prior to deploying the reserve. Be prepared to cutaway.

PILOT CHUTE IN TOW PROCEDURE 2:

Cut away, then immediately deploy the reserve. Because there is a chance the main parachute could deploy during or as a result of the reserve activation, a cutaway might be the best response in some situations.

(3) In some cases, the parachute system used for the jump will require specific procedures that must be followed to reduce the chances of a main/reserve entanglement if the main canopy deploys after the reserve parachute is deployed. Check with the manufacturer of your harness and container for any specific procedures.

PARTIAL MALFUNCTION

1. Identification: A partial malfunction is characterized by deployment (removal from the container) or partial deployment of the main parachute and includes, horseshoe (the container is open but the parachute is not properly deployed because something is snagged on the system), bag lock, streamer, line-over, line pressure knots, major (unlandable) canopy damage, and other open-canopy malfunctions.

2. Procedure: The recommended procedure for responding to partial malfunctions is to cut away the main parachute before deploying the reserve.

3. At some point during descent under a partial malfunction, it becomes too low for a safe cutaway and you must deploy the reserve without cutting away.

4. Consider the operating range of the automatic activation device when determining your personal malfunction response altitudes.

5. Spinning main parachute malfunctions can lose altitude significantly faster and require a rapid response. Checking your altitude more frequently is required to ensure cutting away the main parachute and deploying the reserve is done above your decision altitude.

PREMATURE MAIN CONTAINER OPENING

1. With a throw-out main pilot-chute deployment system (pilot chute deployment prior to closing pin extraction), the container can open before the pilot chute is deployed, causing one type of horseshoe malfunction.

2. Prevention

   a. good equipment and closing system maintenance

   b. careful movement in the aircraft and during climbout and exit

   c. avoiding jumper contact that involves the main closing system

3. Upon discovery that the main container has opened, the recommended response is as follows:

   a. First, attempt to deploy the main pilot chute for no more than two tries or two seconds, whichever comes first.

   b. Failing that, cut away and deploy the reserve.

   c. Out-of-sequence pilot-chute extraction:

      (1) On systems with a bottom-of-container mounted pilot chute, premature extraction of the bag prior to pilot-chute deployment may make the pilot chute difficult to locate and extract.

      (2) On any throw-out hand-deployed system, the pilot chute should be capable of extraction by the jumper or from tension on the main bridle caused by the deployed parachute in the event of this type of malfunction.

TWO CANOPIES OUT

Note: The following recommendations are drawn from experience with larger canopies during tests conducted in the mid-1990s. Smaller canopies may react differently and require a different response.

1. Various scenarios can result in having both parachutes deploy with one of the following outcomes.

2. One canopy inflated, another deploying

   a. Attempt to contain the deploying reserve or main canopy and stuff it between your legs.

   b. If the second canopy deployment is inevitable and there is sufficient altitude, disconnect the reserve static line and cut away the main.

   c. If the second deployment is inevitable and there is insufficient altitude for a cutaway, wait for inflation of the second canopy and evaluate the result.

      (1) The two open canopies typically settle into one of three configurations, biplane, side-by-side, or downplane.

      (2) Trying to force one configuration into a more manageable configuration is typically futile and can be dangerous.

3. Stable biplane

   a. Disconnect the reserve static line if altitude permits.

   b. Unstow the brakes on the front canopy or leave the brakes stowed and steer by pulling on the rear risers and recover gently to full flight.

   c. Leave the brakes stowed on the rear canopy.

   d. Steer the front canopy only as necessary to maneuver for a safe landing.

   e. Use minimal control input as necessary for landing.

   f. Perform a parachute landing fall.

4. Stable side-by-side (choose one procedure):

SIDE-BY-SIDE PROCEDURE 1:

If both canopies are flying without interference or possibility of entanglement and altitude permits:

General Recommendations | 95

5-1 SKYDIVING EMERGENCIES

   (1) Disconnect the reserve static line.
   (2) Cut away the main and steer the reserve to a normal landing.

SIDE-BY-SIDE PROCEDURE 2:

Land both canopies.
   (1) Disconnect the reserve static line if altitude permits.
   (2) Release the brakes of the dominant canopy (larger and more overhead) and steer gently with the toggles, or leave the brakes stowed and steer by pulling on the rear risers.
   (3) Land without flaring and perform a parachute landing fall.

5. Downplane or pinwheel (canopies spinning around each other)
   a. Disconnect the reserve static line if altitude permits.
   b. Cut away the main canopy and steer the reserve to a normal landing.
6. Main-reserve entanglement
   a. Attempt to clear the problem by retrieving the less-inflated canopy.
   b. Perform a parachute landing fall.

F. LANDING EMERGENCIES

WATER LANDINGS

1. Procedures for an unintentional water landing:
   a. Continue to steer to avoid the water hazard.
   b. Activate the flotation device, if available.
   c. Loosen the chest strap to facilitate getting out of the harness after landing in the water.
   d. Disconnect the reserve static line (if applicable) to reduce complications in case the main needs to be cut away after splashing down.
   e. Flare to half brakes at ten feet above the water (this may be difficult to judge, due to poor depth perception over the water).
   f. Prepare for a PLF, in case the water is shallow (it will be nearly impossible to determine the depth from above).
   g. Enter the water with your lungs filled with air.
   h. After entering the water, throw your arms back and slide forward out of the harness.
      (1) Remain in the harness and attached to the canopy until actually in the water.
      (2) If cutting away (known deep water only), do so only after both feet contact the water.
      (3) If flotation gear is not used, separation from the equipment is essential.
      (4) The container can also serve as a flotation device if the reserve canopy is packed in the container.
      (5) Caution must be used to avoid the main canopy suspension lines if the reserve container is used for flotation.
      (6) Tests have shown that a container with a packed reserve will remain buoyant for up to 45 minutes or longer.
   i. Dive deep and swim out from under the collapsed canopy.
   j. If covered by the canopy, follow one seam to the edge of the canopy until clear of it.
   k. In swift or shallow water, pull one toggle in or cut away if under the main canopy.
   l. Refill your lungs at every opportunity.
   m. Swim carefully away upwind or upstream to avoid entangling in the suspension lines.
   n. Remove any full coverage helmets in the event of breathing difficulties.
2. If using the Air Force type (LPU) underarm flotation equipment—
   a. Although worn underneath, the bladders inflate outside the harness, so removal of the harness is not practical without first deflating the bladders.
   b. If you must remove the harness after landing, the bladders should be deflated, extricated from the harness, and reinflated (orally) one at a time.
3. The risks of a water landing are greatly increased when a jumper wears additional weights to increase fall rate.
4. Camera flyers, skysurfers, and other skydivers carrying additional equipment on a jump need to plan their water landing procedures accordingly.
5. Water temperature must always be a consideration
   a. Water temperatures below 70 degrees Fahrenheit can severely limit the amount of time a person can survive while trying to tread water or remain afloat.
   b. Treading water or swimming will cause the body to lose heat more rapidly, because blood moves to the extremities and is then cooled more rapidly.
   c. Depending on the situation, it may be better to try to float rather than swim or tread water while waiting for help to arrive.
6. Other references
   a. SIM Section 2-1, USPA Basic Safety Requirements on water jumping equipment
   b. SIM Section 6-5, Water Landing Recommendations (unintentional and intentional).

POWER LINES

1. Power lines present a serious hazard to all aviators; know where they are near your DZ.
2. Identify power lines in the landing area as early as possible and steer to avoid them.
3. If a low turn is necessary to avoid a power line:
   a. Make the minimum, flat, braked turn necessary to miss the line.
   b. Execute a braked landing and flare.
   c. Prepare for a hard landing (PLF).
4. If a power line landing is unavoidable:
   a. Drop any ripcords or other objects.
   b. Bring a ram-air canopy to slow flight.
   c. With a round canopy, place your hands between the front and rear risers on each side.
   d. Prepare for a PLF with your feet and knees tightly together and turn your head to the side to protect your chin.
   e. Land parallel to the power lines.
   f. Do not touch more than one wire at a time.
   g. If suspended in the wires:
      (1) Wait for help from drop zone and power company personnel; nylon conducts electricity at higher voltages.
      (2) Verify only with the power company that electrical power is off and will stay off.
      (3) If the computer controlling the power distribution senses a fault in the line, computer-controlled resets may attempt to turn the power back on without warning.

SKYDIVING EMERGENCIES 5-1

TREES

1. Avoid trees by careful spotting and a good approach pattern plan for the conditions.
2. The potential dangers of landing in a tree extend until you are rescued and safely on the ground.
3. Make any low-altitude avoidance turns from braked flight to avoid an equally dangerous dive following a turn from full flight.
4. If a tree landing is unavoidable:
   a. With a ram-air canopy, hold the toggles at half brakes until tree contact.
   b. Prepare for a PLF; often the jumper passes through the tree and lands on the ground.
   c. Protect your body.
      (1) Keep feet and knees tightly together.
      (2) Do not cross your feet or legs.
      (3) Cover your face with your hands while holding your elbows tightly against your stomach.
   d. Steer for the middle of the tree, then hold on to the trunk or main branch to avoid falling.
   e. If suspended above the ground, wait for help from drop zone personnel to get down.
   f. Don't attempt to climb down from a tree without competent assistance (rescue personnel or properly trained drop zone staff).

BUILDINGS AND OTHER OBJECTS

1. Plan your landing approach to be well clear of objects.
2. Fly far enough from objects that another jumper or your own misjudgment does not force you into a building or other hazardous object.
3. Focus on clear, open landing areas and steer the parachute to a clear area.
4. Make any low-altitude avoidance turns from braked flight to avoid an equally dangerous dive following a turn from full flight.
5. If landing on a building or object cannot be avoided, prepare for a PLF.
6. Flare at ten feet above the first point of contact with the building or object.
7. Strike the object feet first, whether landing on top or into the side of the object.
8. After landing on top of an object in windy conditions:
   a. Disconnect the reserve static line (if possible) and cut away the main parachute.
   b. If landing with a reserve, retrieve and contain the canopy until removing the harness.
   c. Wait for competent help.

OFF-FIELD LANDINGS

1. Jumpers prefer to land in the planned area, which is usually familiar and free of obstacles; however, circumstances might make that difficult or impossible:
   a. spotting error
   b. unexpected wind conditions
   c. inadvertent high opening
   d. low opening, especially under a reserve canopy
2. Problems resulting from less-than-ideal opening positions over the ground have resulted in injuries and fatalities for students and experienced jumpers:
   a. intentional low turns into an unfamiliar landing area.
   b. unplanned low turns trying to avoid obstacles
   c. landing into or on an obstacle or uneven terrain
   d. errors made after trying to return to the planned landing area or returning lower than planned, when a better choice was available
3. Avoiding off-field landings
   a. Know the correct exit point for the current conditions.
   b. Once at the door of the aircraft, check the spot before exiting and request a go-around if necessary.
   c. In freefall, check the spot soon after exit and adjust opening altitude if necessary and safe to do so, considering the following:
      (1) other groups or individuals in freefall nearby
      (2) jumpers from other planes (multiple-plane operations)
4. If an off-field landing cannot be avoided:
   a. Do not waste altitude trying to reach the main landing area when a viable alternative is available.
   b. Decide on a viable alternative landing area based on your current location and the wind speed and direction.
   c. Plan a descent strategy and landing pattern for the alternative landing area.
   d. Check the alternative landing area carefully for hazards while still high enough to adjust the landing pattern to avoid them.
      (1) When checking for power lines, it is easier to see the poles and towers than the wires themselves.
      (2) Determine the wind direction to predict turbulence created by trees or other obstacles, and plan a landing spot accordingly.
      (3) Fences and hills may be difficult to see from higher altitudes.
      (4) Fences and power lines often form straight lines along the ground
5. Canopy control
   a. A braked approach and braked turns allow for the canopy to be flown at a slower forward speed and descent rate but may lengthen the approach glide.
   b. Altitude-conserving braked turns may be necessary to avoid an obstacle.
   c. A braked turn at a low altitude may not allow enough time for recovery to full flight in time for a landing flare, and a jumper may need to make a braked landing.
   d. Jumpers should practice braked turns and approaches often to prepare for this eventuality.
6. Returning from a long distance:
   a. Flying a long distance in high winds can disorient a jumper for altitude awareness and could lead to a low turn.
   b. High winds at higher altitudes typically diminish near the ground and should not be counted on to carry a jumper over an obstacle or hostile landing area.
   c. A jumper attempting to return from a long distance should keep alternatives in mind along the way

5-1 SKYDIVING EMERGENCIES

and begin an approach into a clear area by 1,000 feet.

   d. Landing into the wind is desirable, but not at the risk of a low turn.

   e. In any off-field landing, a parachute landing fall is a good defense against injury from unknown surface and terrain.

7. Jumpers must respect the property where the landing took place.
    a. Do not disturb livestock.
    b. Leave gates as they were found.
    c. Avoid walking on crops or other cultivated vegetation.
    d. property damage
        (1) Report any property damage to the property owner and make arrangements for repairs.
        (2) USPA membership includes insurance for such situations.

G. FREEFALL COLLISIONS

1. A collision danger faces jumpers exiting in a group or on the same pass when they lose track of each other.
2. Differential freefall speeds may reach upwards of 150 mph horizontally and vertically in combination.
3. Jumpers must take precautions to prevent a collision with freefalling jumpers during and after opening.

H. CANOPY COLLISIONS

1. The best way to avoid a collision is to know where other canopies are at all times.
2. Most canopy collisions occur soon after deployment when two jumpers open too close to each other, or below 1,000 feet while in the landing pattern.
3. Higher break-off altitudes, better planning and tracking farther can help ensure clear airspace during deployment.
4. Remaining vigilant throughout the canopy descent and always looking in the direction of the turn before initiating it can help to identify and avoid other canopies during the descent.
5. If approaching a jumper head on, both canopies should steer to the right unless it is obvious that steering left is necessary to avoid the collision (both jumpers are more offset towards the left).
6. If a collision is inevitable:
    a. Protect your face and operation handles.
    b. Tuck in your arms, legs and head for protection against the impact.
    c. Avoid hitting the suspension lines of the other canopy or the other jumper, if at all possible.
    d. If a collision with the other jumper's suspension lines is unavoidable, it may be possible to spread your legs and one arm, while protecting your handles with the other arm, in order to keep from passing through the suspension lines during the collision. However, a collision at high speed with suspension lines can lead to severe cuts and burns.
    e. Check altitude with respect to the minimum cutaway decision and execution altitude recommended for your experience.
    f. Communicate before taking action:
        (1) The jumper above can strike the jumper below during a cutaway unless one or both are clear or ready to fend off.
        (2) The jumper below can worsen the situation for the jumper above by cutting away before he or she is ready.
        (3) If both jumpers are cutting away and altitude permits, the second jumper should wait until the first jumper clears the area below.
        (4) The first jumper should fly from underneath in a straight line after opening.
        (5) At some point below a safe cutaway altitude (1,000 feet), it may become necessary to deploy one or both reserves (may not be a safe option with an SOS system).
        (6) If both jumpers are suspended under one flying canopy at a low altitude, it may become necessary to land with only that canopy.
        (7) Communications may be difficult if one or both jumpers are wearing full-face helmets.
    g. SIM Section 6-6 F. Emergency procedures contains additional recommendations about dealing with canopy entanglements.

I. LOW TURNS

1. Low turns under canopy are one of the biggest causes of serious injury and death in skydiving.
2. A low turn can be premeditated or result from an error in judgment or experience with a situation.
3. To avoid low turns, fly to a large, uncrowded landing area free of obstacles and—
    a. Fly a planned landing pattern that promotes a cooperative traffic flow.
    b. If landing off-field, plan a landing pattern by 1,000 feet.
4. Once a jumper realizes that a turn has been made at an unsafe altitude:
    a. Use toggle control to get the canopy back overhead and stop the turn.
    b. Stop the dive.
    c. Flare and prepare for a hard landing (PLF).
    d. Manage the speed induced by the turn.
        (1) Expect more responsive flare control with the toggles due to the increased airspeed.
        (2) Expect a longer, flatter flare.
    e. In case of premature contact with the ground, no matter how hard, keep flying the canopy to reduce further injury.

5-2: CURRENCY TRAINING

A. STUDENTS

Students who have not jumped within the preceding 30 days should make at least one jump under the direct supervision of an appropriately rated USPA Instructor.

B. LICENSED SKYDIVERS

1. Skydivers returning after a long period of inactivity encounter greater risk that requires special consideration to properly manage.
2. Care should be taken to regain or develop the knowledge, skills, and awareness needed to satisfactorily perform the tasks planned for the jump.
3. Jumps aimed at sharpening survival skills should precede jumps with other goals.

C. CHANGES IN PROCEDURES

1. If deployment or emergency procedures are changed at any time, the skydiver should be thoroughly trained and practice under supervision in a harness simulator until proficient.
2. Ground training should be followed by a solo jump which includes several practice sequences and deployment at a higher-than-normal altitude.
3. The jumper should repeat ground practice at short intervals, such as before each weekend's jump activities, and continue to deploy at a higher-than-normal altitude until thoroughly familiar with the new procedures.

D. LONG LAY-OFFS

1. Jumpers should receive refresher training appropriate for their skydiving history and time since their last skydive.
    a. Jumpers who were very experienced and current but became inactive for a year or more should undergo thorough training upon returning to the sport.
    b. Skydivers who historically jump infrequently should review training after layoffs of even less than a year.
2. Skydiving equipment, techniques, and procedures change frequently.
    a. During currency training following long periods of inactivity, jumpers may be introduced to new and unfamiliar equipment and techniques.
    b. Procedures change to accommodate developments in equipment, aircraft, flying styles, FAA rules, and local drop zone requirements.
3. Returning skydivers require thorough practical training in the following subject areas:
    a. aircraft procedures
    b. equipment
    c. exit and freefall procedures
    d. canopy control and landings
    e. emergency procedures

A LICENSE

USPA A-license holders who have not made a freefall skydive within the preceding 60 days should make at least one jump under the supervision of a currently rated USPA instructional rating holder until demonstrating altitude awareness, freefall control on all axes, tracking, and canopy skills sufficient for safely jumping in groups.

B LICENSE

USPA B-license holders who have not made a freefall skydive within the preceding 90 days should make at least one jump under the supervision of a USPA instructional rating holder until demonstrating the ability to safely exercise the privileges of that license.

C AND D LICENSE

USPA C and D-license holders who have not made a freefall skydive within the preceding 180 days should make at least one jump under the supervision of a USPA instructional rating holder until demonstrating the ability to safely exercise the privileges of that license.

5-3: EQUIPMENT

A. FEDERAL REGULATIONS ON EQUIPMENT

1. The design, maintenance, and alteration of parachute equipment is regulated by the Federal Aviation Administration of the U.S. Department of Transportation, which publishes Federal Aviation Regulations (FARs).

2. All skydivers should be familiar with the following FARs and their applicability to skydiving (see Section 9-1 and 9-2 of this manual):
   a. Part 65—Certification of Parachute Riggers
   b. Part 91—General Flight Rules
   c. Part 105—Parachute Operations
   d. Advisory Circular 105-2—explains in detail various areas of parachute equipment, maintenance, and modifications.

3. Approval of parachutes is granted to manufacturers in the form of Technical Standard Orders (TSOs).
   a. TSO C-23 is issued to parachutes that comply with the current performance standards.
      (1) NAS 804 for TSO C-23b
      (2) AS-8015A for TSO C-23c
      (3) AS-8015B for TSO C-23d
   b. These standards specify the tests that must be passed for a parachute system and its component parts to receive approval for civilian use.
   c. Procedures for obtaining TSO approval for parachutes or component parts may be found in FAR Part 21 (not included in the SIM).

4. Alterations to approved parachutes may be performed only by those who have been issued an FAA approval for the alteration.
   a. Approval may be obtained by submitting a request and description of the alteration to the manufacturer or to an FAA Flight Standards District Office.
   b. The following are eligible to receive alteration approval:
      (1) FAA master rigger
      (2) manufacturer with an approved quality assurance program
   c. Alterations may not be performed without full documentation of FAA approval for the specific alteration.

B. MAIN PARACHUTE

1. Jumpers should choose canopies that will provide an acceptable landing in a wide range of circumstances, based on several factors including canopy size, wing loading, planform (shape), skill level, and experience.

2. Owners should verify with a rigger that all applicable updates and bulletins have been accomplished.

3. Jumpers should observe the recommendations of the canopy manufacturer for the correct canopy size, usually listed by maximum recommended weight with respect to other factors:
   a. the jumper's experience
   b. drop zone elevation
   c. other conditions, such as density altitude

4. Wing loading, measured as exit weight in pounds per square foot (psf) provides only one gauge of a canopy's performance characteristics.
   a. A smaller canopy at an equal wing loading compared to a larger one of the same design will exhibit a faster and more radical control response, with more altitude loss in any maneuver.
   b. Design, materials, and construction techniques can cause two equally wing-loaded canopies to perform very differently.
   c. Different planforms (square vs. elliptical) will exhibit very different handling characteristics.

5. The Minimum Canopy Recommendations chart represents the minimum recommended canopy size by exit weight and total jumps made on solo equipment with square parachutes. Canopy size for students is at the discretion of the instructor.
   a. Due to the varied sizes of canopies from different manufacturers, any canopy less than 3% smaller than the listed recommendation is acceptable.
   b. Canopy choices for jumpers over 1,000 jumps is at their discretion.
   c. These minimum canopy recommendations may be too aggressive for some jumpers and, in other cases, too conservative. Instructors, canopy coaches and drop zone leadership should assist their skydivers in selecting an appropriate canopy for their jumper's ability and progression.

Minimum Canopy Recommendations

	Exit Weight (Jumper plus all equipment)															
Jumps		100	110	120	130	140	150	160	170	180	190	200	210	220	230	240	250
	0-25	190	190	190	190	190	190	200	200	200	220	220	220	220	240	260	280
	26-50	170	170	170	170	170	190	190	190	190	190	190	200	200	220	240	260
	51-100	170	170	170	170	170	170	170	170	170	190	190	190	200	200	220	240
	101-200	150	150	150	170	170	170	170	170	170	170	170	170	190	200	200	220
	201-300	150	150	150	150	150	150	150	150	170	170	170	170	190	190	190	200
	301-400	135	135	135	150	150	150	150	150	150	150	170	170	170	190	190	190
	401-500	135	135	135	135	135	135	135	150	150	150	170	170	170	190	190	190
	501-750	120	120	120	135	135	135	135	135	135	150	150	170	170	170	170	170
	750-1000	107	120	120	120	135	135	135	135	135	135	150	150	170	170	170	170

C. RESERVE PARACHUTE

1. All skydivers should use a steerable reserve canopy.
2. The FAA requires the reserve parachute assembly, including harness, container, canopy, risers, pilot chute, deployment device, and ripcord, to be approved.
3. Jumpers must observe FARs regarding the manufacturer's maximum certificated weights and speeds for parachutes.
   a. Parachutes approved under FAA Technical Standard Order C-23b, C-23c, and C-23d are subject to different testing standards and operation limits.
   b. The entire parachute system is limited to the maximum certificated load limit of the harness- and-container system or reserve canopy, whichever is less.
   c. Load limits are found in the owner's manual, the manufacturer's website, or placarded on the parachute component itself.
4. For a ram-air reserve, jumpers should not exceed the maximum suspended weight specified by the manufacturer (not necessarily the maximum certificated load limit).
5. A jumper may exceed the rated speeds of a certificated parachute system (harness and/or parachute) by jumping at higher MSL altitudes or falling in vertical freefall orientations.
6. Round reserve canopy
   a. should be equipped with a deployment device to reduce the opening force and control deployment
   b. should have a rate of descent that does not exceed 18 feet per second (fps)
   c. must not exceed a rate of descent of 25 fps at sea level conditions (NAS 804) The following scale indicates the minimum size round reserve canopy recommended for use according to the exit weight of the skydiver:

total suspended weight*	recommended equivalent descent rate (high porosity flat circular)
Up to 149 pounds	24-foot
150 to 199 pounds	26-foot
200 pounds and over	28-foot

*The use of lower porosity materials can reduce the rate of descent.

D. HARNESS AND CONTAINER SYSTEM

1. The FAA requires the harness of a dual parachute assembly to be approved.
2. All harness ends should be folded over and sewn down or wrapped and sewn down to prevent the harness from unthreading through the hardware upon opening.
3. Canopy release systems should be maintained according to the schedule and procedures in the owner's manual.
4. It is desirable for the manufacturing industry to standardize the location of all operational controls.
5. The harness should be equipped with single-point riser releases (one handle releases both risers) for easy and rapid disengagement from the main canopy.
6. Reserve ripcord handles:
   a. Loop type handles should be made of metal.
   b. Plastic and composite reserve ripcord handles are not recommended.
   c. Jumpers should practice peeling and pulling pillow-type reserve ripcord handles until certain they can operate them easily in an emergency.
7. All ripcord housings ends should be secured.
8. Ripcord pins, when seated, should either be started inside the housing or clear the closing loop before entering the housing.
9. A ripcord cable stop should not be used; fatal accidents caused by reserve entanglements with ripcords secured in this manner have been documented.
10. Reserve pilot chute:
    a. The reserve system is usually designed to use a specific type of pilot chute.
    b. It should be properly seated in the container and repacked if it has shifted.
11. Deployment brake systems should provide secure stowage of the steering toggles and slack brake line to prevent brake-line entanglements and premature brake release.

E. MAIN PILOT CHUTE

1. The main pilot chute is designed as part of the main parachute system.
   a. On throw-out hand-deployed systems, the pilot chute and pouch size must be compatible.
   b. Pilot chute size can affect the opening characteristics of the main canopy.
2. Collapsible hand-deployed pilot chutes add complexity and additional maintenance requirements to the system.
   a. additional wear from more moving parts
   b. danger of a high-speed pilot-chute-in-tow malfunction if the pilot chute is not set or cocked
3. Spring loaded and hand-deployed pilot chutes of both types (throw-out and pull-out) each have strengths and weaknesses that affect the user's emergency procedures and other decisions.

F. RESERVE STATIC LINE (RSL)

1. A reserve static line attaches to a main canopy riser to extract the reserve ripcord pin immediately and automatically after separation of the main risers from the harness.
2. An RSL is recommended for all experienced jumpers.
   a. The RSL backs up the jumper by extracting the reserve ripcord pin after a cutaway.
   b. the RSL—
      (1) must be routed and attached correctly to function
      (2) when misrouted, can complicate or prevent a cutaway
   c. RSLs can complicate certain emergency procedures:
      (1) cutaway following a dual deployment
      (2) cutting away from an entanglement after a collision
      (3) unstable cutaway, although statistics show that chances are better from an unstable reserve deployment than delaying after a cutaway
      (4) unstable cutaway with a helmet camera or other protruding device
      (5) cutaway with a surfboard (although an RSL may have prevented two fatal skysurfing accidents)

5-3 | EQUIPMENT

    (6) cutaway on the ground in high winds

    (7) broken riser on the RSL side (results in reserve deployment); prevention—

        (i) inspecting and replacing worn risers

        (ii) packing for soft openings (tight line stows; see manufacturer's instructions)

        (iii) stable deployment at slow speeds

  d. If temporarily disconnecting an RSL, care must be taken so it doesn't interfere with the operation of the parachute system; consult a rigger.

3. When using a reserve static line device, the skydiver must not depend on the static-line device and must manually pull the reserve ripcord immediately after the cutaway.

4. An RSL may not be desirable when attempting linked canopy formations.

5. Unless the manufacturer's instructions state otherwise, a connector device between the left and right main risers should not be used.

G. AUTOMATIC ACTIVATION DEVICE (AAD)

1. An AAD initiates the reserve deployment sequence at a preset altitude (also sometimes used on the main parachute system).

2. An AAD is encouraged for all licensed jumpers.

3. The use of an AAD for activation of the reserve parachute, coupled with proper training in its use, has been shown to significantly increase the chances of surviving a malfunction or loss of altitude awareness.

4. The AAD is used to back up the jumper's deployment and emergency procedures, but no jumper should ever rely on one.

5. The FAA requires that if an AAD is used, it must be maintained in accordance with the manufacturer's instructions (FAR 105.43.c).

6. Each jumper should read and understand the owner's manual for the AAD.

7. An AAD may complicate certain situations, particularly if the jumper deploys the main parachute low enough for the AAD to activate.

8. Understanding and reviewing of the emergency procedures for Two Canopies Out (SIM Section 5-1) is essential.

H. STATIC LINE (MAIN)

1. The FAA requires static line deployment to be either by direct bag or pilot-chute assist.

2. The direct bag is a more positive method of static-line deployment because it reduces the chance of the student interfering with main canopy deployment.

3. The FAA requires an assist device to be used with a static line deployment when rigged with pilot-chute assist.

  a. The assist device must be attached at one end to the static line so that the container is opened before the device is loaded, and at the other end to the pilot chute.

  b. The FAA requires the pilot chute assist device to have a load strength of at least 28 but not more than 160 pounds.

4. The static line should be attached to an approved structural point of the airframe.

  a. A seat belt attachment point is considered part of the airframe, but the static line should pull on it in a longitudinal direction.

  b. Aircraft seats are not considered to be part of the airframe.

5. A static line should be constructed:

  a. with a length of at least eight feet but not more than 15 feet and should never come into contact with the aircraft's tail surfaces

  b. with a locking slide fastener, ID number 43A9502 or MS70120

  c. with webbing of not less than 3,600 pounds tensile strength

I. BORROWING OR CHANGING EQUIPMENT

1. Parachutes should not be rented or loaned to persons unqualified to carry out an intended skydive or to persons of unknown ability.

2. The use of unfamiliar (borrowed, new) equipment without sufficient preparation has been a factor in many fatalities.

3. Equipment changes:

  a. Changes in type of equipment should be avoided or minimized whenever possible during student training.

  b. For all jumpers when changes are made, adequate transition training should be provided.

4. When jumping a new or different main parachute, a jumper should follow the canopy familiarization progression outlined in Categories A-H of the Integrated Student Program (multiple jumps).

J. USE OF ALTIMETERS

1. Skydivers must always know their altitude.

2. There is a great reduction of depth perception over water and at night.

3. Pull altitude and other critical altitudes should be determined by using a combination of visual reference to the ground and to an altimeter.

  a. As a primary reference, each skydiver should learn to estimate critical altitudes (break-off, minimum deployment, minimum cutaway) by looking at the ground and mentally keeping track of time in freefall.

  b. Altimeters provide excellent secondary references for developing and verifying primary altitude-recognition skills.

  c. Some jumpers may desire more than one altimeter and even more than one altimeter of the same type to have a reference available throughout the jump.

  d. Jumpers should wear their altimeters so they are available to them during as many phases of the jump as possible.

4. Some examples of altimeter types and locations include:

  a. visual altimeter worn on the wrist

    (1) easy to read in a variety of freefall positions

    (2) wrist is usually unaffected by burbles

    (3) difficult to read while tracking

  b. visual altimeter worn on the chest or main lift web

    (1) reference for others in a group, particularly when belly flying

    (2) readable during tracking

    (3) subject to error and erratic readings while back-to-earth

c. audible altimeter, typically worn against the ear

   (1) Audibles provide a good reference to key altitudes near the end of the planned freefall.

   (2) Extreme background noise of freefall and a jumper's attention to another event can render audible altimeters ineffective.

   (3) Students should use audible altimeters only after demonstrating a satisfactory level of altitude awareness.

5. Initial and refamiliarization training for altimeter use should include:

   a. Looking at the ground.

   b. Looking at the altimeter and note the altitude.

   c. Repeat this procedure several times per jump to develop the ability to eyeball the altitude.

6. Altimeter errors

   a. Altimeters use electronic and/or mechanical components that are subject to damage and may fail in use.

   b. Minor differences in indicated altitude are to be expected.

   c. Set the altimeter at the landing area and do not readjust the altimeter after leaving the ground.

   d. An altimeter may lag during both ascent and descent; plus or minus 0-500 feet is to be expected.

   e. The needle can stick during both ascent and descent—a visual cross reference with the ground should be used in combination with the altimeter.

   f. When the altimeter is in a burble (as when falling back-to-earth), it may read high by as much as 1,000 feet.

7. Handle altimeters with care and maintain and store them according to the manufacturer's instructions.

K. ACCESSORIES

1. The use of personal equipment should be determined by the type of jump experience and proficiency of the skydiver, weather, and drop zone conditions.

2. Clothing and equipment:

   a. Adequate protective clothing, including jumpsuit, helmet, gloves, goggles, and footwear should be worn for all land jumps.

   b. Gloves are essential when the jump altitude temperature is lower than 40° F.

   c. A jumper should always carry a protected but accessible knife.

   d. A rigid helmet—

   (1) should be worn on all skydives (tandem students may wear soft helmets)

   (2) should be lightweight and not restrict vision or hearing

   e. All jumpers are advised to wear flotation gear when the intended exit, opening, or landing point of a skydive is within one mile of an open body of water (an open body of water is defined as one in which a skydiver could drown).

L. MAIN PARACHUTE PACKING

1. The main parachute of a dual assembly may be packed by—

   a. an FAA rigger

   (1) An FAA rigger may supervise other persons in packing any type of parachute for which that person is rated (FAR 65.125.a and b).

   (2) A non-certificated person may pack a main parachute under the direct supervision of an FAA rigger (FAR 105.43.a).

   b. the person who intends to use it on the next jump (FAR 105.43.a)

2. Packing knowledge:

   a. Each individual skydiver should have the written approval of an S&TA, USPA Instructor, Examiner, or an FAA rigger to pack his or her own parachute.

   b. All parachute packers should know and understand the manufacturer's instructions for packing, maintenance, and use.

3. Tandem main parachutes may be packed by (FAR 105.45.b.1)—

   a. an FAA rigger

   b. the parachutist in command making the next jump with that parachute

   c. a packer under the direct supervision of a rigger

4. Exercise extreme caution when using temporary packing pins.

M. PARACHUTE MAINTENANCE

1. Inspection:

   a. The equipment owner should frequently inspect the equipment for any damage and wear.

   b. Any questionable condition should be promptly corrected by a qualified person.

   c. Detailed owner inspection of the parachute is outlined in the Equipment Section of Category G of the USPA Integrated Student Program, SIM Section 4.

2. Maintenance and repair of the reserve:

   a. The FAA requires the entire reserve assembly to be maintained as an approved parachute.

   b. Repairs to the reserve assembly must be done by an FAA-certificated parachute rigger.

3. Maintenance and repair of the main:

   a. Repairs to the main may be done by an FAA-certificated rigger or by the owner if he or she has adequate knowledge and skill.

   b. The main parachute and its container need not be maintained as "approved."

4. Major repairs and alterations may be performed only by or under the supervision of:

   a. an FAA master rigger

   b. the parachute manufacturer

   c. any other manufacturer the FAA considers competent

5-4: PRE-JUMP SAFETY CHECKS AND BRIEFINGS

A. EQUIPMENT PREPARATION IS ESSENTIAL

1. Preparing all skydiving equipment and procedures prior to each jump is critical to preventing accidents.
2. This information is intended to provide the instructional staff and other experienced jumpers with a reference to use as guidance in developing a personal checklist appropriate to the procedures and equipment in use.
3. In some cases, these checks will be the principal responsibility of others—the pilot, instructor, coach, rigger, ground crew chief, etc., however, no one should assume that these responsibilities have been carried out by others.
    a. Initially, the USPA Instructor performs these pre-jump safety checks and briefings for his or her students.
    b. As students progress, they should begin to learn to do them for themselves.
    c. Through leadership and attitude, the instructional staff has the opportunity to foster a respect for safety that will serve the beginning skydiver well when assuming sole responsibility for all of his or her skydiving activities.
4. Students progressing through the training program and all experienced jumpers should review all of the items on these lists to familiarize themselves with the wide range of details.
5. This section includes checklists for:
    a. aircraft preflight
    b. ground crew briefing
    c. pilot briefing
    d. skydiver briefing
    e. equipment check
    f. before-takeoff check
    g. takeoff
    h. spotting
    i. jump run
    j. descent and landing in aircraft
    k. post-jump debriefing

B. BRIEFINGS

1. Aircraft preflight (primarily the responsibility of the pilot, but the supervising USPA instructional rating holder should check also):
    a. placards: in place (as required)
    b. seats removed (as required)
    c. door stop (under Cessna wing) removed
    d. sharp objects taped
    e. loose objects secured
    f. steps and handholds secure, clean of oil
    g. aircraft altimeter set
    h. filing and activation of notice to airmen (NOTAM)
    i. aircraft radio serviceable
    j. static-line attachment secure
    k. knife in place and accessible
    l. remote spotting correction and communication signals operational (larger aircraft)
    m. winds-aloft report or wind-drift indicators available
    n. seat belts available and serviceable
    o. passenger hand straps near door removed
2. Ground crew briefing: A load organizer (a senior jumper or instructional rating holder) should coordinate to ensure that everyone is in agreement:
    a. communications procedures to meet BSR requirements for ground-to-air communication: smoke, panels, radio, etc.
    b. jump order
    c. distance between groups on exit
    d. landing pattern priorities
    e. control of spectators and vehicles
    f. student operations (USPA Instructor)
        (1) wind limitations
        (2) setting up and maintaining a clear target area
        (3) critiques of student landings
        (4) maintenance of master log
        (5) accident and first-aid procedures
3. Pilot briefing: The load organizer coordinates with the pilot.
    a. jump run altitudes
    b. jump run direction
    c. communications (ground to air, jumpmaster to pilot, air traffic control)
    d. aircraft attitudes during corrections on jump run
    e. jump run speed and cut
    f. locking wheel brake (if applicable), but the parking brake is not to be used
    g. gross weight and center of gravity requirements and limitations
    h. procedures for aircraft emergencies
    i. procedures for equipment emergencies in the aircraft
4. Skydiver briefing
    a. conducted by the load organizer
        (1) seat belt off altitude: 1,500 feet above ground level (AGL) or designated by DZ policy
        (2) movement in the aircraft, especially during jump run
        (3) aircraft emergency procedures, including communication procedures
        (4) parachute equipment emergency procedures
    b. to be conducted by the USPA Instructor:
        (1) review of student log or record
        (2) jump plan
            (i) exit and freefall, including jump commands
            (ii) emergency procedure training or review
            (iii) canopy control and landing pattern
            (iv) drop zone appearance and hazards (an aerial photo or map is recommended)
        (3) protection of operation handles and pins
        (4) conduct in aircraft: mental preparation and movement

C. EQUIPMENT CHECKLIST

1. Equipment check responsibilities before boarding and before exiting:
    a. The USPA Instructor or Coach checks the student's equipment.
    b. Each individual skydiver ensures that his or her own equipment is inspected three times prior to each jump.
        (1) before putting it on

5-4 PRE-JUMP SAFETY CHECKS AND BRIEFINGS

   (2) prior to boarding

   (3) prior to exit

2. Checklist

    a. helmet: proper fit and the chin strap threaded correctly

    b. goggles or glasses secure and clean

    c. canopy releases: properly assembled and periodic maintenance performed

    d. Reserve Static Line (RSL) hooked up and routed correctly (refer to manufacturer's instructions)

    e. altimeters checked and set and ensure that visual altimeters do not block operation handles

    f. main parachute

       (1) main canopy properly sized

       (2) container properly closed, pull-up cord removed, and closing loop in good condition

       (3) activation device

          (i) ripcord: secure in the pocket, housing tacked and secured on both ends, proper movement of the pin or cable in the housing and closing loop, and pilot chute seated correctly

          (ii) throw-out pilot chute: secure in the pouch, bridle routed correctly and secure, pin secure on the bridle and seated in the closing loop, and slack above the pin (this may apply to some rigs; see manufacturer's instructions for details)

          (iii) pull-out pilot chute (not approved for student use) handle secure: pin seated, free movement of the handle through pin extraction (see manufacturer's instructions)

       (4) practice main deployment handle secure (student)

    g. harness:

       (1) straps not twisted and routed correctly

          (i) chest strap

          (ii) leg straps

          (iii) belly band, if applicable

       (2) snaps secured and closed and/or friction adapters properly threaded

       (3) adjusted for proper fit

       (4) running ends turned back and sewn

       (5) loose ends tucked into keepers

    h. belly band (if used):

       (1) correctly routed

       (2) adjusted

       (3) friction adapter properly threaded

    i. reserve:

       (1) proper size for jumper

       (2) pin condition—seated, not bent, and closing loop(s) in good condition

       (3) pilot chute seated

       (4) packing data card in date and seal in place

       (5) ripcord handle pocket condition

       (6) pin cover flap closed

       (7) overall appearance

    j. risers not twisted and toggles secure

    k. suspension and control lines not exposed

    l. static line (students):

       (1) correct length, routing, and slack for operation compatible with that aircraft

       (2) assist device (if required) attached properly

       (3) static-line secured to prevent premature deployment

       (4) closing pin or cable in place

    m. personal:

       (1) footwear—proper type and fit, no open hooks or buckles

       (2) protective clothing

          (i) jumpsuit pockets closed

          (ii) other outerwear compatible with jumping

          (iii) gloves as required

       (3) no unnecessary accessories, such as cameras

       (4) empty pockets

       (5) earplugs

    n. automatic activation device (AAD):

       (1) serviced according to manufacturer's schedule

       (2) calibrated for jump (if required)

       (3) proper routing of cable(s)

       (4) control unit secured in proper location

       (5) armed or turned on as required

    o. radio (students) properly secured and functional (test with base station)

    p. condition of all touch fastener (Velcro®) and tuck tabs

    q. overall fit and appearance

5-5 | WEATHER

5-5: WEATHER

A. DETERMINING WINDS

1. Surface winds must be determined prior to jumping and should be measured at the actual landing area.
2. Winds aloft:
   a. Winds aloft reports available from the FAA flight service are only forecasts.
   b. Observations may be made while in flight using navigation systems, for example, global positioning satellite systems (GPS).
   c. Winds can change at any time, so all available information should be checked by the jumper before and during the jump.

B. HAZARDOUS WEATHER

1. Fronts approach with much warning but can catch the unaware off guard.
   a. Some fronts are preceded by a gust front (a line of sudden and severe weather).
   b. Frontal approach and passage may be associated with rapid and significant changes in the strength and direction of the winds aloft and on the surface.
2. On calm, hot, humid days, thunderstorms can spontaneously generate and move in unpredictable patterns.
3. Dust devils are mini-tornadoes that spontaneously generate on days of high thermal convection activity.
4. Where to get practical information on approaching weather:
   a. the Weather Channel
   b. www.weather.com
   c. TV weathercasts
   d. pilot assistance (legally responsible to know the weather conditions before flight)
   e. continuous observation

C. DENSITY ALTITUDE

1. Parachute performance is measured at sea level in moderate temperatures and humidity.
2. Altitude, heat, and humidity influence the density of air
3. Density altitude is a measure of air density that is calculated according to the temperature and altitude.
4. As density altitude increases, airspeed increases by:
   a. almost five percent per 3,000 feet up to 12,000 feet MSL
   b. more than five percent per 3,000 feet above 12,000 feet MSL
5. As density altitude increases, a ram-air canopy pilot can expect the following:
   a. a higher stall speed
   b. a faster forward speed
   c. a faster descent rate
   d. higher opening forces
6. Additionally, aircraft are affected by higher density altitude in the following ways:
   a. longer distances required for takeoff and landing
   b. reduced propeller effectiveness
   c. poorer turbine and piston engine performance
   d. slower and flatter rate of climb
   e. less useful load
7. The aircraft pilot is responsible to know the density altitude prior to takeoff, and skydivers are advised to consider the effects of density altitude on canopy performance.

5-6: AIRCRAFT

1. Skydivers play a more integral role in aircraft operations than ordinary passengers, because their procedures can dramatically affect the controllability of the aircraft, particularly during exit.
   a. Parasitic drag reduces airspeed necessary for flight and reduces the effectiveness of control surfaces.
   b. Excess weight in the rear of the aircraft can cause the pilot to lose control of the aircraft and cause it to stall.
2. All jumpers should be briefed by a jump pilot on the topics outlined in Aircraft Briefing from Category E of the USPA Integrated Student Program (SIM Section 4).
3. The smallest aircraft to be used for student jumping should be able to carry the pilot and at least three jumpers.
4. High openings
   a. The pilot and all jumpers on board the aircraft should be informed in advance whenever an opening is planned to be above the normal opening altitude (generally 5,000 feet AGL and lower).
   b. When more than one aircraft is being used, the pilots of each aircraft in flight at the time of the jump should be notified.
5. Aircraft fueling
   a. Aircraft fueling operations should occur away from skydiver landing and loading areas, and no person, except the pilot and necessary fueling crew, should be aboard the aircraft during fueling.
   b. USPA accepts the practice of rapid refueling (fueling an aircraft while an engine is running) for certain turbine-powered aircraft when performed in accordance with the guidelines of Parachute Industry Association Technical Standard, TS-122.
6. Entering the aircraft
   a. Students should never approach an aircraft, whether the engine is running or not, unless they are under the direct supervision of a USPA instructional rating holder.
   b. Everyone should always approach a fixed-wing aircraft from behind the wing and always approach a helicopter from the front or the side, only after making eye contact with the pilot.
   c. Everyone should always protect his or her ripcord handles while entering the aircraft and follow procedures to avoid the accidental activation of any equipment.
7. Everyone on board the aircraft is subject to the seating requirements found in FAR 91.107 and the parachute requirements found in FAR 91.307.
8. Ride to altitude
   a. Everyone should have a thorough understanding and be prepared to take the appropriate actions in the event of an accidental activation of parachute equipment in the aircraft.
   b. Seat belts should remain fastened and all hard helmets and other potential projectiles secured until the pilot notifies the jumpers that they may unfasten them.
   c. Students should sit still and move only when specifically directed to do so by their instructor(s) or coach.
   d. Seating arrangements should be determined in advance and will vary according to the particular aircraft and the size and type of the load.
   e. It is important for the load to be properly distributed in the aircraft to maintain the balance in relation to the center of gravity, which is necessary for the aircraft to fly safely.
   f. The jumpers must cooperate fully with the pilot to keep the aircraft within its safe performance envelope throughout the entire flight.
   g. The aircraft must not be loaded with more weight than the maximum allowed in the manufacturer's operating manual.
   h. Failure to maintain proper weight and balance throughout the flight may result in loss of control of the aircraft.
9. When not in use, seat belts should be stowed out of the way but never fastened together unless being worn.
10. All pilots and other occupants of a jump aircraft must wear parachutes when required by the FAA.

5-7: SPOTTING

A. WHY SPOTTING IS IMPORTANT

1. Choosing the correct exit point and guiding the pilot to it (spotting) helps fulfill each skydiver's responsibility to land in an appropriate clear area.
2. Jumpers must demonstrate basic spotting abilities prior to obtaining the USPA A license.
3. Spotting in more difficult circumstances requires continued practice and study.
4. In addition to considerations for getting one jumper or group out of the aircraft at the correct point, spotters must consider the correct exit points for multiple individuals or groups on the same pass from a larger aircraft.

B. PRIORITIES

1. Be familiar with the DZ and surrounding area, including exit and opening points.
   a. Jumpers should observe and talk to those on previous jumps to help determine the correct jump-run direction and exit and opening point.
   b. Methods for estimating the exit and opening point based on winds-aloft forecasts are explained in the Aircraft and Spotting sections of Categories F and G of the Integrated Student Program, Section 4 of this manual.
   c. A wind-drift indicator (WDI) is effective for determining drift under canopy.
      (1) A piece of weighted crepe paper is released at canopy opening altitude over an observed position or at half of the opening altitude so the ground travel will be doubled for the jump.
      (2) The jumpers aboard the aircraft observe the drift of the WDI to determine the distance and direction of the best opening point upwind of the target.
      (3) Jumpers should be responsible for wind drift indicators after they land.
      (4) Observation and calculation of the spot from the winds-aloft report have replaced the WDI for most routine drop zone operations.
2. Look out of the aircraft:
   a. for traffic below
   b. for clouds
   c. to spot
3. Identify the DZ, the climbout point, and the exit point from the open door of the aircraft.
4. Techniques for determining the point straight below the aircraft are discussed in Category D of the ISP.

C. GROUP SEPARATION ON JUMP RUN

1. Slower-falling jumpers and groups are exposed to upper headwinds longer and are blown farther downwind than faster-falling jumpers and groups.
   a. Slower-falling groups should exit before faster-falling groups if jump run is flown into the wind.
   b. On days with strong upper headwinds, allow more time between groups on the same pass to get sufficient horizontal separation over the ground.
      (1) Provide at least 1,000 feet of ground separation between individuals jumping solo.
      (2) Provide at least 1,500 feet of ground separation between small groups, adding more as size of the groups increases.
   c. Once the parachute has opened, delay flying up or down the line of flight until—
      (1) Any slower-falling group that exited before has opened their parachutes and turned toward the landing area.
      (2) The group exiting after has completed their freefall and opened.
2. Flying jump run across the upper winds (crosswind) helps achieve separation between groups.
3. Whether flying one or more aircraft, each pass should allow enough time for jumpers on a previous pass to descend to a safe altitude before dropping jumpers from the next pass.

D. EXIT AND FLIGHT PLAN CONSIDERATIONS FOR DIFFERENT DISCIPLINES

1. Larger jump aircraft may include several different groups of skydivers performing different disciplines, some of which use more airspace than others.
   a. Formation skydivers falling in a belly-to-earth orientation.
   b. Freeflying formations falling in head-down, standing or sitting formations.
   c. Freefall students with instructors.
   d. Tandem students and instructors.
   e. Tracking groups
   f. Angle flying groups
   g. Wingsuit flyers.
2. Some of these groups will tend to descend straight down after exit, drifting horizontally with the effects of wind, but otherwise not moving much in the airspace.
3. These groups include formation skydivers, freeflyers, solo students and tandem students, and they gain adequate separation from one another by exiting in groups largest to smallest per discipline and waiting the appropriate length of time between groups before exiting the airplane.
4. Tracking groups, angle flying groups, and wingsuiters will cover large horizontal distances that must be taken into account when planning a descent strategy.
   a. These groups must fly a specific flight path planned before boarding the aircraft.
   b. Exiting last is the most common exit order for tracking groups, angle flyers and wingsuiters.
   c. Immediately after exit, the group needs to fly perpendicular to the jump run to provide lateral separation from the other groups on the aircraft.
   d. After gaining sufficient lateral distance, the group may then turn in a downwind direction, flying parallel to the other groups that exited earlier.
   e. The jumper leading this type of group must keep the group flying in the planned direction for the entire freefall distance, maintaining adequate lateral separation.
   f. The break-off point must be far enough laterally to allow for these jumpers to gain horizontal separation from each other as well as any of the groups that exited the airplane earlier.
   g. Airplane loads that include more than one group of tracking groups, angle flyers or wingsuiters will add additional complexity to the airspace requirements necessary to allow each group to open in a clear area.
   h. Depending on the situation, it may be safer to restrict each airplane load to only one group of tracking jumpers, angle flyers or wingsuiters.

5-8 INCIDENT REPORTS

A. INCIDENTS

1. USPA rating holders and S&TAs, the leaders in the field, are the key to having skydivers file incident reports. Reporting these incidents can help USPA track current trends in the field and give direction to USPA staff and board members for addressing equipment issues and training methods and for establishing safety procedures.

2. An incident that requires reporting includes any event that requires medical attention or raises a safety concern, but other incidents that should be reported include noteworthy malfunctions, unsafe procedures, unusual or ethically unacceptable skydives, or other extraordinary occurrences concerning skydiving operations.

3. Incident reports are warranted for the following (but NOT limited to):
   a. Fatalities
   b. Injuries requiring medical attention (anything more than local first aid)
   c. Any injuries of a student (including tandem students)
   d. Reserve deployments (intentional or unintentional)
   e. AAD activations
   f. Off-field landing or obstacle landings (buildings and other objects, water, power lines, trees)
   g. Emergency exits from an aircraft
   h. Freefall or canopy collisions
   i. Premature deployments in aircraft or freefall
   j. Harness or canopy damaged during jump
   k. The unplanned dropping of equipment during jump
   l. Anything filed on an insurance claim

B. INVESTIGATION AND REPORTING OF INCIDENTS

1. Fatalities and other significant incidents are an unfortunate part of skydiving that must be addressed. Skydivers learn essential lessons from the mistakes of others. USPA members should take it upon themselves to fill out an incident report when it meets any of the conditions in A.3 of this section, but when appropriate the S&TA can act as an impartial investigator for any incident.

To create an accurate account, USPA needs everyone to gather information about incidents and report them to USPA. When an event requires several reports, including witness accounts and/or the personal observations of the investigator, the efforts should be coordinated through the local S&TA.

USPA keeps reports confidential by following the procedures included in this section. The integrity and effectiveness of the reporting system rely on each USPA official following USPA's procedures precisely as outlined.

C. SUBMISSION AND DISPOSAL OF INCIDENT REPORTS

1. To maintain the confidentiality of the report and to protect the integrity of the USPA incident reporting system, USPA observes the following operating procedures. Everyone should carefully follow the procedures outlined.

   a. The reporting party should use the online submission process but when unavailable print or type a detailed report of each significant incident and send the original report to USPA Headquarters.
   b. USPA Headquarters stores any information to identify trends for USPA and the skydiving industry.
   c. Names and locations are not stored in the electronic database.
   d. The submitted reports are destroyed once the accident information is entered into the electronic database.
   e. Submitting the information using the online incident report form found at uspa.org will help ensure accuracy and keep the data secure.
   f. USPA Headquarters may publish a brief synopsis of the report in Parachutist, excluding the date, specific location and names of anyone involved.

D. THE INCIDENT REPORT FORM

1. Proper use of the accident report form will help to ensure that all the necessary information is submitted to USPA.
2. Detailed information in the narrative will help USPA produce an accurate summary of the accident.
3. The types of injuries must be included in both fatal and non-fatal reports.
4. If the report is non-fatal, provide the prognosis for the jumper's recovery.
5. All of the factors that led to the accident must also be included to help determine how the accident occurred.

E. USPA POLICY REGARDING PROPRIETY AND PRIVILEGED INFORMATION

1. Background
   a. The success of USPA's safety reporting program depends upon the free exchange of information between field reporters (e.g., S&TAs) and USPA Headquarters. If reporting officials believe that the information will be used only for statistical and educational purposes and that the reports themselves will not be released to third parties, the reporting system will continue to serve the best interests of the membership. If, on the other hand, this privileged information is released to third parties for whatever reason, USPA will lose the trust of the field reporters and, with it, valuable safety-generating data.

2. Policy
   a. Documents for use only by the reporting party and USPA officials as necessary to enhance safety through education and training.
   b. All requests by third parties to access such information or documents will be referred to the USPA Executive Director, who, in consultation with the USPA President, will determine the need to refer to counsel.
   c. Failure to adhere to these procedures will subject the violating USPA member to disciplinary action per Section 1-6 of the USPA Governance Manual.

Section 6

ADVANCED PROGRESSION

ADVANCED PROGRESSION | 6

SECTION SUMMARY:

Completing the basic instruction and earning a license presents many new opportunities for advanced progression in skydiving. Advancement in one or more of the areas discussed in this section will help to improve your skills and increase your enjoyment and satisfaction from the sport.

Information in this section provides guidance for night jumping, water landings, canopy formation, high altitude jumps, flying a camera, jumping wingsuits and advanced canopy flight.

These guidelines will also assist you in meeting your skill and knowledge requirements for the USPA B, C, and D licenses and USPA ratings.

IMPORTANT REFERENCE NUMBERS

- group freefall—6-1
- freeflying, freestyle, and skysurfing—6-2
- rate of descent and time table—6-3
- night jumps—6-4
- water landings—6-5
- canopy formation—6-6
- high altitude jumps and oxygen use—6-7
- camera flying—6-8
- wing suits—6-9
- canopy flight fundamentals—6-10
- advanced canopy flight topics—6-11

WHO NEEDS THIS SECTION?

- jumpers planning to engage in new types of skydiving activities
- jumpers planning extraordinary skydives
- jumpers working on advanced USPA licenses and ratings
- USPA Instructors conducting night and water jump briefings
- USPA officials advising jumpers on extraordinary skydives

6-1: GROUP FREEFALL (RELATIVE WORK)

A. WHAT IS RELATIVE WORK?

1. Group skydiving, traditionally called "relative work," may be described as the intentional maneuvering of two or more skydivers in proximity to one another in freefall.
2. The concept of group skydiving is the smooth flow and grace of two or more jumpers in aerial harmony.
   a. Mid-air collisions and funneled formations are not only undesirable but can be dangerous.
   b. The colliding of two bodies in flight can cause severe injuries or death.
   c. The greatest danger exists when jumpers lose sight of each other and open independently, which may set the stage for a jumper in freefall to collide with an open canopy.
   d. Even after opening, there is the possible danger of canopy collisions if proper safety procedures are not followed.

B. TRAINING AND PROCEDURES

1. Before training for group freefall, each student should complete all the training and advancement criteria through Category F of the USPA Integrated Student Program, Section 4 of this manual.
2. Initial training for group freefall skills should begin as soon as the student completes Category F of the ISP—
   a. to maintain interest in skydiving
   b. to encourage relaxation in the air
   c. to develop coordination
   d. to establish participation in group activities
   e. to encourage the development of safe attitudes and procedures
3. Initial training should begin with no more than two jumpers—the trainee and a USPA instructional rating holder.
4. A recommended training outline for beginning group freefall skills is included in Categories G and H of the ISP.

C. BREAKOFF

1. The minimum breakoff altitude should be—
   a. for groups of five or fewer, at least 1,500 feet higher than the highest planned deployment altitude in the group (not counting one camera flyer)
   b. for groups of six or more, at least 2,000 feet higher than the highest planned deployment altitude in the group (not counting a signaling deployment or camera flyers)
   c. higher than these recommendations for the following:
      (1) groups with one or more jumpers of lower experience
      (2) jumpers with slower-opening or faster-flying canopies
      (3) jumpers engaging in freefall activities that involve a fall rate faster than belly to earth terminal velocity
      (4) jumps involving props, toys, or other special equipment, (signs, banners, smoke, flags, hoops, tubes, items released in freefall, etc.)
      (5) jumps taking place over an unfamiliar landing area or in case of an off-field landing (bad spot recognized in freefall)
      (6) other special considerations
2. At the breakoff signal or upon reaching the breakoff altitude, each participant should:
   a. turn 180-degrees from the center of the formation
   b. flat track away to the planned deployment altitude (flat tracking will achieve more separation than diving)
3. Opening:
   a. The pull should be preceded by a distinct wave-off to signal jumpers who may be above.
   b. During the wave-off, one should look up, down and to the sides to ensure that the area is clear.
   c. The low person has the right-of-way, both in freefall and under canopy.

D. OTHER REFERENCES

1. See SIM Section 6-2, "Freeflying, Freestyle Skydiving, and Skysurfing Recommendations" for information about group flying in vertical orientations.
2. See SIM Section 6-4, "Night Jump Recommendations" for guidance on jumping in groups at night.

6-2: FREEFLYING, FREESTYLE AND SKYSURFING

A. THE SCOPE OF FREEFLYING

1. These recommendations provide guidance for vertical freefall body positions, generally associated with significantly higher fall rates and rapid changes in relative speed.
2. The diverse freefall speeds among jumpers engaged in different freefall activities affect separation between individuals and groups exiting on the same pass over the drop zone.
3. The term "freeflying" in this context is applied to all activities that incorporate back, standing, head-down, or sitting freefall positions, including freestyle and skysurfing.

B. QUALIFICATIONS

1. Before engaging in freeflying, the skydiver should either:
   a. hold a USPA A license
   b. receive freeflying instruction from a USPA instructional rating holder with extensive freeflying experience
2. The skydiver should have demonstrated sufficient air skills, including:
   a. consistent altitude awareness
   b. basic formation skydiving skills
   c. ability to track to achieve horizontal separation
   d. understanding of the jump run line of flight
   e. proficiency in movement up, down, forward, backward, and rotation in a backfly position before attempting sit maneuvers.
   f. proficiency in movement up, down, forward, backward, and rotation in a sit position before attempting a standing or head-down maneuvers.

C. EQUIPMENT

1. Gear must be properly secured to prevent premature deployment of either canopy.
   a. A premature opening at the speeds involved in this type of skydiving could result in severe injury to the body or stressing the equipment beyond limits set by the manufacturers.
   b. Deployment systems and operation handles should remain secure during inverted and stand-up flight; therefore, equipment for freeflying should include:
      (1) bottom-of-container mounted throw-out pilot chute pouch, pull-out pilot chute, or ripcord main deployment system
         (i) Exposed leg-strap-mounted pilot chutes present an extreme hazard.
         (ii) Any exposed pilot chute bridle presents a hazard.
         (iii) Use of a tuck-tab is recommended to provide additional security of the pilot chute during high freefall speeds encountered while freeflying.
      (2) closing loops, pin protection flaps, and riser covers well maintained and properly sized
2. Harness straps
   a. Leg straps should be connected with a seat strap to keep the leg straps from moving toward the knees while in a sitting freefall position or making transitions.
   b. Excess leg and chest straps should be tightly stowed.
3. Automatic activation devices are recommended because of the high potential for collisions and loss of altitude awareness associated with freeflying.
4. In the case of skysurfing boards, a board release system that can be activated with either hand without bending at the waist is recommended.
5. Personal accessories for freeflying should include:
   a. audible altimeter (two are recommended)
   b. visual altimeter
   c. hard helmet
   d. clothing or jumpsuit that will remain in place during inverted and stand-up freefall and will not obscure or obstruct deployment or emergency handles or altimeters

D. TRAINING

1. Freeflying has many things in common with face-to-earth formation skydiving.
   a. A beginner will progress much faster and more safely with a coach.
   b. Novices should not jump with each other until—
      (1) receiving basic training in freeflying.
      (2) demonstrating ability to control movement up, down, forward and backward in a sitting position.
2. Prior to jumping with larger groups, progress should follow the same model as for the freefall and canopy formation disciplines: 2-way formations of novice and coach to develop exit, body position, docking, transition, and breakoff skills.

E. HAZARDS ASSOCIATED WITH GROUP FREEFLYING

1. Inadvertently transitioning from a fast-falling body position to a face-to-earth position ("corking") results in rapid deceleration from typically 175 mph to 120 mph.
   a. Freeflying in a group requires the ability to:
      (1) remain in a fast-flying position at all times
      (2) remain clear of the airspace above other freeflyers
   b. Assuming a fast-falling position when the other skydivers are in a slow-falling position puts the freeflyer below the formation, creating a hazard at break-off.
2. Freeflying offers more potential for loss of altitude awareness than traditional skydiving for several reasons.
   a. Higher speeds mean shorter freefalls.
      (1) Face-to-earth freefall time from 13,000 feet to routine deployment altitudes takes about 60-65 seconds.
      (2) Typical freefly times from 13,000 feet may be as short as 40 seconds.
   b. Head-down and sit-fly positions present a different visual picture of the earth; freeflyers may not be visually aware of their altitude.
   c. Visual altimeters can be difficult to read in some body positions.
   d. Audible altimeters can be hard to hear in the higher wind noise associated with freefly speeds.
   e. As with other skydiving disciplines, participants must guard against focusing on an unimportant goal and losing track of the more

6-2 FREEFLYING, FREESTYLE AND SKYSURFING

important aspects of the skydive: time and altitude.

3. Horizontal drift
   a. Novice freeflyers sometimes drift laterally in freefall.
      (1) An experienced coach can correct the problem.
      (2) On solo jumps, freeflyers should practice movement perpendicular to the line of flight (90 degrees to jump run heading).
      (3) Separation from other groups can be enhanced by tracking perpendicular to the line of flight at a routine breakoff altitude.
   b. Experienced freeflyers must also be aware of lateral movement when coaching novices or performing dives involving horizontal movement.
   c. All skydivers on loads mixing freeflyers and traditional formation skydiving must consider the overall effect of the wind on their drift during freefall.
   d. As a general rule, faster-falling groups should leave after slower-falling groups particularly when jump run is flown against a strong headwind.
4. Faster-falling groups should delay canopy flight downwind and remain in position to allow jumpers who exited before them, but who fell slower, to deploy and then turn downwind also.
5. Loss of visual contact with other skydivers:
   a. The rapid changes in vertical separation that can occur in freefly positions makes it easy to lose contact with others on the dive.
   b. Even jumpers with extensive experience in formation skydiving may have trouble locating everyone on a freefly dive.
   c. Breakoff can be more confusing than usual.
   d. Important considerations in planning a freefly dive are:
      (1) Keep the size of the groups small until proficient.
      (2) Plan higher breakoffs than usual.
      (3) Transition from fast-fall rate to normal tracking for separation gradually in case of a skydiver above the formation in a high-speed descent.
      (4) Avoid maneuvers near breakoff that increase vertical separation.
      (5) It is as important to slow down after breakoff as it is to get separation from other jumpers.

6-3: FREEFALL RATE OF DESCENT AND TIME TABLE

A. A LOGGING AID

1. The following table will assist in estimating the approximate amount of freefall time to be expected from a given altitude and in logging the correct amount of freefall time for a given jump.
2. Each skydiver should log every jump made, including the amount of freefall time experienced.
3. The amount of freefall time logged for each jump should be actual time.

B. COMPUTATION

1. Many factors affect the rate of fall or terminal velocity in freefall.
   a. total weight of the jumper including equipment
   b. the surface area-to-weight ratio
   c. jumpsuit
   d. altitude above sea level (air density)
   e. skydiving discipline, e.g., vertical orientations
2. The chart lists freefall times based on three different typical terminal velocities and provides an exit altitude reference for 3,000-foot openings.
   a. 120 mph (176 feet per second) for belly-to earth orientation
   b. 160 mph (235 feet per second) for vertical head-down or standing orientation
   c. 50 mph (73.3 feet per second) for wing-suit jumps
3. To determine the approximate amount of freefall time to expect on a jump and to log a realistic amount of freefall time for a jump, use the following procedures:
   a. Determine your approximate terminal velocity by taking actual measurements of jumps with known exit and opening altitudes (this can be done by timing video tapes, by having someone on the ground time the skydive, or using a recording altimeter).
   b. Subtract your opening altitude from your exit altitude to determine the length of your freefall.
   c. Use the chart to estimate your freefall time according to your approximate terminal velocity and the distance in freefall.

FREEFALL TIME TABLE

Exit Altitude (feet) with opening at 3,000'	Length of freefall (feet)	Time of Freefall (with given terminal velocity)		
		120 mph (horizontal)	160 mph (vertical)	50 mph (wingsuit)
3,500	500	6	5	10
4,000	1,000	9	7	17
4,500	1,500	12	9	24
5,000	2,000	15	12	31
5,500	2,500	18	14	37
6,000	3,000	21	16	44
6,500	3,500	24	18	51
7,000	4,000	26	21	58
7,500	4,500	29	23	65
8,000	5,000	32	25	71
8,500	5,500	35	27	78
9,000	6,000	38	29	85
9,500	6,500	41	31	92
10,000	7,000	43	33	99
10,500	7,500	46	35	105
11,000	8,000	49	38	112
11,500	8,500	52	40	119
12,000	9,000	55	42	126
12,500	9,500	58	44	133
13,000	10,000	60	46	140
13,500	10,500	63	48	146
14,000	11,000	66	50	153
14,500	11,500	69	52	160
15,000	12,000	72	55	167
15,500	12,500	74	57	174

6-4: NIGHT JUMPS

A. WHY JUMP AT NIGHT?

1. Night jumps can be challenging, educational, and fun, but they require greater care on the part of the jumper, pilot, spotter, and ground crew.
2. As with all phases of skydiving, night jumping can be made safer through special training, suitable equipment, pre-planning, and good judgment.
3. Every skydiver, regardless of experience, should participate in night-jump training to learn or review:
   a. techniques of avoiding disorientation
   b. use of identification light, lighted instruments, and flashlight
   c. target lighting
   d. ground-to-air communications
   e. reserve activation
4. To maintain safety and comply with FAA Regulations, any jumps between official sunset and official sunrise are considered as night jumps.
5. Night jumps to meet license requirements and to establish world records must take place between one hour after official sunset and one hour before official sunrise.

B. QUALIFICATIONS

1. Skydivers participating in night jumping should meet all the requirements for a USPA B or higher license.
2. Participants should complete a comprehensive briefing and drill immediately prior to the intended night jump.
   a. The training should be conducted by a USPA S&TA, Examiner, or Instructor, who has completed two-night jumps
   b. The training (including the date and location) should be documented in the jumper's logbook and signed by the USPA S&TA, Examiner, or Instructor.

C. CHALLENGES

1. Night jumps provide the challenge of a new and unusual situation that must be approached with caution because of:
   a. the opportunity for disorientation
   b. the new appearance of the earth's surface and the lack of familiar reference points
   c. Vision and depth perception are greatly impaired by darkness.
   d. Be thoroughly familiar with the effects of hypoxia (oxygen deprivation) on night vision (from the FAA Aeronautical Information Manual (AIM) online at faa.gov:
      (1) One of the first effects of hypoxia, evident as low as 5,000 feet, is loss of night vision.
      (2) It takes approximately 30 minutes to recover from the effects of hypoxia.
      (3) Smokers suffer the effects of hypoxia sooner than non-smokers.
      (4) Carbon monoxide from exhaust fumes, deficiency of Vitamin A in the diet, and prolonged exposure to bright sunlight all degrade night vision.
   e. Night vision requires 30 minutes to fully adjust.
2. A jumper's own shadow cast by the moon can resemble another jumper below and cause confusion.
3. Skydivers infrequently make night jumps, and are less familiar with and less proficient in handling themselves under the conditions of this new environment.
4. Since the skydiver cannot perceive what is taking place as rapidly and easily as in daylight, it takes more time to react to each situation.

D. SPECIAL EQUIPMENT

1. A light visible for at least three statute miles displayed from opening until the jumper is on the ground (an FAA requirement for protection from aircraft)
2. Lighted altimeter
3. Clear goggles
4. Jumper manifest
5. Flashlight to check canopy
6. Whistle
   a. to warn other jumpers under canopy
   b. for after landing to signal other jumpers
   c. to aid rescuers in locating a lost or injured jumper
7. Sufficient lighting to illuminate the target
   a. Lighting can be provided by flashlights, electric lights, or such devices.
   b. Road flares or other pyrotechnics and open flames can be extremely hazardous and should not be used.
   c. Automobiles can be used for lighting, but they clutter the landing area.
8. Cycle the automatic activation device to ensure it is within the time-frame operational limits for the night jump.

E. PROCEDURES

1. General
   a. Night jumps should be conducted in light winds.
   b. visibility
      (1) Night jumps should be made only in clear atmospheric conditions with minimum clouds.
      (2) Moonlight greatly increases visibility and night-jump safety.
   c. advice and notification
      (1) Consult the local S&TA or a USPA Examiner for advice for conducting night jumps (required by the BSRs).
      (2) Notify FAA, state, and local officials as required.
   d. Use a topographical map or photo with FAA Flight Service weather information for appropriate altitude and surface winds to compute jump run compass heading and exit and opening point.
   e. One senior member should be designated jumpmaster for each pass and be responsible for accounting for all members of that pass once everyone has landed.
   f. Each jumper performing a night jump who is not familiar with the drop zone should make at least one jump during daylight hours on the same day, to become familiar with the drop zone and surrounding areas during daylight conditions.
2. Target configuration for accuracy:
   a. Arrange lights in a circle around the target area at a radius of 82 feet from the center.
   b. Remove three or four of the lights closest to the wind line on the downwind side of the target and arrange them in a line leading into the target area.

(1) This will indicate both wind line and wind direction.

(2) By following a flight path over this line of lights, the jumper will be on the wind line and land upwind.

c. Place a red light at dead center, protected by a plexiglass cover flush with the surface.

3. Emergency: Extinguish all lights in the event of adverse weather or other hazardous jump conditions to indicate "no jump."

4. Ground-to-air radio communications should be available.

5. Night Spotting:

   a. Current wind information for both surface and aloft conditions is critical at night.

   b. Spotters should familiarize themselves with the drop zone and surrounding area in flight during daylight, noting ground points that will display lights at night and their relationship to the drop zone and any hazardous areas.

   c. The spotter should plan to use both visual spotting and aircraft instruments to assure accurate positioning of the aircraft.

   d. During the climb to altitude, familiarize each jumper with the night landmarks surrounding the drop zone.

F. GENERAL

1. A jumper making a first night jump should exit solo (no group skydiving).

2. Strobe lights are not recommended for use in freefall, because they can interfere with night vision and cause disorientation.

   a. Constant lights are preferable.

   b. Flashing lights can be used once the jumper has opened and is in full control under canopy.

3. Warning on pyrotechnics:

   a. Road flares and other pyrotechnics exude hot melted chemicals while burning and are hazardous when used by skydivers in freefall.

   b. In addition, the bright glare greatly increases the possibility of disorientation.

G. GROUP JUMPS: FREEFALL AND CANOPY

1. Freefall

   a. It is recommended that night relative work be planned for a full moon.

   b. Skydivers should wear white or light-colored jumpsuits.

   c. A safe progression from a 2-way to larger formations should be made on subsequent night jumps.

   d. Staggering the deployment altitudes can reduce the risk of a canopy collision

      (1) During deployment, in the event there is a lack of horizontal separation

      (2) During the canopy descent and landing pattern, when all canopies are converging above the landing area

      (3) The deployments should be staggered in order, with the lowest wing-loaded jumper deploying at the highest altitude, continuing in order until the highest wing-loaded jumper is deploying at the lowest altitude

2. Under canopy:

   a. With others in the air, jumpers should fly predictably and avoid spirals.

   b. All jumpers on each pass should agree to the same downwind, base, and final approach and the altitudes for turns to each leg of the landing pattern.

3. Jumpers planning canopy formations should practice together during daylight and rehearse prior to boarding for each night jump.

   a. It is recommended that night canopy formation activity be performed during a full moon.

   b. Brightly colored clothing should be worn by all jumpers.

   c. Lighting

      (1) Constant beam lights are preferred.

      (2) Strobes can interfere with night vision and depth perception.

6-5: WATER LANDINGS

A. WHY JUMP IN THE WATER?

1. A number of fatalities have resulted from accidental water landings, usually because of the absence of flotation gear, use of incorrect procedures, and landing in extremely cold water.
2. Water landing training is recommended to improve chances for survival from both intentional and unintentional water landings.
3. The purpose of wet training (required for the USPA B license) is to expose the individual to a worst-case scenario in a controlled situation.
   a. Drownings are usually brought on by panic.
   b. Proper training should decrease the likelihood of panic and therefore decrease the likelihood of a drowning.
4. The potential always exists for unintentional water entry due to spotting error, radical wind changes, malfunctions, and landing under a reserve rather than a main.
5. Intentional water jumps are preplanned jumps into a body of water.
   a. With a few additional precautions, a water jump can be the easiest and safest of all skydives.
   b. Physical injuries and drownings are almost unknown on preplanned, intentional water landings.
6. These recommendations provide the USPA S&TA, Examiner, and Instructor with guidelines to train skydivers to effectively deal with water landings.
7. This section covers recommendations, procedures, and references for the following:
   a. training considerations for unintentional water landings
   b. wet training for water landings, both unintentional and intentional
   c. intentional water jumps

B. TRAINING FOR UNINTENTIONAL WATER LANDINGS

1. In the USPA Integrated Student Program, training recommendations for unintentional water landings are included in the obstacle landing training of Category A (the first-jump course).
2. A more complete and detailed briefing outline is contained in SIM Section 5-1.F.

DRY (THEORETICAL TRAINING)

1. This training (including the date and location) should be documented in the student's logbook and A-license application or on a separate statement and signed by a USPA S&TA, Examiner, or Instructor.
2. Theoretical training should include classroom lessons covering:
   a. techniques for avoiding water hazards
   b. how to compensate for poor depth perception over water
   c. preparation for water entry
   d. additional risks of water landings in cold water temperatures
   e. recovery after landing
3. Practice should combine both ground and training harness drills and should continue until the jumper is able to perform the procedures in a reasonable amount of time.

WET (PRACTICAL TRAINING)

1. Wet training
   a. should be conducted following a class on theory
   b. should take place in a suitable environment such as a swimming pool, lake, or other body of water at least six feet deep
   c. meets the USPA B license training requirements for intentional water landings
2. This training (including the date and location) should be documented in the jumper's logbook and signed by a USPA S&TA, Examiner, or Instructor.
3. Safety personnel should include properly trained and certified lifeguards.
   a. If suitably qualified skydivers are not available, assistance may normally be solicited from the local American Red Cross or other recognized training organization.
   b. Flotation gear and other lifesaving apparatus is recommended for non-swimmers.
   c. Persons conducting this training need to consider the safety of the participants.
4. Review all theoretical and practical training.
5. Initial training may be conducted in swimsuits, but final training is to be conducted in normal jump clothing to simulate a water landing.
   a. Non-swimmer: Training is to include basic skills covering breath control, bobbing, and front and back floating.
   b. Swimmer: Training is to include all of the above, plus the breast stroke, side stroke, back stroke, and treading water.
6. While wearing a parachute harness and container system and all associated equipment, jump into the water.
   a. The USPA Instructor should then cast an open canopy over the jumper before any wave action subsides.
   b. Any type of canopy may be used.
   c. The jumper should then perform the steps necessary to escape from the equipment and the water.
   d. Repeat this drill until proficient.

C. INTENTIONAL WATER LANDINGS

1. Any person intending to make an intentional water landing should:
   a. undergo preparatory training within 60 days of the water jump
      (1) The training should be conducted by a USPA S&TA, Examiner, or Instructor.
      (2) The training (including the date and location) should be documented in the jumper's logbook and signed by a USPA S&TA, Examiner or Instructor.
   b. hold a USPA A license and have undergone wet training for water landings
   c. be a swimmer
2. Theoretical training should include classroom lessons covering:
   a. preparations necessary for safe operations
   b. equipment to be used
   c. procedures for the actual jump

WATER LANDINGS 6-5

    d. recovery of jumpers and equipment

    e. care of equipment

3. Preparation

    a. Obtain advice for the water jump from the local USPA S&TA or Examiner (required by the BSRs).

    b. Check the landing site for underwater hazards.

    c. Use an altimeter for freefalls of 30 seconds or more.

    d. Provide no less than one recovery boat per jumper, or, if the aircraft drops one jumper per pass, one boat for every three jumpers.

    e. Boat personnel should include at least one qualified skydiver and stand-by swimmer with face mask, swim fins, and experience in lifesaving techniques, including resuscitation.

    f. Each jumper should be thoroughly briefed concerning the possible emergencies that may occur after water entry and the proper corrective procedures.

    g. opening altitude

        (1) Jumpers should open no less than 3,000 feet AGL to provide ample time to prepare for water entry.

        (2) This is especially true when the DZ is a small body of water and the jumper must concentrate on both accuracy and water entry.

    h. A second jump run should not be made until all jumpers from the first pass are safely aboard the pickup boat(s).

4. After canopy inflation: In calm conditions with readily accessible pick-up boats, the best procedure is simply to inflate the flotation gear and concentrate on landing in the proper area.

5. Landing

    a. In strong winds, choppy water conditions, in competitive water jump events, or if the flotation gear cannot be inflated, separation from equipment after water entry is essential.

    b. Instruments:

        (1) Water may damage some altimeters and automatic activation devices.

        (2) Skydivers jumping without standard instruments and AADs should use extra care.

D. HIGH-PERFORMANCE LANDINGS IN WATER

1. Water may reduce injuries for jumpers who slightly misjudge high-performance landings, but jumpers have been seriously injured or killed after hitting the water too hard.

2. Jumpers should obtain coaching from an experienced high-performance canopy pilot familiar with water hazard approaches and contact prior to attempting high-performance landings across water.

3. Raised banks at the approach entry and exit from the body of water present a serious hazard.

4. An injury upon landing in a water hazard can increase the jumper's risk of drowning, so high-performance landings involving water should be approached with the standard water landing precautions, including the use of a flotation device.

5. The area around the body of water should be clear of hazards and spectators in case high-speed contact with the water causes the jumper to lose control.

E. WATER JUMP SAFETY CHECKS AND BRIEFINGS

1. A complete equipment check should be performed with particular attention to any additional equipment to be used or carried for the water jump (refer to SIM Section 5-4 on equipment checks).

2. Boat and ground crew briefings:

    a. communications procedures (smoke, radio, buoys, boats)

    b. wind limitations

    c. jump order

    d. control of spectators and other boats

    e. setting up the target

    f. maintenance of master log

    g. how to approach a jumper and canopy in the water (direction, proximity)

6-6: CANOPY FORMATIONS

A. WHAT IS CANOPY RELATIVE WORK?

1. Canopy Formation (CF) is the name of the competition discipline for the skydiving activity commonly called canopy relative work (CRW) or "crew."

2. Canopy formations are built by the intentional maneuvering of two or more open parachute canopies in close proximity to or in contact with one another during flight.

3. The most basic canopy formation is the joining of two canopies vertically during flight as a stack or plane (compressed stack).

4. Canopy formations, both day and night, may be accomplished by experienced canopy formation specialists leading the dives.

B. GENERAL

1. This section recommends procedures considered by canopy formation specialists to be the safest and most predictable, as well as productive.

2. The concept of canopy relative work is that of smooth flow and grace between two or more jumpers and their canopies in flight.

3. Jumper-to jumper collisions or hard docks that result in deflated canopies or entanglements can result in serious injury or death.

C. QUALIFICATIONS AND INITIAL TRAINING

1. Before engaging in canopy formations, a jumper should have:
   a. thorough knowledge of canopy flight characteristics, to include riser maneuvers and an understanding of the relative compatibility of various canopies
   b. demonstrated accuracy capability of consistently landing within 16 feet of a target

2. For the first few jumps, begin with stacks and planes, as offset formations are less stable.

3. Initial training should be conducted with two jumpers—the beginner and a canopy formation specialist—and include lessons in basic docking, break-off procedures, and emergency procedures.

D. EQUIPMENT

1. The following items are essential for safely building canopy formations:
   a. hook knife—necessary for resolving entanglements
   b. ankle protection
      (1) Adequate socks prevent abrasion from canopy lines.
      (2) If boots are used, cover any exposed metal hooks.
   c. gloves for hand protection
   d. Self-retracting or removable pilot chute bridle systems are recommended.
   e. cross connectors
      (1) A secure foothold at the top of the risers is essential for building planes, which can develop greater tension as they grow larger.
      (2) Cross connectors should be attached between the front and rear risers only, not from side to side.
      (3) Side-to-side cross connectors can snag on the reserve container during deployment and cause a dangerous entanglement.

2. The following items are strongly recommended for safely building canopy formations:
   a. altimeter—provides altitude information for dock, abort, and entanglement decisions
   b. protective headgear—should allow adequate hearing capability for voice commands in addition to collision protection
   c. long pants and sleeves for protection from line abrasions
   d. extended or enlarged toggles that can be easily grasped
   e. cascades—recommended to be removed from the two center A lines, which should be marked in red

E. RULES OF ENGAGEMENT

1. Weather considerations:
   a. Avoid jumping in turbulent air or gusty wind conditions.
   b. Early morning and early evening jumps are recommended in areas subject to thermal turbulence and other unstable air conditions.
   c. Avoid passing near clouds, which are associated with unpredictable air conditions.
   d. Use caution in flying formations over plowed fields, paved surfaces, or other areas where thermal conditions often exist.
   e. When encountering bumpy or unexpected turbulent air, it is recommended that all efforts be made to fly the formation directly into the wind.

2. Factors that must be considered in every pre-jump briefing include:
   a. exit order
   b. time between exits
   c. length of freefall
   d. designation of base-pin
   e. canopy wing loading and trim
   f. order of entry
   g. direction of flight and techniques of rendezvous
   h. approach and breakoff traffic patterns
   i. docking procedures
   j. formation flight procedures
   k. one-word verbal commands
   l. breakoff and landing procedures
   m. emergency procedures

3. Exit and opening procedures:
   a. Spotting procedures should allow for upper-wind velocity and direction.
   b. The aircraft pilot should be advised that a canopy formation group is exiting and opening high.
   c. Exits should be made at one- to three-second intervals.
   d. Any opening delay should be adequate to assure clearance from the aircraft, jumper separation, and stable body position at opening.
   e. Each jumper must be prepared to avoid a collision at any time upon leaving the aircraft.

4. Docking procedures:
   a. base-pin
      (1) This position requires the most expertise of all; however, these skills are used in all slots.
      (2) Discuss the methods to be used to dock before boarding the aircraft.
   b. Formation flight course: It is important that the formation pilot

maintain a constant direction of flight along a predetermined course.

c. Traffic patterns: Establish an orderly flight pattern for canopies attempting to dock.

   (1) An orderly pattern will enable approaches to be made without interference and lessen the possibility of canopy collisions.

   (2) No canopies should ever pass in front of a formation; the wake turbulence created will disturb the formation's stability and could lead to a very dangerous situation.

d. Approaches:

   (1) For smoothness and safety, each person entering the formation after base-pin should enter from behind and below, never crossing from one side of the formation to the other.

   (2) Moderate angles of approach are recommended.

e. Docking:

   (1) Only the center section of a docking canopy should be grasped when the canopy closes third or later in a stack formation.

   (2) To complete the stack dock, the top jumper places both feet between both A lines of the center cell of the lower jumper and hooks one by each instep.

   (3) A center cell dock is preferred for beginners.

f. Collapses:

   (1) Improper docks are the most common cause of collapsed canopies.

   (2) Collapsed canopies should be released to allow reinflation only if it will not make the situation worse.

   (3) To prevent dropping an entangled jumper into a potential collision, make sure the area behind and below is clear.

   (4) Experienced participants may be able to reinflate a collapsed canopy by continuing to plane down the lines.

   (5) The jumper with the collapsed canopy can try using brakes or rear risers to back the canopy off and reinflate it.

   (6) The term "drop me" should be used by a jumper wishing to be released from the formation.

      (i) This command is to be obeyed immediately, unless it will drop the jumper into a worse situation.

      (ii) The jumper issuing the command should be sure to check behind for other canopies on approach before asking to be dropped.

5. Formation flight procedures:

   a. Verbal commands should be concise and direct.

   b. There should be no non-essential conversation.

   c. The pilot should fly the formation with limited control movements to minimize oscillations and facilitate docking.

   d. The formation pilot should never use deep brakes in the formation.

   e. Oscillations

      (1) Oscillations are a primary concern in canopy formations, because they can result in collapsed canopies and entanglements.

      (2) To reduce their effect and frequency, jumpers in the formation can—

         (i) when on the bottom of the formation, sit still in the harness and cross their legs

         (ii) maintain an arch

         (iii) if on the bottom, apply the appropriate control to reduce or increase tension

         (iv) manipulate a lower jumper's lines to dampen the oscillation

         (v) drop the bottom jumper before the oscillation develops into something worse

6. Diamonds and offsets

   a. Diamonds and offsets require different flying techniques from vertical formations.

   b. It is imperative to get properly trained before attempting them.

7. Breakoff and landing procedures:

   a. Approaches and docking should stop no lower than 2,500 feet AGL.

CANOPY FORMATION 6-6

   b. Formation pilots should avoid all obstacles, including suspected areas of thermal activity, such as paved surfaces, plowed fields, buildings, etc.

   c. The landing of canopy formations should be attempted by only those with a high level of CRW proficiency.

   d. Breakoff for landing should take place no lower than 2,500 feet AGL because of the danger of entanglement at breakoff time.

   e. Jumpers should not attempt to land formations in high or gusty winds, high density altitudes, or high field elevations.

   f. CRW groups landing off the airport should try to land together.

F. **EMERGENCY PROCEDURES:**

1. Entanglements are the greatest hazards when building canopy formations.

2. Jumpers should know their altitude at all times, because altitude will often dictate the course of action.

3. If a collision is imminent:

   a. The jumpers should spread one arm and both legs as wide as possible to reduce the possibility of penetrating the suspension lines, provided the suspension lines are made from larger diameter Dacron©.

   b. The other hand is used to protect the reserve ripcord.

   c. Canopies with small diameter suspension line, such as Spectra or HMA, can lead to more serious injuries during a collision than canopies using larger diameter suspension lines made from Dacron©.

      (1) Jumpers should tuck in arms, legs and head if the collision involves canopies with small diameter suspension lines.

      (2) Avoid hitting the suspension lines or other jumper, if at all possible.

4. Jumpers should be specific in discussing their intentions.

5. If altitude allows, emergency procedures should proceed only after acknowledgment by other jumper(s).

6-6 CANOPY FORMATION

6. In the event of multiple cutaways and if altitude allows, jumpers should stagger reserve openings to avoid possible canopy collisions.

7. Respond to the given situation.

    a. When entanglements occur, jumpers must be prepared to react quickly and creatively.

    b. In many cases, the emergency is one that can't be prepared for in advance; it may even be a problem no one imagined could happen.

8. If the entanglement occurs with sufficient altitude, the jumpers should attempt to clear the entanglement by following lines out before initiating emergency procedures.

9. Jumpers should try to land together following a canopy relative work emergency.

G. NIGHT CANOPY FORMATIONS

See SIM Section 6-4, "Night Jump Recommendations," for guidance.

6-7: HIGH ALTITUDE AND OXYGEN USE

A. PREPARATION AND PLANNING CRITICAL

1. Skydives from altitudes higher than 15,000 feet above mean sea level (MSL) present the participants with a new range of important considerations.
2. The reduced oxygen, lower atmospheric pressure and temperature, and the higher winds and airspeed above 15,000 feet MSL make skydiving more hazardous in this region than at lower altitudes.
3. Hypoxia, or oxygen deficiency, is the most immediate concern at higher altitudes.
   a. Hypoxia can result in impaired judgment and even unconsciousness and death.
   b. Hypoxia can be prevented by the use of supplemental oxygen and procedures not required for skydives from lower altitudes.
4. With proper training, adequate equipment, and well-planned procedures, high altitude skydives can be conducted within acceptable safety limits; without such precautions, they may result in disaster.

B. SCOPE

1. These recommendations are presented to familiarize skydivers with:
   a. altitude classifications
   b. experience recommendations
   c. training recommendations
   d. equipment recommendations
   e. procedural recommendations
2. General information is provided on the accompanying Planning Chart.

C. ALTITUDE CLASSIFICATIONS

1. Low altitude: below 15,000 feet MSL
2. Intermediate altitude: from 15,000 feet up to 20,000 feet MSL
3. High altitude: from 20,000 feet up to 40,000 feet MSL
4. Extreme altitude: above 40,000 feet MSL

D. EXPERIENCE RECOMMENDED

1. For intermediate-altitude jumps (15,000-20,000 feet MSL), participants should hold at least a USPA B license and have made 100 jumps.
2. For high-altitude jumps (20,000-40,000 feet MSL), participants should:
   a. hold a USPA C license
   b. have made at least one jump from 15,000 feet MSL or below using the same functioning bailout oxygen system
3. For extreme-altitude jumps (40,000 feet MSL and higher), participants should:
   a. hold a USPA D license
   b. have made at least two jumps from below 35,000 feet MSL using the same functioning bailout oxygen and pressure systems

E. TRAINING RECOMMENDATIONS

1. It is a benefit for participants on intermediate-altitude skydives to have completed physiological flight training (PFT) within the preceding 12 months.
2. It is essential for all participants on high- and extreme-altitude skydives to have completed PFT within the preceding 12 months.
3. PFT availability:
   a. The FAA's Civil Aerospace Medical Institute offers a one-day aviation physiology course at the Mike Monroney Aeronautical Center site in Oklahoma City, OK with a hypobaric chamber that creates high-altitude and rapid-decompression scenarios.
   b. Additional locations run by private companies are available in various locations across the U.S.
   c. To attend training, applicants for PFT must hold at least a current FAA class 3 medical certificate.
4. The PFT course:
   a. familiarizes the skydiver with the problems encountered in the high-altitude environment
   b. introduces basic high-altitude oxygen and pressure equipment and its use
   c. provides the opportunity to discover individual reactions to hypoxia and other altitude diseases through simulated high-altitude flights in a decompression chamber
5. Applications:
   a. First, view the CAMI web site at: www.faa.gov/pilots/training/airman_education/aerospace_physiology/
   b. Directions and enrollment instructions can be found at: www.faa.gov/pilots/training/airman_education/aerospace_physiology/cami_enrollment/

F. RECOMMENDED EQUIPMENT

1. General:
   a. A sensitive altimeter and adequate protective clothing are recommended for skydives from above 15,000 feet MSL in addition to the oxygen and body pressurization equipment listed below.
   b. In the event of a malfunction in the primary systems and components, backup oxygen systems and components should be available on board the aircraft.
2. Intermediate-altitude jumps: A separate oxygen mask should be provided for each skydiver and aircrew member, although a common central oxygen bottle and regulator system may be used.
3. High-altitude jumps:
   a. All skydivers must be equipped with an appropriate on-board oxygen source and compatible bailout oxygen system, preferably with a backup bottle (see Planning Chart following this section).
   b. An automatic activation device (AAD) is recommended.
4. Extreme-altitude jumps:
   a. All skydivers must be equipped with compatible on-board and bailout oxygen and body pressurization systems appropriate to the goal altitude (see Planning Chart following this section).
   b. An AAD is recommended.

G. RECOMMENDED PREPARATIONS

1. General:
   a. All jumps must be coordinated in advance with the appropriate local, state, and federal aviation authorities.
   b. All jumps should be coordinated in advance with USPA for safety and for establishing new national and international skydiving records under the FAI Sporting Code.
2. Oxygen monitor:
   a. For group jumps from above 15,000 feet MSL, it is helpful to appoint an

6-7 HIGH ALTITUDE AND OXYGEN USE

oxygen monitor whose duties are to:

   (1) inspect, operate, and monitor the oxygen systems during their use

   (2) watch for symptoms of hypoxia and other altitude diseases in all jumpers

   (3) initiate appropriate remedial measures in the event of oxygen equipment malfunction or jumper illness

   (4) see that oxygen equipment is properly stowed before exit

   b. There should be one oxygen monitor for each six persons or each oxygen bottle, whichever is fewer.

3. Communications in the aircraft are extremely limited by the wearing of oxygen masks.

   a. The spotter and oxygen monitor should establish with the jumpers and aircrew a standard set of hand signals for the commands, inquiries, and responses required during flight.

   b. A small blackboard or similar device may be helpful for communicating lengthier messages.

4. Warning: Oxygen explosively accelerates burning.

   a. To prevent damage to aircraft and equipment and injury to persons from oxygen-fed flash fires, the aircraft should be electrically grounded during all ground practice.

   b. No smoking should be permitted in the vicinity of the aircraft, either on the ground or aloft, while oxygen equipment is on board.

5. Ground practice

   a. Ground practice is essential because of—

      (1) restrictions on communication

      (2) the additional pre-exit activities required

      (3) restricted vision (by the mask)

      (4) restricted movement

         (i) results from bulkier clothing

         (ii) is often further irritated by long periods of sitting and low cabin temperatures during the climb to jump altitude

   b. Signals and exit procedures should be practiced on the ground in the actual jump aircraft until everyone can perform the procedures—

      (1) by hand-signal command

      (2) smoothly and without discussion

   c. Practice will prevent confusion aloft that may result from inadequate rehearsal.

6. Equipment checks:

   a. Equipment should be checked prior to loading the aircraft and especially before exit.

   b. In addition, the oxygen monitor should perform the "P.D. McCRIPE" oxygen equipment inspection:

   Pressure gauge
   Diaphragm
   Mask
   Connections at mask
   Connections at disconnect
   Regulator
   Indicator
   Portable unit (walk-around bottle)
   Emergency cylinders (bailout bottles)

H. OXYGEN USE PROCEDURES

Oxygen use procedures will vary with the equipment used, but the following are basic.

1. Intermediate altitude:

   a. All participants should put on masks and begin breathing oxygen at 8,000 feet MSL.

      (1) Breathing should be continuous throughout the remainder of the climb and jump run.

      (2) This procedure should be conducted under the supervision of the oxygen monitor.

      (3) This procedure is important (even if it doesn't seem necessary), especially if more than one jump per day is planned.

   b. Two minutes from exit—

      (1) The spotter signals "get ready."

      (2) At this time, all jumpers move into the ready position and prepare to remove their oxygen masks.

   c. prior to exit—

      (1) Jumpers should stay on oxygen for as long as possible, removing their masks at the "climbout" or "exit" signal.

      (2) The spotter need do nothing further than signal or lead the exit.

   d. In the event of an aborted jump run, the oxygen masks should be redistributed and donned, a wide orbit made, and the process repeated, with all skydivers again breathing oxygen until within 30 seconds of exit.

2. High altitude:

   a. All skydivers should pre-breathe 100% oxygen under the supervision of the oxygen monitor for 30 minutes prior to takeoff when goal altitude is above 25,000 feet MSL.

   b. When goal altitude is lower than 25,000 feet MSL, all skydivers should begin breathing from their on-board oxygen source at 8,000 feet MSL, under the supervision of the oxygen monitor.

   c. Five minutes before exit, the spotter signals "get ready."

   d. Two minutes from exit—

      (1) The spotter signals two fingers and gives the command to activate bailout bottles, activates his own and, when he feels its pressure, disconnects from the aircraft oxygen system.

      (2) To prevent goggles from fogging, jumpers should leave their goggles raised until bailout bottle activation is completed.

   e. Once on the bailout bottle, the spotter goes back to spotting.

      (1) The oxygen monitor gives the spotter the "thumbs up" signal when all other jumpers have functioning bailout bottles and are disconnected from the aircraft oxygen.

      (2) The spotter then need only signal or lead the exit.

   f. In the event of malfunction of the skydiver's first bailout bottle, there is sufficient time (two minutes) to switch to the backup bottle.

      (1) In the event that no backup bottle is carried, the skydiver would be forced to remain connected to the aircraft oxygen system.

(2) After the other jumpers exit, the jumper should descend to 20,000 feet MSL or lower, then jump or land with the aircraft.

3. Extreme altitude: Standard procedures are not established, but must be developed for the specific mission and equipment.

I. SPOTTING PROCEDURES

1. Direction of the wind at altitude and on the surface may not coincide.
   a. Winds aloft may also be stronger than surface winds (the jet stream is found at high altitude).
   b. Adjust the exit point for freefall drift to allow for winds aloft.
   c. Exit point and opening point will not coincide.
2. The higher ground speeds attained by an aircraft indicating the same airspeed as usual at lower altitude radically increases the distance of forward throw that will be encountered on exit.
3. To calculate the exit point, consult FAA Flight Service for the winds aloft up to the planned exit altitude.
   a. Using an average freefall rate of 10,000 feet per minute, compute the time required to freefall through each different layer of wind direction and speed reported.
   b. Insert the time and wind speed figure into the following equation and solve for wind drift through each layer:

   Drift = Wind Velocity x Time of Exposure

   (1) The time component of wind speed and time of exposure must both be expressed in or converted to the same units, (i.e., feet per second and seconds, miles per hour and hours).
   (2) The drift distance will then be expressed in the same unit as the distance unit of the wind speed figure.
4. Use a sheet of acetate, a grease pencil, and a map or aerial photo of the DZ and surrounding area to plot the exit point.
   a. On the acetate, mark a north-south reference line.
   b. Then beginning with the topmost wind layer and proceeding to the lowest layer:

   (1) In the same scale as the map or photo, plot the computed wind drift for each by a line.
   (2) Join the beginning of the line representing the drift anticipated in the next lower layer to the end of the line from the one above.
   c. The resulting zigzag line represents the total wind drift expected during freefall, without tracking.
   d. In the opposite direction of the exit altitude wind drift (or in the direction of the jump run if it is not to coincide with the wind direction) add 2,000 feet to compensate for forward throw from the aircraft.
5. Throw wind-drift indicators at the planned opening altitude to determine the opening point, then, orient the acetate over the photo or map.
   a. Place the end of the freefall wind drift line on the opening point indicated by the wind drift indicators.
   b. The other end of the wind drift line now indicates the exit point.
6. Jump run should be oriented directly into the wind at exit altitude to prevent lateral drift if spotting is to be primarily visual.
7. Navigational aids may be used as the primary spotting reference, but the spot should always be confirmed visually prior to exit.

J. HAZARDS OF OPENINGS AT HIGHER ALTITUDES

1. As terminal velocity increases, so does the rate of change in speed from freefall to open canopy.
   a. At normal opening altitude, terminal velocity is about 160 feet per second (fps) and the rate of descent under open canopy is about 15 fps; thus, the change in velocity at opening is about 145 fps.
   b. By comparison, the figures for an opening at 40,000 feet MSL are 336 minus 40, or a 296 fps change in velocity in the same period of time.
   c. At 60,000 feet MSL the change in velocity is even more striking: 543 minus 64, or 479 fps.
2. Because of the higher terminal velocity at the higher altitudes—
   a. It is clear that an inadvertent opening can cause serious injury as result of the greater opening shock experienced.
   b. In addition, the equipment may not be able to withstand the load without damage.
3. Even if a skydiver were not injured and the equipment not damaged, he or she would still face an extended period of exposure to the extreme cold at altitude.
4. Another hazard of a canopy opening at higher altitude is hypoxia.

6-7 HIGH ALTITUDE AND OXYGEN USE

HIGHER ALTITUDE PLANNING CHART

Goal Altitude (MSL)	Classification	License Recommended	Equipment Required[1]						
			Mask	Aircraft Onboard Oxygen Source			Bailout Oxygen Source		Pressure Suit
				Regulator	Setting		Freefall Descent	Canopy Descent	
					Auto	Manual			
70,000	Extreme	USPA Class D	Pressure suit helmet-integrated breathing apparatus required.					No suitable "off the shelf" hardware available at this time.	Full pressure required.
60,000									
50,000				Emergency		Above 45M	Standard emergency "bailout bottle" assembly.		Partial pressure required.
45,000						45M			
43,000						43M			
40,000						41M			
35,000	High	USPA Class C	Positive Pressure	Pressure breathing	100% Oxygen[2]	Safety	Average duration 10-12 mins.	Standard "bailout bottle"	None required
33,000									
30,000			Diluter demand	Diluter demand	On normal oxygen	Normal oxygen			
25,000									
20,000									
15,000	Intermediate	USPA Class B with 100 jumps	Constant flow	Continuous flow	On	On	None required	None required	None required
			Use supplemental oxygen on board above 8,000 ft. MSL until exit.						
10,000	Low	None required	Supplemental oxygen on board aircraft. Use above 10,000 ft. MSL, whenever elapsed time above 8,000 ft. MSL is expected to exceed 30 minutes.						
8,000									
Sea level									

[1] Minimum equipment listed. Equipment shown for higher altitudes satisfies all requirements for lower altitudes.

[2] Oxygen systems for high-altitude flights and skydiving should be filled with aviator's oxygen, not medical oxygen. Medical oxygen has a high moisture content which can cause oxygen mask valves to ice over in high-altitude operations.

HIGHER ALTITUDE PLANNING CHART

HIGH ALTITUDE AND OXYGEN USE | 6-7

Training Recommended[3]	Average Freefall for 2,000 ft. AGL Opening (sec)	Time of Useful Consciousness Without Oxygen or Pressure (mm:ss)	Aircraft Required	Hypoxia Symptoms	Special Consideration
	Unknown	00:09	Gas Balloon		In this region, supersonic speeds may be attained during the freefall. The effects of trans-sonic and supersonic freefall on sky divers and their equipment are not known at this time. At 63,000 feet MSL, the critical pressure of your blood and body fluids is reached. Without pressurization, or in the event of a failure of pressurization at or above this altitude, your blood and body fluids will boil. In the event of an inadvertent parachute deployment at high or extreme altitude, the parachutist (if conscious) should break away from that parachute and freefall to a lower altitude, if there is insufficient oxygen for a canopy descent to 15,000 feet MSL. The opening shock and malfunction probability of a deploying parachute increases radically with altitude. A final equipment check before leaving the aircraft will help prevent premature deployment.
	190	00:20	Turbo Jet		
	178	01:00			
	160	01:30			
Physiological flight training course and at least one jump from below 15,000 feet or below using full oxygen gear in freefall.		02:30	Turboprop	• loss of: » consciousness[4] » muscular control » judgment » memory » reasoning » time sense • convulsions • repeated purposeless movements • emotional outbursts	Above 25,000 feet MSL, the skydiver is subject to decompression sickness including the bends, chokes, and cramps, resulting from the nitrogen in the bloodstream coming out of solution and forming a froth of bubbles around joints. Decompression sicknesses are avoided to a large extent by denitrogenization of the bloodstream by breathing 100% oxygen for at least one hour before reaching an altitude of 25,000 feet MSL. Air temperature above 20,000 feet MSL may be expected to be below zero, year-round. All skin should be protected from wind blast by clothing since exposed skin areas are subject to severe frostbite.
	140	05:00	Turbocharged engine		
	120		Reciprocating engine		
Physiological flight training course				• false sense of well-being • narrowing field of attention • blurring vision • overconfidence • poor memory • faulty reasoning • fatigue • drowsiness • poor judgment • headache • sluggishness • deterioration of night vision	All airspace above 18,000 feet is designated as Class A airspace. Refer to FAR Part 105 for special rules governing the conduct of skydiving operations in this area.

[3] Always rehearse oxygen, communication, and exit procedures before takeoff.

[4] AADs are recommended as a backup system on all high-altitude jumps, due to the possibility of the skydiver being rendered unconscious by oxygen system failure.

6-8: CAMERA FLYING RECOMMENDATIONS

A. INTRODUCTION

1. Skydiving provides a wealth of visual stimulation that can be readily captured through still and video photography.
2. Smaller and lighter cameras have made it easier and less expensive to take cameras on a jump.
3. Jumpers need to exercise caution with respect to camera flying:
   a. camera equipment and its interaction with the parachute system
   b. activities on the jump
   c. breakoff procedures
   d. special emergency procedures for camera flyers
4. Once a camera flyer has become completely familiar with the equipment and procedures of the discipline, he or she will be able to experiment and perform creatively.

B. BACKGROUND

1. In the early days:
   a. Early pioneer camera flyers had to solve the obvious problems presented by big, cumbersome camera equipment and parachutes.
   b. Only the most experienced jumpers and photographers would brave the activity of filming others.
2. More recently:
   a. Miniature digital still and video cameras appear to present less of a challenge, encouraging more jumpers to use cameras on their jumps.
   b. Skydivers have become less concerned about the skill of a camera flyer jumping with their group.

C. PURPOSE

1. Recommendations for flying cameras should educate potential camera flyers and those making jumps with them.
2. Jumpers should realize that flying a camera is a serious decision and that it requires additional effort and attention on each jump.

D. EQUIPMENT

1. A camera flyer should consult another experienced camera flyer and a rigger before using any new or modified piece of equipment on a camera jump:
   a. helmet
   b. parachute
   c. deployment device modification
   d. camera
   e. camera mount
   f. flash
   g. switch and mounting
   h. camera suit
   i. other
      (1) sky surfboard or skis
      (2) tubes or other freefall toys
      (3) wingsuit
2. Prior to filming other skydivers, each new or additional piece of equipment should be jumped until the camera flyer is completely familiar with it and has adjusted any procedures accordingly.
3. Camera equipment
   a. Small cameras are not necessarily safer to jump than larger ones.
   b. Regardless of location, any camera mount should be placed and rigged with respect to the deploying parachutes.
   c. All edges and potential snag areas should be covered, taped, or otherwise protected.
      (1) Necessary snag points on helmet-mounted cameras should at least face away from the deploying parachute.
      (2) A pyramid shape of the entire camera mounting system may deflect lines better than an egg shape.
      (3) Deflectors can help protect areas that can't be otherwise modified to reduce problems.
      (4) All gaps between the helmet and equipment, including mounting plates, should be taped or filled (hot glue, etc.).
      (5) Protrusions, such as camera sights, should be engineered to present the least potential for snags.
      (6) Ground testing should include dragging a suspension line over the camera assembly to reveal snag points.
   d. Sharp edges and protrusions can injure other jumpers in the event of a collision or emergency aircraft landing.
   e. Cameras mounted on a jumper's extremities need to be kept clear during deployment.
   f. Camera operation devices (switches, cables) need to be simple and secure.
   g. Each added piece of equipment needs to be analyzed for its potential interaction with the overall camera system and the parachute.
4. Helmets and camera mounts
   a. All camera platforms, whether custom or off the shelf, should be evaluated for safety and suitability to the camera flyer's purpose.
      (1) by a rigger
      (2) by an experienced camera flyer
   b. The helmet should provide full visibility for the camera flyer:
      (1) in freefall
      (2) under canopy
      (3) during emergency procedures
   c. Empty camera mounts should be covered and taped to prevent snags.
5. Helmet releases
   a. An emergency release is recommended for camera helmets in the event of an equipment entanglement.
   b. Emergency helmet releases should be easy to operate with either hand.
   c. Using a reliable helmet closure or clasp that can also be used as an emergency release promotes familiarity with the system.
6. Parachute
   a. Camera flyers should use a reliable parachute that opens slowly and on heading.
   b. The deployment system needs to be compatible with the camera suit, if used.
   c. Camera suit wings and lower connections must not interfere with the camera flyer's parachute operation handles or main bridle routing in any freefall orientation.
   d. The pilot chute and bridle length must be sufficient to overcome the additional burble created by a camera suit, if worn.
   e. If the camera flyer generally opens higher than the other jumpers, a slower descending canopy may help reduce traffic conflicts.

f. The camera flyer should weigh the advantages against the disadvantages of a reserve static line in the event of a partial malfunction.

   (1) Advantages: could assist after a low cutaway or when disoriented during cutaway procedures

   (2) Disadvantages: could deploy the reserve during instability following a cutaway, increasing the chances for the reserve entangling with the camera system, especially a poorly designed one

g. As always, proper attention to packing and maintenance, especially line stowage, helps prevent hard openings and malfunctions.

7. Recommended accessory equipment

   a. audible altimeter

   b. visual altimeter that can be seen while photographing

   c. hook knife

E. PROCEDURES

1. General

   a. Prior to jumping with a camera, a skydiver should have enough general jump experience to be able to handle any skydiving emergency or minor problem easily and without stress.

   b. A camera flyer should possess freefall flying skills well above average and applicable to the planned jump.

      (1) belly-to-earth

      (2) freeflying (upright and head-down)

      (3) canopy formation

      (4) multiple (for skysurfing, filming student training jumps, etc.)

   c. A USPA C license is recommended.

   d. The jumper should have made at least 50 recent jumps on the same parachute equipment to be used for camera flying,

   e. The camera flyer should know the experience and skills of all the jumpers in the group.

   f. Deployment:

      (1) The deployment altitude should allow time to deal with the additional equipment and its associated problems.

      (2) The camera flyer must remain aware of other jumpers during deployment.

   g. Each camera flyer should conduct a complete camera and parachute equipment check before rigging up, before boarding the plane, and again prior to exit.

   h. Camera jumps should be approached procedurally, with the same routine followed on every jump.

   i. The priorities on the jump should be the parachute equipment and procedures first, then the camera equipment and procedures.

   j. Introduce only one new variable (procedure or equipment) at a time.

   k. A camera jump requires additional planning and should never be considered just another skydive.

2. Aircraft

   a. Cameras should be worn or secured during take off and landing to prevent them from becoming a projectile in the event of sudden movement.

   b. A camera flyer needs to be aware of the additional space the camera requires:

      (1) Use caution when the door is opening to prevent getting hit by door components.

      (2) Practice climbout procedures in each aircraft to prevent injury resulting from catching the camera on the door or other part of the aircraft.

      (3) To prevent injury and damage to the aircraft, the camera flyer should coordinate with the pilot before attempting any new climbout position.

3. Exit

   a. Unless the plan calls for the camera flyer to be part of the exit, he or she should remain clear of the group, being mindful of the airspace opposite the exiting jumpers' relative wind.

   b. A collision can be more serious with a jumper wearing a camera helmet.

   c. Student jumpers can become disoriented if encountering a camera flyer unexpectedly.

   d. A tandem parachutist in command requires clear airspace to deploy a drogue.

   e. Skydivers occasionally experience inadvertent openings on exit.

4. Freefall

   a. The jumpers should prepare a freefall plan with the camera flyer, to include:

CAMERA FLYING RECOMMENDATIONS 6-8

      (1) the camera flyer's position in relation to the group

      (2) any planned camera flyer interaction with the group

   b. The jumpers and the camera flyer should follow the plan.

5. Exit and breakoff

   a. All jumpers on the load should understand the camera flyer's breakoff and deployment plan.

   b. Two or more camera flyers must coordinate the breakoff and deployment more carefully than when only one camera flyer is involved.

   c. Filming other jumpers through deployment should be planned in consideration of the opening altitudes of all the jumpers involved and with their cooperation.

   d. The camera flyer should maintain awareness of his or her position over the ground and deploy high enough to reach a safe landing area.

6. Deployment

   a. The camera flyer must exercise added caution during deployment:

      (1) to prevent malfunctions

      (2) to assure an on-heading deployment and reduce the likelihood of line twist

      (3) to avoid neck injury

   b. New camera flyers should consult with experienced camera flyers for specific techniques to prevent accidents during deployment and inflation.

   c. Malfunction, serious injury, or death could occur if the lines of a deploying parachute become snagged on camera equipment.

7. Parachute emergencies

   a. The additional equipment worn for filming can complicate emergency procedures.

   b. Each camera flyer should regularly practice all parachute emergency procedures under canopy or in a training harness while fully rigged for a camera jump.

   c. Emergency procedure practice should include removing the helmet with either hand in response to certain malfunctions.

6-8 CAMERA FLYING RECOMMENDATIONS

   d. Routine emergency procedures should be practiced during every jump.
   e. When to release the helmet:
      (1) equipment entanglements
      (2) obstacle landings (water, trees, building, power lines)
      (3) whenever a dangerous situation presents itself

F. **CONSIDERATIONS FOR FILMING STUDENTS**

1. Refer to the USPA Instructional Rating Manual for additional guidelines for flying camera for student training jumps.
   a. A skydiver should have extensive camera flying experience with experienced jumpers prior to photographing or videoing student jumps.
      (1) At least 300 group freefall skydives
      (2) At least 50 jumps flying camera with experienced jumper
   b. The USPA Instructor supervising the jump should conduct a thorough briefing with the camera flyer prior to boarding.
   c. All procedures and the camera plan should be shared among the USPA Coach or Instructor, the camera flyer, and the student making the jump.
2. The instructors' full attention is supposed to be on the student, and the student is incapable of considering the movements and needs of the camera flyer.
3. The camera flyer should avoid the area directly above or below a student or instructor(s).
   a. Students may deploy without warning.
   b. Disturbing the student's or instructors' air could compromise their performance and the safety of the jumpers.
4. Exit
   a. The camera flyer should plan an exit position that avoids contact with the student or the instructor(s).
   b. During the exit, students often give erratic exit counts, making exit timing difficult for the camera flyer.
      (1) The camera flyer may leave slightly before the student exits if the count is reliable.
      (2) The camera flyer should follow slightly after the student's exit whenever the student's exit timing is uncertain.
   c. When filming tandem jumpers, the camera flyer must remain clear of the deploying drogue
5. The camera flyer needs to maintain independent altitude awareness and never rely on the student or instructor(s).
6. Opening
   a. The camera flyer is responsible for opening separation from the student and the instructor(s).
   b. While dramatic, aggressive filming of openings compromises the safety of the student, the instructor(s), and the camera flyer.
7. When using larger aircraft, student groups typically exit farther upwind, which may require a higher opening for the camera flyer to safely return to the landing area.
8. When using a handcam to film students, the tandem instructor should review the information contained in the tandem section of the Instructional Rating Manual Tandem Section 4-5 regarding handcam training.

6-9: WINGSUIT FIRST FLIGHT COURSE (FFC) SYLLABUS

Note: As used here, "Coach" describes an experienced wingsuiter. "Student" describes a first-time wingsuit jumper required to have a minimum of 200 jumps per BSR 2-1. It is also recommended that at least 200 jumps have been completed in the past 18 months before completing a wingsuit first jump course and making a wingsuit jump. Wingsuit manufacturers offer instructional ratings for their products. All jumpers, regardless of experience in other disciplines, are recommended to seek thorough training that covers all of the elements below.

A. CLASSROOM TOPICS

1. Equipment Considerations
   a. Canopy selection
      (1) Non-elliptical, docile main canopies with consistent opening characteristics, with a wing loading of not more than 1.3, and having a bridle length of at least six feet from pin to pilot chute are strongly recommended for First Flight Course (FFC) jumps.
      (2) Students should be familiar with any canopy used on FFC jumps.
   b. Pilot Chutes and Deployment Systems
      (1) Wingsuits create a large burble above and to the back of a skydiver, and may not provide the pilot chute enough air for a clean inflation and extraction of the deployment bag from the pack tray.
      (2) Pilot chutes smaller than 24 inches are not recommended, due to wingsuiters' slower fall rates, which may result in reduced snatch force.
      (3) If wingsuiting becomes the student's primary skydiving activity, bridle length should be increased as the wingsuiter moves into larger suits that create larger burbles.
      (4) The bottom-of-container throw-out pilot chute is the only deployment system that should be used for wingsuit skydiving.
      (5) It is recommended that a pilot chute handle that is as light as possible be used on the main pilot chute.
   c. Helmets and Automatic Activation Devices
      (1) Students should wear a helmet for FFC jumps.
      (2) Use of an Automatic Activation Device is recommended for all wingsuit flights.
   d. Audible Altimeters
      (1) Use of at least one audible altimeter is recommended for all FFC flights.
      (2) The first warning alarm should be set for 6,500 feet in preparation for wave-off and deployment.
      (3) The second alarm should be set for 5,500 feet (deployment altitude).
      (4) The third alarm should be set for 4,500 feet (low altitude warning).
2. Wingsuit Selection
   a. Wingsuit Designs
      (1) Provide a general overview of the popular wingsuit models and advantages and disadvantages of different designs.
      (2) Mono-wing and tri-wing designs;
      (3) Wing sizes and shapes, and their advantages and disadvantages for flocking, aerobatics, distance and slow flight.
   b. Discuss popular cutaway and emergency systems in general.
   c. Wingsuits for Use in FFC Jumps
      (1) Wingsuit Coaches should select a wingsuit for FFC jumps that is appropriate for use by a novice wingsuiter according to manufacturer's guidelines.
      (2) Wingsuit Coaches should explain why a particular suit has been selected and should ask the students questions to confirm that they understand these concerns.
      (3) Students should be encouraged to continue to use suits appropriate for novice wingsuiters following completion of the FFC. In no event should students be encouraged in the FFC to use or purchase an expert or advanced suit.
3. Wingsuit Attachment
   a. The Coach must ensure that the student is fully capable of properly connecting the wingsuit to the parachute harness system used in a FFC, according to manufacturer guidelines.
   b. Wingsuit Coaches should demonstrate to the student the proper method of attaching the wingsuit to the container.
   c. The student must receive training for attaching each specific type of wingsuit to the container prior to making any jump with that wingsuit.
4. Wingsuit Pre-Jump Inspections
   a. For a Cable Thread System, assure the cables are threaded correctly through the tabs, all the way up, with the wing cutaway handles properly secured.
   b. For a Zipper Attachment System, look to see if the zipper is attached properly and completely. If applicable, check that the Velcro breakaway system isn't bunched or pinched
   c. Tug on the wing to make certain that it is properly attached.
      (1) Students must be capable of connecting the parachute harness system to the wingsuit and demonstrate a gear check prior to being allowed to make their first FFC jump.
      (2) The Coach is responsible for checking the wingsuit and parachute harness system prior to the first flight to ensure they are properly connected and the student is wearing the harness correctly.
5. Wingsuiting Special Concerns
   a. Restrictions on Motion
      (1) Arm movements are generally more restricted during a wingsuit skydive, although the amount of restriction is model-specific.
      (2) Some suits do allow for a full range of arm motion, although pressurized cells in the wingsuit may make full arm movement more difficult.
   b. Fall Rates
      (1) A typical belly-to-earth skydiver has a vertical (downward) descent speed of approximately 120 miles per hour and a horizontal (forward) speed of zero.
      (2) A typical wingsuit skydiver has a vertical (downward) descent speed of approximately 65 mph

6-9 WINGSUIT RECOMMENDATIONS

and horizontal (forward) speeds ranging between 40 to 90 mph.

(3) The deployment of the parachute following a wingsuit skydive results in the canopy leaving the pack tray at approximately a 45-degree angle from the flight direction.

c. Importance of Navigation

(1) Wingsuits are capable of traveling tremendous distances from standard exit altitudes when compared to traditional skydivers.

(2) This means great care must be taken when planning exit points.

(3) Winds aloft must be taken into account, as should the potential for other canopy and aircraft traffic.

(4) Wingsuit flight within 500 feet vertically or horizontally of any licensed skydiver under canopy requires prior planning and agreement between the canopy pilot and wingsuit pilot.

(5) The USPA Basic Safety Requirements prohibit wingsuit flight within 500 feet vertically or horizontally of any solo or tandem student under canopy.

d. Water Landings

(1) If the wingsuit flight occurs near a coastline or other large body of water, remain close enough to the shoreline to ensure each wingsuit flyer can make it to the designated landing area or another suitable landing area

(2) In case of a water landing, it is critical that the arm wings and leg wing and booties are released before landing in the water to allow the jumper as much freedom of movement as possible after entering the water.

6. Exits

a. Exit Order

(1) The minimum exit altitude for a first flight should be 9,000 feet AGL.

(2) Wingsuiters should be the last to exit the aircraft (i.e., after tandems).

b. Exit Position

(1) Regardless of the aircraft, Wingsuit Coaches should always choose an exit position for the student that allows the student to exit safely:

(2) The exit should allow the student to exit the aircraft in a stable manner.

(3) The student must be trained for an exit that allows for safely clearing the tail of the aircraft.

(4) The student should maintain eye contact with the Coach.

(5) The Coach must maintain proximity to the student.

(6) The Coach must maintain stability and eye contact with the student

(7) The Coach must not create a distraction or collide with the student.

c. Typical FFC Jump Exit:

(1) Coach checks the spot with student.

(2) Coach signals for an engine cut (if applicable).

(3) Student takes position at Coach's direction.

(4) Student uses an exit technique that directs his or her face toward the propeller of the aircraft.

(5) This method not only provides a clean exit for both skydivers, but also provides for a good angle for video of the student exit.

(6) Exit procedures should be practiced on the ground several times at the mock-up until the student can physically and verbally demonstrate all points of the exit clearly and with confidence.

d. Avoiding Tail Strikes

(1) Students should be informed of the danger of collision with the tail of the aircraft if they open their wings immediately upon exit.

(2) Students should demonstrate a two-second delay between exit and opening of their wings.

(3) Instruct the student to open wings after clearing the tail of the aircraft.

7. Body Position for Flight

a. Demonstrate Basic Neutral Body Position

(1) The Coach should demonstrate a basic neutral position for the suit that the student will be flying in the FFC jump.

(2) Have the student practice in both horizontal and vertical positions.

b. Demonstrate How to Accelerate.

(1) The Coach should demonstrate how to accelerate.

(2) Have the student practice this position.

c. Demonstrate How to Decelerate

(1) The Coach should demonstrate how to decelerate.

(2) Have the student practice this position.

d. Demonstrate How to Turn

(1) The Coach should demonstrate how to turn.

(2) Have the student practice these motions.

e. Flat Spins and Tumbling

(1) Poorly aligned body position and overly aggressive turns can result in flat spins or tumbling.

(2) Students should be instructed in how to best manage flat spins per manufacturer guidelines.

(3) If the student's flat spin is uncontrolled after 10 seconds, or if the flat spin occurs below 6,000 feet AGL, the student should immediately deploy.

(4) Have the student practice this process.

f. Signals

(1) Present any hand signals that the Coach intends to use during the first flight.

(2) Quiz the student on these signals after presentation and periodically throughout the remainder of the FFC.

8. Deployment Procedures

a. At 5,500 feet AGL, the student should wave off and deploy by 5,000 feet. This altitude provides ample time to deal with any emergency procedures and provides ample time to unzip/release and stow any parts of the wingsuit that may require release.

(1) Wave off by clicking the heels together three times; this is mandatory on every skydive.

(2) Collapse all wings simultaneously while

maintaining proper symmetrical body position.
- (3) Pull at correct altitude.
- (4) Collapse both arm wings and grasp the pilot chute handle.
- (5) Throw the pilot chute: the left hand makes a simultaneous symmetrical "fake throw" as the right hand throws the actual pilot chute.
- (6) Following release of the pilot chute, bring both hands forward symmetrically to the front of the harness.
- (7) Keep tail wing closed until the canopy is fully deployed.
b. Wingsuit Coaches should stress the importance of maintaining body symmetry and closed wings throughout the deployment sequence to avoid difficulties with deployment (e.g., line twists due to asymmetry or a pilot chute caught in the leg wing burble).

9. Emergency Procedures
a. Arm wings may restrict movement and prevent the jumper from grabbing risers until the wings are released
b. Leg wings also restrict movement, and the large wing surface can have an effect on which way a body moves following a cutaway if the wing is still inflated.
c. Any wingsuit, regardless of the model, should allow enough range of motion to pull the cut-away and reserve ripcord handles without having to disconnect the arm wings.
d. In the event of a main canopy malfunction, immediately pull the cutaway handle followed by the reserve ripcord. Do not waste time by disconnecting the arm wings first.
e. It may be necessary to release arm wings in order to reach as high as the risers in the event the main canopy opens with line twists and the jumper needs to reach the risers.

10. Procedures After Normal Canopy Inflation
a. Clear airspace.
b. Unzip arm wings first; remove thumb loops (if necessary); unzip leg zippers and remove booties.
c. Tuck away or snap up leg wing (the student must do this on the ground until it can be done without looking, so student can keep eyes on surrounding airspace under canopy).
d. If video of the first flight is being recorded, the videographer (or Coach, as applicable) should attempt to obtain footage of the complete deployment sequence.
e. Post-deployment Awareness
   (1) Wingsuit skydivers often share canopy airspace with tandems and jumpers still on student status (as well as other jumpers that may have deployed higher than 3,000 feet AGL).
   (2) As experienced skydivers, the FFC student should exercise care around these other canopies to avoid canopy collisions.

11. Navigation and Descent Plans
a. Navigation
   (1) Because wingsuiters can travel miles from exiting the aircraft to the point at which they deploy, navigation is a critically important skill.
   (2) Winds aloft should be determined prior to FFC jumps by consulting the pilot or winds aloft forecasts.
b. Wingsuits generally fly a standard flight pattern, which may vary with the drop zone and air traffic concerns.
   (1) In a typical "left-hand pattern," the wingsuiter exits the aircraft and immediately turns 90 degrees from the line of flight for 10 to 30 seconds. They make a second 90-degree turn back along the line of flight, with significant separation between the wingsuiter and any deploying canopies.
   (2) Wingsuit Coaches should plan the navigation for the jump using an aerial photograph of the drop zone and surrounding areas.
   (3) After outlining the desired pattern, the Coach should plan the skydive with the student.
   (4) The student should be able to plan a basic exit point, flight path, and deployment point that assures vertical and horizontal separation from other skydivers on the load.
   (5) Wingsuiters often deploy at altitudes where large canopy traffic may be found (e.g., tandems and AFF students). The planned flight path must take this into account. Emphasis should be placed on deploying at a safe distance from tandems.
   (6) If multiple groups of wingsuiters are to exit on the same load, the groups should exit and fly in opposite patterns (e.g., the first wingsuit group to exit may fly a left-hand pattern, and the second group may fly a right-hand pattern).
   (7) There should be a minimum 10-second separation between wingsuit groups.
   (8) Wingsuit Coaches should anticipate possible student out-landings and communicate a plan with the drop zone's management. Students should be encouraged to carry a cell phone with them on all wingsuit jumps.
   (9) If a student makes any gross navigation mistakes, the Coach should require another jump before signing off on the FFC.

12. Clouds and Visibility
a. A hole in the clouds suitable for typical skydivers (see SIM Section 9, Part 105), may not be sufficient for wingsuit skydivers.
b. Wingsuit skydivers must meet the requirements of (it is recommended that they exceed the requirements of) FAR 105.17.
c. Below 10,000 MSL:
   (1) Three mile flight visibility;
   (2) Not less than 500 feet below clouds;
   (3) Not less than 1,000 feet above clouds; and
   (4) Not less than 2,000 feet horizontally from clouds.
d. Above 10,000 MSL:
   (1) Five mile flight visibility;
   (2) Not less than 1,000 feet below clouds;
   (3) Not less than 1,000 feet above clouds; and
   (4) Not less than one mile horizontally from clouds.

6-9 WINGSUIT RECOMMENDATIONS

  e. Wingsuit Coaches should avoid taking students on first flights if weather conditions may present visual obstructions.
  f. In the event of inadvertently entering a cloud, students must be trained to maintain a straight-line flight path and avoid making any radical turns while in the cloud.
13. Communication with Pilots and Other Skydivers
  a. Pilot Considerations
    (1) Pilots should not be distracted during takeoff or jump run.
    (2) Wingsuit Coaches should communicate with the pilot either on the ground, or between 4,000 and 10,000 feet AGL.
    (3) Wingsuit Coaches should inform the pilot of intended flight direction, any special needs, the number of wingsuiters exiting, and of any wingsuit floating exits.
  b. Pilots
    (1) Wingsuit skydivers often exit the aircraft following tandems, and are usually the last to exit the aircraft.
    (2) Inform the pilot if wingsuiters will remain in the plane for a minute or more following the exit of the last of the "traditional" skydivers (especially when there are significant winds aloft)
    (3) Inform the pilot in advance if wingsuiters need an extended jump run requiring the pilot to power up the aircraft again prior to the wingsuiters' exit.
    (4) A solid engine cut is necessary for wingsuiters to avoid colliding with the tail during the exit, particularly in low-tail aircraft.
  c. Other Skydivers
    (1) Wingsuiters should be aware of the deployment altitudes and types of skydiving activities (e.g., tandem, FS, freeflying, etc.) that are being conducted on their loads.
    (2) Wingsuiters should be aware of any skydivers on the load intending to deploy above 6,000 feet.
14. Confirm the Student's Understanding
  a. Ask Questions
    (1) Wingsuit Coaches should ask questions throughout the FFC to make sure that the student understands the material.
    (2) At the conclusion of the FFC, the Coach should encourage the student to ask questions.
    (3) The Coach should repeat any material that appears to have been misunderstood or which requires additional explanation.
  b. Perform a walkthrough following the completion of the ground portion of the FFC, the Coach should walk the student through the complete FFC jump.
    (1) The student should be able to verbally relate the flight plan without prompting or coaching.
    (2) The Coach should confirm that the student knows any hand signals that the Coach intends to use, and that the student is aware Coach may guide student via flight pattern.
    (3) The student should be able to complete all of the activities without prompting by the Coach.

B. GEARING UP AND PRE-FLIGHT GEAR CHECKS

1. Gear Checks
  a. Three Gear Checks. Wingsuit Coaches should perform a complete gear check at least three times:
    (1) Before rigging up;
    (2) Before boarding; and
    (3) Before exit.
  b. Checking the Rig
    (1) Always check the wingsuit and rig in a logical order, such as top to bottom, back to front.
    (2) Automatic activation device switched on.
    (3) Closing loop tight for properly closed container
    (4) Pilot chute handle easily reached
    (5) Flap closing order and bridle routing correct
    (6) Slack above the curved pin
    (7) Pin fully seated
    (8) Tight closing loop, with no more than 10-percent visible fraying
    (9) Pin secured to bridle with no more than 10-percent fraying
    (10) Collapsible pilot chute cocked
    (11) Pilot chute and bridle with no more than 10-percent damage at any wear point
    (12) Main deployment handle in place
    (13) Canopy release system and RSL
    (14) Cutaway handle
    (15) Reserve ripcord handle
    (16) Leg straps threaded properly
    (17) Chest strap threaded properly through the friction adapter and excess stowed securely
  c. Checking the Wingsuit
    (1) All zippers intact
    (2) No rips, tears or excess fabric that may cover handles
    (3) Handles not pulled into or covered by wingsuit
    (4) All cables neatly secured (if applicable)
  d. Checking the Helmet
    (1) Adequate protection
    (2) Fit and adjustment
  e. Audible – settings (for example):
    (1) 6,500 feet
    (2) 5,500 feet
    (3) 4,500 feet
  f. Altimeter
    (1) Readable by student
    (2) Zeroed
  g. Goggles
    (1) Clear and clean
    (2) Tight
2. Attaching the Wingsuit to the Parachute Harness System
  a. Student Responsibility
    (1) The student is responsible for attaching the wingsuit to the harness under the supervision of the Coach.
    (2) The student should be able to attach the wingsuit with minimal guidance from the Coach.
  b. Coach Responsibility
    (1) The Coach is responsible for inspecting the attached wingsuit/harness system once it has been attached by the student.

(2) Any mis-attachments or errors should be pointed out to the student for correction by the student.

(3) Consider delaying the FFC jump to focus on gear issues if the student appears to have difficulty with this subject.

3. Putting on the Gear
   a. Student Responsibility
      (1) The student is responsible for attaching and putting on the gear.
      (2) The student should be able to put on the wingsuit and parachute harness system without input (but while under supervision) from the Coach.
   b. Coach Responsibility
      (1) The Coach is responsible for inspecting the gear once it has been put on by the student. The Coach should complete the second complete gear check at this point.
      (2) Wingsuit Coaches should pay particular attention at this point to harness attachment systems (i.e., leg straps and chest straps):
      (3) Wingsuit Coaches should instruct the student to feel his or her leg straps through the wingsuit fabric to make sure that they are on and tight.
      (4) Wingsuit Coaches should have the student shrug and the student should feel tension from the leg straps if they are on properly.
      (5) The Coach should visually affirm that the leg straps are properly tightened around both legs of the student.
      (6) Consider delaying the FFC jump to focus on gear issues if the student appears to have difficulty with this subject.
      (7) Once the gear is on, the student should be instructed not to remove any gear without informing the Coach.

C. WALK-THROUGH; BOARDING; RIDE TO ALTITUDE

1. Full Walkthrough
   a. Complete a full, geared up walk through of the skydive, from climb out to deployment.
   b. Demonstrate several hand signals that may be used by the Coach to confirm that the student understands them.
   c. The student should be able to complete the walk-through with minimal input from the Coach.

2. Confirm Weather Conditions
   a. Confirm that the Coach has an up-to-date weather forecast.
   b. Confirm surface winds and winds aloft are appropriate for wingsuiting.
   c. Confirm sufficient daylight is remaining.

3. Boarding the Aircraft
   a. Student Equipment
      (1) Monitor the student's equipment.
      (2) Encourage wingsuit and gear awareness.
   b. Coach's Equipment
      (1) if other experienced wingsuiters are present, ask for a gear check from one of them.
      (2) This demonstration highlights to the student that even experienced wingsuiters seek out gear checks.

4. Pre-exit Gear Checks
   a. Conduct a complete pre-exit equipment check with the student at 3,000 feet below exit altitude.
   b. Have the student shrug and feel the leg straps to confirm that they are properly routed.
   c. Remind the student to be aware of his movement in the aircraft during climb out.

5. Spotting
   a. Coach Responsibility
      (1) The Coach should ask the student to identify the proper spot for exit.
      (2) The Coach is responsible for confirming the spot and should not allow the first flight to occur unless the spot is appropriate.

D. WINGSUIT EXIT AND FLIGHT

1. Spotting
   a. Proper spotting techniques will help to assure an on-field landing.
   b. Flying a standard box pattern will help to avoid other skydiver traffic and will increase the likelihood of making it back to the drop zone.
   c. The student should make a visual confirmation of the landing area as well as make a note of where other jumpers are relative to the drop zone.
   d. The airspace also needs to be checked for aircraft or any other air traffic.

2. Climb Out and Exit
   a. Climb out or set up in door, breathe and prepare to exit as per Coach instruction.
   b. The Coach should observe the exit to evaluate:
      (1) the students' stability; and
      (2) that the student delayed opening their wings as instructed to avoid the horizontal stabilizer.
   c. The student should establish stability as soon as possible.

3. Practice Pulls/Touches and Circle of Awareness
   a. After establishing stability, the student should complete three wave offs and practice pulls/touches as taught in the ground portion of the FFC.
   b. The student should demonstrate awareness by responding to hand signals from the Coach and by being aware of his altitude.

6-9 WINGSUIT RECOMMENDATIONS

4. Navigation
    a. The student should fly a standard pattern with minimal input or prompting from the Coach.
    b. The Coach should note any discrepancies between the student's actual flight path as compared to his planned flight path.
5. Formation Flights
    a. Due to the significant forward speed generated by wingsuits, each wingsuit flyer should fly parallel flight paths with one another.
    b. Flying head-on toward another wingsuit flyer should never be attempted.
    c. Flying an intersecting flight at 90-degree angles should never be attempted.
    d. Reducing any significant lateral distances should be accomplished by flying towards the other wingsuiter at a gradual angle of 30 degrees or less.
6. Deployment
    a. The student will wave off at 5,500 feet AGL and deploy not lower than 5,000 feet AGL.
    b. If possible, the deployment sequence should be captured on video.

E. DEBRIEF

1. Verify that the student has landed and returned safely to the hangar.
2. Provide a post-flight debrief.
    a. Conduct a walk and talk, allowing the student to act out his or her perceptions of the jump first.
    b. Particular attention should be paid to whether the student was aware of any mistakes he made during the jump.
    c. Explain the jump from the Coach's viewpoint.
        (1) Accentuate the positive.
        (2) Discuss areas for improvement.
        (3) Review the video, if available.
    d. Provide any necessary corrective training.
    e. Conduct or overview the training for the next jump.
    f. Record the jump in the student's logbook.

6-10: CANOPY FLIGHT FUNDAMENTALS

A. INTRODUCTION AND PURPOSE

1. The same ram-air parachute technology that has led to soft openings and landings, flat glides, and small pack volume has opened the door for higher performance with increased wing loadings (the jumper's exit weight divided by the area of the parachute canopy, expressed in the U.S. in pounds per square foot).

    a. Skilled and practiced jumpers who choose to fly this equipment aggressively may achieve desirable results, given the right training and the use of good judgment.

    b. In the hands of untrained, uncurrent, unskilled, and unpracticed pilots, this equipment and these techniques pose a potential threat to the pilot and others sharing the airspace.

    c. The recommended training in USPA's Integrated Student Program given in preparation for the USPA A license is not adequate to prepare jumpers for advanced canopy flight.

    d. Routine canopy descents and landings alone do not provide the kind of skills and experience necessary to safely perform advanced maneuvers under more highly loaded canopies.

2. Jumpers, particularly those new to the sport, need to understand the potential dangers of flying this kind of equipment in the skydiving flight environment.

    a. The ram-air parachutes used in skydiving, even those considered moderately loaded, can cover a large amount of horizontal and vertical distance when handled aggressively during descent.

    b. High-performance landings are a part of a demanding and unforgiving discipline requiring careful study, practice, and planning.

    c. The reference for what equipment and techniques might be considered conservative or aggressive varies according to a jumper's experience, canopy size and canopy design.

        (1) Skydivers who jump highly loaded canopies may have different goals than others they advise.

        (2) Most successful high-performance canopy pilots have practiced extensively with larger canopies before experimenting with higher wing loadings.

        (3) It is difficult for a jumper who is accustomed to more advanced equipment and techniques to remember the challenges facing less-experienced jumpers.

B. SCOPE OF PERFORMANCE

1. "Advanced" refers to practices that combine equipment and control techniques to increase descent and landing approach speeds.

    a. A canopy designed for more performance may exhibit relatively docile characteristics with a light wing loading and when flown conservatively.

    b. A canopy designed for docile performance that is flown aggressively and jumped with a higher wing loading can exhibit high-performance characteristics.

2. The types of errors that novice canopy flyers make on docile canopies without getting hurt could have serious consequences when made on more advanced equipment.

3. Advanced equipment generally refers to canopies loaded as follows:

    a. above 230 square feet, 1.1 pounds per square foot or higher

    b. from 190 to 229 square feet, 1.0 pounds per square foot or higher

    c. from 150 to 189 square feet, .9 pounds per square foot or higher

    d. canopies smaller than 150 square feet at any wing loading

4. Canopy design can play a significant role in skewing these numbers one way or the other.

    a. Some canopies are designed for flaring with less-than-expert technique.

    b. Some canopies are designed to perform better with higher wing loadings but require skillful handling.

    c. Earlier canopy designs, particularly those using 0-3 cfm canopy fabric ("F-111"), can be more challenging to land, even with relatively light wing loadings.

5. Advanced technique generally refers to control manipulation to induce speeds greater than stabilized, hands-off, level flight (natural speed) during descent and on the final landing approach.

6. Canopy flight characteristics and control become more challenging as field elevation, temperature, and humidity increase.

7. These recommendations do not consider the specialized information and expertise required to safely fly canopies at wing loadings approaching 1.5 pounds per square foot and beyond or canopies approaching 120 square feet or smaller.

8. Each progressive step in downsizing, technique, and canopy design should be a conscious decision, rather than considered a routine part of a skydiver's progression:

    a. Jumpers downsizing to get a smaller or lighter container should also be prepared to handle the added responsibility of jumping a higher-performance canopy.

    b. Jumpers at drop zones with a high-performance canopy culture need to understand that neglecting the individual training required to pursue that discipline safely can lead to serious consequences for themselves and for others.

    c. Jumpers need to understand the design intents of the canopies they purchase to see whether those canopies match their overall expectations and goals.

    d. The decision to progress to advanced canopy skills and equipment should include others who can be affected, including jumpers in the air and landing area who could be affected by a canopy piloting error.

C. PERFORMANCE PROGRESSION

1. Jumpers will advance at different rates.

2. The "Canopy" sections (B.) in each category of the USPA Integrated Student Program outline a series of exercises valuable for exploring the flight characteristics and performance envelope of any unfamiliar canopy.

    a. The jumper should become familiar with a standard controllability check to determine a baseline for later comparison in the event of a minor malfunction (broken line,

6-10 | CANOPY FLIGHT FUNDAMENTALS

detached steering control, fabric damage, etc.).

b. A jumper should review the basics on each new canopy before proceeding with more advanced maneuvers; skipping the foundations of flight control will show up later with potentially serious consequences.

3. Before attempting any advanced landing maneuvers, each jumper should be familiar with the following under his or her current canopy at altitudes above 2,500 feet AGL:

   a. reverse toggle turns (90 degrees reversing abruptly to 180 degrees)
   b. canopy formation approaches and at least non-contact canopy formation flight
   c. back-riser turns and flaring
      (1) If, due to a control problem, a jumper has decided to land a canopy using back risers, the jumper should be familiar with the technique.
      (2) A jumper may decide after experimentation and practice that a canopy is not safe to land with back risers.
      (3) A jumper should consider this decision before contemplating advanced maneuvers or wing loadings where dropping or breaking a control line on final approach becomes more significant.
   d. front-riser control, including single and double front riser maneuvers (all performed with toggles in hand)
   e. altitude loss in a variety of diving and turning maneuvers (check the altimeter at the beginning and end of a turn)
   f. aborting a turn and recovery to flare
   g. slow-flight gliding and maneuvering (braked turns)
   h. braked approach and landing

D. DOWNSIZING PROGRESSION

1. Before moving to a smaller size, a jumper should be familiar and comfortable with the following landing maneuvers on his or her current canopy:

   a. landing flare from full, natural-speed flight
   b. flaring for landing from slow (braked) flight
   c. consistent soft, stand-up landings within 32 feet of a planned target in a variety of wind conditions, including downwind
   d. beginning to flare, turning to ten-degree bank, and returning to wings-level before landing

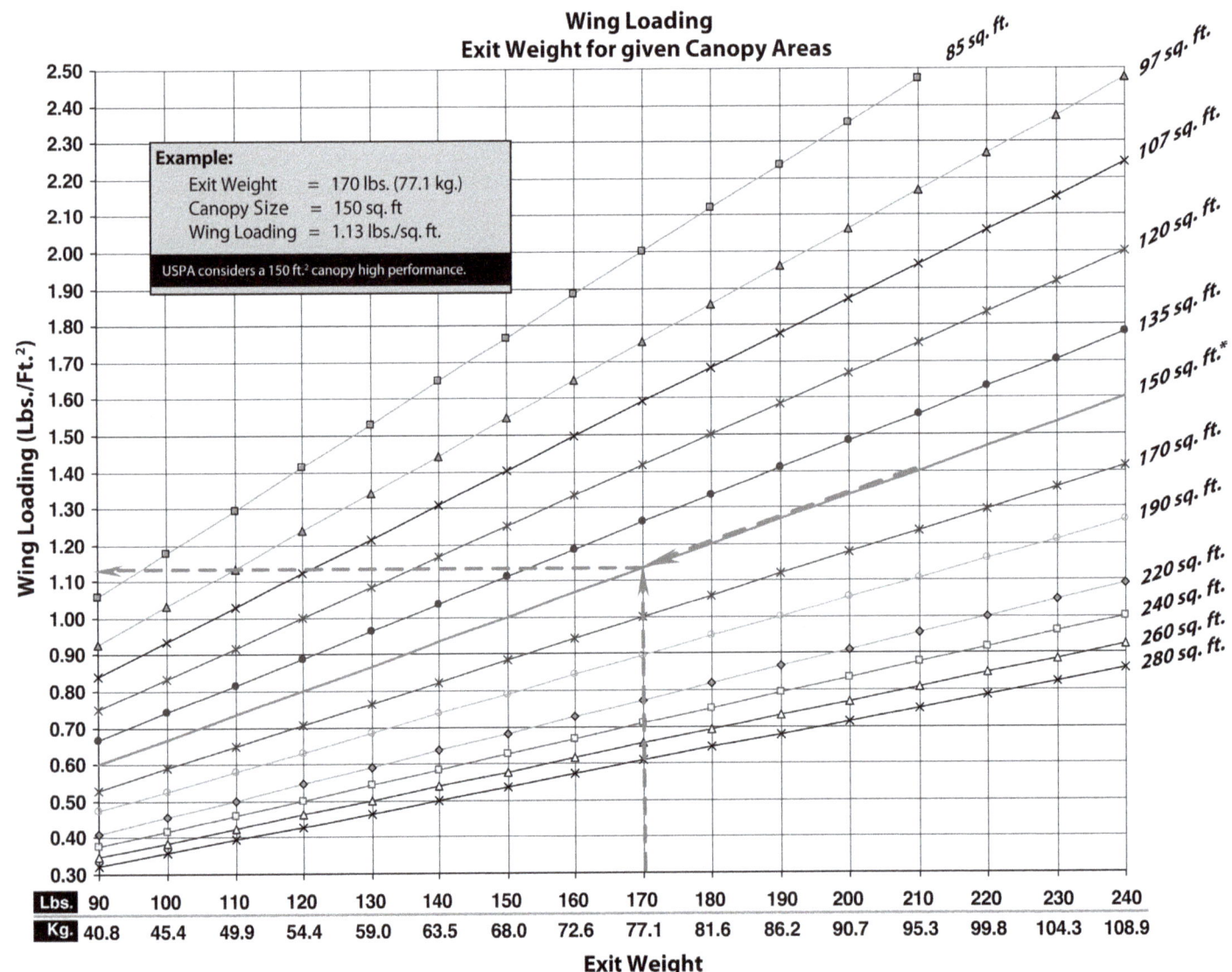

2. Downsize increments on the same canopy design
   a. above 230 square feet, 30 square feet
   b. from 229 to 150 square feet, 20 square feet
   c. from 149 to 120 square feet, 15 square feet
   d. below 120 square feet in smaller increments
3. Before downsizing, jumpers should be familiar with any maneuver they plan to attempt or might encounter on a smaller canopy, including induced-speed landing approaches and braked landing approaches (low speed).
4. A jumper who has downsized without performing advanced maneuvers at each increment should practice them on a larger canopy first before trying them on his or her current canopy.

E. DESIGN PROGRESSION

1. Jumpers should explore only one new design element until completing and becoming comfortable with all recommended maneuvers.
2. Design increments (one design characteristic at a time at the same square footage before downsizing)
   a. tapered or elliptical planform (degree of taper or ellipse varies according to design)
   b. cross-bracing or other airfoil flattening or stiffening design
   c. modifications requiring additional in-flight procedures, for example, removable pilot chutes, deployment bags, and sliders

F. PRACTICE AREA

1. To avoid danger to other jumpers, all practice of high-performance activities must take place in a landing area where other jumpers are not on approach.
   a. Separate by exit altitude.
      (1) Canopy pilots exiting and opening high must consider other high-opening jumpers (students, tandems, and others) to avoid descending into their airspace during approach.
      (2) Canopy pilots exiting on a lower pass must fly clear of the opening and canopy descent area before other jumpers exit higher.
      (3) All jumpers should be aware of other canopies in their airspace, but it is especially critical that jumpers who choose to jump a high-performance parachute be aware of all canopy traffic that may be a factor during their descent and landing.
   b. Separate by landing area.
      (1) Landing areas must be separated according to wind direction so that no jumper is over the practice approach and landing area below 1,000 feet.
      (2) Canopy pilots descending into the practice landing area must be alert for errant jumpers.
2. Advanced maneuvers, turns over 90 degrees, in a common landing area must never be attempted.
   a. It is a violation of the USPA Group Member pledge to allow high-performance landings to take place into common canopy traffic landing areas.
   b. High-performance canopy landings with turns greater than 90-degrees must be separated by space by using a separate landing area, or by time, by providing a separate pass.
   c. Whichever method is used to separate the canopy traffic, the high-performance landings must be separated from those who are flying a standard landing approach in such a way that the chances of a canopy collision are eliminated.
3. Canopy pilots should be completely familiar with all advanced landing characteristics and techniques in a variety of weather conditions and using a variety of approaches before—
   a. attempting flight into a competition-style course.
   b. landing in the vicinity of any hazard, including water.

6-11: ADVANCED CANOPY PILOTING TOPICS

OVERVIEW

A. INTRODUCTION

1. USPA recognizes that effective advanced canopy pilot training beyond the required training for the first certificate of proficiency (skydiving license) can improve jumper skills and confidence and reduce the risk of canopy flight accidents.
2. USPA encourages the development of effective canopy piloting training courses.
3. The Advanced Canopy Piloting Topics outline provides canopy piloting instructors with a list of topics in a logical presentation order to advance the canopy flight knowledge and skills of licensed jumpers.

B. BACKGROUND

1. Canopy design and flying techniques have advanced beyond what is expected of a USPA Instructor when preparing a skydiving student for the USPA A license.
2. Skydiving culture encourages skydivers to purchase and jump equipment that requires additional training to be jumped safely.
3. Analysis of accident reports indicates that jumpers are at risk without advanced canopy training beyond the A license.
    a. Jumpers who have progressed without advanced training to average designs at average wing loadings are largely unprepared for how their canopy will handle in difficult landing situations.
    b. Jumpers who pursue induced-speed landing techniques without training put themselves and other jumpers at extreme risk.
4. Rather than limit jumper flying style and equipment choice, USPA has pursued an "education, not regulation" strategy in coordination with expert canopy pilots, advanced canopy training schools, and canopy manufacturers.
    a. basic but comprehensive canopy flight training and discovery in the USPA Integrated Student Program, leading to the A license
    b. articles on basic and advanced canopy topics in *Parachutist*
    c. SIM Section 6-10, "Advanced Canopy Flight"
    d. this course outline for use preferably by USPA Instructors with additional qualifications as listed

C. SCOPE

1. To get the most from the topics presented in this outline, a jumper should have completed all the exercises listed under "Canopy" in SIM Section 4, Categories A-H of the ISP, and hold a USPA A license.
2. Jumpers who complete a course of instruction covering the topics listed here, including evaluations jumps and continued practice, should be better prepared to make choices regarding advanced equipment and maneuvers, as discussed in SIM Section 6-10.
3. USPA encourages all jumpers to engage in a course of instruction with a qualified course director including these topics, particularly when preparing to jump advanced equipment or perform advanced maneuvers.
4. The course conductor should organize the course to accommodate attendees according to their goals and objectives.
    a. sufficient staff to assign to subgroups, according to performance or equipment objectives
    b. separate courses on different dates and tailored for jumpers with like goals

D. INSTRUCTOR QUALIFICATIONS

1. USPA does not issue instructional ratings specifically for canopy coaching.
2. It is essential that the information contained in this course be presented correctly.
3. Those who intend to teach an advanced canopy piloting course should hold a USPA Instructor rating and have extensive knowledge of canopy flight.
    a. Instructors who intend to teach this material must realistically assess their level of knowledge regarding canopy flight and instruction.
    b. Before teaching this course, instructors must work through the outlined canopy skills using a variety of canopy designs and wing loadings.
    c. Attending any one of several commercially available factory-sponsored canopy schools as a student is highly recommended before teaching this course.
    d. For USPA B-license requirements, a S&TA must approve the course director and sign the Canopy Piloting Proficiency Card once the course is completed.

E. USPA B LICENSE REQUIREMENTS

1. Every USPA B license must also include a completed and signed copy of the Canopy Piloting Proficiency Card.
2. The completed Canopy Piloting Proficiency Card must be signed by a current USPA S&TA, Examiner, or USPA Board member.
    a. The supervising official must ensure that a qualified course director conducts the training in this section.
    b. In some situations, the best candidate to teach this material may not hold any USPA ratings, but may have extensive knowledge about canopy control and landings.
    c. These training jumps may be completed in a structured course with all five jumps completed in succession or the jumps may be completed individually.
    d. The term course director applies to the person teaching this material, but is not an actual rating issued by USPA.
    e. Each of the five training jumps listed on the USPA Canopy Piloting Proficiency card must be signed by a Verifying Official, who is responsible for supervision and training for the jump.
    f. The final signature of the supervising official on the proficiency card is to verify that the training has been satisfactorily completed by the candidate.

F. EVALUATION

1. There is no "pass" or "fail" for a course of this nature, but attendees should be better able to self-assess their canopy aptitude and proficiency based on their own experience with the control maneuvers and an accurate evaluation of each approach and landing from a course director.

2. The course director should sign and date the entries on the Canopy Piloting Proficiency Card as jumpers complete the items listed.
    a. control maneuvers
    b. loss of altitude in turns
    c. landing pattern
    d. varied approaches
    e. approach and landing accuracy objectives
    f. aborted approach
    g. carving landings
3. The Canopy Piloting Proficiency Card can assist drop zone management in assessing a jumper's canopy skills.
4. Each jumper should begin a new Canopy Piloting Proficiency Card for every new model and size canopy.

G. RISK ASSUMPTION

1. USPA warns all jumpers that skydiving comes with inherent and sometimes unforeseen hazards and risks that may or may not be preventable.
2. While the goal of any skydiving training is to reduce risk, neither USPA nor the course director can predict the outcome or success of the training.
3. USPA warns all jumpers that some of the maneuvers described to develop understanding of canopy flight involve a greater risk of injury, even serious injury or death, than a routine parachute landing using a straight-in approach flown at the canopy's natural speed until flaring.
4. A canopy pilot should receive as much coaching as possible to reduce the risks under canopy; however, USPA warns all jumpers that any pilot who manipulates the canopy controls to induce additional speed prior to landings presents a greater hazard to himself or herself and others.
5. Before jumping begins, USPA advises the course director to require each participant to complete an assumption-of-risk agreement in conjunction with a comprehensive liability risk-management program applied in accordance with applicable local and state laws.
6. USPA accepts no liability for the use of this outline and does not authorize its use in any course of instruction; ideas presented here come with no implied or expressed suitability for any purpose or application.

GROUND SCHOOL TOPICS

PART 1: EQUIPMENT

A. EQUIPMENT CHOICE CONSIDERATIONS

1. Because of certain advantages smaller canopies offer, a misconception pervades the sport that all jumpers are better off overall using a smaller canopy.
    a. Smaller canopies make for more compact and comfortable parachute systems.
    b. Smaller canopies, especially the newer designs, can be easier to land than larger wings in ideal conditions.
    c. Properly flown, smaller canopies provide greater versatility in higher winds.
2. Studies of USPA serious injury and fatality summaries reveal a trend where jumpers under canopies popularly considered "average sized" or "conservatively loaded" frequently mishandle them in non-routine landing situations.
3. Jumpers should seek out reliable information before changing to smaller canopies.
4. The sport of skydiving includes a series of specialized activities that require exclusive equipment, for example:
    a. classic accuracy
    b. canopy formation
    c. competition freefall formation skydiving
    d. large freefall formations
    e. wingsuits
    f. camera flying
    g. high-performance landings
    h. competition swooping
5. All jumpers should
    a. set goals in the sport
    b. choose the best equipment to meet their needs
    c. learn how to use that equipment
    d. skydive within the limits of their equipment and capabilities

B. WING LOADING

1. Size v. wing loading
    a. The shorter lines of a smaller canopy will cause it to respond differently than a larger one of the same design with an equal wing loading.

ADVANCED CANOPY PILOTING TOPICS 6-11

   b. Compared to a canopy with longer lines, a shorter-lined canopy will have—
      (1) quicker turns
      (2) quicker flare response
      (3) quicker pendulum action (quicker to dive after an early flare)
   c. A canopy with a shorter chord (front-to-back measurement) responds more quickly to flare input.
   d. A canopy with a shorter span (wingtip-to-wingtip measurement) will respond more quickly to turn input.
2. In theory, glide angle doesn't change with wing loading.
3. Most jumpers can get a lot more performance from their canopies without needing to downsize.

C. PERFORMANCE ENHANCING DESIGNS

1. Tapered shape (planform)
   a. more dimensional stability (less distortion)
   b. faster forward speed from lower and cleaner drag
   c. faster turns and less flight stability
2. High-aspect ratio
   a. flat glide
   b. easier flare
      (1) lighter toggle pressure
      (2) shorter toggle stroke (some models)
      (3) quicker flare response
3. Higher rib frequency to reduce billowing between ribs
   a. seven-cell v. nine-cell
   b. cross bracing
4. Thickness (after inflation)
   a. thicker: slow speed, more predictable and gentle stall
   b. thinner: faster speed, more abrupt stalls at a higher speed

D. DRAG REDUCTION

1. Zero-P fabric
2. Small-diameter lines

6–11 ADVANCED CANOPY PILOTING TOPICS

3. Collapsible pilot chute
4. Collapsible slider:
   a. cloth or metal links with covers
   b. larger v. smaller slider grommets
5. Risers
6. Outerwear
7. Removable Deployment Systems
8. Body Position

E. CONTROLS: TOGGLES AND BEYOND

1. Brakes
   a. toggle types for ease of handling
   b. steering line length to allow front riser maneuvers (toggles in hand)
2. Front risers and control enhancement discussion (loops, blocks, etc.)
3. Back risers and how they work
4. Front risers and how they work
5. Harness turns

F. ACCESSORIES

1. Jumpsuit (reinforced butt and knees)
2. Hard helmet
3. Gloves, pros and cons
4. Altimeter
   a. altimeter use under canopy
   b. digital v. analog
5. Weights

G. SPEED

1. The pilot perceives the forward speed more than the downward speed, so a faster canopy can seem a lot scarier to fly.
2. The faster the canopy goes, the more effect adding drag (by using a control) will have on the flight path.

H. GLIDE

1. Skydiving canopies: approximately 2.5:1 in natural flight
2. Changing the glide
   a. using brakes or rear risers
   b. using induced speed to temporarily add lift

PART 2: MAINTENANCE

A. ENVIRONMENT

1. Dirt degrades of the fabric, lines, and slider
2. Ultraviolet degrades nylon.
   a. sunlight
   b. fluorescent lighting (50% of the strength of sunlight)
3. Water distorts reinforcement tapes

B. COLLAPSIBLE PILOT CHUTE AND SLIDER

1. Wear results from friction as the line moves through its channel.
2. Pilot chute centerlines shrink with use.

C. SUSPENSION LINES

1. Spectra can't stretch and shrinks a lot with use.
2. Vectran is stable in both directions but abrades.
3. HMA is stable but breaks when it still looks new.
4. Dacron stretches on opening, is stable and durable, but fat.

D. BRAKE LINES

1. wear
2. shrinkage
3. the results of a broken line
   a. upon flaring
   b. landing a smaller canopy using risers

E. PACKING FOR AN ON-HEADING OPENING:

1. Even risers
2. Symmetrical bag
3. Line-stow placement and tension
4. 24 inches of unstowed line

F. EQUIPMENT INSPECTION

1. Pre-jump
2. During packing (various times throughout the course)

PART 3: BREAK-OFF, OPENING, SEPARATION, AND CANOPY TRAFFIC

A. BREAKOFF

1. Breakoff altitude should allow enough time to open clear of others and handle both routine and abnormal circumstances.
2. Tracking review
   a. conserving altitude during turning and tracking
   b. body position and flat-track technique
   c. opening when clear at the optimum altitude
3. Flying through the opening
   a. shoulders level (use this time to look again at the spot)
   b. flying the canopy through inflation
      (1) back risers
      (2) hips and legs stay even through the
   c. deployment (feet together)
4. Dealing with the standard problems becomes more difficult as canopy performance increases.
   a. Discuss the following from the perspective of higher-performance canopies:
      (1) line twist
      (2) premature brake release
      (3) locked brake(s)
      (4) slider-brake system fouling
   b. Spinning with a smaller canopy results in rapid altitude loss.
5. Cut away defensively: Look below and behind to make sure you are clear of others.

B. TRAFFIC

1. As canopies fly faster, jumpers must pay better attention to other canopy traffic on descent.
2. Altitude management
   a. use of brakes to stay aloft
   b. relative wing loading
      (1) self-assessment
      (2) knowing the wing loading of others
   c. placement in the aircraft
   d. a dive plan, such as stacked approaches, to promote vertical separation under canopy
3. Awareness of others
   a. Know or judge others' canopies, wing loading, and habits.
   b. Fly the landing pattern or land elsewhere.
   c. Fly a straight final approach avoiding S-turns.
   d. Dealing with other's errors:
      (1) In the event of a traffic issue, discuss the problem with the canopy pilots who were involved

- (2) canopy wake turbulence, (yours and others')
- (3) only need to miss by a little—no low turns necessary

4. Off-wind landings (technique)
   a. crosswind
   b. downwind
5. Landing away from the crowd
   a. less pressure; room to practice
   b. familiarity and consistency with using the same landing area every time
6. Situations that pop up:
   a. Crowded landing area: Follow someone you trust closely and let them know you're there.
   b. Cutaways disrupt the plan for a normal canopy descent and landing planned for the main canopy.
   c. Landing accidents on the ground can lead to confusion and chaos.
   d. Off-field landing
      (1) Plan and follow a sensible pattern.
      (2) Keep your eyes open.
      (3) Perform a PLF.

ADVANCED EXERCISES

A. FLIGHT PLAN

1. The course director should assist the class with an aircraft, canopy flight, and landing plan prior to each jump included in the course.
2. The plan should include an individualized progression plan for each student, according to experience and goals.
3. The plan should consider:
   a. winds
   b. DZ layout and target areas
   c. traffic management to keep clear of other jumpers not participating
   d. landing separation between canopy students
4. Landings should be videotaped for debriefing by the course director.

B. UNDER CANOPY

1. The aircraft should fly multiple passes as necessary.
2. Jumpers should arrange their exit order and opening altitudes according to wing loading.
3. Maintain vertical and horizontal separation; higher canopies should use brakes to slow descent if needed.
4. Each jumper needs to allow enough separation for the course director to video each final approach and landing individually.

JUMP 1—EVALUATION JUMP

1. The first jump in the course follows the presentation and discussion of the ground school topics.
2. The course director evaluates each student's accuracy and landing skills.
   a. Demonstration of a straight-in approach and natural-speed landing provides the course director with a baseline evaluation of flaring and landing skills.
   b. Each student should try for a target, with the first priority being a good landing from a straight-in approach, to provide the course director a starting point for accuracy improvement.
3. Each course candidate should inspect the canopy's steering lines while in full flight, with the brakes released.
   a. The steering lines on most canopies should bow slightly behind the back of the canopy and its suspension lines, while in full flight
   b. Check with the manufacturer to see what is recommended for steering line adjustments
   c. For jumpers who use front risers, the steering lines should have enough slack that the riser can be pulled with the toggle in hand and still not deflect the tail of the canopy.
   d. A parachute rigger should adjust the length of the steering lines if necessary, before the next jump.

JUMP 2—BASIC AERODYNAMICS, EFFECTIVE FLARING AND RISER TURNS

1. Lift
   a. Air passing over an airfoil creates a force called lift.
   b. Lift is always perpendicular to the velocity.
   c. The ram-air is trimmed nose down, by cutting the A lines shorter and each group behind them a little longer.
2. Drag
   a. The resistance created by air as an object moves is called drag.
   b. Drag is always parallel to the velocity.

ADVANCED CANOPY PILOTING TOPICS | 6-11

   c. The lines, pilot chute, slider, jumper's body, and even the surface of the canopy itself produce drag (parasitic drag).
3. Gravity
   a. Gravity is a constant in the equation of forces acting on the jumper and canopy.
   b. Using the force created by gravity, the airfoil deflects the air to make the canopy glide.
4. Momentum (force)
   a. Mass: Doubling the mass of a moving object gives it twice as much energy.
   b. Speed
      (1) The term "speed" refers to the magnitude of velocity.
      (2) Energy increases as the square of the speed.
         (i) Doubling the speed produces four times the energy.
         (ii) Tripling the speed produces nine times the energy.
      (3) Inertia: The term "inertia," means that an object in motion will stay in motion until resisted.
5. Flaring
   a. While turning or landing your parachute, the location of your body in relation to the canopy changes.
   b. In a turn, momentum swings your body out from under the canopy.

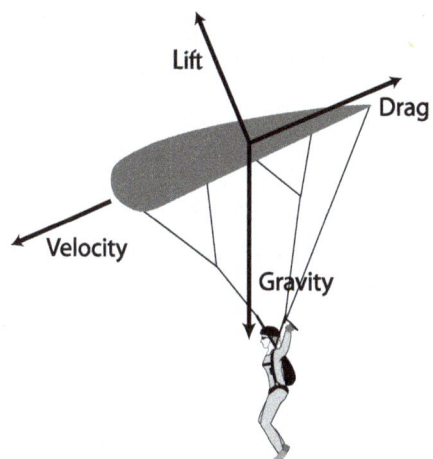

Figure 6-1. The forces acting upon a canopy in flight.

6-11 ADVANCED CANOPY PILOTING TOPICS

c. During the recovery arc, your body begins to swing back under the canopy.

d. On final approach in natural flight your body is below the center of the canopy.

e. During initial flare, using toggles or rear risers, the canopy rocks slightly behind the jumper, raising the nose in relation to the tail and temporarily increasing lift (higher angle of attack).

f. Pulling the toggles gradually further adds drag on the tail, keeping the canopy at the correct angle and providing the most lift for the remainder of the flare.

g. Effective flare techniques with emphasis on finishing the flare.

   (1) Enter the flare with the ideal stroke rate and depth that causes the canopy to fly as flat as possible, and remain flying flat as long as possible.

   (2) Follow through by gradually pulling more toggle, timing the rate of the stroke to finish landing just prior to the stall.

   (3) Focus on flying your canopy as long as possible before allowing your feet to touch the ground, and finish the flare completely even after your feet first touch the ground.

   (4) Avoid a common bad habit: Many jumpers stop flying their parachute just as their feet reach the ground, raising the toggles and running out the remaining forward speed.

6. Riser turns

   a. During this jump you will make a series of riser turns above the traffic pattern altitude.

   b. Most jumpers should have already been trained and practiced riser maneuvers as a requirement for the USPA A License.

   c. Jumpers who are completely unfamiliar with riser turns should make a separate training jump to focus solely on riser turns.

7. Under canopy

   a. Flare the canopy five times while observing the wing throughout the flare.

   b. Pay particular attention to your relative position under the canopy during the various stages of the flare.

   c. Check airspace frequently to maintain separation during the practice exercises.

   d. Repeat the five practice flares with eyes closed, paying close attention to the physical sensation during each phase of the practice flare.

   e. Check altitude, position and traffic, and initiate two alternating 90-degree turns using rear risers.

   f. Check altitude, position and traffic, and initiate two alternating 180-degree turns using rear risers.

   g. Check altitude, position and traffic, and initiate two alternating 360-degree turns using rear risers.

   h. Jumpers must stop any riser maneuver at 1,000 feet or higher above the ground.

   i. Due to the energy required for flaring and riser maneuvers, it may be necessary for jumpers to complete these maneuvers over a series of jumps

   j. On landing

      (1) Make a straight-in approach facing into the wind, with minimal input for the last ten seconds before the landing flare.

      (2) Practice an effective flaring technique, focusing on a smooth finish.

JUMP 3—STALLS

1. Dynamic stall

   a. Occurs after a dynamic pitch maneuver and is followed by the jumper swinging back under the canopy

   b. Can cause an abrupt dive once the jumper has reached the end of toggle effectiveness in a flare

   c. Sometimes occurs less noticeably at the end of the recovery arc following a diving maneuver, such as a turn

2. Aerodynamic stall

   a. Point that loss of lift occurs as the pilot gradually applies brakes or back risers

      (1) decreased glide

      (2) higher rate of descent

      (3) stable mode of flight for a ram-air parachute, because of the extremely low center of gravity

   b. Also called "sink" or "steady state stall"

   c. Used in classic accuracy with low-aspect ratio seven-cell canopies

3. Full ram-air stall (reverse flight)

   a. Radical stall reached when the tail is held below the level of the nose for an extended period

   b. Can be entered following a dynamic or steady-state stall using toggles or rear risers

   c. Requires a smooth, gentle recovery to prevent entanglement or line twist

   d. Reverse flight using toggles not recommended for some canopies

4. High-speed stall

   a. Occurs at any speed when the canopy reaches too high of an angle of attack

   b. Easily induced as a result of distorting the wing too far during a rear-riser flare

5. Common stall characteristics

   a. Separation of air from the upper surface of the wing

   b. Wing loading and stalls (helpful knowledge for landings):

      (1) Higher wing loadings stall at faster forward speeds.

      (2) Decreasing the wing loading by putting your feet on the ground allows the canopy to fly slower before it stalls.

6. Stall practice

   a. Full ram-air stalls using toggles

      (1) Gently apply brakes to a point where forward flight diminishes and the canopy begins to sink.

      (2) Continue to depress the brakes fully down until the canopy "bow ties."

      (3) Slowly raise the toggles until resuming forward flight.

      (4) High-performance canopies:

         (i) Full stalls may induce a line-twist malfunction with cross-braced or highly elliptical canopies and are not recommended.

         (ii) Cross-braced and fully elliptical parachutes may be

flown to very slow flight and a dynamic or aerodynamic stall without entering reverse flight or "bow tying" the canopy.

  b. Stalls using rear risers
     (1) Slowly pull down the rear risers until forward flight ceases.
     (2) Adding more riser input, the canopy will eventually sink and begin to descend in a backward direction.
     (3) Risers should be slowly raised to recover to forward flight.
     (4) Rear riser stalls are not as violent but occur more abruptly than toggle-induced stalls.
7. Under canopy
  a. Practice riser flares and stalls
     (1) Rear riser flare without stalling the canopy
     (2) Full ram-air stalls using rear risers
     (3) Full ram-air stalls using toggles
  b. Plan and execute an appropriate downwind, base leg and final approach landing into the wind.

JUMP 4—FLAT TURNS AND CROSS-WIND LANDINGS

1. Reasons for flying in brakes
  a. Vertical separation from canopy traffic
  b. Slow forward speed and descent rate
  c. Returning from a long spot
  d. Flat turns as a defense tool at low altitudes
2. Techniques for initiating a braked turn
  a. Bring both toggles to mid-stall position to start.
  b. Raise one toggle slightly to turn in the opposite direction.
  c. Pull one toggle down slightly to initiate a turn in the same direction.
  d. Most effective method for flat turns: Raise one toggle slightly and pull the opposite toggle down slightly to initiate a turn in the direction which the toggle is pulled down
  e. Avoid stalling the canopy.
3. Effect of brakes on glide
  a. Slower forward speed
  b. Lower descent rate
  c. Change in glide:
     (1) The pilot needs to experiment to determine the change in glide path at different degrees of flying in brakes.
     (2) Most modern nine-cell canopies fly flatter when a slight amount of brakes are applied.
     (3) Some lower-aspect canopies are designed to sink for a classic accuracy approach, which is less effective when performed under a higher-aspect ratio canopy in low-wind conditions.
4. Flaring from a braked position
  a. Expect a different glide on a braked final approach.
  b. Expect a shorter and quicker stroke needed to flare.
  c. Prepare for a harder landing.
5. Under canopy
  a. Practice flaring several times from the quarter-, half-, and three-quarter-braked positions, and focus on making an effective flare from each position.
  b. Practice braked turns using all the methods discussed.
  c. Fly a landing pattern that allows for a crosswind final approach and landing.
     (1) For purposes of training and familiarization, the crosswind landing should only be performed in winds up to five miles per hour.
     (2) All jumpers on the same pass must use the same landing pattern to promote a smooth flow of traffic.
  d. On final approach, focus on crosswind correction necessary to prevent crabbing.
  e. A crosswind landing may require pulling the upwind toggle deeper than the downwind toggle to keep the jumper going in the same direction and reduce the ground speed upon landing. Performing an uneven flare in this manner increases the stall speed of the canopy. A parachute landing fall is recommended for any unusual landing

ADVANCED CANOPY PILOTING TOPICS | 6-11

JUMP 5—LONG SPOT

1. Projected landing point
  a. Discovery of how to locate the point on the ground the parachute will reach while flying at natural speed
  b. Altering the glide using brakes and rear risers
     (1) Minimize the drag.
        (i) Collapse the slider.
        (ii) Pull legs up, arms in, and arch to reduce air resistance
        (iii) Loosen the chest strap to improve glide.
     (2) If holding brakes, reducing fatigue by hooking your thumbs in the harness. (Be careful not to hook onto your cutaway or reserve ripcord handles.)
     (3) Decide by 1,500 feet about a new landing area.
        (i) Allow enough altitude for the final turn.
        (ii) Expect the winds to weaken as you get lower.
  c. Choose an alternate landing area if necessary, and follow off-field landing recommendations.
2. Under canopy
  a. Exit the aircraft at 5,000 feet AGL at least 1.5 miles upwind of the main landing area.
  b. Determine the glide path of the canopy and the landing point using the projected landing point to determine the point on the ground which is neither rising or sinking.
  c. Alter the glide
     (1) using brakes
     (2) using rear risers
     (3) comparison of effectiveness
  d. If the intended landing area cannot be reached by an altitude which allows for a safe landing, a reasonable alternative should be used.
  e. On landing, follow the flight plan and continue to work on effective flaring

6-12 | MOVEMENT JUMPS

6-12: MOVEMENT JUMPS

A. INTRODUCTION

1. These recommendations provide guidance for a skydive that entails one or more skydivers who are intentionally moving away from the point at which they were dropped, generally in a horizontal orientation that changes pitch and speed throughout the jump.
2. The term "movement" in this context includes but is not limited to tracking jumps and angle flying.
3. Wingsuit jumps are movement jumps but are covered separately in section 6-9 due to several unique considerations.

B. QUALIFICATIONS

1. Before engaging in movement jumps outside of the USPA Integrated Student Program, a participating skydiver (not a leader) should:
   a. Hold a USPA A license.
   b. Demonstrate proficiency at tracking while maintaining situational awareness.
2. Before engaging in movement jumps as the leader, the skydiver should have:
   a. At a minimum, qualified for the USPA C-license.
   b. The ability to maintain consistent awareness of altitude and location
   c. Proficiency and experience in the discipline
   d. Received formal instruction on:
      (1) DZ terrain (changing ground levels, bodies of water or any other ground obstacles) and alternate landing areas (outs).
      (2) exit order
      (3) navigation (move in the correct direction and ability to deploy where planned)
      (4) communication with drop zone authorities, other jumpers and the pilot (to determine jump run and spot)
      (5) understanding weather (including reading a winds-aloft forecast, and maintaining awareness of clouds prior to jumping)
      (6) Making a flight plan (including exit order, breakoff and designated deployment area) and adjusting that flight plan as necessary to accommodate changing conditions to avoid other groups.
3. Jumpers can use the graph below to determine their skill levels:

	BEGINNER	INTERMEDIATE	ADVANCED
Group Size	1-3	4-7	8+
Angle of Jump	Flat	Shallow	Steep
Transitions	0	1-3	4+
Relativity	Can fly in a quadrant on head (belly and back)	Can fly in quadrant or on level on head (belly and back), manage speed and pitch	Ability to maintain slot and stability in any orientation and matching speed and pitch
Breakoff	Fan out, choose a clear path and airspace	Can accelerate, choose a clear path and airspace to flatten out	Can accelerate, choose a clear path and airspace to flatten out, while mitigating congestion
Wind Conditions at Altitude	Calm	Calm-Mild	Calm-Extreme
Wind Speeds and Weather	No-to-light ground winds	Medium ground winds	High ground winds, wind shear between uppers and canopy winds, clouds, emerging weather

C. EQUIPMENT

1. Gear must be properly secured to prevent premature deployment of either canopy.
   a. A premature opening at the speeds involved in this type of skydiving could result in severe injury to the body or stressing the equipment beyond limits set by the manufacturers.
   b. Deployment systems and operation handles should remain secure during inverted and stand-up flight; therefore, equipment for movement jumps should include:
      (1) bottom-of-container-mounted throw-out pilot-chute pouch, pull-out pilot chute, or ripcord main deployment system
         (i) Exposed leg-strap-mounted pilot chutes present an extreme hazard.
         (ii) Any exposed pilot-chute bridle presents a hazard.
         (iii) Use of a tuck-tab is recommended to provide additional security of the pilot chute during high freefall speeds encountered while movement flying.
      (2) Closing loops, pin-protection flaps, and riser covers well maintained and properly sized
2. Harness straps
   a. Leg straps should be connected with a seat strap to keep the leg straps from moving toward the knees.
   b. Excess leg and chest straps should be tightly stowed.
3. Automatic activation devices are recommended because of the high potential for collisions and loss of altitude awareness associated with movement jumps.
4. Personal accessories for movement jumps should include:
   a. audible altimeter (two are recommended)
   b. visual altimeter
   c. hard helmet
   d. clothing or jumpsuit that will remain in place during movement flights and will not obscure or obstruct deployment, emergency handles or altimeters
   e. GPS

MOVEMENT JUMPS | 6-12

D. TRAINING

1. Movement flying has many things in common with face-to-earth formation skydiving.
   a. A beginner will progress faster and safer with a coach.
   b. Novices should not jump with each other until they have—
      (1) received specific training in movement jumps
      (2) demonstrated the ability to control navigation, pitch and speed
2. Prior to jumping with larger groups, progress should follow the same model as for the freefall and canopy formation disciplines: Novices should begin with coached 2-way formations to develop exit, body position, pitch and speed control and breakoff skills, and progress gradually to larger and more complex movement jumps

E. HAZARDS ASSOCIATED WITH MOVEMENT JUMPS

1. Understanding navigation is of utmost importance. Jumpers must plan accordingly to:
   a. Move off the aircraft's line of flight
   b. Consider other movement groups on the load
   c. Avoid other groups in freefall and under canopy
   d. Open where they've pre-determined
   e. Account for the DZ terrain
   f. Have a backup plan if landing out
2. Weather is important in the planning phase to determine:
   a. Navigation
   b. Exit Order
   c. Coordination with other movement groups
   d. The current and changing cloud conditions during freefall and canopy flight
3. Communication
   a. Prior to boarding, it is of the utmost importance to communicate your intentions with the drop zone authorities (such as manifest, an S&TA or a load master) and the entire load in order to:
      (1) Understand local drop zone restrictions and requirements for movement jumps
      (2) Share your flight plan
      (3) Determine exit order
   b. It is also important that everyone in the group understand the DZ terrain, hazards, and alternate landing areas (outs)
4. Movement groups per load. Several factors (e.g., local DZ rules and terrain, weather and leader experience) influence how many movement groups may be safely accommodated per load; however, the general recommendation is to limit movement groups to two per load.
5. Exit order
   a. The exit order will depend on weather (freefall drift), DZ terrain, deployment altitudes, other groups and DZ rules and considerations
   b. Group leader must communicate with the S&TA, DZ, pilot and others on the load
6. Varied skill levels considerations
   a. Every jump should meet the skill level of the lowest experienced jumper in order to execute the flight plan and open in the determined spot
   b. Opening in the correct, predetermined spot is crucial for safety, so jumpers must be able to demonstrate proficiency on beginner-level movement jumps before progressing to intermediate or advanced jumps. Jumpers who are unable to follow intermediate or advanced movement jumps may cause their groups to conflict with others on the load.
   c. Adding speed and pitch changes and transitions greatly increases the difficulty of the jump, requiring an expert leader to consider all the variables of the jump so as to avoid collisions, maintain the flight plan and open in the predetermined spot.
7. Relativity
   a. Maintain visual contact with the leader to adapt if you are far behind, above, to the side of or low relative to the group. To avoid collisions, continue moving in the same direction as the group, even if you are far away.
   b. Maintain the same heading (direction) as the rest of the group. Off-heading collisions are more dangerous than collisions between jumpers heading in the same direction.
   c. Never turn 180 degrees from the group's heading, even if you think there is nobody behind you.
   d. If you've passed the group, slow down and let it catch up. If you are flying to the side of the group and the group starts turning toward you, turn toward the same heading, even if you are far away.
8. Breakoff. It is crucial to understand the elements of breakoff to avoid congestion and collisions.
   a. Choose a clear path (line) and fan out from the other jumpers while flattening the pitch to a track
   b. Maintain awareness by looking in all directions
   c. If you are on your back at breakoff, avoid flipping to a belly-to-earth orientation until you are on a clear trajectory with no one above you. Once on your belly, continue to track off until it's time to clear airspace and pull

F. PRE-FLIGHT CHECKLIST

This pre-flight checklist can help you determine the specifics of your jump. Draw the flight plan on the map of your DZ and share it with the drop zone, load and pilot to confirm you can perform your skydive safely:

- ☐ What is jump run for your load?
- ☐ What are the forecasted winds aloft at these points during your jump?
  - ☐ Exit altitude
  - ☐ Freefall
  - ☐ Canopy
  - ☐ Landing Pattern
- ☐ How many groups and other jumpers on your load?
- ☐ What is your exit order?
  - ☐ Are there any other movement jumps on your load?
- ☐ What are the DZ terrain factors to consider in navigation?
- ☐ What is the intended landing pattern and holding area for the jump?
- ☐ Have you ensured that your flight path does not interfere with jump run?
- ☐ Does your flight plan take into consideration freefall, DZ terrain, canopy flight path and weather?
- ☐ Is your flight plan appropriate for the skill level of jumpers on your movement jump?

6-12 | MOVEMENT JUMPS

Section 7

EXHIBITION JUMPING AND RATING

EXHIBITION JUMPING AND RATING — 7

SECTION SUMMARY:

A demonstration jump, also called a display or exhibition jump, is a jump at a location other than an existing drop zone done for the purpose of reward, remuneration, or promotion and principally for the benefit of spectators. One purpose of USPA is to promote successful demonstration jumps as part of an overall public relations program for the sport.

These recommendations cover the following: experience, ability and attitude, the Professional Exhibition (PRO) Rating, landing area size, technical considerations, insurance, and how to complete the FAA authorization request form.

NOTE: All intentional off airport parachute jumps require a certificate of authorization (FAR 105.21). Submit FAA form 7711-2 with the local FSDO to obtain a certificate of authorization. Any jumps made without a certificate of authorization may not be covered under USPA third party liability insurance.

IMPORTANT REFERENCE NUMBERS

- USPA and FAA definitions of landing areas—Table 7.A
- exhibition jump approval requirements—7-1.N
- PRO Rating requirements for application, renewal, and requalification—7-2
- FAA instructions for completing Form 7711-2—7-3

WHO NEEDS THIS SECTION?

- jumpers preparing for the USPA PRO Rating
- jumpers planning exhibition jumps
- USPA officials advising jumpers on exhibition jumps

7-1: EXHIBITION JUMPING

Note: Requirements for obtaining demonstration jump insurance may differ from the recommendations listed in this section.

A. DEFINITION

An exhibition jump, also called a demonstration or display jump, is a jump at a location other than an existing drop zone done for the purpose of reward, remuneration, or promotion and principally for the benefit of spectators.

B. HOW TO APPROACH A DEMO JUMP

1. As with all jumps, safety must be the first consideration.
2. Next, the most important aspect of a demonstration jump is landing in the target area.
   a. Good aerial work is not impressive if the jumpers land out.
   b. A stand-up landing in the target area is usually the most visible and impressive portion of a demonstration jump.
3. Demo jumps have many variables which must be considered, including wind speed and direction, approach types, equipment type, jumper experience, target areas, and alternate landing areas.
4. Each proposed demo needs to be evaluated on an individual basis.

C. EXPERIENCE AND ABILITY

1. Open Field and Level 1, as defined by USPA and accepted by the FAA (all of the following):
   a. USPA C license or higher
   b. minimum 200 jumps
   c. 50 jumps within the past 12 months
   d. five jumps within the previous 60 days using the same model and size canopy to be used on the demonstration jump
   e. For tandem jumps, the above requirements do not apply to the tandem student
2. Level 2 and Stadium, as defined by USPA and accepted by the FAA (all of the following):
   a. hold the USPA PRO rating (required by the BSRs)
   b. 50 jumps within the past 12 months
   c. five jumps within the previous 60 days using the same model and size canopy to be used on the demonstration jump

D. ATTITUDE

1. While a good demonstration jump provides great public relations for the sport, a poorly performed one may severely damage skydiving's image.
   a. Therefore, it is important to recognize and understand that sometimes it may be in the best interest of the individual jumper and skydiving in general not to make the jump at all.
   b. A mature attitude should be exhibited at all times.
2. Promise no more than you can produce and then perform with expertise and efficiency.
3. Take no unnecessary chances.
4. Know what you are getting into before getting there.
5. Recognize and deal with the air of excitement that surrounds a demo jump.
6. Make mature and professional judgments in dealing with unforeseen circumstances.
7. Delay or cancel the demo when conditions are not right for a safe jump.
8. Jumpers and support staff should have a sharp, clean appearance to make a better impression and present a professional image.

E. LANDING AREAS

1. All FAA-authorized demonstration jumps are classified as either Open Field, Level 1, Level 2, or Stadium.
2. USPA with the FAA's concurrence defines these areas as described in Table 7.A, Size and Definition of Landing Areas (inset on previous page).
3. Minimum landing areas for PRO Rating holders:
   a. For PRO Rating holders, there should be no less than 5,000 square feet of landing area per four jumpers.
   b. An additional 800 square feet per jumper is required for any jumper landing within 30 seconds of the last of any four jumpers.
4. Alternate landing areas (run-offs or escape areas) must be considered when evaluating a demonstration jump.
5. Open bodies of water may be considered for measuring landing area

TABLE 7.A— SIZE AND DEFINITION OF LANDING AREAS

OPEN FIELD
1. A minimum-sized area that will accommodate a landing area no less than 500,000 square feet.
2. Allows a jumper to drift over the spectators with sufficient altitude (250 feet) so as not to create a hazard to persons or property on the ground
3. Will accommodate landing no closer than 100 feet from the spectators

LEVEL 1
1. An area that will accommodate a landing area no smaller than at least 250,000 square feet up to 500,000 square feet
2. Or an area with the sum total that equals 250,000 square feet, up to 500,000 square feet) with a one-sided linear crowd line
3. Allows jumpers to drift over the spectators with sufficient altitude (250 feet) so as not to create a hazard to persons or property on the ground
4. Will accommodate landing no closer than 50 feet from the spectators
5. Many Open-Field athletic areas constitute a Level 1 area.

LEVEL 2
1. An area that will not accommodate a 250,000 square-foot landing area but will allow an area no smaller than 5,000 square feet per four jumpers
2. Allows jumpers to fly under canopy no lower than 50 feet above the crowd and land no closer than 15 feet from the crowd line
3. Parachutists who certify that they will use both ram-air main and ram-air reserve parachutes will be permitted to exit over or into a congested area but not exit over an open-air assembly of people.
4. This area would require an FAA Form 7711-2 to conduct an approved demo.

STADIUM
1. A Level 2 landing area smaller than 450 feet in length by 240 feet in width and bounded on two or more sides by bleachers, walls, or buildings in excess of 50 feet high
2. This area would also require an FAA Form 7711-2 to conduct an approved demonstration jump.

requirements for open-field, level 1 and level 2 landing areas. However, the vertical and horizontal distance limits from any spectator outlined in Table 7.A still apply.

F. TURBULENCE AND TARGET PLACEMENT

1. Recommended minimum distances from major obstacles should never be disregarded, especially in windy conditions.
    a. Major obstacles affect air currents and can cause turbulence.
    b. Major obstacles include large buildings and trees.
    c. A single tree, pole, fence, etc., is not considered as a major obstacle.
    d. Stadium jumps usually involve turbulence that should be considered.
2. Jumpers should be thoroughly familiar with the turbulent-air flight characteristics of their canopies.

G. MAXIMUM WINDS

1. When considering wind limits, include wind turbulence and the capabilities of the reserve canopy.
2. USPA recommends that all demonstration jumps be conducted with a maximum 15-mph ground wind limitation.
3. For stadium jumps, the wind should be measured at the top of the stadium, and turbulence should always be anticipated.

H. EQUIPMENT

1. Main canopy:
    a. Open Field, Level 1, Level 2 and Stadium: ram-air type recommended by USPA
    b. Level 2 and Stadium: ram-air required by FAA
2. Reserve canopy:
    a. Open Field: should be steerable
    b. Level 1, Level 2, and Stadium: ram-air reserve required by FAA
3. Smoke should be hand-carried or attached to an easily ejectable boot bracket.
4. Depending on the type of demonstration jump; it is recommended to use an AAD and an RSL.

Warning: military type (M-18) smoke grenades are extremely hot and should not be hand held.

I. AERIAL MANEUVERS

1. Aerial maneuvers should be rehearsed, just as any professional would give a show a dry run.
    a. Participants should be aware of their exit point, freefall drift, and opening point.
    b. Landing on target takes priority over air work.
    c. One should be prepared to break off, track, or pull high if necessary.
2. Some suggested freefall maneuvers:
    a. barber pole:
        (1) Two or more jumpers with two or more colors of smoke exit and hook up.
        (2) The jumpers then spin the formation creating a giant barber pole.
    b. starburst: Three or more jumpers exit and form a star, then break, make a 180° turn, and track apart.
    c. cutaway:
        (1) One jumper opens, cuts away, and deploys a second main canopy.
        (2) The jumper is required to wear three parachutes, one of which must be a TSO'ed reserve, and the reserve must be attached to a TSO'ed harness.
3. Some suggested canopy maneuvers:
    a. smoke
        (1) After opening, ignite smoke and drop on a ten-foot line.
        (2) Make a series of turns in one direction.
        (3) The line should be releaseable from the upper end if it becomes necessary.
        (4) Be careful in crossing over obstacles on approach.
        (5) Make sure the smoke container won't burn through the line.
    b. flag
        (1) A flag may be attached to the rear lines or dropped below the jumper on a weighted line attached to the leading edge.
        (2) A ground crew should catch the flag so that it won't touch the ground.
        (3) Larger flags must be folded into a bag or pouch designed to contain the flag and the weight that is attached to the lower leading edge of the flag.
        (4) The flag should be deployed over an uncongested area to protect people and property in the event the weight detaches from the flag.
        (5) Before jumping with an unfamiliar flag system, seek out training and advice from a PRO Rated jumper who is familiar with the rigging of the flag and associated components.
    c. canopy formation
        (1) Canopy maneuvers should be performed by only experienced CRW jumpers.
        (2) Efforts to build canopy formations should stop no lower than 2,500 feet AGL.
        (3) It is much more difficult and dangerous to land a canopy stack on target than it is to land canopies separately.
    d. Radical canopy maneuvers should not be performed below 500 feet.

J. CROWD CONTROL

1. Collisions with spectators present a great danger to the spectator, the jumper, and the well-being of the sport.
    a. Reasonable precautions should be taken to keep the spectators out of the landing area.
    b. People not sitting may move toward the target, but they will not always move out of the way of the landing jumper.
2. Jumpers should pick up their equipment immediately after landing.
    a. Some spectators may decide that skydiving equipment makes good souvenirs.
    b. Jumpers who plan on packing in the crowd should protect against equipment damage by spectators' drinks and cigarettes.

K. GROUND SIGNALS

1. Ground-to-air communication must be maintained (BSRs).
    a. This may be accomplished by a radio, smoke, or a panel.

7-1 EXHIBITION JUMPING

b. It is best if a backup to the primary signal exists in case the primary signal fails.

2. If a Certificate of Authorization (FAA Form 7711-1) is issued, it may require ground-to-air radio communication.

L. ANNOUNCER

1. An experienced skydiver on the public address system contributes to a quality demonstration jump.

2. The announcer can point out the aircraft, explain each phase of the jump, give general information, and explain any unusual occurrences, such as a reserve activation or a jumper missing the target.

3. The announcer can contribute to crowd control by asking spectators not to enter the target area.

M. OTHER ACTIVITIES

1. Activities after the jump add to the entertainment of the spectators.

2. Packing demonstration:
   a. Team members pack their parachutes in view of the spectators.
   b. Jumpers should pack slowly, explaining each step and answering questions.
   c. Often, this facet of the demonstration is more effective if one person packs while another does the talking.

3. Answering questions:
   a. Respond to spectator questions politely and factually.
   b. Direct persons interested in jumping to USPA or distribute brochures advertising a drop zone.

N. ADVICE AND APPROVAL

1. Approval may need to be secured from federal, state, or local officials before a demonstration jump can be performed.

2. Local approval
   a. It may be necessary to contact local authorities prior to a jump.
   b. The FARs require airport management approval prior to a jump onto the airport (FAR 105.23).
   c. A call to the local police is recommended.
      (1) They may offer to help in crowd control.
      (2) With prior knowledge of the jump, they are less likely to respond to a call, such as, "There has been a mishap, and people are falling out of the sky."

3. State approval
   a. It may be necessary to contact the state department of aviation.
   b. The local S&TA or Examiner notified of the demonstration jump should be able to assist the organizers in meeting all state requirements.

4. FAA approval: Almost every jump requires either that the FAA be notified or an air traffic control authorization be received (FAR 105.25).
   a. For any jump, the air traffic control facility having jurisdiction over the airspace at the first intended exit altitude must be notified at least one hour before the jump.
   b. Congested areas and open air assembly of persons:
      (1) FAR 105.21.a. states that no jump be made over or into a congested area or an open air assembly of persons until a certificate of authorization has been issued (FAA Form 7711-1).
      (2) Application for authorization, if required, must be filed with the local Flight Standards District Office.
      (3) The FAA's instructions on how to fill out the application, FAA Form 7711-2, are included in SIM Section 7-3.
      (4) The local S&TA or Examiner notified of the demo should be able to assist the organizers in meeting all federal requirements.
      (5) An aerial photo and aviation sectional chart marking the location of the jump may be required by the local FSDO.

5. Notification and advice:
   a. The jumper is required by the BSRs to contact the local S&TA or an Examiner for demonstration jump advice.
   b. The information should be provided as outlined in FAR 105.15.a.
   c. The S&TA or an Examiner providing advice for a demonstration jump should use this section as a guideline.
   d. The Examiner whose advice was sought should contact the S&TA for the area or the drop zone at which the flight will originate.
   e. The S&TA should assist the jumpers in meeting all applicable state and federal requirements and check that the requirements have been met.
   f. All authorizations and permits should be carried on the jump by the organizer or team captain.
   g. The S&TA should investigate both the proposed area and the participants.
      (1) The S&TA or Examiner may recommend the use of specific jumpers or advise the organizer to use only individuals meeting certain experience requirements.
      (2) General advice allows the organizer greater flexibility in making last-minute substitutions of aircraft and participants.
   h. When consulted for a demonstration jump, the S&TA may recommend certain additional limitations such as wind speed and direction, altitude, etc.
   i. The S&TA should consider the information in this section when making recommendations and should ask the question, "All things considered, are the chances of performing a safe and professional demonstration jump reasonably good?"

O. INSURANCE

1. USPA individual membership liability skydiving insurance (property damage and bodily injury), which is included as a benefit of USPA membership, is not valid for demonstration jumps.

2. Contact USPA Headquarters for information on demonstration jump insurance.

P. RELATED READINGS

1. FAA Part 105, Parachute Operations
2. FAA AC 105-2, Sport Parachute Jumping
3. FAA AC 91-45, Waivers: Aviation Events

7-2: PROFESSIONAL EXHIBITION RATING

A. WHAT IS A PRO RATING?

1. Working in conjunction with the FAA, USPA issues Professional Exhibition (PRO) Ratings to any USPA member who has met the current requirements for the rating.

    a. This rating identifies the jumper as highly proficient and accurate in canopy control.

    b. A PRO Rating holder is also knowledgeable in the areas of coordination with the Federal Aviation Administration, obtaining insurance coverage, and providing a professional demonstration of skills on a wing loading of 1.5:1 and below.

    c. A high-performance (HP) endorsement allows PRO-rated members to make exhibition jumps with wing loadings above 1.5:1.

2. A USPA PRO Rating is not required for all demonstration jumps but may be a valuable advantage in working with the FAA.

3. The PRO Rating is recognized by the FAA and serves as a certificate of proficiency.

B. QUALIFICATIONS AND PROCEDURES

1. To initially qualify for a PRO Rating, an applicant must:

    a. be a current member of USPA

    b. possess a USPA D license

    c. have made two-night jumps (recommended that the first one be a solo and one in a group) with a freefall of at least 20 seconds:

        (1) with verification of prior night jump training from a USPA Instructor holding a USPA D license, who has also successfully completed two-night jumps (does not have to be within twelve months of PRO rating application)

        (2) with the advice of an S&TA, in accordance with USPA BSRs

    d. make a series of 10 solo jumps with a stand-up landing into an area 40 feet long by 20 feet wide using the same model and size canopy, at a wing loading 1.5:1 or below.

        (1) The applicant must pre-declare each jump to count toward the requirements for the PRO rating.

            (i) All of the declared jumps must be recorded on video that clearly shows the PRO rating applicant's final approach and landing into a defined area 40 feet long by 20 feet wide.

            (ii) Video footage of each approach and landing must be submitted to the appropriate Regional Director, or the director of safety and training at USPA Headquarters, along with the PRO rating application.

            (iii) Video footage may be submitted via online sharing or by sending the video files on a portable hard drive.

        (2) Once the applicant has started the series, he or she may make non-declared jumps; however, non-declared jumps may not count toward the accuracy requirements for the rating.

        (3) All of the 10 pre-declared jumps in the series must be successful for any in the series to count toward the rating; and in the event of an unsuccessful jump, the applicant must start a new series. At least two must be crosswind approaches and landings into an area 40 feet long by 20 feet wide. The final approach must be 90-degrees to the direction of the wind. Wind speed must be at least five miles per hour and no more than 15 miles per hour.

        (4) On each declared jump, the applicant must make the first contact and stop within the designated landing area.

        (5) All declared jumps must be witnessed by either a S&TA, Examiner, USPA Judge or USPA Regional or National Director.

        (6) The applicant must obtain signatures of the eligible verifying official for each of the ten jumps.

    e. To qualify for a HP (high performance) endorsement for the PRO rating, applicants flying a parachute at a wing-loading greater than 1.5:1, make a series of five solo jumps into an area 40 feet long by 20 feet wide using the same model and size canopy.

        (1) The applicant must pre-declare each jump to count toward the requirements for the HP endorsement for the PRO rating.

            (i) All of the declared jumps must be recorded on video that clearly shows the PRO rating applicant's final approach and landing into a defined area 40 feet long by 20 feet wide.

            (ii) Video footage of each approach and landing must be submitted to the appropriate Regional Director, or the director of safety and training at USPA Headquarters, along with the PRO rating application.

            (iii) Video footage may be submitted via online sharing or by sending the video files on a portable hard drive.

        (2) At least one landing must demonstrate a crosswind approach and landing into an area 40 feet long by 20 feet wide. The final approach must be 90degrees to the direction of the wind. Wind speed must be at least five miles per hour and no more than 15 miles per hour.

        (3) At least two approaches and landings must demonstrate a heading change of at least 45 degrees during the final 150 feet of canopy flight. The heading change must be started and completed no higher than 25 feet AGL. This flared, carving turn is to demonstrate the ability to change heading during the swoop portion of the landing and still maintain control of the parachute.

        (4) All the five pre-declared jumps in this series must be successful for any in the series to count toward the rating; and in the event of an unsuccessful jump, the applicant must start a new series.

7-2 PROFESSIONAL EXHIBITION RATING

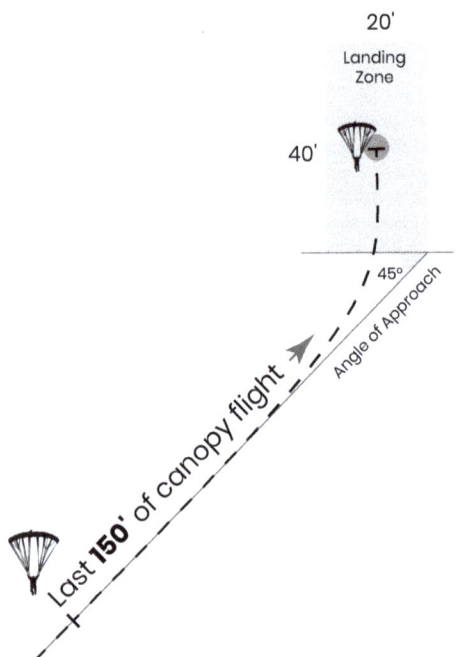

Illustration 7-2.1: High performance endorsement approach and landing requirements as described in 7-2.B.1.f.(3)

    f. The PRO Rating exam is administered by a USPA S&TA, Examiner, Judge or board member and the examining official:

        (1) gives the applicant an answer sheet and the questions to the exam

            (i) No references or other assistance are permitted during the exam.

            (ii) After the test, the examining official collects the materials and grades the exam.

            (iii) A score of 75% is required to pass.

        (2) The score is recorded on the license application and in the applicant's logbook.

            (i) An applicant not passing the paper exam will be eligible to retake this exam after seven days.

            (ii) Applicants who have not passed the USPA online testing program may retest using the same method immediately for a total of three attempts per day.

    g. forward the completed application form to his or her USPA Regional Director for signature and include:

        (1) the completed PRO Rating exam

        (2) the rating fee

        (3) the PRO Rating Proficiency Card signed off by an Examiner, S&TA, or PRO Rating holder indicating that the PRO Rating applicant has received training in the following areas:

            (i) ground crew—and served as a ground crew member on at least one Level 1 or Level 2 demo jump

            (ii) flag rigging—and made at least one jump with a flag

            (iii) smoke rigging—and made at least one jump with smoke

            (iv) NOTAM filing and certificates of authorization

            (v) crowd control

            (vi) post-jump procedures

    h. Except for the minimum 500 ram-air jump requirements, all training listed must be made within the previous 12 months of the application.

2. The USPA Regional Director will forward the initial application to USPA Headquarters.

3. Conditions

    a. The canopy used during qualification will be the smallest size canopy to be used for minimum landing area (Level 2) jumps, and the canopy size will be noted on the USPA membership card.

    b. USPA will issue an annual PRO Rating with an expiration date that will coincide with the applicant's membership expiration date.

    c. The rating must be renewed annually in order to remain current.

    d. If a PRO Rating holder's competence is questioned by a FAA or USPA official (including S&TAs), the PRO Rating holder may be required to reaffirm his or her proficiency.

C. TO REQUALIFY ON SMALLER CANOPIES

1. To requalify on a smaller canopy with a wing loading of 1.5:1 or below:

    a. The rating holder must make three successive, pre-declared jumps, making the first contact and stopping within an area 40 feet long by 20 feet wide.

        (1) All of the declared jumps must be recorded on video that clearly shows the PRO-rating applicant's final approach and landing into a defined area 40 feet long by 20 feet wide.

        (2) Video footage of each approach and landing must be submitted to the appropriate Regional Director, or the director of safety and training at USPA Headquarters, along with the PRO rating application.

        (3) Video footage may be submitted via online sharing or by sending the video files on a portable hard drive.

    b. All landings must be made standing up and be verified by a USPA Examiner, S&TA, Judge or board member.

    c. The three landings must be logged on the PRO rating application and signed by the witness who verified the jump.

    d. The application may then be submitted to USPA Headquarters for processing.

2. To re-qualify on a smaller canopy with a wing loading greater than 1.5:1:

    a. The rating holder must first meet the qualifications for HP endorsement listed above (ie. five HP qualification jumps must be done first).

    b. The rating holder must make three successive, pre-declared jumps, making the first contact and stopping within an area 40 feet long by 20 feet wide.

        (1) All of the declared jumps must be recorded on video that clearly shows the PRO rating applicant's final approach and landing into a defined area 40 feet long by 20 feet wide.

        (2) Video footage of each approach and landing must be submitted to the appropriate Regional Director, or the director of safety and training at USPA Headquarters, along with the PRO rating application.

        (3) Video footage may be submitted via online sharing or by sending the video files on a portable hard drive.

    c. One jump must be made landing into the wind in any wind speeds up to 15 miles per hour.

d. One jump must be a crosswind landing. The final approach must be 90-degrees to the direction of the wind. Wind speed must be at least five miles per hour and no more than 15 miles per hour.

e. One jump approach and landing must demonstrate a heading change of at least 45 degrees during the final 150 feet of canopy flight. The heading change must be started and completed no higher than 25 feet AGL. This flared, carving turn is to demonstrate the ability to change heading during the swoop portion of the landing and still maintain control of the parachute.

f. All landings must be verified by a USPA Examiner, S&TA, Judge or board member.

g. The three landings must be logged on the PRO rating application and signed by the witness who verified the jump.

h. The application may then be submitted to USPA Headquarters for processing.

D. ANNUAL RENEWAL REQUIREMENTS:

1. Within the previous 12 months the PRO holder must perform all the following, verified by the signature of a current USPA S&TA, Examiner, Judge or Board member (you may not renew yourself) and forward a completed PRO renewal application to USPA Headquarters:

   a. Make at least 50 jumps.

   b. Include the current renewal fee.

   c. PRO rating for wing loadings of 1.5:1 and below, in the presence of a USPA Examiner, S&TA, Judge or board member:

      (1) perform two stand-up landings, making the first contact and stopping within an area 40 feet long by 20 feet wide.

      (2) or perform two Level 2 demo jumps (as defined by USPA and accepted by the FAA) with a wing loading 1.5:1 or lower.

   d. HP endorsement for wing loadings over 1.5:1, in the presence of any of a USPA Examiner, S&TA, Judge or board member:

      (1) meet requirements for wing loadings of 1.5:1 and below, perform two landings, one each to meet the criteria outlined in C.2.d and e of this section making the first contact and stopping within an area 40 feet long by 20 feet wide.

      (2) or meet requirements for wing loadings of 1.5:1 and below and perform two Level 2 demo jumps (as defined by USPA and accepted by the FAA) with a wing loading above 1.5:1.

   e. The canopy used to meet annual renewal requirements will be the smallest-sized canopy allowed to be used on demonstration jumps.

E. LAPSED PRO-RATING RENEWAL REQUIRMENTS

1. For persons with an expired PRO rating (up to two years), in the presence of a USPA Examiner, S&TA, Judge or board member:

   a. for wing loadings of 1.5:1 and below, perform two stand-up landings, making the first contact and stopping within an area 40 feet long by 20 feet wide.

   b. for wing loadings over 1.5:1, meet requirements for wing loadings of 1.5:1 and below, perform two landings, one each to meet the criteria outlined in C.2.d and e of this section, making the first contact and stopping within an area 40 feet long by 20 feet wide.

2. If a PRO Rating holder allows his or her rating to lapse for two years or longer, the initial landing qualification requirements must be met.

3. If the canopy size used for requalification is larger than the one originally qualified on, it will become the smallest-sized canopy allowed to be used for demonstrations.

7-3: INSTRUCTIONS FOR COMPLETING FAA FORM 7711-2

Parachute demonstration or exhibitions jumps conducted into aviation events, congested areas on the surface, or open-air assemblies, require an FAA Certificate of Authorization to be issued by the FAA Flight Standards District Office with jurisdiction where the jump(s) will occur. FAA Form 7711-2—the application for that authorization—can be found on both the FAA and USPA websites. Submit the application to the FSDO after completing the form using the following FAA instructions:

Applications for parachute jump authorizations made over or into a congested area or open-air assembly of people should be presented at least 10 working days before an event if possible to allow for processing time. Approval or denial of the application must be completed within 5 working days of receipt by the FSDO.

Item 1. [Name of organization] The organization sponsoring the event shall retain sole responsibility for safeguarding persons and property on the surface and shall inform the [Name of issuing FSDO] Flight Standards District Office (FSDO) in writing of the person named to ensure operational safety of the event. When applicable, IIC's should insert the name of the responsible person, found in Item 2 of the application, into the text of the special provisions to indicate the holder of the Certificate of Waiver or Authorization.

Item 2. The responsible person must have been determined to be competent and knowledgeable concerning the terms and provisions of this Certificate of Authorization. The application may be submitted by the organizer for a sanctioned military team but must be submitted by a team member if not a sanctioned military team. This person will be responsible to the Federal Aviation Administration (FAA) for the safe conduct of the event on all authorization matters.

Item 3. This information refers to the holder of the Certificate of Authorization listed in either Item 1 or 2. If no organization is listed in Item 1 then the information pertains to the name in Item 2.

Item 4. N/A should be entered unless the application is for banner towing.

Item 5. N/A should be entered unless the application is for banner towing.

Item 6. Enter NONE.

Item 7. Example: A four-person skydiving exhibition with flags, banners, smoke and pyrotechnics.

Item 8. Example 1: 1.0 Nm in radius from a point 7.3 Nm on the CVG 270 degree radial from surface to 8,000 feet MS or Example 2: 1.0 Nm in radius from the center of W66 airport.

Item 9a. The beginning date and hour of the first jump using UTC (GMT aka Zulu time) pertains to the time the jump aircraft arrives over the jump site.

Item 9b. The date and hour the last jumper is on the ground using UTC.

Item 10. Aircraft make and model to be used, back-up aircraft, pilot(s) name(s) certificate number(s), and home address (also include N-number of aircraft in block (a) if known).

Items 11 through 16 are not required for parachuting authorizations, however, the jumpers' names, USPA certificate level and number (if USPA members) should be submitted either in the remarks block or on a separate sheet of paper attached.

Section 8

MEMBERSHIP AWARDS PROGRAMS

SECTION SUMMARY:

USPA presents awards to individual members in recognition of their accomplishments in skydiving. These awards programs have been established to provide both goals and recognition in a variety of fields. Each of these awards represents a significant milestone achieved by an individual skydiver.

Service awards are reserved for special USPA members whose contributions to the organization and the sport meet the criteria established by the award.

Achievement awards are earned by accumulating numbers of jumps (by thousands) or freefall time (12-hour increments).

Performance awards are presented for accomplishments in canopy formations.

Tenure awards are granted for longevity, measured by years of USPA membership.

IMPORTANT REFERENCE NUMBERS

- USPA Chesley H. Judy Safety Award instructions—8-1.3
- Service awards, including recipients of the USPA Lifetime Achievement Award and Gold Medal for Meritorious Service—8-1.4-5
- Achievement awards, including rules for accumulating number of jumps or freefall time—8-2
- Performance awards, including rules for accomplishments in canopy formation—8-3
- Tenure Awards—8-4

WHO NEEDS THIS SECTION?

- jumpers applying for USPA awards
- jumpers nominating others for USPA awards
- USPA officials verifying awards
- USPA Board members seeking procedures for awards nominations and selection
- anyone interested in reviewing some of the most notable USPA members over the years

8-1: SERVICE AWARDS

8-1: SERVICE AWARDS

A. INTRODUCTION

1. The USPA Membership Services Committee is charged by the USPA Board of Directors with the preparation of recommendations of USPA members who are eligible for major national and international awards, medals, and other special recognitions.

2. Final action on these recommendations is the responsibility of the full board of directors, but all members of the association are invited to submit nominations to the Membership Services Committee, via USPA Headquarters, for any and all awards.

3. The Membership Services Committee will consider only nominees who have served the cause and interests of skydiving in general and the USPA in particular.

4. No current member of the USPA Board of Directors will be recommended by USPA for any award during the term of office.

B. PROCEDURES

Note: the following procedures apply to all service awards except the USPA Chesley H. Judy Safety Award, which is provided in the section for that specific award.

1. Nominations
   a. Identify the nominee, including address and telephone number.
   b. Identify the nominator, including email address and telephone number.
   c. Prepare the citation in 30 words or less capturing the essence of the achievement for which the nominee's name has been submitted.
   d. In 100 words or less, give complete, concise details justifying the award to the nominee, with pertinent background information to assist the committee.
   e. Nominations for all USPA awards must be received at USPA Headquarters at least 10 business days prior to the summer USPA Board of Directors meeting.
   f. Nominations for all non-USPA awards must be received at USPA Headquarters before the next upcoming USPA Board of Directors meeting.
   g. Previous nominations may be considered by the Membership Services Committee in future years without resubmission.

2. Selection
   a. After a review of all nominees proposed, the Membership Services Committee will present to the full board a list of those nominees for which the board's endorsement is requested.
   b. By a two-thirds majority and secret ballot in closed session, the USPA Board of Directors will select the candidates for the year being considered from those nominations presented by the committee.
   c. If the USPA Board approves nominations for NAA and/or FAI awards, the chair of the Membership Services Committee will forward appropriate letters of recommendation not later than the deadline imposed for the specific award, in support of each candidate endorsed by the USPA Board, together with necessary supporting documents and evidence to the National Aeronautic Association.

3. Follow-up
   a. The chair will then follow up personally if necessary with each of the aviation organizations sponsoring the various national and international awards to ensure that USPA nominees are properly evaluated.
   b. Within 24 hours of the decision by the USPA Board of Directors to select or nominate a recipient, the President or his designee should notify the recipient of the board's decision.
   c. Once notification is made, USPA Headquarters will make the decision public.
   d. The Chair of the USPA Membership Services Committee will compose or delegate an author for a suitable article to appear in *Parachutist* magazine explaining the merits of the recipient and the reasons for the decision of the board.
   e. Headquarters should consult with the recipient on the time and venue for presentation of the award and it should be presented at an appropriate USPA event where many USPA members are likely to be present.

8-1.1: FÉDÉRATION AÉRONAUTIQUE INTERNATIONALE (FAI) GENERAL AWARDS

A. PAUL TISSANDIER DIPLOMA

1. The Tissandier Diploma is awarded to those who have served the cause of aviation in general and sporting aviation in particular, by their work, initiative, devotion, or in other ways.

2. Each year, the United States may submit the names of up to three candidates.

B. FAI HONORARY GROUP DIPLOMA

1. As its name implies, the FAI Honorary Group Diploma may be awarded to groups of people (design offices, scientific bodies, aeronautical publications, etc.) that have contributed significantly to the progress of aeronautics or astronautics during the previous year or years.

2. Each year, an FAI member may submit the names of two candidates, one for aeronautics and one for astronautics.

C. FAI PARACHUTING AWARDS

(FAI parachuting awards are subject to approval by the FAI Parachuting Commission.)

1. The FAI Gold Parachuting Medal
   a. The FAI Gold Medal may be awarded annually for an outstanding accomplishment in connection with parachuting, in the realm of sport, safety, or an invention.
   b. The medal was created by an endowment fund provided by Mr. J.A. Istel, President of Honour of the FAI Parachuting Commission.

2. The Leonardo da Vinci Diploma is awarded to a parachutist who has any one of the following:
   a. at least three times consecutively won a national overall championship title
   b. at least once won the world absolute individual parachuting championship and twice the title of combined champion (male or female) at a recognized international parachuting competition
   c. served twice as chief judge at a recognized international competition and at least once at a recognized world parachuting championships or served at least

three times consecutively as an international judge at a recognized world parachuting championships

d. established at least three world parachuting records

e. served at least twice as meet director at a recognized international parachuting competition and at least once at a recognized world parachuting championship

f. been nominated as honorary president of the International Parachuting Committee (IPC)

g. served for at least ten consecutive years, including the current year, as a national delegate to the IPC

3. The Faust Vrancic Medal is awarded for technical innovation or achievement in parachuting.

8-1.2: NATIONAL AERONAUTIC ASSOCIATION (NAA) SERVICE AWARDS

A. FRANK G. BREWER TROPHY

The NAA Brewer Trophy, awarded annually, is given to an individual, group or organization for significant contributions of enduring value to aerospace education in the United States.

B. DISTINGUISHED STATESMAN OF AVIATION

1. The NAA Distinguished Statesman Award honors outstanding Americans who, by their efforts over a period of years, have made contributions of significant value to aeronautics and have reflected credit upon America and themselves

2. A nominee must
   a. be a citizen of the U.S. who has for at least 15 years been actively identified with aeronautics
   b. be at least 60 years of age
   c. be well and favorably known as a person of ability and character

8-1.3: USPA SERVICE AWARDS

A. USPA LIFETIME ACHIEVEMENT AWARD

1. Introduction
   a. Perhaps the most respected honor which is offered by the United States Parachute Association is the USPA Lifetime Achievement Award, which was originally conceived and created in 1970, as a result of an initial gift of $3,000 from an "Anonymous Donor."
   b. The sum was eventually enlarged to a total of $30,000 over a period of years and the funds were placed on deposit with the National Aeronautic Association, which agreed to administer them on behalf of the United States Parachute Association, for the purpose of underwriting the cost of a variety of perpetual competition trophies, as well as the Achievement Award.
   c. The fund ceased to exist in 1982 when the final money available was used to construct the floor-to-ceiling display cases at USPA's Headquarters in Alexandria, Virginia.
   d. The agreement signed on May 13, 1970, between Attorney John Kerr Wilson, acting for the "Anonymous Donor;" General Brooke E. Allen, Executive Director of the National Aeronautic Association, acting for the National Aeronautic Association; and Dr. Edward A. Fitch, president of the United States Parachute Association, acting for USPA, stipulates (among other things) that at any time on or after May 13, 1975, the "Anonymous Donor" may identify himself and direct that any and all awards created through his gift carry his name. To date the "Anonymous Donor" has not seen fit to exercise this privilege.

2. Qualifications for the award: The May 13, 1970, agreement, as accepted by USPA, describes the award itself and the qualifications required of recipients, using this language:

"To provide a bowl or other suitable trophy to be known initially as 'The United States Parachute Association Achievement Award' [renamed 'USPA Lifetime Achievement Award' in July, 2004], which shall be perpetual and will be awarded annually to an expert active or retired sport parachute jumper in recognition of outstanding sportsmanship, skill, or personal contribution to the sport of parachuting and the United States Parachute Association, its goals and purposes. The recipient of such award will be selected by the board of directors by a majority vote during a closed regular or special meeting. In the event a majority of the board of directors cannot agree upon a recipient of such award on account of a lack of preeminence of the sport parachutist in any one year, the award will be made at least once each two years. Such trophy will be kept permanently in an appropriate location to be determined by the board of directors."

3. Description of trophy
   a. The trophy itself is a sterling silver bowl, 15 inches in diameter, seated on an octagonal teakwood base which bears carved wooden replicas of the USPA emblem on four faces and sterling silver plates listing the names and qualifications of recipients of the award on the other four faces.
   b. Traditionally, each year the recipient receives a smaller, eight-inch diameter replica sterling-silver bowl as his or her personal possession.

4. Other considerations
   a. Traditionally the award is made for the year prior to the year in which it is presented.
   b. While the deed of gift requires that the award be given only to an individual, in 1974, the presentation was made to the United States Army Parachute Team, which suggests that the language in the deed is usable more as a guideline than as a strict requirement.
   c. The Membership Services Committee and the board has usually regarded the statement, "In recognition of personal contribution to the United States Parachute Association, its goals and purposes" as an overriding requirement (i.e., achievements in sport parachuting unrelated to the United States Parachute Association would normally not be considered sufficient to qualify a recipient, lacking specific contributions to USPA).
   d. While the deed of gift states that the award must be made at least once every two years, neither in 1991 nor in 1992 was a recipient named, thereby again suggesting that this particular language serves more as a guideline than as a requirement.
   e. No current member of the USPA Board of Directors may be recommended for the USPA Lifetime Achievement Award during his or her term as a member of the board.

8-1 SERVICE AWARDS

(1) In practice, this requirement has been extended to forbid a nomination for at least two full years after the end of board service.

(2) It is enlarged to include as ineligible current or former USPA employees, also until at least two years after their employment ends.

B. USPA GOLD MEDAL FOR MERITORIOUS SERVICE

1. Background
   a. The USPA Gold Medal for Meritorious Service was established on July 13, 1997, by the USPA Board of Directors.
   b. The award given to no more than three recipients per year, in the form of a struck brass medal which measures three inches in diameter, weighs approximately five ounces and is slotted at the top for attachment of a 30-inch gold fabric ribbon.
   c. For permanent display at USPA Headquarters is a large wooden plaque measuring two feet by four feet and adorned with an exact replica of the medal along with brass metal strips bearing the name and date of each recipient.

2. Criteria for the award
   a. The USPA Gold Medal for Meritorious Service is to honor outstanding USPA members who, by their efforts over a period of years, have made significant contributions to the skydiving community.
   b. Each recipient must be or have been a USPA member and been active in sport parachuting for at least 20 years in the areas of, but not limited to judging, instruction, jumpmastering, camera (film and video), competition, and safety.
   c. No current member of the USPA Board of Directors may be considered for the award and no past member of the board of directors of USPA may be considered for the award until at least two years after retiring from the board.
   d. No current employee of USPA may be considered for the award and no past employee of USPA may be considered for the award until at least two years after leaving USPA employment.

C. USPA REGIONAL ACHIEVEMENT AWARD

1. Background
   a. Many outstanding individuals have contributed to the sport more on a local or regional level. To recognize the contribution of these individuals, the Board of Directors has created this award.
   b. The award is presented to no more than five recipients per year total, in the form of a certificate.

2. Criteria for the award
   a. The USPA Regional Achievement Award is to honor an outstanding member of a USPA region who, by their efforts over a period of time or one outstanding act, has made a significant contribution to that region's skydiving community.
   b. No current member of the USPA Board of Directors may be considered for the award and no past member of the Board of Directors of USPA may be considered for the award until they have been off the board for at least two years.
   c. No current employee of USPA may be considered for the award and no past employee of USPA may be considered for the award until at least two years after leaving USPA employment.

D. USPA CHESLEY H. JUDY SAFETY AWARD

1. Background
   a. A fund was established at USPA in 1997 to honor the memory of Ches Judy, former USPA Director of Safety and Training, killed in a skydiving plane crash two years earlier.
   b. Distribution of the fund was in abeyance pending the development of a suitable safety-related program.

2. Purpose of the award
   a. In 2004, USPA developed a safety award to honor members who had promoted safety in our sport.
   b. The USPA Board determined that the new award was consistent with the original intent of the Ches Judy Safety Fund, so therefore designated the new award as the USPA Chesley H. Judy Safety Award.

3. USPA Headquarters developed the certificate, which is available at no charge to each drop zone to honor the local USPA member who is most deserving of the award.

4. The award is to be presented on USPA Safety Day in conjunction with the other planned activities for the annual event.

5. Criteria for the award: The selection for the award recipient should be based on the previous year's actions or accomplishments of any current USPA member who, through example, deed, training, or innovation, had promoted safe skydiving in a substantive way.

6. Selection and administrative procedures
   a. The USPA S&TA in consultation with the drop zone owner selects one individual from the drop zone to which the award is appointed based on the above criteria.
   b. By February 15th, the S&TA requests a certificate from headquarters, either in writing (attention: Safety & Training), or by email to safety@uspa.org.
   c. The request should include the correctly spelled name of the recipient and the name of the drop zone.
   d. USPA will provide the completed certificate to the requesting S&TA for presentation during that year's Safety Day activities.

8-1.4: RECIPIENTS OF THE USPA LIFETIME ACHIEVEMENT AWARD

Note: In absent years, no award was presented.

1971 Joe Crane (*posthumously*), C-1—
"For unselfish and dedicated service as founder, president, and chairman of the board of the National Parachute Jumpers and Riggers and its successor, the Parachute Club of America."

1972 Lew Sanborn, D-1—
"For originating safe and reliable parachute equipment, for pioneering work in freefall photography, and for many other contributions to the sport and USPA."

1973 Steve Snyder, D-5—
"For pioneering contributions through the years to the saving of lives and the improvement of parachute equipment."

1974 United States Army Parachute Team—
"Generous and dedicated sportsmen, celebrated competitors, respected leaders who since 1961 have introduced parachuting at its best to worldwide millions and have brought honor and distinction to the sport."

1975 Lowell Bachman, D-700 —
"For service to the United States Parachute Association and all competitors as judge and chief judge at countless national championships, and as a dedicated leader in the development of judging excellence."

1977 Russ Gunby, C-350—
"A founding spirit who saw the future when others doubted. As author, executive director, and P.C.A. president, he gave countless hours to build the early framework of our sport."

1978 Len Potts, D-220—
"In recognition of personal sacrifice and countless contributions to skydiving and this organization spanning our decades as a sport. His past is our present."

1980 Dan Poynter, D-454—
"Prolific author, distinguished instructor, preeminent parachutist, whose service to skydiving spans more than 20 active years."

1981 Norman E. Heaton, D-565—
"In eleven years of devoted service as executive director, he contributed substantially and uniquely to USPA's greatest growth."

1983 James F. "Curt" Curtis, D-1407—
"A total contributor to our sport and USPA: competitive champion, headquarters executive, drop zone owner, safety officer, director, board chairman." [For some reason, his service as USPA president was not recorded.]

1984 Chuck MacCrone, D-526—
"In recognition of outstanding contributions to sport parachuting and as a testament to his unparalleled service as president, FAI-IPC."

1986 Jack Bergman (*posthumously*), D-357—
"USPA Director 1967-1984, Treasurer 1967-1984, National Championships Meet Director 1975-1984. With selfless devotion he gave a quarter century to skydiving and USPA."

1987 Carl Boenish (*posthumously*), D-2556—
"A prolific and talented skydiver whose lifetime of pioneering freefall photography brought unforgettable images and better understanding to fellow jumpers and the public."

1989 J. Scott Hamilton, D-514—
"For service to USPA and the skydiving world 1967-1979, a Collegiate League director, Safety and Training Committee chairman, and USPA president."

1990 Ken Coleman (*posthumously*), D-12630 —
"World and national champion who created the accelerated freefall program."

1993 Loy Brydon, D-12 —
"In recognition of major contributions to parachuting in the development of equipment, freefall techniques and competition—an original role model of the total skydiver."

1994 William H. Ottley, D-298 —
"In recognition of more than three decades of dedicated service to skydiving and USPA, as board member, vice president and executive director."

1995 Dick Barber, C-2375—
"For dedicated service to all competitors as a judge at countless U.S. Nationals and world championships, and for the inspiration provided to judges."

1997 Clint Vincent, D-7624—
"Selfless service for the betterment of all aspects of skydiving and in support of all skydivers."

1998 Patrick M. Moorehead, D-2962—
"For unselfish dedication to the United States Parachute Association since 1969 as an ambassador extraordinaire while traveling the world as a member of the board of directors and as a professional skydiving performer."

2002 Jerry (*posthumously*) and Sherry Schrimsher, D-7916—
"For their selfless dedication to USPA's competition and instructional programs and as leaders of the community while serving on USPA's board of directors."

2003 Al Krueger, D-3663—
"For almost 40 years of dedication to the sport and especially USPA as a board member, U.S. Nationals meet director, world skydiving champion, and inspirational visionary."

2004 Gene Paul Thacker, D-167—
"For over 40 years of contributions to USPA and the sport of skydiving, particularly in the Style & Accuracy community as an athlete, coach, leader, inspiration, volunteer, conscience and catalyst."

2007 Jacques-Andre Istel, D-2—
"In recognition of his pioneering spirit as he promoted skydiving in America, United States Parachute Teams, and collegiate parachuting competition while serving the United States Parachute Association and its predecessors."

8-1 SERVICE AWARDS

2010 Chris Needels, D-1765—
"For almost a half-century of total commitment to USPA as a board member, officer, executive director, and skydiving museum trustee, providing unparalleled leadership, vision and lasting stability."

2011 Paul Sitter, D-2714—
"For nearly three decades of service to the U.S. Parachute Association and its members, particularly in the area of safety and training by helping to educate and improve safety for skydivers everywhere."

2012 King Morton, D-2954—
"For improving the sport, enhancing collegiate skydiving and raising the stature of USPA as a competitor, jumpmaster and instructor and by serving 20 years on the USPA

2013 Larry K. Bagley, D-4522—
"For selfless dedication and commitment to the core values of the United States Parachute Association and the skydiving community as advocate, leader and wise counsel for nearly half a century."

2015 B.J. Worth, D-3805—
"For truly dedicated leadership over more than three decades, serving as USPA National Director, Chairman of the Board and IPC delegate; for promoting the sport through world records and demonstration jumps in front of millions."

2016 Alvin Lee Schlichtemeier, D-16256—
"In recognition of his unwavering dedication to USPA's financial well-being, his wise counsel as a career-long USPA board member and his contribution to the competition community as a national and international judge."

2018 Pat Thomas—
"For nearly three decades of advancing the sport of skydiving by sponsoring U.S. competitors and teams, being a leader in the harness-and-container industry and masterfully organizing the Parachute Industry Association Symposium."

2019 Ray Ferrell, D-5748—
"For more than 40 years of advancing the skydiving industry in myriad ways, including jumper and pilot training, rigging and aviation innovation, world records, competition, business and service to USPA, all while maintaining the highest standards and principles."

2021 Marylou Laughlin, D-12418—
"For unsurpassed selfless contribution to the sport of skydiving and the United States Parachute Association as a leader, competitor, judge and U.S. representative within the international skydiving community."

2022 Jim Crouch D-16979 —
"For his steadfast dedication to safety as a multi-rated instructor and examiner, jump pilot, rigger, drop zone owner and Parachutist author, and for his service to USPA members as Director of Safety and Training from 2000-2018, a time that saw a drastic reduction in skydiver fatalities and injuries due in large part to his many efforts."

8-1.5: RECIPIENTS OF THE USPA GOLD MEDAL FOR MERITORIOUS SERVICE

1997 Lorrie Young—
"In recognition of outstanding achievement as a National and International Judge in all skydiving disciplines. Her unwavering dedication to fairness and integrity brought honor, as well as equality, to the judging profession."

1999 Jimmy Godwin, D-126—
"For outstanding and meritorious service to the skydiving community and for sharing his knowledge for over three decades as a Drop Zone owner, rigger examiner, pilot, instructor, and Conference Director."

1999 Jerry Bird, D-3299—
"For outstanding and meritorious service to the skydiving community for over thirty years, inspiring jumpers into becoming competitors and for unselfish training and organizing in the field of relative work."

2000 Sandra Williams, D-5829—
"For your unparalleled encouragement to women's participation in skydiving and helping set the benchmark for achievement in our sport."

2001 Dave DeWolf, D-1046—
"In recognition of your decades of service to the sport as a rigging school operator, seminar host and mentor."

2002 Bill Booth, D-3546—
"For over three decades of quality parachute equipment design and manufacture, especially his personal contribution to the concept and promotion of the tandem skydiving system."

2002 Ted Strong, D-16—
"For almost a half-century of contribution to the skydiving community as a competitor, a sponsor of numerous US parachute teams, and, most notably, his unique innovation in parachute equipment design including the tandem skydiving system and its importance to the growth of the sport in general and USPA in particular."

2003 Tom Morrison, D-2273—
"In recognition of more than 40 years as an ambassador for the sport of skydiving worldwide and for serving as an inspiration to skydivers of all ages."

2003 Fredrick W. "Bill" Wenger, D-3774—
"For over thirty years of leadership and support of the skydiving competition community as a board member, judge, team coach, and national and world champion."

2004 Michael J. McGowan, D-5709—
"For promoting our sport through professional aerial photography as a freefall cameraman, and for his innovation in developing freefall photography techniques."

2005 Tom Sanders, D-6503—
"For over a quarter of a century of promoting skydiving in general and USPA in particular as a professional aerial photographer, contributing often to the USPA calendar and Parachutist magazine."

2006 James (Jim) Wallace, D-3497—
"In recognition of almost 40 years dedicated to the skydiving community, and especially USPA, with boundless energy and enthusiasm as an instructor, demonstration jumper, U.S. Team member, and movie stuntman."

2006 Norman Kent D-8369—
"For nearly 30 years of contributions to skydiving and the USPA. Norman's work has put the highest artistic touch on images of our sport that have been seen by millions."

2006 Michael Truffer, D-3863—
"For service to the USPA membership as national director and for his vision and guidance in establishing the U.S. Parachute Team Trust Fund, which has and will continue to support those teams for many years."

2007 Judy Celaya—
"For almost three decades of dedicated contributions to the worldwide skydiving community as a national and international competition judge, judge course director, and ambassador of the sport."

2007 Chris Gay, D-11504—
"For innovations that have redefined the discipline of canopy formation. Chris Gay made the USA the dominant force in international competitions, improved safety and was instrumental in the 100-way world record organization."

2007 Mike Lewis, D-2071—
"For being one of CRW's original pioneers. Mike Lewis has been an integral part of every aspect of the discipline's development including safety, equipment, training, competition and organizing the 100-way world record."

2011 Bill Wood, D-9085—
"For acting as a true worldwide ambassador of skydiving as both a demonstration jumper and leader of the Parachutists Over Phorty Society, and for earning an international reputation as a traveling good-vibes skydiver."

2011 Jeff Steinkamp, A-3451—
"For nearly four decades of service to the competition community as a nationally rated judge and to the accuracy community in particular as an innovator of accuracy events and scoring systems."

2012 Perry Stevens, B-106—
"D-51, is recognized for Meritorious Achievement for his reserve-static-line invention, which has saved many skydivers with quick, reliable openings."

2013 Pat Works, D-1813—
"For over 50-years of contribution as a teacher, innovator, author, competitor - and for encouraging and inspiring countless skydivers to advance their skills and find joy in the blue sky."

2014 Roger Ponce de Leon, D-5104—
"For forty-six years, Roger "Ponce" has advanced skydiving as a leader and participant on numerous large formation world records, and promoted skydiving as a coach and load organizer throughout the world."

8-1 SERVICE AWARDS

2015 Carol Clay, D-3347—
"For more than 45 years of skydiving and inspiring jumpers around the world as a competitor, record holder and organizer: for mentoring new skydivers and serving as a role model to women entering the sport."

2015 Kate Cooper-Jensen, D-7333—
"For advancing big-way formation skydiving throughout the U.S. and abroad as an organizer and multiple world-record holder. Over the decades, Kate has mentored countless skydivers and been a role model to women skydivers around the world."

2015 Alicia Moorehead, D-9821—
"For volunteering for 28 years for the Parachutists Over Phorty Society, serving as USA TopPOP #9, World TopPOP #2 and POPS records administrator: for spreading goodwill around the globe and encouraging others to skydive in their later years."

2016 Bill Jones, D-924—
"For more than six decades of sharing his expertise in both the civilian and military skydiving worlds as a visionary, pioneer, innovator, competitor, coach, master parachute rigger, aircraft mechanic, mentor, drop zone owner and multiple world record holder."

2016 Robert J Laidlaw, D-32405—
"For more than 40 years of advancing training methods that have produced professional, highly skilled skydiving coaches and instructors; for developing Skydive University; and for sharing that knowledge with USPA for our student and instructional rating programs."

2017 Chuck Karcher, D-9603—
"For his instrumental role in testing and developing the tandem skydiving system, as well as sport parachute designs; for his groundbreaking work in freefall photography and videography; and for helping to pioneer sit-flying."

2017 Ben L. Crowell (*posthumously*), D-15715—
"For developing tandem equipment modifications to enable people with disabilities to experience tandem skydiving and for extensively sharing his expertise to both civilian and military rigging and parachuting."

2017 Mark C Baur, D-6108—
"For his contributions and innovations in parachute rigging and equipment, and for many years of teaching and mentoring riggers and skydiving instructors to improve the skill levels of all involved."

2018 Greg Windmiller, D-20004—
"For representing true sportsmanship in the U.S. and international skydiving communities as a U.S. Army Golden Knight, multiple national champion, world record holder and U.S. Team leader and for promoting safety as an instructor and canopy piloting coach."

2018 Mike Horan, D-881—
"For his instrumental role in preserving the history of skydiving and USPA by serving as the organization's archivist, assembling more than a century of the sport's history and sharing the information freely with USPA and the skydiving community."

2018 Mary Bauer, D-8123 and Bob Stumm, D-3604—
"For helping grow the sport by instructing and mentoring countless students, dedicating themselves to running a club drop zone, fostering a culture of safety both at their home DZ and beyond and being pillars in the Wisconsin skydiving community for decades."

2019 Bryan Burke, D-8866—
"For three decades of helping improve the safety of the sport by analyzing and sharing accident data and developing procedures for landing and airspace safety; and for serving as meet director for countless national and international competitions."

2019 Thomas Jenkins (*posthumously*), D-7707—
"For 39 years of dedicated service to skydiving as an instructor, competitor, judge, organizer, mentor and motivator; and for showing a steadfast commitment to skydivers around the world by developing safe practices and leading by example."

2019 Kirk Knight, D-6709—
"For over 40 years of dedication to skydiving, both military and civilian, as an international judge, competitor and role model, and for his immense contributions to the International Skydiving Museum and Hall of Fame."

2020 Kurt Gaebel, D-18635—
"For connecting and inspiring formation skydivers in the U.S. and worldwide by hosting competitions, providing news coverage and promoting the sport through the National Skydiving League for 20-plus years."

2020 Yong Chisholm —
"For being a pioneering female skydiver, instructional rating holder and competitor and for having a standout career marked by selflessness, caring, humility, enormous skill and a commitment to excellence."

2021 Bram Clement, D-14597—
"For establishing and operating Skydive Ratings, a full-time instructional rating school that offers friendly, structured, professional courses for all USPA ratings and has qualified thousands of highly proficient instructors."

2021 Joannie Murphy, C-9720—
"For 50 years dedicated to skydiving, in which she set records, pioneered safety standards, preserved the sport's history and, above all, kept skydiving available to the world in Zephyrhills, Florida."

2021 Morris "Moe" Viletto, D-5853—
"For 50 years of rigging innovation, stunt work, technical sewing and mentorship of riggers and jumpers, and for being the architect and pioneer of equipment and techniques for the advancement of the sport through a passionate approach toward improvement, precision and safety."

2022 Daniel L. Brodsky-Chenfeld D-8424—
"For inspiring fellow skydivers and the general public as a multi-time world and national champion competitor, record organizer, mentor, DZ manager, educator, motivational speaker and author, and for generously sharing his time, advocating for safety and being one of the foremost ambassadors of the sport for more than 40 years."

SERVICE AWARDS | 8-1

2022 JaNette Lefkowitz C-35536—
"For raising the level of skydiving worldwide as a top-class competitor, prolific coach, developer of educational materials and organizer of high-profile events, and for working tirelessly to create a strong community for both men and women in the sport."

2022 Cheryl Stearns D-4020—
"For advancing the image of skydiving across the globe as the first female member of the U.S. Army Golden Knights; her unparalleled skill as a three-time world military women's style and accuracy champion, two-time civilian world champion and multiple world record holder; and for her professionalism and boundless enthusiasm as an exhibition jumper during her 40-plus years of skydiving and more than 21,000 jumps."

8-1: SERVICE AWARDS

8-1.6: RECIPIENTS OF THE USPA REGIONAL ACHIEVEMENT AWARD

2014 *(Southern)* **James L. Horak, D-9524**
"For dedicating 34 years to the sport of skydiving. As an instructor, examiner, PRO jumper and rigger, Jim introduced many new individuals to the sport, as well as advanced many through the sport. His love for aviation was reflected in his many ratings and awards involving numerous aeronautical activities."

2014 *(Northeast)* **Gary G. Pond, D-6969—**
"For unselfish dedication to our Sport, the Massachusetts Sport Parachute Club, Jumptown and the New England Region. Father, Mentor. Example."

2014 *(Western)* **Eike H. Hohenadl, D-11851—**
"A Gentleman in every respect! Eike had thousands of jumps under his belt and held numerous U.S. Parachute Association licenses and ratings, including safety and training advisor. He was loved by everyone who knew him and will be sorely missed."

2014 *(Eastern)* **Michael E. Schultz, D-1180—**
"In recognition of nearly a half-century of outstanding and varied contributions to sport parachuting in areas of leadership, instruction, drop-zone and aircraft operations, regional and national competition and research and development."

2014 *(Southwest)* **Radoslav Mulik, D-12537—**
"Who founded the Stefan Banic Parachute Foundation, named for the designer of emergency parachutes that saved many aviators' lives in World War I. Since 1977, Mulik has made tireless efforts to promote the foundation and present gold medals to those who have made outstanding contributions to sport parachuting."

2015 *(Foreign)* **Gary Lincoln-Hope, D-33675—**
"For his outstanding efforts in bringing the sport of skydiving to Kenya, introducing newcomers to the sport and developing activities for experienced skydivers; he transformed skydiving in Kenya from a handful of enthusiasts to a full-fledged sport."

2015 *(Northeast)* **Fran Strimenos, D-4957—**
"For promoting skydiving throughout the New England Region with a passion for the sport and love of the skydiving community. Over the years, Fran's generosity has shown through her words and actions. She has quietly moved skydiving forward while setting an example for all skydivers, and especially women, in the Northeast to follow."

2015 *(Mid-Atlantic)* **Edward Ristaino, D-3645—**
"For skillfully and selflessly piloting a hot-air balloon in extremely threatening weather, putting the safety of his passengers ahead of his own; for nobly sacrificing his own life to save others, gracefully handling unusually challenging circumstances."

2016 *(Mountain)* **Brianne M. Thompson, D-30035—**
"For her inspiration, motivation and tireless attention to include and train first-time jumpers, students and veterans with challenges and making a way for them to comfortably enter into the sport of skydiving."

2016 *(North Central)* **Donald J. Solberg, D-4270—**
"For being a true skydiving pioneer who embodies the indomitable spirit, relentless passion, and unshakeable steadfastness in working to establish and grow the sport of skydiving in North Dakota."

2016 *(Northeast)* **Kenneth D. Newman, D-19754—**
"For their partnership in their advocacy and outstanding dedication in encouraging safe teaching for students and the skydiving sport."

2016 *(Foreign)* **David Clark Cohen, D-33786—**
"For his advocacy and efforts in removing the ban on skydiving in Costa Rica and for inspiring an entire country and a whole new generation of Central American skydivers."

2016 *(Mid-Atlantic)* **Randy K. Hamberlin, D-21552—**
"For his extreme friendliness, professionalism and his efforts at making skydiving the best and safest sport throughout the community."

2016 *(Northeast)* **Randy Sherman, D-20213—**
"For their partnership in their advocacy and outstanding dedication in encouraging safe teaching for students and the skydiving sport."

2017 *(North Central)* **Miles J. Hubbard, D-5808—**
"For 44 years of continuous jumping at least once a month; for helping bring the AFF program to the Midwest; for mentoring both students and instructors throughout the region; and for his unwavering love of the sport of skydiving."

2017 *(Southern)* **Harry Ervin, D-14192—**
"For his 50-plus years of dedication to the sport of skydiving as a participant, instructor, mentor and rigger in and around Tennessee."

2017 *(Gulf)* **Dewayne A. Bruette, D-3136—**
"For more than 50 years of dedication to skydiving, including participating in numerous records, volunteering to fund and perform demonstration jumps for children and veterans and showing the public a positive image of the sport."

2017 *(Western)* **Doug and Marilyn Wuest, D-6883 and D-6504—**
"For 30 years of sharing the fun and camaraderie of skydiving by organizing the well-known Wuest Ways formation skydives at Skydive Perris and Skydive Elsinore and by mentoring countless new skydivers as they progress in the sport."

2018 *(Mid-Atlantic)* **Kevin D. Carver, D-18229—**
"For more than 20 years of training and mentoring students, instructors and DZ staff, creating a community of dedicated skydiving professionals and promoting safety and a love of the sport among both civilian and military jumpers in North Carolina and the entire region."

SERVICE AWARDS 8-1

2018 *(Southeast)* **Brandon D. Radcliff, D-31962—**
"For his tireless dedication to fostering a cooperative learning environment that is both safe and fun with high standards of professionalism and creating continuing education that is accessible to all skydivers."

2018 *(Foreign)* **Marc S. DeTrano, D-22324—**
"For keeping skydiving alive in Costa Rica, enforcing safety standards, co-founding the first USPA DZ in the country and being instrumental in getting Civil Aviation to recognize skydiving as a safe and organized activity."

2018 *(Pacific)* **Stephen R. Rafferty, D-12337—**
"For more than three decades as an instructor and mentor, introducing more than 15,000 students to the sport, sharing his knowledge and passion and inspiring everyone lucky enough to learn from him."

2019 *(Northwest)* **John T. Mitchell, D-6462—**
"For being a mainstay in the Northwest skydiving community for more than 40 years as an instructor, organizer, fun jumper and mentor; for providing insight to jump pilots as an air traffic controller; and for organizing the annual Leap for Lupus charity boogie."

2019 *(Pacific)* **John M. Dobleman, D-7790—**
"For nearly four decades of promoting the sport in the Pacific region as a load organizer, fun jumper and world record holder, always supporting safe skydiving and fostering a fun and welcoming drop zone environment for jumpers of all skill levels."

2019 *(Northeast)* **Logan R. Donovan, D-31751—**
"For aiding in the advancement of canopy piloting in the Eastern region, providing guidance on canopy progression and flight to newer jumpers and organizing local competitions; and for developing the scoring system for canopy piloting competitions that is used both locally and internationally."

2019 *(Mid-Atlantic)* **James E. Burriss, D-9540—**
"For more than 40 years of dedication to skydivers in the Mid-Atlantic region as an instructor, pilot, rigger, Safety & Training Advisor and mentor, always maintaining the highest standards of safety and professionalism and welcoming countless people into the sport."

2019 *(Eastern)* **Marc P. Nadeau, D-14782—**
"For more than 40 years of service to skydivers in the Eastern region as a rigging and skydiving instructor, drop zone owner and Safety & Training Advisor, providing wisdom, insight and expertise to countless skydivers over the years."

2020 *(Northeast)* **Matthew F. Madden, D-30212—**
"For supporting and advising instructors in the New England Region and for enhancing safety and professionalism in the USPA instructional rating program."

2020 *(Central)* **Lee Baney, D-10487—**
For dedication to the sport of skydiving for 50 years, including as an instructor and demonstration jumper, and for being inspirational to countless new skydivers as they advance their skills."

2020 *(Mid-Atlantic)* **Steven W. Hetrick, D-8585—**
"For 38 years of promoting safety to students and licensed skydivers as an instructor, instructor examiner, Safety and Training Advisor and mentor."

2021 *(Pacific)* **Benjamin T. Devine, D-36111—**
"For supporting skydiving in the Pacific Islands and creating the Save Dillingham Airfield organization, leading the fight to keep one of the most popular skydiving destinations open."

2021 *(Mountain)* **Dustin J. White, D-35877—**
"For his attention to detail and awareness while acting as a tandem instructor, which resulted in saving the life of an AFF student by catching a critical gear error before the student exited."

2021 *(Southern)* **Elizabeth Young D-35348—**
"For tireless dedication to the sport and the instruction and mentorship of students, specifically through the sisters in Skydiving program, and for supporting women in skydiving and funding women's cancer research in the Southern region."

2021 *(Northeast)* **Douglas Hendrix, D-34552—**
"For his dedication and leadership in the New England Region as a Safety and Training Advisor, instructor, competitor, record-setter and judge, and for his innovative approaches to promoting safety within the sport."

2021 *(Northeast)* **Robert J. Goldman, D-10269—**
"For outstanding dedication, innovation and leadership in the New England Region's fun-jumping community, and for his unwavering motivation to help skydivers become better flyers and team players."

8-2: ACHIEVEMENT AWARDS

A. ACHIEVEMENT AWARDS FOR JUMP EXPERIENCE

1. These two types of freefall awards are intended to provide a special kind of recognition to those United States Parachute Association members who have accumulated significant levels of experience in both number of freefall skydives and amount of freefall time.
2. USPA proudly recognizes those members.

B. CUMULATIVE JUMPS AND FREEFALL TIME

1. Expert Wings are awarded for freefall jumps in 1,000-jump increments.
2. Freefall Badges are awarded for freefall time in 12-hour increments.

C. GENERAL REQUIREMENTS

1. To be eligible for any of these awards a person must:
    a. have completed the required number of freefall skydives or accumulated the required amount of freefall time
    b. have made each jump being presented as qualification in compliance with the USPA BSRs
    c. be a current USPA member at the time of application for the award
    d. be the holder of a current USPA C license or its accepted foreign equivalent
    e. have no record of a BSR violation on file with USPA
    f. have met the requirements of the previous award
2. Logging:
    a. The applicant must present logbook evidence of the required number of freefall skydives or amount of freefall time for which the award is being made.
    b. For jumps made after December 31, 1987, each jump must be listed as a separate entry and contain at least:
        (1) the jump number
        (2) date
        (3) location
        (4) exit altitude
        (5) freefall length
        (6) type of jump (formation skydiving, accuracy, jumpmaster, photography, etc.)
        (7) signatures of witnessing jumpers or pilots (encouraged but not required)
3. Verification of the required number of freefall skydives or freefall time and other requirements will be made by:
    a. a USPA Regional or National Director
    b. a USPA administrative officer
    c. in case of hardship or extraordinary conditions, other persons deemed acceptable to USPA Headquarters or the USPA Board of Directors
4. The verifying official will submit to USPA Headquarters a completed application verifying that the applicant has met all requirements.
5. Upon receipt of the completed application, USPA Headquarters will issue the award as directed by the verifying official.
6. All awards will be issued by USPA Headquarters in the order the qualified application is received.
7. In the case of special circumstances or hardships, waiver of these requirements and procedures may be applied for through the USPA Board of Directors.

D. PRESENTATION

1. Because of the particular significance of the milestone represented by the award of Expert Wings and Freefall Badges, it is in the best interest of the United States Parachute Association and the sport of skydiving that these awards be presented to the recipient with appropriate ceremony and recognition.
2. Except when not practical, these awards should be presented by a USPA National or Regional Director, to whom the award will normally be entrusted before presentation.
3. It is also recommended and urged that all recipients of Expert Wings and Badges be publicized as widely as possible through skydiving publications and local news media.
4. Whenever possible, a brief report and photograph of the presentation should be emailed to communications@uspa.org or mailed to:

Editor
Parachutist
5401 Southpoint Centre Blvd.
Fredericksburg, VA 22407

8-3: PERFORMANCE AWARDS

A. AWARDS FOR SKYDIVING SKILL

The performance awards program is an international awards program of the United States Parachute Association.

1. Canopy formation performance awards
    a. These awards recognize each applicant's progression towards higher levels of canopy control, maneuverability, and proficiency.
    b. In receiving and exhibiting these awards, the recipient agrees to exercise good judgment and wisdom in promoting safe canopy relative work among his or her peers, among those less experienced than himself or herself, and toward observers of the sport.

B. PREREQUISITES

1. Each applicant must be either a current USPA member or a member of another FAI Aero Club.
2. Jumps used to qualify for these awards are to comply with the USPA Basic Safety Requirements.

C. CANOPY AWARD CATEGORIES

1. The 4-Stack Award is available for building a canopy formation of four or more canopies.
2. The CCR (Canopy Crest Recipient) or 8-Stack Award is available for building a canopy formation of eight or more canopies.
3. The CCS (Canopy Crest Solo) Award is available for entering eighth or later in a complete eight-canopy or larger formation.
4. Night versions of each of these awards are available for those who have completed these formations at night.

D. QUALIFICATIONS

1. The formations completed for this award may come from the USPA Skydiver's Competition Manual or may be other recognizable formations.
2. All formations must be planned in advance.
3. All participants must be in position and on grips for the formation to be considered complete.
4. The completed formation must be held for a minimum of ten seconds.

E. APPLICATION

Send the completed application to:

USPA Headquarters
5401 Southpoint Centre Blvd.
Fredericksburg, VA 22407

or fax to (540) 604-9741 and include:

1. the applicant's name as it is to appear on official certificates
2. the location of the jump: city, state, country (if not USA)
3. diagram or name of each completed formation
4. a list of the other participants (signatures not required)
5. the date of the jump that qualified the applicant for the award
6. the holding time for the formation
7. the award applied for
8. the appropriate fee for the award and any additional materials requested, such as decals, pins, or additional certificates

8-4: MEMBERSHIP TENURE CERTIFICATES

A. TENURE AWARDS

1. Membership tenure certificates are issued to acknowledge support of skydiving through membership in USPA for significant periods of time.
2. USPA membership tenure certificates are issued at the completion of ten years of accumulated membership and at each five years thereafter.

B. QUALIFICATIONS

1. Computation of tenure:
   a. The ten-year certificate is issued when a full ten years of membership has been accumulated.
   b. In other words, the certificate is issued at the end of the tenth year of membership.
   c. Lapses in membership are subtracted from the total time of membership.
2. Certificates are issued upon request either by submitting the information online through the USPA website, or by contacting the membership department at USPA Headquarters.

8-5: SPORTSMANSHIP AWARD

A. TED STRONG AWARD FOR EXTRAORDINARY SPORTSMANSHIP

1. Established in 2012 to honor extraordinary sportsmanship displayed by teams or individuals at a USPA National Championships.

2. Description of and criteria for this award are in the Skydiver's Competition Manual.

B. RECIPIENTS OF THE TED STRONG AWARD FOR EXTRAORDINARY SPORTSMANSHIP

2012 Jarrett Martin, D-28900

2014 Team "Spaceland Lite 8"

2018 John "Jack" Berke, D-5195

8-5 | SPORTSMANSHIP AWARD

Section 9

FAA DOCUMENTS

SECTION SUMMARY:

The Federal Aviation Administration (FAA) of the U.S. Department of Transportation has the responsibility for regulating airspace usage in the United States. Concerning skydiving activities, the FAA fulfills this responsibility by specifically regulating certain aspects of skydiving and by relying upon the self-regulation of the participants through the guidelines and recommendations published by USPA.

The FAA's main responsibility is to provide for the safety of air traffic, as well as persons and property on the ground. The FAA does this by certificating pilots, mechanics, air traffic controllers and parachute riggers and by requiring approval data for aircraft and parachutes. The agency has the authority to impose fines and suspend or revoke certificates it has issued. In the case of a skydiving violation, the FAA can fine the pilot, rigger, and the jumpers, as well as suspend or revoke the certificates of pilots and riggers.

The FAA relies upon self policing from within the skydiving community for most training and operational requirements.

IMPORTANT REFERENCE NUMBERS

- FAR Part 61 (excerpts), pilot certification
- FAR Part 65 (excerpts), parachute riggers
- FAR 91 (excerpts), general flight rules pertaining to skydiving operations
- FAR Part 105 (all), skydiving
- FAR Part 119 (excerpts), limits of jump flights
- AC 90-66B, multi-users at uncontrolled airports
- AC 105-2E, sport parachuting
- FAA Air Traffic Bulletins, information for air traffic controllers

WHO NEEDS THIS SECTION?

- jumpers studying for licenses and ratings
- jumpers planning exhibition jumps or jumps off the regular DZ
- parachute riggers and packers
- jump pilots
- drop zone management

9-1: FEDERAL AVIATION REGULATIONS

SUBCHAPTER D—AIRMEN

PART 61—CERTIFICATION: PILOTS, FLIGHT INSTRUCTORS, AND GROUND INSTRUCTORS

SEC. 61.1: APPLICABILITY AND DEFINITIONS

(a) This part prescribes:

  (1) The requirements for issuing pilot, flight instructor, and ground instructor certificates and ratings; the conditions under which those certificates and ratings are necessary; and the privileges and limitations of those certificates and ratings.

  (2) The requirements for issuing pilot, flight instructor, and ground instructor authorizations; the conditions under which those authorizations are necessary; and the privileges and limitations of those authorizations.

  (3) The requirements for issuing pilot, flight instructor, and ground instructor certificates and ratings for persons who have taken courses approved by the Administrator under other parts of this chapter.

SEC. 61.3: REQUIREMENT FOR CERTIFICATES, RATINGS, AND AUTHORIZATIONS

(a) *Required pilot certificate for operating a civil aircraft of the United States.* No person may serve as a required pilot flight crewmember of a civil aircraft of the United States, unless that person:

  (1) Has in the person's physical possession or readily accessible in the aircraft when exercising the privileges of that pilot certificate or authorization—

    (i) A pilot certificate issued under this part and in accordance with § 61.19;

  (2) Has a photo identification that is in that person's physical possession or readily accessible in the aircraft when exercising the privileges of that pilot certificate or authorization.

(c) Medical certificate.

  (1) A person may serve as a required pilot flight crewmember of an aircraft only if that person holds the appropriate medical certificate issued under part 67 of this chapter, or other documentation acceptable to the FAA, that is in that person's physical possession or readily accessible in the aircraft.

    (l) Inspection of certificate. Each person who holds an airman certificate, medical certificate, authorization or license required by this part must present it and their photo identification as described in paragraph (a)(2) of this section for inspection upon a request from:

      (1) The Administrator;

      (2) An authorized representative of the National Transportation Safety Board;

      (3) Any Federal, State, or local law enforcement officer; or

      (4) An authorized representative of the Transportation Security Administration.

SEC. 61.23: MEDICAL CERTIFICATES: REQUIREMENT

(a) Operations requiring a medical certificate.

  (2) Must hold at least a second class medical certificate when exercising:

    (ii) Privileges of a commercial pilot certificate;

SEC. 61.51: PILOT LOGBOOKS

(i) Presentation of required documents.

  (1) Persons must present their pilot certificate, medical certificate, logbook, or any other record required by this part for inspection upon a reasonable request by—

    (i) The Administrator;

    (ii) An authorized representative from the National Transportation Safety Board; or

    (iii) Any Federal, State, or local law enforcement officer.

SEC. 61.56: FLIGHT REVIEW

(c) Except as provided in paragraphs (d), (e), and (g) of this section, no person may act as pilot in command of an aircraft unless, since the beginning of the 24th calendar month before the month in which that pilot acts as pilot in command, that person has—

  (1) Accomplished a flight review given in an aircraft for which that pilot is rated by an authorized instructor and

  (2) A logbook endorsed from an authorized instructor who gave the review certifying that the person has satisfactorily completed the review.

SEC. 61.57: RECENT FLIGHT EXPERIENCE: PILOT IN COMMAND

(a) General experience.

  (1) Except as provided in paragraph (e) of this section, no person may act as a pilot in command of an aircraft carrying passengers or of an aircraft certificated for more than one pilot flight crewmember unless that person has made at least three takeoffs and three landings within the preceding 90 days, and—

    (i) The person acted as the sole manipulator of the flight controls; and

    (ii) The required takeoffs and landings were performed in an aircraft of the same category, class, and type (if a type rating is required), and, if the aircraft to be flown is an airplane with a tailwheel, the takeoffs and landings must have been made to a full stop in an airplane with a tailwheel.

SEC. 61.133: COMMERCIAL PILOT PRIVILEGES AND LIMITATIONS

(a) Privileges —

  (1) General. A person who holds a commercial pilot certificate may act as pilot in command of an aircraft—

    (i) Carrying persons or property for compensation or hire, provided the person is qualified in accordance with this part and with the applicable parts of this chapter that apply to the operation; and

    (ii) For compensation or hire, provided the person is qualified in accordance with this part and with the applicable parts of this chapter that apply to the operation.

FEDERAL AVIATION REGULATIONS 9-1

If you hold	And on the date of examination for your most recent medical certificate you were	And you are conducting an operation requiring	Then your medical certificate expires, for that operation, at the end of the last day of the
(1) A first-class medical certificate	(i) Under age 40	an airline transport pilot certificate for pilot-in-command privileges, or for second-in-command privileges in a flag or supplemental operation in part 121 requiring three or more pilots	12th month after the month of the date of examination shown on the medical certificate
	(ii) Age 40 or older	an airline transport pilot certificate for pilot-in-command privileges, for second-in-command privileges in a flag or supplemental operation in part 121 requiring three or more pilots, or for a pilot flightcrew member in part 121 operations who has reached his or her 60th birthday	6th month after the month of the date of examination shown on the medical certificate
	(iii) Any age	a commercial pilot certificate or an air traffic control tower operator certificate	12th month after the month of the date of examination shown on the medical certificate
	(iv) Under age 40	a recreational pilot certificate, a private pilot certificate, a flight instructor certificate (when acting as pilot in command or a required pilot flight crewmember in operations other than glider or balloon), a student pilot certificate, or a sport pilot certificate (when not using a U.S. driver's license as medical qualification)	60th month after the month of the date of examination shown on the medical certificate
	(v) Age 40 or older	a recreational pilot certificate, a private pilot certificate, a flight instructor certificate (when acting as pilot in command or a required pilot flight crewmember in operations other than glider or balloon), a student pilot certificate, or a sport pilot certificate (when not using a U.S. driver's license as medical qualification)	24th month after the month of the date of examination shown on the medical certificate
(2) A second-class medical certificate	(i) Any age	an airline transport pilot certificate for second-in-command privileges (other than the operations specified in paragraph (d)(1) of this section), a commercial pilot certificate, or an air traffic control tower operator certificate	12th month after the month of the date of examination shown on the medical certificate
	(ii) Under age 40	a recreational pilot certificate, a private pilot certificate, a flight instructor certificate (when acting as pilot in command or a required pilot flight crewmember in operations other than glider or balloon), a student pilot certificate, or a sport pilot certificate (when not using a U.S. driver's license as medical qualification)	60th month after the month of the date of examination shown on the medical certificate
	(iii) Age 40 or older	a recreational pilot certificate, a private pilot certificate, a flight instructor certificate (when acting as pilot in command or a required pilot flight crewmember in operations other than glider or balloon), a student pilot certificate, or a sport pilot certificate (when not using a U.S. driver's license as medical qualification)	24th month after the month of the date of examination shown on the medical certificate
(3) A third-class medical certificate	(i) Under age 40	a recreational pilot certificate, a private pilot certificate, a flight instructor certificate (when acting as pilot in command or a required pilot flight crewmember in operations other than glider or balloon), a student pilot certificate, or a sport pilot certificate (when not using a U.S. driver's license as medical qualification)	60th month after the month of the date of examination shown on the medical certificate
	(ii) Age 40 or older	a recreational pilot certificate, a private pilot certificate, a flight instructor certificate (when acting as pilot in command or a required pilot flight crewmember in operations other than glider or balloon), a student pilot certificate, or a sport pilot certificate (when not using a U.S. driver's license as medical qualification)	24th month after the month of the date of examination shown on the medical certificate

9-1 FEDERAL AVIATION REGULATIONS

PART 65—CERTIFICATION: AIRMEN OTHER THAN FLIGHT CREWMEMBERS

SEC. 65.1: APPLICABILITY

This part prescribes the requirements for issuing the following certificates and associated ratings and the general operating rules for the holders of those certificates and ratings:

(a) Air-traffic control-tower operators.

(b) Aircraft dispatchers.

(c) Mechanics.

(d) Repairmen.

(e) Parachute riggers.

SEC. 65.11: APPLICATION AND ISSUE

(a) Application for a certificate and appropriate class rating, or for an additional rating, under this part must be made on a form and in a manner prescribed by the Administrator. Each person who applies for airmen certification services to be administered outside the United States or for any certificate or rating issued under this part must show evidence that the fee prescribed in appendix A of part 187 of this chapter has been paid.

(b) An applicant who meets the requirements of this part is entitled to an appropriate certificate and rating.

(c) Unless authorized by the Administrator, a person whose air traffic control tower operator, mechanic, or parachute rigger certificate is suspended may not apply for any rating to be added to that certificate during the period of suspension.

(d) Unless the order of revocation provides otherwise—

(1) A person whose air traffic control tower operator, aircraft dispatcher, or parachute rigger certificate is revoked may not apply for the same kind of certificate for 1 year after the date of revocation; and

(2) A person whose mechanic or repairman certificate is revoked may not apply for either of those kinds of certificates for 1 year after the date of revocation.

SEC. 65.12: OFFENSES INVOLVING ALCOHOL OR DRUGS

(a) A conviction for the violation of any Federal or state statute relating to the growing, processing, manufacture, sale, disposition, possession, transportation, or importation of narcotic drugs, marihuana, or depressant or stimulant drugs or substances is grounds for—

(1) Denial of an application for any certificate or rating issued under this part for a period of up to 1 year after the date of final conviction; or

(2) Suspension or revocation of any certificate or rating issued under this part.

(b) The commission of an act prohibited by § 91.19(a) of this chapter is grounds for—

(1) Denial of an application for a certificate or rating issued under this part for a period of up to 1 year after the date of that act; or

(2) Suspension or revocation of any certificate or rating issued under this part.

SEC. 65.15: DURATION OF CERTIFICATES

(a) Except for repairman certificates, a certificate or rating issued under this part is effective until it is surrendered, suspended, or revoked.

(b) Unless it is sooner surrendered, suspended, or revoked, a repairman certificate is effective until the holder is relieved from the duties for which the holder was employed and certificated.

(c) The holder of a certificate issued under this part that is suspended, revoked, or no longer effective shall return it to the Administrator.

(d) Except for temporary certificates issued under § 65.13, the holder of a paper certificate issued under this part may not exercise the privileges of that certificate after March 31, 2013.

SEC. 65.16: CHANGE OF NAME: REPLACEMENT OF LOST OR DESTROYED CERTIFICATE

(a) An application for a change of name on a certificate issued under this part must be accompanied by the applicant's current certificate and the marriage license, court order, or other document verifying the change. The documents are returned to the applicant after inspection.

(b) An application for a replacement of a lost or destroyed certificate is made by letter to the Department of Transportation, Federal Aviation Administration, Airman Certification Branch, Post Office Box 25082, Oklahoma City, OK 73125. The letter must—

(1) Contain the name in which the certificate was issued, the permanent mailing address (including zip code), social security number (if any), and date and place of birth of the certificate holder, and any available information regarding the grade, number, and date of issue of the certificate, and the ratings on it; and

(2) Be accompanied by a check or money order for $2, payable to the Federal Aviation Administration.

(c) An application for a replacement of a lost or destroyed medical certificate is made by letter to the Department of Transportation, Federal Aviation Administration, Aerospace Medical Certification Division, Post Office Box 26200, Oklahoma City, OK 73125, accompanied by a check or money order for $2.00.

(d) A person whose certificate issued under this part or medical certificate, or both, has been lost may obtain a telegram from the FAA confirming that it was issued. The telegram may be carried as a certificate for a period not to exceed 60 days pending his receiving a duplicate certificate under paragraph (b) or (c) of this section, unless he has been notified that the certificate has been suspended or revoked. The request for such a telegram may be made by prepaid telegram, stating the date upon which a duplicate certificate was requested, or including the request for a duplicate and a money order for the necessary amount. The request for a telegraphic certificate should be sent to the office prescribed in paragraph (b) or (c) of this section, as appropriate. However, a request for both at the same time should be sent to the office prescribed in paragraph (b) of this section.

SEC. 65.17: TESTS: GENERAL PROCEDURE

(a) Tests prescribed by or under this part are given at times and places, and by persons, designated by the Administrator.

(b) The minimum passing grade for each test is 70 percent.

SEC. 65.18: WRITTEN TESTS: CHEATING OR OTHER UNAUTHORIZED CONDUCT

(a) Except as authorized by the Administrator, no person may—

(1) Copy, or intentionally remove, a written test under this part;

(2) Give to another, or receive from another, any part or copy of that test;

(3) Give help on that test to, or receive help on that test from, any person during the period that test is being given;

(4) Take any part of that test in behalf of another person;

(5) Use any material or aid during the period that test is being given; or

(6) Intentionally cause, assist, or participate in any act prohibited by this paragraph.

(b) No person who commits an act prohibited by paragraph (a) of this section is eligible for any airman or ground instructor certificate or rating under this chapter for a period of 1 year after the date of that act. In addition, the commission of that act is a basis for suspending or revoking any airman or ground instructor certificate or rating held by that person.

SEC. 65.19: RETESTING AFTER FAILURE

An applicant for a written, oral, or practical test for a certificate and rating, or for an additional rating under this part, may apply for retesting—

(a) After 30 days after the date the applicant failed the test; or

(b) Before the 30 days have expired if the applicant presents a signed statement from an airman holding the certificate and rating sought by the applicant, certifying that the airman has given the applicant additional instruction in each of the subjects failed and that the airman considers the applicant ready for retesting.

SEC. 65.20: APPLICATIONS, CERTIFICATES, LOGBOOKS, REPORTS, AND RECORDS: FALSIFICATION, REPRODUCTION, OR ALTERATION

(a) No person may make or cause to be made—

(1) Any fraudulent or intentionally false statement on any application for a certificate or rating under this part;

(2) Any fraudulent or intentionally false entry in any logbook, record, or report that is required to be kept, made, or used, to show compliance with any requirement for any certificate or rating under this part;

(3) Any reproduction, for fraudulent purpose, of any certificate or rating under this part; or

(4) Any alteration of any certificate or rating under this part.

(b) The commission by any person of an act prohibited under paragraph (a) of this section is a basis for suspending or revoking any airman or ground instructor certificate or rating held by that person.

SEC. 65.21: CHANGE OF ADDRESS

Within 30 days after any change in his permanent mailing address, the holder of a certificate issued under this part shall notify the Department of Transportation, Federal Aviation Administration, Airman Certification Branch, Post Office Box 25082, Oklahoma City, OK 73125, in writing, of his new address.

SEC. 65.111: CERTIFICATE REQUIRED

(a) No person may pack, maintain, or alter any personnel-carrying parachute intended for emergency use in connection with civil aircraft of the United States (including the reserve parachute of a dual parachute system to be used for intentional parachute jumping) unless that person holds an appropriate current certificate and type rating issued under this subpart and complies with §§ 65.127 through 65.133.

(b) No person may pack any main parachute of a dual-parachute system to be used for intentional parachute jumping in connection with civil aircraft of the United States unless that person—

(1) Has an appropriate current certificate issued under this subpart;

(2) Is under the supervision of a current certificated parachute rigger;

(3) Is the person making the next parachute jump with that parachute in accordance with § 105.43(a) of this chapter; or

(4) Is the parachutist in command making the next parachute jump with that parachute in a tandem parachute operation conducted under § 105.45(b)(1) of this chapter.

(c) No person may maintain or alter any main parachute of a dual-parachute system to be used for intentional parachute jumping in connection with civil aircraft of the United States unless that person—

(1) Has an appropriate current certificate issued under this subpart; or

(2) Is under the supervision of a current certificated parachute rigger;

(d) Each person who holds a parachute rigger certificate shall present it for inspection upon the request of the Administrator or an authorized representative of the National Transportation Safety Board, or of any Federal, State, or local law enforcement officer.

(e) The following parachute rigger certificates are issued under this part:

(1) Senior parachute rigger.

(2) Master parachute rigger.

(f) Sections 65.127 through 65.133 do not apply to parachutes packed, maintained, or altered for the use of the armed forces.

SEC. 65.113: ELIGIBILITY REQUIREMENTS: GENERAL

(a) To be eligible for a parachute rigger certificate, a person must—

(1) Be at least 18 years of age;

(2) Be able to read, write, speak, and understand the English language, or, in the case of a citizen of Puerto Rico, or a person who is employed outside of the United States by a U.S. air carrier, and who does not meet this requirement, be issued a certificate that is valid only in Puerto Rico or while he is employed outside of the United States by that air carrier, as the case may be; and

(3) Comply with the sections of this subpart that apply to the certificate and type rating he seeks.

(b) Except for a master parachute rigger certificate, a parachute rigger certificate that was issued before, and was valid on, October 31, 1962, is equal to a senior parachute rigger certificate, and may be exchanged for such a corresponding certificate.

SEC. 65.115 SENIOR PARACHUTE RIGGER CERTIFICATE: EXPERIENCE, KNOWLEDGE, AND SKILL REQUIREMENTS

Except as provided in § 65.117, an applicant for a senior parachute rigger certificate must—

(a) Present evidence satisfactory to the Administrator that he has packed at

9-1 FEDERAL AVIATION REGULATIONS

least 20 parachutes of each type for which he seeks a rating, in accordance with the manufacturer's instructions and under the supervision of a certificated parachute rigger holding a rating for that type or a person holding an appropriate military rating;

(b) Pass a written test, with respect to parachutes in common use, on—

   (1) Their construction, packing, and maintenance;
   (2) The manufacturer's instructions;
   (3) The regulations of this subpart; and

(c) Pass an oral and practical test showing his ability to pack and maintain at least one type of parachute in common use, appropriate to the type rating he seeks.

SEC. 65.117: MILITARY RIGGERS OR FORMER MILITARY RIGGERS: SPECIAL CERTIFICATION RULE

In place of the procedure in § 65.115, an applicant for a senior parachute rigger certificate is entitled to it if he passes a written test on the regulations of this subpart and presents satisfactory documentary evidence that he—

(a) Is a member or civilian employee of an Armed Force of the United States, is a civilian employee of a regular armed force of a foreign country, or has, within the 12 months before he applies, been honorably discharged or released from any status covered by this paragraph;

(b) Is serving, or has served within the 12 months before he applies, as a parachute rigger for such an Armed Force; and

(c) Has the experience required by § 65.115(a).

SEC. 65.119: MASTER PARACHUTE RIGGER CERTIFICATE: EXPERIENCE, KNOWLEDGE, AND SKILL REQUIREMENTS.

An applicant for a master parachute rigger certificate must meet the following requirements:

(a) Present evidence satisfactory to the Administrator that he has had at least 3 years of experience as a parachute rigger and has satisfactorily packed at least 100 parachutes of each of two types in common use, in accordance with the manufacturer's instructions—

   (1) While a certificated and appropriately rated senior parachute rigger; or
   (2) While under the supervision of a certificated and appropriately rated parachute rigger or a person holding appropriate military ratings.

An applicant may combine experience specified in paragraphs

(a) (1) and (2) of this section to meet the requirements of this paragraph.

(b) If the applicant is not the holder of a senior parachute rigger certificate, pass a written test, with respect to parachutes in common use, on—

   (1) Their construction, packing, and maintenance;
   (2) The manufacturer's instructions; and
   (3) The regulations of this subpart.

(c) Pass an oral and practical test showing his ability to pack and maintain two types of parachutes in common use, appropriate to the type ratings he seeks.

SEC. 65.121: TYPE RATINGS

(a) The following type ratings are issued under this subpart:

   (1) Seat
   (2) Back
   (3) Chest
   (4) Lap

(b) The holder of a senior parachute rigger certificate who qualifies for a master parachute rigger certificate is entitled to have placed on his master parachute rigger certificate the ratings that were on his senior parachute rigger certificate.

SEC. 65.123: ADDITIONAL TYPE RATINGS: REQUIREMENTS

A certificated parachute rigger who applies for an additional type rating must—

(a) Present evidence satisfactory to the Administrator that he has packed at least 20 parachutes of the type for which he seeks a rating, in accordance with the manufacturer's instructions and under the supervision of a certificated parachute rigger holding a rating for that type or a person holding an appropriate military rating; and

(b) Pass a practical test, to the satisfaction of the Administrator, showing his ability to pack and maintain the type of parachute for which he seeks a rating.

SEC. 65.125: CERTIFICATES: PRIVILEGES

(a) A certificated senior parachute rigger may—

   (1) Pack or maintain (except for major repair) any type of parachute for which he is rated; and
   (2) Supervise other persons in packing any type of parachute for which that person is rated in accordance with § 105.43(a) or § 105.45(b)(1) of this chapter.

(b) A certificated master parachute rigger may—

   (1) Pack, maintain, or alter any type of parachute for which he is rated; and
   (2) Supervise other persons in packing, maintaining, or altering any type of parachute for which the certificated parachute rigger is rated in accordance with § 105.43(a) or § 105.45(b)(1) of this chapter.

(c) A certificated parachute rigger need not comply with §§ 65.127 through 65.133 (relating to facilities, equipment, performance standards, records, recent experience, and seal) in packing, maintaining, or altering (if authorized) the main parachute of a dual parachute pack to be used for intentional jumping.

SEC. 65.127: FACILITIES AND EQUIPMENT

No certificated parachute rigger may exercise the privileges of his certificate unless he has at least the following facilities and equipment available to him:

(a) A smooth top table at least three feet wide by 40 feet long
(b) Suitable housing that is adequately heated, lighted, and ventilated for drying and airing parachutes
(c) Enough packing tools and other equipment to pack and maintain the types of parachutes that he services
(d) Adequate housing facilities to perform his duties and to protect his tools and equipment

SEC. 65.129 PERFORMANCE STANDARDS

No certificated parachute rigger may—
(a) Pack, maintain, or alter any parachute unless he is rated for that type;
(b) Pack a parachute that is not safe for emergency use;
(c) Pack a parachute that has not been thoroughly dried and aired;
(d) Alter a parachute in a manner that is not specifically authorized by the Administrator or the manufacturer;

(e) Pack, maintain, or alter a parachute in any manner that deviates from procedures approved by the Administrator or the manufacturer of the parachute; or

(f) Exercise the privileges of his certificate and type rating unless he understands the current manufacturer's instructions for the operation involved and has—

  (1) Performed duties under his certificate for at least 90 days within the preceding 12 months; or

  (2) Shown the Administrator that he is able to perform those duties.

SEC. 65.131: RECORDS

(a) Each certificated parachute rigger shall keep a record of the packing, maintenance, and alteration of parachutes performed or supervised by him. He shall keep in that record, with respect to each parachute worked on, a statement of—

  (1) Its type and make;

  (2) Its serial number;

  (3) The name and address of its owner;

  (4) The kind and extent of the work performed;

  (5) The date when and place where the work was performed; and

  (6) The results of any drop tests made with it.

(b) Each person who makes a record under paragraph (a) of this section shall keep it for at least 2 years after the date it is made.

(c) Each certificated parachute rigger who packs a parachute shall write, on the parachute packing record attached to the parachute, the date and place of the packing and a notation of any defects he finds on inspection. He shall sign that record with his name and the number of his certificate.

SEC. 65.133: SEAL

Each certificated parachute rigger must have a seal with an identifying mark prescribed by the Administrator, and a seal press. After packing a parachute he shall seal the pack with his seal in accordance with the manufacturer's recommendation for that type of parachute.

SUBCHAPTER F—AIR TRAFFIC AND GENERAL OPERATING RULES

PART 91—GENERAL OPERATING AND FLIGHT RULES

SEC. 91.1: APPLICABILITY

Source: Docket No. 18334, 54 FR 34292, Aug. 18, 1989, unless otherwise noted.

(a) Except as provided in paragraphs (b) and (c) of this section and Secs. 91.701 and 91.703, this part prescribes rules governing the operation of aircraft (other than moored balloons, kites, unmanned rockets, and unmanned free balloons, which are governed by part 101 of this chapter, and ultralight vehicles operated in accordance with part 103 of this chapter) within the United States, including the waters within 3 nautical miles of the U.S. coast.

(b) Each person operating an aircraft in the airspace overlying the waters between 3 and 12 nautical miles from the coast of the United States shall comply with Secs. 91.1 through 91.21; Secs. 91.101 through 91.143; Secs. 91.151 through 91.159; Secs. 91.167 through 91.193; Sec. 91.203; Sec. 91.205; Secs. 91.209 through 91.217; Sec. 91.221; Secs. 91.303 through 91.319; Sec. 91.323; Sec. 91.605; Sec. 91.609; Secs. 91.703 through 91.715; and 91.903.

(c) This part applies to each person on board an aircraft being operated under this part, unless otherwise specified.

SEC. 91.3: RESPONSIBILITY AND AUTHORITY OF THE PILOT IN COMMAND

(a) The pilot in command of an aircraft is directly responsible for, and is the final authority as to, the operation of that aircraft.

(b) In an in-flight emergency requiring immediate action, the pilot in command may deviate from any rule of this part to the extent required to meet that emergency.

(c) Each pilot in command who deviates from a rule under paragraph (b) of this section shall, upon the request of the Administrator, send a written report of that deviation to the Administrator.

SEC. 91.5: PILOT IN COMMAND OF AIRCRAFT REQUIRING MORE THAN ONE REQUIRED PILOT

No person may operate an aircraft that is type certificated for more than one required pilot flight crewmember unless the pilot in command meets the requirements of Sec. 61.58 of this chapter.

SEC. 91.7: CIVIL AIRCRAFT AIRWORTHINESS

(a) No person may operate a civil aircraft unless it is in an airworthy condition.

(b) The pilot in command of a civil aircraft is responsible for determining whether that aircraft is in condition for safe flight. The pilot in command shall discontinue the flight when unairworthy mechanical, electrical, or structural conditions occur.

SEC. 91.11: PROHIBITION ON INTERFERENCE WITH CREWMEMBERS

No person may assault, threaten, intimidate, or interfere with a crewmember in the performance of the crewmember's duties aboard an aircraft being operated.

SEC. 91.13: CARELESS OR RECKLESS OPERATION

(a) Aircraft operations for the purpose of air navigation. No person may operate an aircraft in a careless or reckless manner so as to endanger the life or property of another.

(b) Aircraft operations other than for the purpose of air navigation. No person may operate an aircraft, other than for the purpose of air navigation, on any part of the surface of an airport used by aircraft for air commerce (including areas used by those aircraft for receiving or discharging persons or cargo), in a careless or reckless manner so as to endanger the life or property of another.

SEC. 91.15 DROPPING OBJECTS

No pilot in command of a civil aircraft may allow any object to be dropped from that aircraft in flight that creates a hazard to persons or property. However, this section does not prohibit the dropping of any object if reasonable precautions are taken to avoid injury or damage to persons or property.

SEC. 91.17: ALCOHOL OR DRUGS

(a) No person may act or attempt to act as a crewmember of a civil aircraft—

9-1 FEDERAL AVIATION REGULATIONS

(1) Within 8 hours after the consumption of any alcoholic beverage;

(2) While under the influence of alcohol;

(3) While using any drug that affects the person's faculties in any way contrary to safety; or

(4) While having .04 percent by weight or more alcohol in the blood.

(b) Except in an emergency, no pilot of a civil aircraft may allow a person who appears to be intoxicated or who demonstrates by manner or physical indications that the individual is under the influence of drugs (except a medical patient under proper care) to be carried in that aircraft.

(c) A crewmember shall do the following:

(1) On request of a law enforcement officer, submit to a test to indicate the percentage by weight of alcohol in the blood, when—

(i) The law enforcement officer is authorized under State or local law to conduct the test or to have the test conducted; and

(ii) The law enforcement officer is requesting submission to the test to investigate a suspected violation of State or local law governing the same or substantially similar conduct prohibited by paragraph (a)(1), (a)(2), or (a)(4) of this section.

(2) Whenever the Administrator has a reasonable basis to believe that a person may have violated paragraph (a)(1), (a)(2), or (a)(4) of this section, that person shall, upon request by the Administrator, furnish the Administrator, or authorize any clinic, hospital, doctor, or other person to release to the Administrator, the results of each test taken within 4 hours after acting or attempting to act as a crewmember that indicates percentage by weight of alcohol in the blood.

(d) Whenever the Administrator has a reasonable basis to believe that a person may have violated paragraph (a)(3) of this section, that person shall, upon request by the Administrator, furnish the Administrator, or authorize any clinic, hospital, doctor, or other person to release to the Administrator, the results of each test taken within 4 hours after acting or attempting to act as a crewmember that indicates the presence of any drugs in the body.

(e) Any test information obtained by the Administrator under paragraph (c) or (d) of this section may be evaluated in determining a person's qualifications for any airman certificate or possible violations of this chapter and may be used as evidence in any legal proceeding under section 602, 609, or 901 of the Federal Aviation Act of 1958.

SEC. 91.19: CARRIAGE OF NARCOTIC DRUGS, MARIHUANA, AND DEPRESSANT OR STIMULANT DRUGS OR SUBSTANCES

(a) Except as provided in paragraph (b) of this section, no person may operate a civil aircraft within the United States with knowledge that narcotic drugs, marihuana, and depressant or stimulant drugs or substances as defined in Federal or State statutes are carried in the aircraft.

(b) Paragraph (a) of this section does not apply to any carriage of narcotic drugs, marihuana, and depressant or stimulant drugs or substances authorized by or under any Federal or State statute or by any Federal or State agency.

SEC. 91.101: APPLICABILITY

Source: Docket No. 18334, 54 FR 34294, Aug. 18, 1989, unless otherwise noted.

This subpart prescribes flight rules governing the operation of aircraft within the United States and within 12 nautical miles from the coast of the United States.

SEC. 91.103 PREFLIGHT ACTION

Each pilot in command shall, before beginning a flight, become familiar with all available information concerning that flight. This information must include—

(a) For a flight under IFR or a flight not in the vicinity of an airport, weather reports and forecasts, fuel requirements, alternatives available if the planned flight cannot be completed, and any known traffic delays of which the pilot in command has been advised by ATC;

(b) For any flight, runway lengths at airports of intended use, and the following takeoff and landing distance information:

(1) For civil aircraft for which an approved Airplane or Rotorcraft Flight Manual containing takeoff and landing distance data is required, the takeoff and landing distance data contained therein; and

(2) For civil aircraft other than those specified in paragraph (b)(1) of this section, other reliable information appropriate to the aircraft, relating to aircraft performance under expected values of airport elevation and runway slope, aircraft gross weight, and wind and temperature.

SEC. 91.107: USE OF SAFETY BELTS, SHOULDER HARNESSES, AND CHILD RESTRAINT SYSTEMS

(a) Unless otherwise authorized by the Administrator—

(1) No pilot may take off a U.S.-registered civil aircraft (except a free balloon that incorporates a basket or gondola, or an airship type certificated before November 2, 1987) unless the pilot in command of that aircraft ensures that each person on board is briefed on how to fasten and unfasten that person's safety belt and, if installed, shoulder harness.

(2) No pilot may cause to be moved on the surface, take off, or land a U.S.-registered civil aircraft (except a free balloon that incorporates a basket or gondola, or an airship type certificated before November 2, 1987) unless the pilot in command of that aircraft ensures that each person on board has been notified to fasten his or her safety belt and, if installed, his or her shoulder harness.

(3) Except as provided in this paragraph, each person on board a U.S.-registered civil aircraft (except a free balloon that incorporates a basket or gondola or an airship type certificated before November 2, 1987) must occupy an approved seat or berth with a safety belt and, if installed, shoulder harness, properly secured about him or her during movement on the surface, takeoff, and landing. For seaplane and float equipped rotorcraft operations during movement on the surface, the person pushing off the seaplane or rotorcraft from the dock and the person mooring the seaplane or rotorcraft at the dock are excepted from the preceding seating and

safety belt requirements. Notwithstanding the preceding requirements of this paragraph, a person may:

- (i) Be held by an adult who is occupying an approved seat or berth, provided that the person being held has not reached his or her second birthday and does not occupy or use any restraining device;
- (ii) Use the floor of the aircraft as a seat, provided that the person is on board for the purpose of engaging in sport parachuting;

SEC. 91.111: OPERATING NEAR OTHER AIRCRAFT

(a) No person may operate an aircraft so close to another aircraft as to create a collision hazard.

(b) No person may operate an aircraft in formation flight except by arrangement with the pilot in command of each aircraft in the formation.

(c) No person may operate an aircraft, carrying passengers for hire, in formation flight.

SEC. 91.113: RIGHT-OF-WAY RULES: EXCEPT WATER OPERATIONS

(a) Inapplicability. This section does not apply to the operation of an aircraft on water.

(b) General. When weather conditions permit, regardless of whether an operation is conducted under instrument flight rules or visual flight rules, vigilance shall be maintained by each person operating an aircraft so as to see and avoid other aircraft. When a rule of this section gives another aircraft the right-of-way, the pilot shall give way to that aircraft and may not pass over, under, or ahead of it unless well clear.

(c) In distress. An aircraft in distress has the right-of-way over all other air traffic.

(d) Converging. When aircraft of the same category are converging at approximately the same altitude (except head-on, or nearly so), the aircraft to the other's right has the right-of-way. If the aircraft are of different categories—

- (1) A balloon has the right-of-way over any other category of aircraft;
- (2) A glider has the right-of-way over an airship, airplane, or rotorcraft; and
- (3) An airship has the right-of-way over an airplane or rotorcraft. However, an aircraft towing or refueling other aircraft has the right-of-way over all other engine-driven aircraft.

(e) Approaching head-on. When aircraft are approaching each other head-on, or nearly so, each pilot of each aircraft shall alter course to the right.

(f) Overtaking. Each aircraft that is being overtaken has the right-of-way and each pilot of an overtaking aircraft shall alter course to the right to pass well clear.

(g) Landing. Aircraft, while on final approach to land or while landing, have the right-of-way over other aircraft in flight or operating on the surface, except that they shall not take advantage of this rule to force an aircraft off the runway surface which has already landed and is attempting to make way for an aircraft on final approach. When two or more aircraft are approaching an airport for the purpose of landing, the aircraft at the lower altitude has the right-of-way, but it shall not take advantage of this rule to cut in front of another which is on final approach to land or to overtake that aircraft.

SEC. 91.119: MINIMUM SAFE ALTITUDES: GENERAL

Except when necessary for takeoff or landing, no person may operate an aircraft below the following altitudes:

(a) Anywhere. An altitude allowing, if a power unit fails, an emergency landing without undue hazard to persons or property on the surface.

(b) Over congested areas. Over any congested area of a city, town, or settlement, or over any open air assembly of persons, an altitude of 1,000 feet above the highest obstacle within a horizontal radius of 2,000 feet of the aircraft.

(c) Over other than congested areas. An altitude of 500 feet above the surface, except over open water or sparsely populated areas. In those cases, the aircraft may not be operated closer than 500 feet to any person, vessel, vehicle, or structure.

(d) Helicopters. Helicopters may be operated at less than the minimums prescribed in paragraph (b) or (c) of this section if the operation is conducted without hazard to persons or property on the surface. In addition, each person operating a helicopter shall comply with any routes or altitudes specifically prescribed for helicopters by the Administrator.

SEC. 91.126: OPERATING ON OR IN THE VICINITY OF AN AIRPORT IN CLASS G AIRSPACE

(a) General. Unless otherwise authorized or required, each person operating an aircraft on or in the vicinity of an airport in a Class G airspace area must comply with the requirements of this section.

(b) Direction of turns. When approaching to land at an airport without an operating control tower in Class G airspace—

- (1) Each pilot of an airplane must make all turns of that airplane to the left unless the airport displays approved light signals or visual markings indicating that turns should be made to the right, in which case the pilot must make all turns to the right; and
- (2) Each pilot of a helicopter must avoid the flow of fixed-wing aircraft.

(c) Flap settings. Except when necessary for training or certification, the pilot in command of a civil turbojet-powered aircraft must use, as a final flap setting, the minimum certificated landing flap setting set forth in the approved performance information in the Airplane Flight Manual for the applicable conditions. However, each pilot in command has the final authority and responsibility for the safe operation of the pilot's airplane, and may use a different flap setting for that airplane if the pilot determines that it is necessary in the interest of safety.

(d) Communications with control towers. Unless otherwise authorized or required by ATC, no person may operate an aircraft to, from, through, or on an airport having an operational control tower unless two-way radio communications are maintained between that aircraft and the control tower. Communications must be established prior to 4 nautical miles from the airport, up to and including 2,500 feet AGL. However, if the aircraft radio fails in flight, the pilot in command may operate that aircraft and land if weather conditions are at or

9-1 FEDERAL AVIATION REGULATIONS

above basic VFR weather minimums, visual contact with the tower is maintained, and a clearance to land is received. If the aircraft radio fails while in flight under IFR, the pilot must comply with Sec. 91.185.

SEC. 91.127 OPERATING ON OR IN THE VICINITY OF AN AIRPORT IN CLASS E AIRSPACE

(a) Unless otherwise required by part 93 of this chapter or unless otherwise authorized or required by the ATC facility having jurisdiction over the Class E airspace area, each person operating an aircraft on or in the vicinity of an airport in a Class E airspace area must comply with the requirements of Sec. 91.126.

(b) Departures. Each pilot of an aircraft must comply with any traffic patterns established for that airport in part 93 of this chapter.

(c) Communications with control towers. Unless otherwise authorized or required by ATC, no person may operate an aircraft to, from, through, or on an airport having an operational control tower unless two-way radio communications are maintained between that aircraft and the control tower. Communications must be established prior to 4 nautical miles from the airport, up to and including 2,500 feet AGL. However, if the aircraft radio fails in flight, the pilot in command may operate that aircraft and land if weather conditions are at or above basic VFR weather minimums, visual contact with the tower is maintained, and a clearance to land is received. If the aircraft radio fails while in flight under IFR, the pilot must comply with Sec. 91.185.

SEC. 91.151 FUEL REQUIREMENTS FOR FLIGHT IN VFR CONDITIONS

(a) No person may begin a flight in an airplane under VFR conditions unless (considering wind and forecast weather conditions) there is enough fuel to fly to the first point of intended landing and, assuming normal cruising speed—

(1) During the day, to fly after that for at least 30 minutes; or

(2) At night, to fly after that for at least 45 minutes.

(b) No person may begin a flight in a rotorcraft under VFR conditions unless (considering wind and forecast weather conditions) there is enough fuel to fly to the first point of intended landing and, assuming normal cruising speed, to fly after that for at least 20 minutes.

SEC. 91.155: BASIC VFR WEATHER MINIMUMS

(a) Except as provided in paragraph (b) of this section and Sec. 91.157, no person may operate an aircraft under VFR when the flight visibility is less, or at a distance from clouds that is less, than that prescribed for the corresponding altitude and class of airspace in the following table:

(b) Class G Airspace. Notwithstanding the provisions of paragraph (a) of this section, the following operations may be conducted in Class G airspace below 1,200 feet above the surface:

(1) Helicopter. A helicopter may be operated clear of clouds if operated at a speed that allows the pilot adequate opportunity to see any air traffic or obstruction in time to avoid a collision.

(2) Airplane. When the visibility is less than 3 statute miles but not less than 1 statute mile during night hours, an airplane may be operated clear of clouds if operated in an airport traffic pattern within one-half mile of the runway.

(c) Except as provided in Sec. 91.157, no person may operate an aircraft beneath the ceiling under VFR within the lateral boundaries of controlled airspace designated to the surface for an airport when the ceiling is less than 1,000 feet.

(d) Except as provided in Sec. 91.157 of this part, no person may take off or land an aircraft, or enter the traffic pattern of an airport, under VFR, within the lateral boundaries of the surface areas of Class B, Class C, Class D, or Class E airspace designated for an airport—

(1) Unless ground visibility at that airport is at least 3 statute miles; or

(2) If ground visibility is not reported at that airport, unless flight visibility during landing or takeoff, or while

	Distance from Airspace	Flight Visibility	Clouds
Class A		Not Applicable	Not Applicable
Class B		3 statute miles	Clear of Clouds
Class C		3 statute miles	500 feet below. 1,000 feet above. 2,000 feet horizontal.
Class D		3 statute miles	500 feet below. 1,000 feet above. 2,000 feet horizontal.
Class E	Less than 10,000 feet MSL	3 statute miles	500 feet below. 1,000 feet above. 2,000 feet horizontal.
Class E	At or above 10,000 feet MSL	5 statute miles	1,000 feet below. 1,000 feet above. 1 statute mile horizontal.
Class G	1,200 feet or less above the surface (regardless of MSL altitude).		
Class G	*Day*, except as provided in Sec. 91.155(b).	1 statute mile	Clear of Clouds
Class G	*Night*, except as provided in Sec. 91.155(b).	3 statute mile	500 feet below. 1,000 feet above. 2,000 feet horizontal.
Class G	More than 1,200 feet above the surface but less than 10,000 feet MSL		
Class G	Day	1 statute mile	500 feet below. 1,000 feet above. 2,000 feet horizontal.
Class G	Night	3 statute mile	500 feet below. 1,000 feet above. 2,000 feet horizontal.
Class G	More than 1,200 feet above the surface and at or above 10,000 feet MSL.	5 statute miles	1,000 feet below. 1,000 feet above. 1 statute mile horizontal.

operating in the traffic pattern is at least 3 statute miles.

(e) For the purpose of this section, an aircraft operating at the base altitude of a Class E airspace area is considered to be within the airspace directly below that area.

SEC. 91.211: SUPPLEMENTAL OXYGEN

(a) General. No person may operate a civil aircraft of U.S. registry—

(1) At cabin pressure altitudes above 12,500 feet (MSL) up to and including 14,000 feet (MSL) unless the required minimum flight crew is provided with and uses supplemental oxygen for that part of the flight at those altitudes that is of more than 30 minutes duration;

(2) At cabin pressure altitudes above 14,000 feet (MSL) unless the required minimum flight crew is provided with and uses supplemental oxygen during the entire flight time at those altitudes; and

(3) At cabin pressure altitudes above 15,000 feet (MSL) unless each occupant of the aircraft is provided with supplemental oxygen.

SEC. 91.215: ATC TRANSPONDER AND ALTITUDE REPORTING EQUIPMENT AND USE

(a) *All airspace: U.S.-registered civil aircraft.* For operations not conducted under part 121 or 135 of this chapter, ATC transponder equipment installed must meet the performance and environmental requirements of any class of TSO-C74b (Mode A) or any class of TSO-C74c (Mode A with altitude reporting capability) as appropriate, or the appropriate class of TSO-C112 (Mode S).

(b) *All airspace.* Unless otherwise authorized or directed by ATC, and except as provided in paragraph (e)(1) of this section, no person may operate an aircraft in the airspace described in paragraphs (b)(1) through (5) of this section, unless that aircraft is equipped with an operable coded radar beacon transponder having either Mode 3/A 4096 code capability, replying to Mode 3/A interrogations with the code specified by ATC, or a Mode S capability, replying to Mode 3/A interrogations with the code specified by ATC and intermode and Mode S interrogations in accordance with the applicable provisions specified in TSO C-112, and that aircraft is equipped with automatic pressure altitude reporting equipment having a Mode C capability that automatically replies to Mode C interrogations by transmitting pressure altitude information in 100-foot increments. The requirements of this paragraph (b) apply to—

(1) *All aircraft.* In Class A, Class B, and Class C airspace areas;

(2) *All aircraft.* In all airspace within 30 nautical miles of an airport listed in appendix D, section 1 of this part from the surface upward to 10,000 feet MSL;

(3) Notwithstanding paragraph (b)(2) of this section, any aircraft which was not originally certificated with an engine-driven electrical system or which has not subsequently been certified with such a system installed, balloon or glider may conduct operations in the airspace within 30 nautical miles of an airport listed in appendix D, section 1 of this part provided such operations are conducted—

   (i) Outside any Class A, Class B, or Class C airspace area; and

   (ii) Below the altitude of the ceiling of a Class B or Class C airspace area designated for an airport or 10,000 feet MSL, whichever is lower; and

(4) All aircraft in all airspace above the ceiling and within the lateral boundaries of a Class B or Class C airspace area designated for an airport upward to 10,000 feet MSL; and

(5) All aircraft except any aircraft which was not originally certificated with an engine-driven electrical system or which has not subsequently been certified with such a system installed, balloon, or glider—

   (i) In all airspace of the 48 contiguous states and the District of Columbia at and above 10,000 feet MSL, excluding the airspace at and below 2,500 feet above the surface; and

   (ii) In the airspace from the surface to 10,000 feet MSL within a 10-nautical-mile radius of any airport listed in appendix D, section 2 of this part, excluding the airspace below 1,200 feet outside of the lateral boundaries of the surface area of the airspace designated for that airport.

(c) *Transponder-on operation.* Except as provided in paragraph (e)(2) of this section, while in the airspace as specified in paragraph (b) of this section or in all controlled airspace, each person operating an aircraft equipped with an operable ATC transponder maintained in accordance with §91.413 shall operate the transponder, including Mode C equipment if installed, and shall reply on the appropriate code or as assigned by ATC, unless otherwise directed by ATC when transmitting would jeopardize the safe execution of air traffic control functions.

(d) *ATC authorized deviations.* Requests for ATC authorized deviations must be made to the ATC facility having jurisdiction over the concerned airspace within the time periods specified as follows:

(1) For operation of an aircraft with an operating transponder but without operating automatic pressure altitude reporting equipment having a Mode C capability, the request may be made at any time.

(2) For operation of an aircraft with an inoperative transponder to the airport of ultimate destination, including any intermediate stops, or to proceed to a place where suitable repairs can be made or both, the request may be made at any time.

(3) For operation of an aircraft that is not equipped with a transponder, the request must be made at least one hour before the proposed operation.

SEC. 91.223: TERRAIN AWARENESS AND WARNING SYSTEM

(a) Airplanes manufactured after March 29, 2002. Except as provided in paragraph (d) of this section, no person may operate a turbine-powered U.S.-registered airplane configured with six or more passenger seats, excluding any pilot seat, unless that airplane is equipped with an approved terrain awareness and warning system that as a minimum meets the requirements for Class B equipment in Technical Standard Order (TSO)-C151.

(b) Airplanes manufactured on or before March 29, 2002. Except as provided in

9-1 FEDERAL AVIATION REGULATIONS

paragraph (d) of this section, no person may operate a turbine-powered U.S.-registered airplane configured with six or more passenger seats, excluding any pilot seat, after March 29, 2005, unless that airplane is equipped with an approved terrain awareness and warning system that as a minimum meets the requirements for Class B equipment in Technical Standard Order (TSO)-C151. (Approved by the Office of Management and Budget under control number 2120-0631)

(c) Airplane Flight Manual. The Airplane Flight Manual shall contain appropriate procedures for—

  (1) The use of the terrain awareness and warning system; and

  (2) Proper flight crew reaction in response to the terrain awareness and warning system audio and visual warnings.

(d) Exceptions. Paragraphs (a) and (b) of this section do not apply to—

  (1) Parachuting operations when conducted entirely within a 50 nautical mile radius of the airport from which such local flight operations began.

SEC. 91.225: AUTOMATIC DEPENDENT SURVEILLANCE-BROADCAST (ADS-B) OUT EQUIPMENT AND USE

(a) After January 1, 2020, unless otherwise authorized by ATC, no person may operate an aircraft in Class A airspace unless the aircraft has equipment installed that—

  (1) Meets the performance requirements in TSO-C166b, Extended Squitter Automatic Dependent Surveillance-Broadcast (ADS-B) and Traffic Information Service-Broadcast (TIS-B) Equipment Operating on the Radio Frequency of 1090 Megahertz (MHz); and

  (2) Meets the requirements of §91.227.

(b) After January 1, 2020, except as prohibited in paragraph (i) (2) of this section or unless otherwise authorized by ATC, no person may operate an aircraft below 18,000 feet MSL and in airspace described in paragraph (d) of this section unless the aircraft has equipment installed that—

  (1) Meets the performance requirements in—

    (i) TSO-C166b; or

    (ii) TSO-C154c, Universal Access Transceiver (UAT) Automatic Dependent Surveillance-Broadcast (ADS-B) Equipment Operating on the Frequency of 978 MHz;

  (2) Meets the requirements of §91.227.

(c) Operators with equipment installed with an approved deviation under §21.618 of this chapter also are in compliance with this section.

(d) After January 1, 2020, except as prohibited in paragraph (i) (2) of this section or unless otherwise authorized by ATC, no person may operate an aircraft in the following airspace unless the aircraft has equipment installed that meets the requirements in paragraph (b) of this section:

  (1) Class B and Class C airspace areas;

  (2) Except as provided for in paragraph (e) of this section, within 30 nautical miles of an airport listed in appendix D, section 1 to this part from the surface upward to 10,000 feet MSL;

  (3) Above the ceiling and within the lateral boundaries of a Class B or Class C airspace area designated for an airport upward to 10,000 feet MSL;

  (4) Except as provided in paragraph (e) of this section, Class E airspace within the 48 contiguous states and the District of Columbia at and above 10,000 feet MSL, excluding the airspace at and below 2,500 feet above the surface; and

  (5) Class E airspace at and above 3,000 feet MSL over the Gulf of Mexico from the coastline of the United States out to 12 nautical miles.

(e) The requirements of paragraph (b) of this section do not apply to any aircraft that was not originally certificated with an electrical system, or that has not subsequently been certified with such a system installed, including balloons and gliders. These aircraft may conduct operations without ADS-B Out in the airspace specified in paragraphs (d)(2) and (d)(4) of this section. Operations authorized by this section must be conducted—

  (1) Outside any Class B or Class C airspace area; and

  (2) Below the altitude of the ceiling of a Class B or Class C airspace area designated for an airport, or 10,000 feet MSL, whichever is lower.

(f) Except as prohibited in paragraph (i)(2) of this section, each person operating an aircraft equipped with ADS-B Out must operate this equipment in the transmit mode at all times unless—

  (1) Otherwise authorized by the FAA when the aircraft is performing a sensitive government mission for national defense, homeland security, intelligence or law enforcement purposes and transmitting would compromise the operations security of the mission or pose a safety risk to the aircraft, crew, or people and property in the air or on the ground; or

  (2) Otherwise directed by ATC when transmitting would jeopardize the safe execution of air traffic control functions.

(g) Requests for ATC authorized deviations from the requirements of this section must be made to the ATC facility having jurisdiction over the concerned airspace within the time periods specified as follows:

  (1) For operation of an aircraft with an inoperative ADS-B Out, to the airport of ultimate destination, including any intermediate stops, or to proceed to a place where suitable repairs can be made or both, the request may be made at any time.

  (2) For operation of an aircraft that is not equipped with ADS-B Out, the request must be made at least 1 hour before the proposed operation.

SEC. 91.307: PARACHUTES AND PARACHUTING

(a) No pilot of a civil aircraft may allow a parachute that is available for emergency use to be carried in that aircraft unless it is an approved type and—

  (1) If a chair type (canopy in back), it has been packed by a certificated and appropriately rated parachute rigger within the preceding 180 days; or

  (2) If any other type, it has been packed by a certificated and rated parachute rigger—

    (i) Within the preceding 180 days, if its canopy, shrouds, and harness are composed exclusively of nylon, rayon, or other similar synthetic fiber or materials that are substantially resistant to damage from mold, mildew, or other fungi and other rotting agents propagated in a moist environment; or

  (ii) Within the preceding 60 days, if any part of the parachute is composed of silk, pongee, or other natural fiber, or materials not specified in paragraph (a)(2)(i) of this section.

(b) Except in an emergency, no pilot in command may allow, and no person may conduct, a parachute operation from an aircraft within the United States except in accordance with part 105 of this chapter.

(c) Unless each occupant of the aircraft is wearing an approved parachute, no pilot of a civil aircraft carrying any person (other than a crewmember) may execute any intentional maneuver that exceeds—

  (1) A bank of 60 degrees relative to the horizon; or

  (2) A nose-up or nose-down attitude of 30 degrees relative to the horizon.

(d) Paragraph (c) of this section does not apply to—

  (1) Flight tests for pilot certification or rating; or

  (2) Spins and other flight maneuvers required by the regulations for any certificate or rating when given by—

    (i) A certificated flight instructor; or

    (ii) An airline transport pilot instructing in accordance with Sec. 61.67 of this chapter.

(e) For the purposes of this section, approved parachute means—

  (1) A parachute manufactured under a type certificate or a technical standard order (C-23 series); or

  (2) A personnel-carrying military parachute identified by an NAF, AAF, or AN drawing number, an AAF order number, or any other military designation or specification number.

SEC. 91.403: GENERAL

(a) The owner or operator of an aircraft is primarily responsible for maintaining that aircraft in an airworthy condition, including compliance with part 39 of this chapter.

(b) No person may perform maintenance, preventive maintenance, or alterations on an aircraft other than as prescribed in this subpart and other applicable regulations, including part 43 of this chapter.

(c) No person may operate an aircraft for which a manufacturer's maintenance manual or instructions for continued airworthiness has been issued that contains an airworthiness limitations section unless the mandatory replacement times, inspection intervals, and related procedures specified in that section or alternative inspection intervals and related procedures set forth in an operations specification approved by the Administrator under part 121 or 135 of this chapter or in accordance with an inspection program approved under § 91.409(e) have been complied with.

SEC. 91.409: INSPECTIONS

(a) Except as provided in paragraph (c) of this section, no person may operate an aircraft unless, within the preceding 12 calendar months, it has had—

  (1) An annual inspection in accordance with part 43 of this chapter and has been approved for return to service by a person authorized by § 43.7 of this chapter; or

  (2) An inspection for the issuance of an airworthiness certificate in accordance with part 21 of this chapter.

No inspection performed under paragraph (b) of this section may be substituted for any inspection required by this paragraph unless it is performed by a person authorized to perform annual inspections and is entered as an "annual" inspection in the required maintenance records.

(b) Except as provided in paragraph (c) of this section, no person may operate an aircraft carrying any person (other than a crewmember) for hire, and no person may give flight instruction for hire in an aircraft which that person provides, unless within the preceding 100 hours of time in service the aircraft has received an annual or 100-hour inspection and been approved for return to service in accordance with part 43 of this chapter or has received an inspection for the issuance of an airworthiness certificate in accordance with part 21 of this chapter. The 100-hour limitation may be exceeded by not more than 10 hours while en route to reach a place where the inspection can be done. The excess time used to reach a place where the inspection can be done must be included in computing the next 100 hours of time in service.

(c) Paragraphs (a) and (b) of this section do not apply to—

  (1) An aircraft that carries a special flight permit, a current experimental certificate, or a light-sport or provisional airworthiness certificate;

  (2) An aircraft inspected in accordance with an approved aircraft inspection program under part 125 or 135 of this chapter and so identified by the registration number in the operations specifications of the certificate holder having the approved inspection program;

  (3) An aircraft subject to the requirements of paragraph (d) or (e) of this section; or

  (4) Turbine-powered rotorcraft when the operator elects to inspect that rotorcraft in accordance with paragraph (e) of this section.

(d) *Progressive inspection.* Each registered owner or operator of an aircraft desiring to use a progressive inspection program must submit a written request to the responsible Flight Standards office, and shall provide—

  (1) A certificated mechanic holding an inspection authorization, a certificated airframe repair station, or the manufacturer of the aircraft to supervise or conduct the progressive inspection;

  (2) A current inspection procedures manual available and readily understandable to pilot and maintenance personnel containing, in detail—

    (i) An explanation of the progressive inspection, including the continuity of inspection responsibility, the making of reports, and the keeping of records and technical reference material;

    (ii) An inspection schedule, specifying the intervals in hours or days when routine and detailed inspections will be performed and including instructions for exceeding an inspection interval by not more than 10 hours while en route and for changing an inspection interval because of service experience;

9-1 FEDERAL AVIATION REGULATIONS

  (iii) Sample routine and detailed inspection forms and instructions for their use; and

  (iv) Sample reports and records and instructions for their use;

(3) Enough housing and equipment for necessary disassembly and proper inspection of the aircraft; and

(4) Appropriate current technical information for the aircraft.

The frequency and detail of the progressive inspection shall provide for the complete inspection of the aircraft within each 12 calendar months and be consistent with the manufacturer's recommendations, field service experience, and the kind of operation in which the aircraft is engaged. The progressive inspection schedule must ensure that the aircraft, at all times, will be airworthy and will conform to all applicable FAA aircraft specifications, type certificate data sheets, airworthiness directives, and other approved data. If the progressive inspection is discontinued, the owner or operator shall immediately notify the responsible Flight Standards office, in writing, of the discontinuance.

(e) *Large airplanes (to which part 125 is not applicable), turbojet multiengine airplanes, turbopropeller-powered multiengine airplanes, and turbine-powered rotorcraft.* No person may operate a large airplane, turbojet multiengine airplane, turbopropeller-powered multiengine airplane, or turbine-powered rotorcraft unless the replacement times for life-limited parts specified in the aircraft specifications, type data sheets, or other documents approved by the Administrator are complied with and the airplane or turbine-powered rotorcraft, including the airframe, engines, propellers, rotors, appliances, survival equipment, and emergency equipment, is inspected in accordance with an inspection program selected under the provisions of paragraph (f) of this section, except that, the owner or operator of a turbine-powered rotorcraft may elect to use the inspection provisions of § 91.409(a), (b), (c), or (d) in lieu of an inspection option of § 91.409(f).

(f) *Selection of inspection program under paragraph (e) of this section.* The registered owner or operator of each airplane or turbine-powered rotorcraft described in paragraph (e) of this section must select, identify in the aircraft maintenance records, and use one of the following programs for the inspection of the aircraft:

(1) A continuous airworthiness inspection program that is part of a continuous airworthiness maintenance program currently in use by a person holding an air carrier operating certificate or an operating certificate issued under part 121 or 135 of this chapter and operating that make and model aircraft under part 121 of this chapter or operating that make and model under part 135 of this chapter and maintaining it under § 135.411(a)(2) of this chapter.

(2) An approved aircraft inspection program approved under § 135.419 of this chapter and currently in use by a person holding an operating certificate issued under part 135 of this chapter.

(3) A current inspection program recommended by the manufacturer.

(4) Any other inspection program established by the registered owner or operator of that airplane or turbine-powered rotorcraft and approved by the Administrator under paragraph (g) of this section. However, the Administrator may require revision of this inspection program in accordance with the provisions of § 91.415.

Each operator shall include in the selected program the name and address of the person responsible for scheduling the inspections required by the program and make a copy of that program available to the person performing inspections on the aircraft and, upon request, to the Administrator.

(g) *Inspection program approved under paragraph (e) of this section.* Each operator of an airplane or turbine-powered rotorcraft desiring to establish or change an approved inspection program under paragraph (f)(4) of this section must submit the program for approval to the responsible Flight Standards office. The program must be in writing and include at least the following information:

(1) Instructions and procedures for the conduct of inspections for the particular make and model airplane or turbine-powered rotorcraft, including necessary tests and checks. The instructions and procedures must set forth in detail the parts and areas of the airframe, engines, propellers, rotors, and appliances, including survival and emergency equipment required to be inspected.

(2) A schedule for performing the inspections that must be performed under the program expressed in terms of the time in service, calendar time, number of system operations, or any combination of these.

(h) *Changes from one inspection program to another.* When an operator changes from one inspection program under paragraph (f) of this section to another, the time in service, calendar times, or cycles of operation accumulated under the previous program must be applied in determining inspection due times under the new program.

PART 105—PARACHUTE OPERATIONS

SEC. 105.1 APPLICABILITY

(a) Except as provided in paragraphs (b) and (c) of this section, this part prescribes rules governing parachute operations conducted in the United States.

(b) This part does not apply to a parachute operation conducted—

  (1) In response to an in-flight emergency, or

  (2) To meet an emergency on the surface when it is conducted at the direction or with the approval of an agency of the United States, or of a State, Puerto Rico, the District of Columbia, or a possession of the United States, or an agency or political subdivision thereof.

(c) Sections 105.5, 105.9, 105.13, 105.15, 105.17, 105.19 through 105.23, 105.25(a)(1) and 105.27 of this part do not apply to a parachute operation conducted by a member of an Armed Force—

  (1) Over or within a restricted area when that area is under the control of an Armed Force.

  (2) During military operations in uncontrolled airspace.

SEC. 105.3 DEFINITIONS

For the purposes of this part—

APPROVED PARACHUTE means a parachute manufactured under a type certificate or a Technical Standard Order (C-23 series), or a personnel-carrying U.S. military parachute (other than a high altitude, high speed, or ejection type) identified by a Navy Air Facility, an Army Air Field, and Air Force-Navy drawing number, an Army Air Field order number, or any other military designation or specification number.

AUTOMATIC ACTIVATION DEVICE means a self-contained mechanical or electro-mechanical device that is attached to the interior of the reserve parachute container, which automatically initiates parachute deployment of the reserve parachute at a pre-set altitude, time, percentage of terminal velocity, or combination thereof.

DIRECT SUPERVISION means that a certificated rigger personally observes a non-certificated person packing a main parachute to the extent necessary to ensure that it is being done properly, and takes responsibility for that packing.

DROP ZONE means any pre-determined area upon which parachutists or objects land after making an intentional parachute jump or drop. The center-point target of a drop zone is expressed in nautical miles from the nearest VOR facility when 30 nautical miles or less; or from the nearest airport, town, or city depicted on the appropriate Coast and Geodetic Survey World Aeronautical Chart or Sectional Aeronautical Chart, when the nearest VOR facility is more than 30 nautical miles from the drop zone.

FOREIGN PARACHUTIST means a parachutist who is neither a U.S. citizen or a resident alien and is participating in parachute operations within the United States using parachute equipment not manufactured in the United States.

FREEFALL means the portion of a parachute jump or drop between aircraft exit and parachute deployment in which the parachute is activated manually by the parachutist at the parachutist's discretion or automatically, or, in the case of an object, is activated automatically.

MAIN PARACHUTE means a parachute worn as the primary parachute used or intended to be used in conjunction with a reserve parachute.

OBJECT means any item other than a person that descends to the surface from an aircraft in flight when a parachute is used or is intended to be used during all or part of the descent.

PARACHUTE DROP means the descent of an object to the surface from an aircraft in flight when a parachute is used or intended to be used during all or part of that descent.

PARACHUTE JUMP means a parachute operation that involves the descent of one or more persons to the surface from an aircraft in flight when an aircraft is used or intended to be used during all or part of that descent.

*editor's note: It is assumed that the FAA intended to say "... from an aircraft in flight when a parachute is used or intended to be used during all or part of that descent."

PARACHUTE OPERATION means the performance of all activity for the purpose of, or in support of, a parachute jump or a parachute drop. This parachute operation can involve, but is not limited to, the following persons: parachutist, parachutist in command and passenger in tandem parachute operations, drop zone or owner or operator, jump master, certificated parachute rigger, or pilot.

PARACHUTIST means a person who intends to exit an aircraft while in flight using a single-harness, dual parachute system to descend to the surface.

PARACHUTIST IN COMMAND means the person responsible for the operation and safety of a tandem parachute operation.

PASSENGER PARACHUTIST means a person who boards an aircraft, acting as other than the parachutist in command of a tandem parachute operation, with the intent of exiting [sic] the aircraft while in-flight using the forward harness of a dual harness tandem parachute system to descend to the surface.

PILOT CHUTE means a small parachute used to initiate and/or accelerate deployment of a main or reserve parachute.

RAM-AIR PARACHUTE means a parachute with a canopy consisting of an upper and lower surface that is inflated by ram air entering through specially designed openings in the front of the canopy to form a gliding airfoil.

RESERVE PARACHUTE means an approved parachute worn for emergency use to be activated only upon failure of the main parachute or in any other emergency where use of the main parachute is impractical or use of the main parachute would increase risk.

SINGLE-HARNESS, DUAL PARACHUTE SYSTEM means the combination of a main parachute, approved reserve parachute, and approved single-person harness and dual-parachute container. This parachute system may have an operational automatic activation device installed.

TANDEM PARACHUTE OPERATION means a parachute operation in which more than one person simultaneously uses the same tandem parachute system while descending to the surface from an aircraft in flight.

TANDEM PARACHUTE SYSTEM means the combination of a main parachute, approved reserve parachute, and approved harness and dual parachute container, and a separate approved forward harness for a passenger parachutist. This parachute system must have an operational automatic activation device installed.

SEC. 105.5 GENERAL

No person may conduct a parachute operation, and no pilot in command of an aircraft may allow a parachute operation to be conducted from an aircraft, if that operation creates a hazard to air traffic or to persons or property on the surface.

SEC. 105.7 USE OF ALCOHOL AND DRUGS

No person may conduct a parachute operation, and no pilot in command of an aircraft may allow a person to conduct a parachute operation from that aircraft, if that person is or appears to be under the influence of—

(a) Alcohol, or

(b) Any drug that affects that person's faculties in any way contrary to safety.

SEC. 105.9 INSPECTIONS

The Administrator may inspect any parachute operation to which this part applies (including inspections at the site where the parachute operation is being conducted) to determine compliance with the regulations of this part.

SEC. 105.13 RADIO EQUIPMENT AND USE REQUIREMENTS

(a) Except when otherwise authorized by air traffic control-

  (1) No person may conduct a parachute operation, and no pilot in command of an aircraft may allow a parachute operation to be conducted from that aircraft, in or into controlled airspace unless, during that flight-

   (i) The aircraft is equipped with a functioning two-way radio communication system

9-1 FEDERAL AVIATION REGULATIONS

Altitude	Flight Visibility	Distance From Clouds
(1) 1,200 feet or less above the surface regardless of MSL altitude.	3 statute mile	500 feet below. 1,000 feet above. 2,000 feet horizontal.
(2) More than 1,200 feet above the surface but less than 10,000 feet MSL.	3 statute mile	500 feet below. 1,000 feet above. 2,000 feet horizontal.
(3) More than 1,200 feet above the surface and at or above 10,000 feet MSL.	5 statute miles	1,000 feet below. 1,000 feet above. 1 statute mile horizontal.

appropriate to the air traffic control facilities being used; and

(ii) Radio communications have been established between the aircraft and the air traffic control facility having jurisdiction over the affected airspace of the first intended exit altitude at least 5 minutes before the parachute operation begins. The pilot in command must establish radio communications to receive information regarding air traffic activity in the vicinity of the parachute operation.

(2) The pilot in command of an aircraft used for any parachute operation in or into controlled airspace must, during each flight—

(i) Continuously monitor the appropriate frequency of the aircraft's radio communications system from the time radio communications are first established between the aircraft and air traffic control, until the pilot advises air traffic control that the parachute operation has ended for that flight.

(ii) Advise air traffic control when the last parachutist or object leaves the aircraft.

(b) Parachute operations must be aborted if, prior to receipt of a required air traffic control authorization, or during any parachute operation in or into controlled airspace, the required radio communications system is or becomes inoperative.

SEC. 105.15 INFORMATION REQUIRED AND NOTICE OF CANCELLATION OR POSTPONEMENT OF A PARACHUTE OPERATION

(a) Each person requesting an authorization under Secs. 105.21(b) and 105.25(a)(2) of this part and each person submitting a notification under Sec. 105.25(a)(3) of this part must provide the following information (on an individual or group basis):

(1) The date and time the parachute operation will begin.

(2) The radius of the drop zone around the target expressed in nautical miles.

(3) The location of the center of the drop zone in relation to—

(i) The nearest VOR facility in terms of the VOR radial on which it is located and its distance in nautical miles from the VOR facility when that facility is 30 nautical miles or less from the drop zone target; or

(ii) The nearest airport, town, or city depicted on the appropriate Coast and Geodetic Survey World Aeronautical Chart or Sectional Aeronautical Chart, when the nearest VOR facility is more than 30 nautical miles from the drop zone target.

(4) Each altitude above mean sea level at which the aircraft will be operated when parachutists or objects exit the aircraft.

(5) The duration of the intended parachute operation.

(6) The name, address, and telephone number of the person who requests the authorization or gives notice of the parachute operation.

(7) The registration number of the aircraft to be used.

(8) The name of the air traffic control facility with jurisdiction of the airspace at the first intended exit altitude to be used for the parachute operation.

(b) Each holder of a certificate of authorization issued under Secs. 105.21(b) and 105.25(b) of this part must present that certificate for inspection upon the request of the Administrator or any Federal, State, or local official.

(c) Each person requesting an authorization under Secs. 105.21(b) and 105.25(a)(2) of this part and each person submitting a notice under Sec. 105.25(a)(3) of this part must promptly notify the air traffic control facility having jurisdiction over the affected airspace if the proposed or scheduled parachute operation is canceled or postponed.

SEC. 105.17 FLIGHT VISIBILITY AND CLEARANCE FROM CLOUD REQUIREMENTS

No person may conduct a parachute operation, and no pilot in command of an aircraft may allow a parachute operation to be conducted from that aircraft-

(a) Into or through a cloud, or

(b) When the flight visibility or the distance from any cloud is less than that prescribed in the following table:

SEC. 105.19 PARACHUTE OPERATIONS BETWEEN SUNSET AND SUNRISE

(a) No person may conduct a parachute operation, and no pilot in command of an aircraft may allow a person to conduct a parachute operation from an aircraft between sunset and sunrise, unless the person or object descending from the aircraft displays a light that is visible for at least 3 statute miles.

(b) The light required by paragraph (a) of this section must be displayed from the time that the person or object is under a properly functioning open parachute until that person or object reaches the surface.

SEC. 105.21 PARACHUTE OPERATIONS OVER OR INTO A CONGESTED AREA OR AN OPEN-AIR ASSEMBLY OF PERSONS

(a) No person may conduct a parachute operation, and no pilot in command of an aircraft may allow a parachute operation to be conducted from that aircraft, over or into a congested area of a city, town, or settlement, or an open-air assembly of persons unless a certificate of authorization for that parachute operation has been issued under this section. However, a parachutist may drift over a congested area or an open-air assembly of persons with a fully deployed and properly functioning parachute if that parachutist is at a sufficient altitude to avoid creating a hazard to persons or property on the surface.

(b) An application for a certificate of authorization issued under this section must—

  (1) Be made in the form and manner prescribed by the Administrator, and

  (2) Contain the information required in Sec. 105.15(a) of this part.

(c) Each holder of, and each person named as a participant in a certificate of authorization issued under this section must comply with all requirements contained in the certificate of authorization.

(d) Each holder of a certificate of authorization issued under this section must present that certificate for inspection upon the request of the Administrator, or any Federal, State, or local official.

SEC. 105.23 PARACHUTE OPERATIONS OVER OR ONTO AIRPORTS

No person may conduct a parachute operation, and no pilot in command of an aircraft may allow a parachute operation to be conducted from that aircraft, over or onto any airport unless—

(a) For airports with an operating control tower:

  (1) Prior approval has been obtained from the management of the airport to conduct parachute operations over or on that airport.

  (2) Approval has been obtained from the control tower to conduct parachute operations over or onto that airport.

  (3) Two-way radio communications are maintained between the pilot of the aircraft involved in the parachute operation and the control tower of the airport over or onto which the parachute operation is being conducted.

(b) For airports without an operating control tower, prior approval has been obtained from the management of the airport to conduct parachute operations over or on that airport.

(c) A parachutist may drift over that airport with a fully deployed and properly functioning parachute if the parachutist is at least 2,000 feet above that airport's traffic pattern, and avoids creating a hazard to air traffic or to persons and property on the ground.

SEC. 105.25 PARACHUTE OPERATIONS IN DESIGNATED AIRSPACE

(a) No person may conduct a parachute operation, and no pilot in command of an aircraft may allow a parachute operation to be conducted from that aircraft—

  (1) Over or within a restricted area or prohibited area unless the controlling agency of the area concerned has authorized that parachute operation;

  (2) Within or into a Class A, B, C, D airspace area without, or in violation of the requirements of, an air traffic control authorization issued under this section;

  (3) Except as provided in paragraph (c) and (d) of this section, within or into Class E or G airspace area unless the air traffic control facility having jurisdiction over the airspace at the first intended exit altitude is notified of the parachute operation no earlier than 24 hours before or no later than 1 hour before the parachute operation begins.

(b) Each request for a parachute operation authorization or notification required under this section must be submitted to the air traffic control facility having jurisdiction over the airspace at the first intended exit altitude and must include the information prescribed by Sec. 105.15(a) of this part.

(c) For the purposes of paragraph (a)(3) of this section, air traffic control facilities may accept a written notification from an organization that conducts parachute operations and lists the scheduled series of parachute operations to be conducted over a stated period of time not longer than 12 calendar months. The notification must contain the information prescribed by Sec. 105.15(a) of this part, identify the responsible persons associated with that parachute operation, and be submitted at least 15 days, but not more than 30 days, before the parachute operation begins. The FAA may revoke the acceptance of the notification for any failure of the organization conducting the parachute operations to comply with its requirements.

(d) Paragraph (a)(3) of this section does not apply to a parachute operation conducted by a member of an Armed Force within a restricted area that extends upward from the surface when that area is under the control of an Armed Force.

SEC. 105.41 APPLICABILITY

This subpart prescribed rules governing parachute equipment used in civil parachute operations.

SEC. 105.43 USE OF SINGLE-HARNESS, DUAL-PARACHUTE SYSTEMS

No person may conduct a parachute operation using a single-harness, dual-parachute system, and no pilot in command of an aircraft may allow any person to conduct a parachute operation from that aircraft using a single-harness, dual-parachute system, unless that system has at least one main parachute, one approved reserve parachute, and one approved single person harness and container that are packed as follows:

(a) The main parachute must have been packed within 180 days before the date of its use by a certificated parachute rigger, the person making the next jump with that parachute, or a non-certificated person under the direct supervision of a certificated parachute rigger.

(b) The reserve parachute must have been packed by a certificated parachute rigger—

  (1) Within 180 days before the date of its use, if its canopy, shroud, and harness are composed exclusively of nylon, rayon, or similar synthetic fiber or material that is substantially resistant to damage from mold, mildew, and other fungi, and other rotting agents propagated in a moist environment; or

  (2) Within 60 days before the date of its use, if it is composed of any amount of silk, pongee, or other natural fiber, or material not specified in paragraph (b)(1) of this section.

(c) If installed, the automatic activation device must be maintained in accordance with manufacturer instructions for that automatic activation device.

FEDERAL AVIATION REGULATIONS

SEC. 105.45 USE OF TANDEM PARACHUTE SYSTEMS

(a) No person may conduct a parachute operation using a tandem parachute system, and no pilot in command of an aircraft may allow any person to conduct a parachute operation from that aircraft using a tandem parachute system, unless—

(1) One of the parachutists using the tandem parachute system is the parachutist in command, and meets the following requirements:

   (i) Has a minimum of 3 years of experience in parachuting, and must provide documentation that the parachutist—

   (ii) Has completed a minimum of 500 freefall parachute jumps using a ram-air parachute, and

   (iii) Holds a master parachute license issued by an organization recognized by the FAA, and

   (iv) Has successfully completed a tandem instructor course given by the manufacturer of the tandem parachute system used in the parachute operation or a course acceptable to the Administrator.

   (v) Has been certified by the appropriate parachute manufacturer or tandem course provider as being properly trained on the use of the specific tandem parachute system to be used.

(2) The person acting as parachutist in command:

   (i) Has briefed the passenger parachutist before boarding the aircraft. The briefing must include the procedures to be used in case of an emergency with the aircraft or after exiting the aircraft, while preparing to exit and exiting the aircraft, freefall, operating the parachute after freefall, landing approach, and landing.

   (ii) Uses the harness position prescribed by the manufacturer of the tandem parachute equipment.

(b) No person may make a parachute jump with a tandem parachute system unless—

(1) The main parachute has been packed by a certificated parachute rigger, the parachutist in command making the next jump with that parachute, or a person under the direct supervision of a certificated parachute rigger.

(2) The reserve parachute has been packed by a certificated parachute rigger in accordance with Sec. 105.43(b) of this part.

(3) The tandem parachute system contains an operational automatic activation device for the reserve parachute, approved by the manufacturer of that tandem parachute system. The device must—

   (i) Have been maintained in accordance with manufacturer instructions, and

   (ii) Be armed during each tandem parachute operation.

(4) The passenger parachutist is provided with a manual main parachute activation device and instructed on the use of that device, if required by the owner/operator.

(5) The main parachute is equipped with a single-point release system.

(6) The reserve parachute meets Technical Standard Order C23 specifications.

SEC. 105.47 USE OF STATIC LINES

(a) Except as provided in paragraph (c) of this section, no person may conduct a parachute operation using a static line attached to the aircraft and the main parachute unless an assist device, described and attached as follows, is used to aid the pilot chute in performing its function, or, if no pilot chute is used, to aid in the direct deployment of the main parachute canopy. The assist device must—

(1) Be long enough to allow the main parachute container to open before a load is placed on the device.

(2) Have a static load strength of—

   (i) At least 28 pounds but not more than 160 pounds if it is used to aid the pilot chute in performing its function; or

   (ii) At least 56 pounds but not more than 320 pounds if it is used to aid in the direct deployment of the main parachute canopy; and

(3) Be attached as follows:

   (i) At one end, to the static line above the static-line pins or, if static-line pins are not used, above the static-line ties to the parachute cone.

   (ii) At the other end, to the pilot chute apex, bridle cord, or bridle loop, or, if no pilot chute is used, to the main parachute canopy.

(b) No person may attach an assist device required by paragraph (a) of this section to any main parachute unless that person is a certificated parachute rigger or that person makes the next parachute jump with that parachute.

(c) An assist device is not required for parachute operations using direct-deployed, ram-air parachutes.

SEC. 105.49 FOREIGN PARACHUTISTS AND EQUIPMENT

(a) No person may conduct a parachute operation, and no pilot in command of an aircraft may allow a parachute operation to be conducted from that aircraft with an unapproved foreign parachute system unless—

(1) The parachute system is worn by a foreign parachutist who is the owner of that system.

(2) The parachute system is of a single-harness dual parachute type.

(3) The parachute system meets the civil aviation authority requirements of the foreign parachutist's country.

(4) All foreign non-approved parachutes deployed by a foreign parachutist during a parachute operation conducted under this section shall be packed as follows—

   (i) The main parachute must be packed by the foreign parachutist making the next parachute jump with that parachute, a certificated parachute rigger, or any other person acceptable to the Administrator.

   (ii) The reserve parachute must be packed in accordance with the foreign parachutist's civil aviation authority requirements, by a certificated parachute rigger, or any other person acceptable to the Administrator.

SUBCHAPTER G—AIR CARRIERS AND OPERATORS FOR COMPENSATION OR HIRE: CERTIFICATION AND OPERATIONS

PART 119—CERTIFICATION: AIR CARRIERS AND COMMERCIAL OPERATORS

SEC. 119.1 APPLICABILITY

(a) This part applies to each person operating or intending to operate civil aircraft—

 (1) As an air carrier or commercial operator, or both, in air commerce; or

 (2) When common carriage is not involved, in operations of U.S.-registered civil airplanes with a seat configuration of 20 or more passengers, or a maximum payload capacity of 6,000 pounds or more.

(b) This part prescribes—

 (1) The types of air operator certificates issued by the Federal Aviation Administration, including air carrier certificates and operating certificates;

(e) Except for operations when common carriage is not involved conducted with airplanes having a passenger-seat configuration of 20 seats or more, excluding any required crewmember seat, or a payload capacity of 6,000 pounds or more, this part does not apply to—

 (6) Nonstop flights conducted within a 25-statute-mile radius of the airport of takeoff carrying persons or objects for the purpose of conducting intentional parachute operations.

9-2: ADVISORY CIRCULARS

AC 90-66B—RECOMMENDED STANDARD TRAFFIC PATTERNS AND PRACTICES FOR AERONAUTICAL OPERATIONS AT AIRPORTS WITHOUT OPERATING CONTROL TOWERS

Department of Transportation—Federal Aviation Administration. 2/25/19 • Initiated by: AFS-800

1 PURPOSE OF THIS ADVISORY CIRCULAR (AC). This AC calls attention to regulatory requirements, recommended operations, and communications procedures for operating at an airport without a control tower or an airport with a control tower that operates only part time. It recommends traffic patterns, communications phraseology, and operational procedures for use by aircraft, lighter-than-air aircraft, gliders, parachutes, rotorcraft, and ultralight vehicles. This AC stresses safety as the primary objective in these operations. This AC is related to the right-of-way rules under Title 14 of the Code of Federal Regulations (14 CFR) part 1, § 1.1 (traffic pattern), and part 91, §§ 91.113 and 91.126.

8 BACKGROUND AND SCOPE.

8.1 In the interest of promoting safety, the FAA, through its AIM, Chart Supplements, ACs, and other publications, provides frequency information, good operating practices, and procedures for pilots to use when operating at an airport without an operating control tower. The FAA believes that observance of a standard traffic pattern and the use of CTAF procedures as detailed in this AC will improve the safety and efficiency of aeronautical operations at airports without operating control towers.

8.2 Regulatory provisions relating to traffic patterns are found in 14 CFR parts 91, 93, and 97. The airport traffic patterns described in part 93 relate primarily to those airports where there is a need for unique traffic pattern procedures not provided for in part 91. Part 97 addresses instrument approach procedures (IAP). At airports without operating control towers, part 91 requires only that pilots of airplanes approaching to land make all turns to the left, unless light signals or visual markings indicate that turns should be made to the right (see approved light gun signals in § 91.125, visual markings and right-hand patterns in the PHAK, Chapter 14, Airport Operations, and the AIM, Chapter 4, Section 3, Airport Operations).

8.2.1 The FAA does not regulate traffic pattern entry, only traffic pattern flow. For example, an aircraft on an instrument approach flying on the final approach course to land would follow the requirements dictated by the approach procedure. A visual flight rules (VFR) aircraft on a long, straight-in approach for landing never enters the traffic pattern unless performing a go-around or touch and go after landing (see paragraph 9.5).

8.2.1.1 Traffic pattern entry information is advisory, provided by using this AC or by referring to the AIM and the PHAK. Approaching to land in relation to traffic patterns by definition would mean aircraft in the traffic pattern landing or taking off from an airport. An aircraft not in the traffic pattern would not be bound by § 91.126(b) (see paragraph 11.3 for aircraft crossing over midfield above pattern altitude to enter the pattern). Requirements for traffic pattern flow under § 91.126 continue to apply to other airspace classification types under § 91.127 (Class E airspace), § 91.129 (Class D airspace), and § 91.130 (Class C airspace), particularly when a towered airport is currently operating as a non-towered airport.

9 GENERAL OPERATING PRACTICES.

9.1 Left Traffic. Use of standard traffic patterns (left turns) for all aircraft and CTAF procedures by radio-equipped aircraft are required at all airports without operating control towers unless indicated otherwise by visual markings, light gun signals, airport publications, or published approach procedure. It is recognized that other traffic patterns (right turns) may already be in common use at some airports or that special circumstances or conditions exist that may prevent use of the standard traffic pattern. Right-hand patterns are noted at airports on an aeronautical chart with an "RP" designator and the applicable runway next to the airport symbol.

9.2 Collision Avoidance. The pilot in command's (PIC) primary responsibility is to see and avoid other aircraft and to help them see and avoid his or her aircraft. Keep lights and strobes on. The use of any traffic pattern procedure does not alter the responsibility of each pilot to see and avoid other aircraft. Pilots are encouraged to participate in "Operation Lights On," a voluntary pilot safety program described in the AIM, paragraph 4-3-23, that is designed to improve the "see-and-avoid" capabilities.

9.2.1 <u>Unmanned Aircraft.</u> Unmanned aircraft (commonly known as drones or model aircraft), like manned aircraft, are allowed to operate in Class G airspace without specific air traffic control (ATC) authorization and without required radio communications. The remote PIC and the Unmanned Aircraft System (UAS) operator must always yield right-of-way to a manned aircraft and not interfere with manned aircraft operations. Additional information regarding unmanned aircraft operations may be found in AC 91-57, AC 107-2, and 14 CFR part 107.

Note: Operators of UAS are required to obtain ATC authorization prior to operating in Class B, C, D, and surface Class E airspaces.

9.3 Preflight Actions. As part of the preflight familiarization with all available information concerning a flight, each pilot should review all appropriate publications (e.g., Chart Supplements, the AIM, and NOTAMs), for pertinent information on current traffic patterns at the departure and arrival airports.

9.4 Traffic Flow. It is recommended that pilots use visual indicators, such as the segmented circle, wind direction indicator, landing direction indicator, and traffic pattern indicators that provide traffic pattern information. If other traffic is present in the pattern, arriving or departing aircraft should use the same runway as these aircraft. Transient aircraft may not know local ground references, so pilots should use standard pattern phraseology, including distances from the airport.

9.5 **Straight-In Landings.** The FAA encourages pilots to use the standard traffic pattern when arriving or departing a non-towered airport or a part-time-towered airport when the control tower is not operating, particularly when other traffic is observed or when operating from an unfamiliar airport. However, there are occasions where a pilot can choose to execute a straight-in approach for landing when not intending to enter the traffic pattern, such as a visual approach executed as part of the termination of an instrument approach. Pilots should clearly communicate on the CTAF and coordinate maneuvering for and execution of the landing with other traffic so as not to disrupt the flow of other aircraft. Therefore, pilots operating in the traffic pattern should be alert at all times to aircraft executing straight-in landings, particularly when flying a base leg prior to turning final.

9.6 **Instrument Flight Rules (IFR) Traffic.** Pilots conducting instrument approaches in visual meteorological conditions (VMC) should be particularly alert for other aircraft in the pattern so as to avoid interrupting the flow of traffic and should bear in mind they do not have priority over other VFR traffic. Pilots are reminded that circling approaches require left-hand turns unless the approach procedure explicitly states otherwise. This has been upheld by prior FAA legal interpretations of § 91.126(b).

9.6.1 Non-instrument-rated pilots might not understand radio calls referring to approach waypoints, depicted headings, or missed approach procedures. IFR pilots often indicate that they are on a particular approach, but that may not be enough information for a non-IFR-rated pilot to know your location. It is better to provide specific direction and distance from the airport, as well as the pilot's intentions upon completion of the approach. For example, instead of saying, "PROCEDURE TURN INBOUND V-O-R APPROACH 36," it should be "6 MILES SOUTH … INBOUND V-O-R APPROACH RUNWAY 36, LOW APPROACH ONLY" or "6 MILES SOUTH … INBOUND V-O-R APPROACH RUNWAY 36, LANDING FULL STOP."

9.7 **No-Radio Aircraft.** Pilots should be aware that procedures at airports without operating control towers generally do not require the use of two-way radios; therefore, pilots should be especially vigilant for other aircraft while operating in the traffic pattern. Pilots of inbound aircraft that are not capable of radio communications should determine the runway in use prior to entering the traffic pattern by observing the landing direction indicator, the wind indicator, landing and departing traffic, previously referring to relevant airport publications, or by other means.

9.8 **Wake Turbulence.** All aircraft generate wake turbulence. Therefore, pilots should be prepared to encounter turbulence while operating in a traffic pattern and especially when in the trail of other aircraft. Wake turbulence can damage aircraft components and equipment. In flight, avoid the area below and behind the aircraft generating turbulence, especially at low altitude where even a momentary wake encounter can be hazardous. All operators should be aware of the potential adverse effects that their wake, rotor, or propeller turbulence has on light aircraft and ultralight vehicles.

9.9 **Other Approaches to Land.** Pilots should be aware of the other types of approaches to land that may be used at an airport when a pilot indicates they are doing so, which may or may not be initiated from the traffic pattern. The more common types of these include a short approach, low approach, or overhead approach.

9.9.1 A short approach is executed when the pilot makes an abbreviated downwind, base, and final legs turning inside of the standard 90-degree base turn. This can be requested at a towered airport for aircraft spacing, but is more commonly used at a non-towered airport or a part-time-towered airport when the control tower is not operating, when landing with a simulated engine out or completing a power-off 180-degree accuracy approach commercial-rating maneuver.

9.9.2 A low approach is executed when an aircraft intends to overfly the runway, maintaining runway heading but not landing. This is commonly used by aircraft flying practice instrument approaches.

9.9.3 An overhead approach is normally performed by aerobatic or high-performance aircraft and involves a quick 180-degree turn and descent at the approach end of the runway before turning to land (described in the AIM, paragraph 5-4-27, Overhead Approach Maneuvers).

10 **COMMUNICATIONS PROCEDURES.** The following information is intended to supplement the AIM, paragraph 4-1-9, Traffic Advisory Practices at Airports Without Operating Control Towers.

10.1 **Recommended Traffic Advisory Practices.** All traffic within a 10-mile radius of a non-towered airport or a part-time-towered airport when the control tower is not operating should continuously monitor and communicate, as appropriate, on the designated CTAF until leaving the area or until clear of the movement area. After first monitoring the frequency for other traffic present passing within 10 miles from the airport, self-announcing of your position and intentions should occur between 8 and 10 miles from the airport upon arrival. Departing aircraft should continuously monitor/communicate on the appropriate frequency from startup, during taxi, and until 10 miles from the airport, unless 14 CFR or local procedures require otherwise.

10.1.1 To achieve the greatest degree of safety, it is essential that:

1. All radio-equipped aircraft transmit/receive on a common frequency identified for the purpose of airport advisories, as identified in appropriate aeronautical publications.

2. Pilots use the correct airport name, as identified in appropriate aeronautical publications, when exchanging traffic information to reduce the risk of confusion. For example, using "Midwest National Traffic" instead of the town name "Mosby Traffic" or "Clay County Traffic" at KGPH when the airport

name is printed "Midwest National" on aeronautical charts.

3. To help identify one airport from another, the correct airport name should be spoken at the beginning and end of each self-announce transmission.

4. Pilots clarify intentions if a communication sent by either their aircraft or another aircraft was potentially not received or misunderstood.

5. Pilots limit communications on CTAF frequencies to safety-essential information regarding arrivals, departures, traffic flow, takeoffs, and landings. The CTAF should not be used for personal conversations.

10.2 Information Provided by UNICOM. UNICOM stations may, upon request, provide pilots with weather information, wind direction, the recommended runway, or other necessary information. If the UNICOM frequency is designated as the CTAF, it will be identified in appropriate aeronautical publications. If wind and weather information is not available, it may be obtainable from nearby airports via the Automatic Terminal Information Service (ATIS) or Automated Weather Observing System (AWOS). UNICOM operators are not required to communicate with pilots, and if they do, there are no standards for the information conveyed.

10.3 Self-Announce Position and/or Intentions. "Self-announce" is a procedure whereby pilots broadcast their aircraft call sign, position, altitude, and intended flight activity or ground operation on the designated CTAF. This procedure is used almost exclusively at airports that do not have an operative control tower on the airport. If an airport has a control tower that is either temporarily closed or operated on a part-time basis, pilots should use the published CTAF to self-announce position and/or intentions when entering within 10 miles of the airport.

10.3.1 Self-announce transmissions may include aircraft type to aid in identification and detection. Paint schemes and color or style descriptions may be added to the use of the aircraft call sign and type, but should not replace type or call sign. For example, "MIDWEST TRAFFIC, TWIN COMMANDER FIVE ONE ROMEO FOXTROT TEN MILES NORTHEAST" or "MIDWEST TRAFFIC, FIVE ONE ROMEO FOXTROT TWIN COMMANDER TEN MILES NORTHEAST." In some cases, where the type of aircraft may not be familiar to pilots, the color and description may be added to the type and call sign. For instance, "MIDWEST TRAFFIC, EXPERIMENTAL SKYBOLT NOVEMBER THREE TWO DELTA SIERRA, ORANGE AND WHITE BIPLANE TEN MILES NORTHEAST." When referring to a specific runway, pilots should use the runway number and not use the phrase "Active Runway," because there is no official active runway at a non-towered airport. To help identify one airport from another when sharing the same frequency, the airport name should be spoken at the beginning and end of each self-announce transmission.

Note: Pilots are reminded that the use of the phrase, "ANY TRAFFIC IN THE AREA, PLEASE ADVISE," is not a recognized self-announce position and/or intention phrase and should not be used under any condition. Any traffic that is present at the time of your self-announcement that is capable of radio communications should reply without being prompted to do so.

10.4 Confusing Language. To avoid misunderstandings, pilots should avoid using the words "to" and "for" whenever possible. These words might be confused with runway numbers or altitudes. The use of "inbound for landing" should also be avoided. For example, instead of saying, "MIDWEST TRAFFIC, EIGHT ONE TANGO FOXTROT TEN MILES TO THE NORTHEAST, INBOUND FOR LANDING RUNWAY TWO TWO MIDWEST," it is more advisable to say, "MIDWEST TRAFFIC, EIGHT ONE TANGO FOXTROT TEN MILES NORTHEAST OF THE AIRPORT, LANDING STRAIGHT IN RUNWAY TWO TWO, MIDWEST," so it does not confuse runway 4, runway 22, or the use of an IAP on arrival.

10.5 Unlisted Frequencies. Where there is no tower, CTAF, or UNICOM station depicted for an airport on an aeronautical chart, use MULTICOM frequency 122.9 for self-announce procedures. Such airports should be identified in appropriate aeronautical information publications.

10.6 Practice Instrument Approaches in VFR Conditions. Pilots conducting practice instrument approaches should be particularly alert for other aircraft that may be departing in the opposite direction or on a base leg or final approach to the runway associated with the approach. Conducting any practice instrument approach, regardless of its direction relative to other airport operations, does not take priority over other VFR aircraft. Pilots should be ready to communicate on CTAF, discontinue the approach, and enter a traffic pattern as needed, based on the traffic saturation of the airport and/or the current runway in use, to maintain aircraft separation and aviation safety. Pilots are reminded that circling approaches, practice or actual, require left-hand turns unless the approach procedure explicitly states otherwise. This has been upheld by prior FAA legal interpretations of § 91.126(b).

10.7 Disagreements. Do not correct other pilots on frequency (unless it is safety critical), particularly if you are aware you are correcting a student pilot. If you disagree with what another pilot is doing, operate your aircraft safely, communicate as necessary, clarify their intentions and, if you feel you must discuss operations with another pilot, wait until you are on the ground to have that discussion. Keep in mind that while you are communicating, you may block transmissions from other aircraft that may be departing or landing in the opposite direction to your aircraft due to IFR operations, noise abatement, obstacle avoidance, or runway length requirements. An aircraft might be using a runway different from the one favoring the prevailing winds. In this case, one option is to simply point out the current winds to the other pilots and indicate which runway you plan on using because of the current meteorological conditions.

11 RECOMMENDED STANDARD TRAFFIC PATTERN. The following information is intended to supplement the AIM, paragraph 4-3-3, Traffic Patterns, and the PHAK, Chapter 14.

11.1 Traffic Pattern Design. Airport owners and operators, in coordination with the FAA, are responsible for establishing traffic patterns. The FAA encourages airport owners and operators to establish traffic patterns as recommended in this AC. Further, left traffic patterns should be established, except where obstacles, terrain, and noise-sensitive areas dictate otherwise (see Appendix A, Traffic Patterns).

11.2 Determination of Traffic Pattern. Prior to entering the traffic pattern at an airport without an operating control tower, aircraft should avoid the flow of traffic until established on the entry leg. For example, the pilot can check wind and landing direction indicators while at an altitude above the traffic pattern, or by monitoring the communications of other traffic that communicate the runway in use, especially at airports with more than one runway. When the runway in use and proper traffic pattern direction have been determined, the pilot should then proceed to a point well clear of the pattern before descending to and entering at pattern altitude.

11.3 Traffic Pattern Entry. Arriving aircraft should be at traffic pattern altitude and allow for sufficient time to view the entire traffic pattern before entering. Entries into traffic patterns while descending may create collision hazards and should be avoided. Entry to the downwind leg should be at a 45 degree angle abeam the midpoint of the runway to be used for landing. The pilot may use discretion to choose an alternate type of entry, especially when intending to cross over midfield, based upon the traffic and communication at the time of arrival.

Note: Aircraft should always enter the pattern at pattern altitude, especially when flying over midfield and entering the downwind directly. A midfield crossing alternate pattern entry should not be used when the pattern is congested. Descending into the traffic pattern can be dangerous, as one aircraft could descend on top of another aircraft already in the pattern. All similar types of aircraft, including those entering on the 45 degree angle to downwind, should be at the same pattern altitude so that it is easier to visually acquire any traffic in the pattern.

11.4 Traffic Pattern Altitudes. It is recommended that airplanes observe a 1,000 foot above ground level (AGL) traffic pattern altitude. Large and turbine-powered airplanes should enter the traffic pattern at an altitude of 1,500 feet AGL or 500 feet above the established pattern altitude. Ultralight vehicles should operate no higher than 500 feet below the powered aircraft pattern altitude. A pilot may vary the size of the traffic pattern depending on the aircraft's performance characteristics.

11.5 Descent and Base Turn. The traffic pattern altitude should be maintained until the aircraft is at least abeam the approach end of the landing runway on the downwind leg. The base leg turn should commence when the aircraft is at a point approximately 45 degrees relative bearing from the approach end of the runway.

11.6 Runway Preference. Landing and takeoff should be accomplished on the operating runway most nearly aligned into the wind. However, if a secondary runway is used (e.g., for length limitations), pilots using the secondary runway should avoid the flow of traffic to the runway most nearly aligned into the wind.

11.7 Takeoff and Go-Around. Airplanes on takeoff should continue straight ahead until beyond the departure end of the runway. Aircraft executing a go-around maneuver should continue straight ahead, beyond the departure end of the runway, with the pilot maintaining awareness of other traffic so as not to conflict with those established in the pattern. In cases where a go-around was caused by an aircraft on the runway, maneuvering parallel, or sidestepping to the runway may be required to maintain visual contact with the conflicting aircraft.

Note: Ask an instructor, Fixed-Base Operator (FBO) employee, or other pilots at your departure airport about special procedures such as noise abatement departure routes or local protocols if they are not apparent or directly communicated by the FAA. Not every airport has official noise abatement procedures, nor does every airport consistently share this information with transient pilots. One inconsiderate act, even if inadvertent, can undo months of effort by local pilots and the airport.

11.8 Turning Crosswind. Airplanes remaining in the traffic pattern should not commence a turn to the crosswind leg until beyond the departure end of the runway and within 300 feet below traffic pattern altitude. Pilots should make the turn to downwind leg at the traffic pattern altitude.

Note: Pilots should be aware that the crosswind leg may be longer or shorter due to weather conditions that are unusually hot or cold.

11.9 Departing the Pattern. When departing the traffic pattern, airplanes should continue straight out or exit with a 45-degree left turn (right turn for right traffic pattern) beyond the departure end of the runway after reaching pattern altitude. Pilots need to be aware of any traffic entering the traffic pattern prior to commencing a turn.

11.10 Airspeed Limitations. Airplanes should not be operated in the traffic pattern at an indicated airspeed of more than 200 knots (230 mph).

11.11 Right-of-Way. Throughout the traffic pattern, right-of-way rules apply as stated in § 91.113; any aircraft in distress has the right-of-way over all other aircraft. In addition, when converging aircraft are of different categories, a balloon has the right-of-way over any other category of aircraft; a glider has the right-of-way over an airship, airplane, or rotorcraft; and an airship has the right-of-way over an airplane or rotorcraft.

Note: Parachute operations are subject to 14 CFR part 105. Parachute operators are required to coordinate their operations with the airport manager before they take place, and utilize proper radio notification during operations.

12 OTHER TRAFFIC PATTERNS. Airport operators routinely establish local procedures for the operation of gliders, parachutists, lighter-than-air aircraft, helicopters, and ultralight vehicles. Appendix B, Glider Operations, and Appendix C, Parachute Operations, illustrate these operations as they relate to recommended standard traffic patterns.

9-2 ADVISORY CIRCULARS

12.5 Parachute Operations.

12.5.1 All activities are normally conducted under a NOTAM noting the location, altitudes, and time or duration of jump operations. The Chart Supplement lists airports where permanent Drop Zones (DZ) are located.

12.5.2 Jumpers normally exit the aircraft either above, or well upwind of, the airport and at altitudes well above traffic pattern altitude. Parachutes are normally deployed between 2,000 feet and 5,000 feet AGL and can be expected to be below 3,000 feet AGL within 2 miles of the airport.

12.5.3 Pilots of jump aircraft are required by part 105 to establish two-way radio communications with the ATC facility that has jurisdiction over the affected airspace prior to jump operations for the purpose of receiving information in the aircraft about known air traffic in the vicinity. In addition, when jump aircraft are operating at or in the vicinity of an airport, pilots are also encouraged to provide advisory information on the CTAF. For example, "Chambersburg traffic, jumpers away over Chambersburg."

12.5.4 When a DZ has been established at an airport, parachutists are expected to land within the DZ. At airports that have not established DZs, parachutists should avoid landing on runways, taxiways, aprons, and their associated safety areas. Pilots and parachutists should both be aware of the limited flight performance of parachutes and take steps to avoid any potential conflicts between aircraft and parachute operations.

12.5.5 Appendix C depicts operations conducted by parachutists.

APPENDIX A. TRAFFIC PATTERNS
Single Runway (Diagram from the AIM, Paragraph 4-3-3)

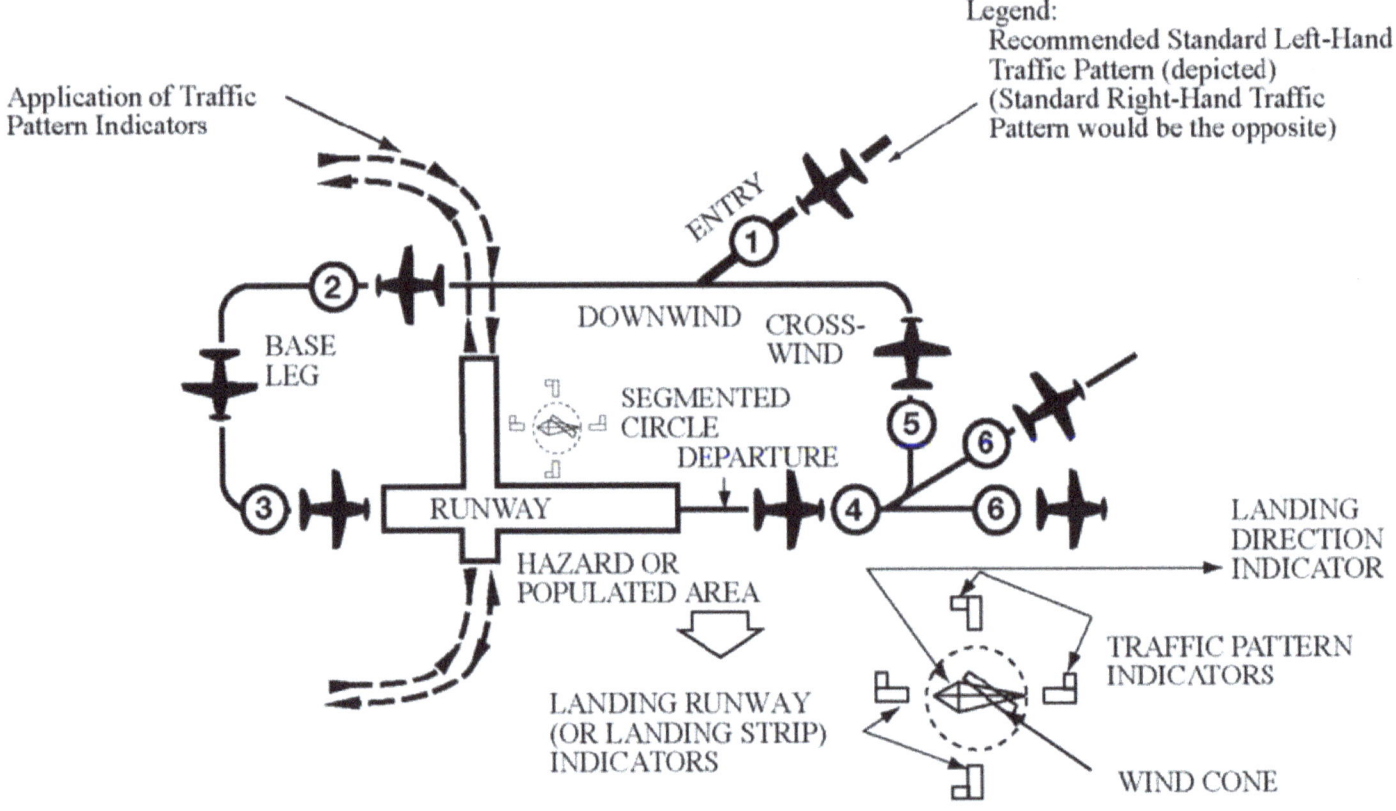

EXAMPLE–

Key to traffic pattern operations

1. Enter pattern in level flight, abeam the midpoint of the runway, at pattern altitude.
2. Maintain pattern altitude until abeam approach end of the landing runway on downwind leg, begin descent and turn base at approximately 45 degrees from the intended landing point.
3. Complete turn to final at least ¼ mile from the runway.
4. Continue straight ahead until beyond departure end of runway.
5. If remaining in the traffic pattern, commence turn to crosswind leg beyond the departure end of the runway within 300 feet of pattern altitude.
6. If departing the traffic pattern, continue straight out, or exit with a 45-degree turn (to the left when in a left-hand traffic pattern; to the right when in a right-hand traffic pattern) beyond the departure end of the runway, after reaching pattern altitude.

PARACHUTE OPERATIONS

SIDE VIEW

TOP VIEW

NOTE: THIS DEPICTS AN AIRPORT WHERE NO DROP ZONE HAS BEEN ESTABLISHED.

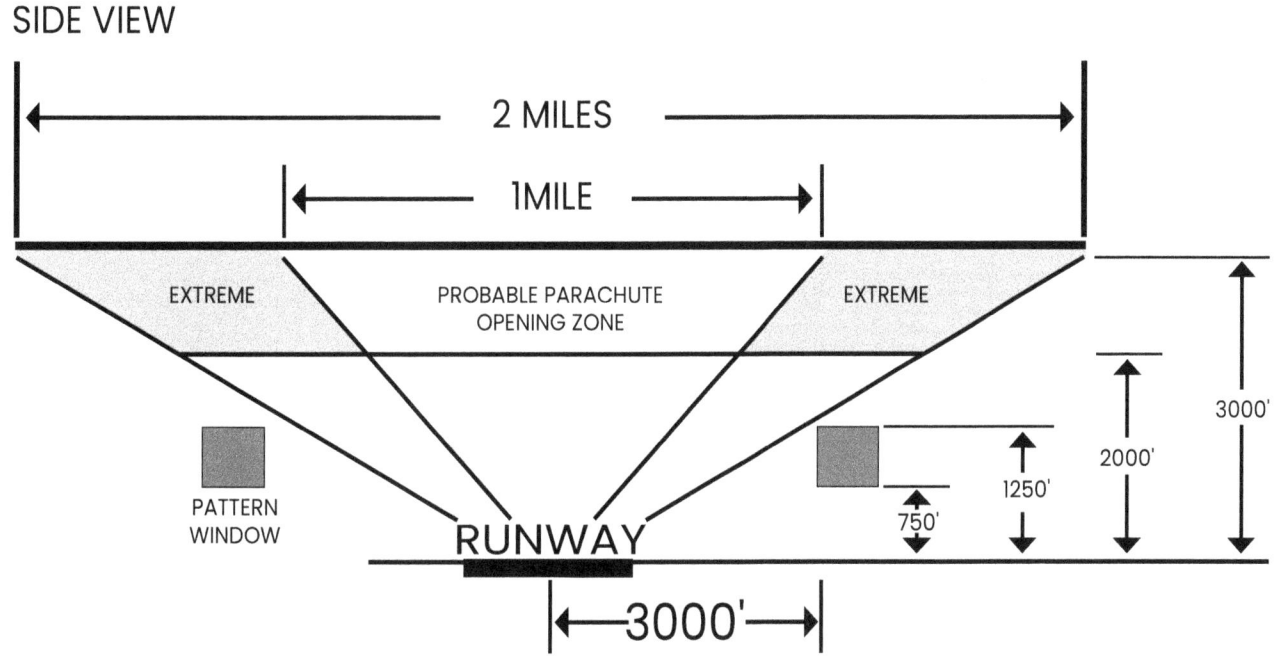

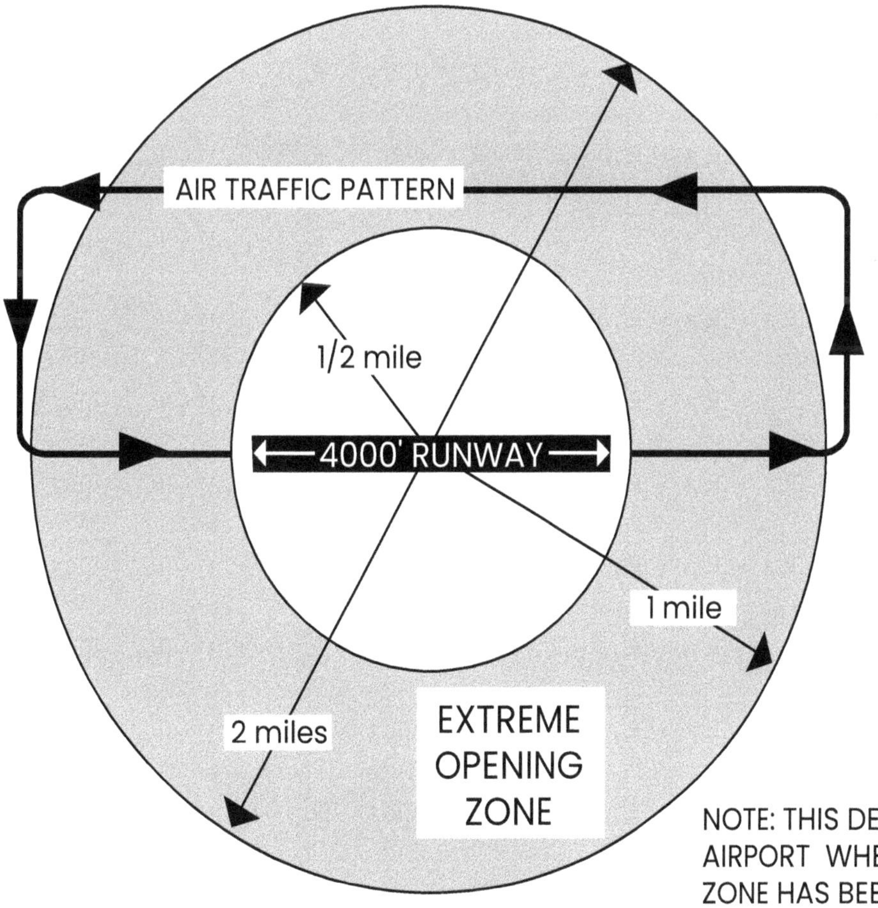

9-2 ADVISORY CIRCULARS

AC 105-2E— SPORT PARACHUTING

Department of Transportation—Federal Aviation Administration. 12/4/13 • Initiated by: AFS-800

1. **PURPOSE.** This advisory circular (AC) provides suggestions to improve sport parachuting safety and disseminates information to assist all parties associated with sport parachuting to be conducted in compliance with Title 14 of the Code of Federal Regulations (14 CFR) part 105. It also contains information for jumpers and riggers on parachuting equipment, on-airport parachuting operations, jump pilot training, aircraft maintenance programs, parachute rigging, and procedures for Federal Aviation Administration (FAA) authorization for flight operations with a removed or modified door.

2. **CANCELLATION.** This AC cancels AC 105-2D, Sport Parachuting, dated May 18, 2011.

3. **RELATED 14 CFR PARTS AND PUBLICATIONS.** The FAA's primary responsibility with respect to skydiving is the protection of air traffic and persons and property on the ground. Part 105 was developed to accomplish this task.

    a. **Title 14 CFR.** This paragraph describes the 14 CFR parts that are of interest to skydivers, parachute riggers, and jump aircraft pilots. They may be downloaded from the FAA's website at: http://www.faa.gov/regulations_policies/faa_regulations/. Since the Federal regulations and other publications may be amended at any time, all FAA regulations, ACs, and other documents are also available for download from the FAA's website for continued compliance with current requirements.

    (1) **Part 65, Certification: Airmen Other Than Flight Crewmembers.** Subpart F concerns parachute riggers, their eligibility requirements, privileges, and performance standards.

    (2) **Part 91, General Operating and Flight Rules.** Parachute operators and jump pilots must comply with all applicable sections of part 91.

    (3) **Part 105, Parachute Operations.** This part is especially important to parachutists, parachute riggers, and the pilots who fly parachutists, since it contains regulations governing intentional parachute jumping.

    (4) **Part 119, Certification.** Air Carriers and Commercial Operators (§ 119.1(e)(6)). Pilots who conduct parachute operations within a 25 statute mile (sm) radius of the airport of departure may conduct them as commercial operations under part 91.

    b. **Technical Standard Order (TSO)-C23, Personnel Parachutes Assemblies.** The TSO-C23 series contains the minimum performance standards for parachute assemblies and components. Manufacturers design and test new parachutes to the most current TSO standards, although they may continue to produce parachutes approved under earlier TSO standards. The most current TSO-C23 document may be obtained from the FAA Web site: faa.gov/regulations_policies/faa_regulations/.

    c. **Parachuting Symbols on Charts, Electronic Navigation Equipment, and Related Publications.** Having parachuting symbols on aeronautical charts, electronic navigation equipment, and related publications helps alert pilots to the location of parachuting Drop Zones (DZ) and the need for extra caution in those areas. The FAA Aeronautical Information Services (AJV-5) collects, stores, and distributes static parachute jumping activities (PAJA) data for use in FAA publications, charts, and navigation databases.

    (1) Operators conducting parachute operations should report any additions, deletions, or changes to static PAJA data to the FAA air traffic control (ATC) facility with jurisdiction over the affected airspace. Operators should submit changes as outlined in part 105, § 105.15.

    (2) ATC facilities that have jurisdiction over the affected airspace should report any additions, deletions, or changes to static PAJA data to AJV-5. At a minimum, include location; distance and radial from the nearest very high frequency omni-directional range (VOR); maximum altitude; DZ radius; day/time of use; and the ATC frequency. Submit static PAJA changes to the Aeronautical Data, National Flight Data Center (NFDC) website at: faa.gov/air_traffic/flight_info/aeronav/Aero_Data/.

4. **BACKGROUND**

    a. **Parachuting as an FAA-Recognized Aeronautical Activity.** Sport parachuting (skydiving) continues to increase in popularity and is an FAA-recognized aeronautical activity even though parachutists are not certificated airmen. As an FAA-recognized aeronautical activity, regulations require airports that have received FAA funding to accommodate this activity unless the FAA determines that compatibility issues prohibit parachuting operations at a particular airport. FAA Order 5190.6, FAA Airport Compliance Manual, has more information regarding airport obligations.

    b. **Training, Licensing, and Instructor Rating.** Sport parachuting has certain inherent risks for all participants. The FAA encourages sport parachutists to complete formal training courses offered by nationally recognized organizations or organizations that have equivalent training programs. The United States Parachute Association (USPA) is an FAA-accepted, nationally recognized skydiving organization that licenses skydivers in the United States. Many local skydiving clubs, schools, and drop zone operators (DZO) require documentation of experience and competency before using their equipment and/or parachuting facilities. This documentation usually consists of a logbook with endorsements and/or a skydiving license issued by a nationally recognized organization.

    c. **Parachute Equipment.** Parachuting as a sport depends on equipment manufacturers, materials suppliers, parachute riggers, government and military agencies, and other industry professionals. The Parachute Industry Association (PIA) is an international trade association that brings all of these interests together for the purpose of advancing the technology and safety of parachutes and parachuting activities. The PIA creates, publishes, and maintains materials, technical, and certification standards relating to parachutes, accessible on their web site: http://www.pia.com.

5. SKYDIVER SAFETY

a. Basic Safety Requirements (BSR). The USPA developed basic safety requirements and information for skydiving activities. These requirements and information are for training, checking equipment, and conducting a wide variety of sport parachuting activities. While not approved by the FAA, the BSRs are considered industry best practices and are widely accepted for use by individuals and parachute centers. The BSRs may be obtained from: The United States Parachute Association, 5401 Southpoint Centre Boulevard, Fredericksburg, VA 22407. The association's phone number is (540) 604-9740 and the USPA Web site is http://www.uspa.org. The FAA encourages skydivers to use facilities that conduct their operations in accordance with the USPA BSRs or other similar skydiving association best practices.

b. Medical Certificates. While the regulations do not require an FAA medical certification, the FAA urges prospective skydivers to receive a physical examination prior to their first jump and on a periodic basis thereafter. The skydiver should inform the physician of the purpose of the examination.

c. Training Methods. The skydiving industry has developed various methods of first-jump instruction. The FAA recommends that beginning skydivers seek instruction from instructors that have met the qualifications set forth by a nationally recognized parachuting organization.

d. Safety Devices and Equipment

(1) **Deployment Assist Device.** Section 105.47 requires that all persons making a parachute jump with a static line attached to the aircraft and main parachute use an assist device to aid the pilot chute in performing its function. An assist device is also required if no pilot chute is used in direct deployment of a round, main parachute canopy. The regulations do not require an assist device for direct deployment of a ram-air main parachute canopy.

(2) **Automatic Activation Device (AAD).** An AAD is a self-contained mechanical or electromechanical device attached to the parachute container that automatically releases the parachute closing system when it meets specific parameters, such as exceeding a specific vertical velocity and being at or below a specific altitude. Parachutists may attach this device to the main, reserve, or both. However, it is normally only attached to the reserve. An AAD does not physically open the parachute container or deploy the canopy, but rather initiates the container opening by pulling the ripcord pin or by cutting the container closing loop, allowing the canopy to deploy in a similar manner as when pulling the ripcord manually.

(a) The FAA requires that all tandem parachutes have an AAD installed on the reserve parachute. Many skydiving schools and clubs follow USPA BSRs and require the use of an AAD for all unlicensed skydivers.

(b) The FAA has not established minimum operational performance standards (MOPS) or a TSO for AADs. Therefore, the FAA recommends that anyone using an AAD review manufacturer's reports conforming to the PIA Technical Standard TS-120, AAD Design and Testing Report Format, and independent third-party reports attesting to the AAD's performance standard in order to make an educated decision prior to the use of any particular make or model AAD. The FAA recommends that jumpers using AADs to satisfy the requirements set forth in part 105 purchase them from manufacturers who provide such reports. Each parachute manufacturer approves the installation of the AAD on their equipment.

(c) Users of AADs should be aware of the device's level of reliability and its operating limitations, be knowledgeable about the various parameters of the device, and be trained on the specific use and setting for the particular AAD. Users should be well informed about the use of the AAD and have access to the manufacturer's instructions.

(d) Users should understand that AADs are strictly backup devices and are not intended to replace training or timely manual execution of emergency procedures. AADs may or may not initiate reserve parachute deployment at a sufficient altitude, depending upon various combinations of circumstances.

(e) Jumpers should make a pre-jump check using the manufacturer's recommended procedures for proper setting, arming, and operational status verification to ensure the proper functioning of the AAD. This pre-jump check is usually made prior to boarding the aircraft to ensure that it is set at the proper altitude and under current weather conditions to aid in accuracy. This is especially important when using an AAD that has selectable or adjustable activation settings, or when the intended landing area is at an elevation different from that of the departure airfield.

(f) AADs may have selectable or adjustable altitude activation settings. Some AADs are preset for the intended type of operation (e.g., Tandem or Student), while others may be user-selectable. The model, version, and settings, must be appropriate for the particular type of equipment and jump. Different manufacturers may have different arming altitudes, as well as different activation altitudes and vertical speeds for the similar settings.

(g) Since body position and other factors may cause a delay in the actual parachute opening altitude, the devices should only be used as a backup to manually deploying the reserve parachute.

9-2 ADVISORY CIRCULARS

When the situation requires the use of the reserve parachute, the jumper should always manually pull the reserve ripcord using the established procedures for reserve deployment before ever reaching AAD activation altitude. The procedures for deployment of the reserve parachute are usually the same whether an AAD is installed or not.

(h) AAD malfunctions and activations should be reported to the AAD and container manufacturers, as well as to the USPA.

e. **Weather.** Strong or gusty winds can be dangerous, especially to student jumpers. In addition, skydivers and pilots should ensure adequate ceiling and visibility to maintain the required weather minimums.

f. **Parachute Landing Areas.** The FAA recommends that areas used as parachute landing areas remain unobstructed, with sufficient minimum radial distances to the nearest hazard. The guidelines in the USPA's BSRs can be used in determining if the landing area is adequate.

g. **Water Safety Equipment.** Flotation gear should be worn whenever the intended exit point or landing point of a skydiver is within 1 mile of an open body of water.

h. **Advanced Parachuting.** Many of the safety suggestions presented in this AC are intended primarily for the student parachutist, who should make all jumps in a controlled training environment. Individual experience and judgment dictate what additional training should be obtained before undertaking more advanced parachuting activities. All parachutists should acquire experience and training before using unfamiliar or high-performance equipment.

i. **Pre-Jump Equipment Checks.** The parachute system user has primarily responsibility for the airworthiness of his equipment at the time of use. Prior to each jump, the user should inspect his equipment for serviceability, including at least general condition, AAD serviceability (see subparagraph 5d(2)), pilot chute bridle routing, main and reserve pin seating, and Reserve Static Line (RSL) routing and connection.

6. **PARACHUTE OPERATIONS ONTO AIRPORTS**

a. **Stipulations for Landing at or Flying Over an Airport.** Most parachute operations take place at airports, including having the parachute landing area located on the airport property. Section 105.23 requires approval from airport management prior to skydiving onto any airport. However, § 105.23(c) allows a parachutist to drift over an airport with an open parachute without airport management approval as long as the parachutist remains at least 2,000 feet above that airport's traffic pattern. Airport traffic patterns are generally 1,000 to 1,500 feet above ground level (AGL).

b. **Additional Aviation Activities.** A large number of airports that accommodate parachute operations also have different kinds of aviation activities taking place simultaneously, including flight training, glider and helicopter operations, emergency medical services, sightseeing operations, and aerobatic practice over or in the immediate vicinity of the airport. Many airports accommodate a large volume of transient traffic during skydiving operations.

c. **Shared Facility Airports.** The FAA recommends that shared facility airports have operating procedures so that each activity can operate safely by knowing the procedures for each of the other activities. Representatives of each type of activity can operate more effectively by knowing the procedures for each of the other activities. Representatives of each type of airport user group should develop procedures specific to their activity and share these procedures with other user groups. Airport management must ensure that airport policies and procedures are kept current, which can be accomplished via regularly scheduled meetings with all airport user groups.

(1) **Traffic Patterns.** With a minimum parachute opening altitude of 2,000 feet AGL (most parachutists open much higher), parachutes are nearly always open 800 feet or more above the traffic pattern altitude for any airport. Parachutes descend relatively slowly and are easy for pilots to acquire visually. Parachutists and pilots have a shared responsibility to see and avoid each other. Refer to the current edition of AC 90-66, Recommended Standard Traffic Patterns and Practices for Aeronautical Operations at Airports without Operating Control Towers, for information on traffic patterns and parachute operations.

(2) **Parachute Landings on Airports.** Airports may designate suitable parachute landing areas. While skydivers attempt to land in such areas, at times there may be inadvertent landings in other grass or hard-surfaced areas. This could include landings on runways, taxiways, and other hard-surfaced areas. Areas such as runways, taxiways, clearways, and Obstacle Free Zones (OFZ) are not prohibited areas but should not be designated as a primary landing area and should be vacated as soon as practical. Flying a parachute over runways at low altitudes should be avoided where possible. The FAA recommends that airport management work with parachute operators to develop standard operating procedures (SOP) for activities conducted by parachutists. Airports that receive or have received Federal funding or grant assurances may have additional requirements or restrictions to parachute landing areas. For additional information, see the current editions of FAA Order 5190.6, FAA Airport Compliance Manual, AC 150/5190-7, Minimum Standards for Commercial Aeronautical Activities; and AC 150/5300-13, Airport Design. 7

7. **JUMP AIRCRAFT MAINTENANCE AND JUMP PILOTS**

Whenever flights are offered for compensation or hire, the flight is considered a commercial operation under part 91, and Federal regulations require:

a. **Aircraft Inspections.** The operator must ensure the aircraft is maintained in accordance with part 91, § 91.409 as applicable:

(1) Section 91.409(a) and (b), annual and 100-hour inspection programs;

(2) Section 91.409(d), progressive inspection program;

(3) Section 91.409(f)(3), manufacturer's inspection program; or

(4) Section 91.409(f)(4), approved inspection program.

b. **Aircraft Inspection Quality Assurance (QA).** Aircraft operated commercially under part 91 must be inspected by a person authorized to perform inspections under a 100-hour/annual program or an FAA-approved progressive inspection program consistent with the requirements for part 91 operations. Operators must maintain aircraft operated under 14 CFR part 125 or 135 under an FAA-approved maintenance program. The FAA recommends the use of an aircraft status sheet for QA.

c. **Additional Information on Acceptable Maintenance Programs.** Anyone conducting parachuting operations should contact his or her local FAA Flight Standards District Office (FSDO) for additional information on acceptable maintenance programs. Reviewing aircraft maintenance records can be simplified by the use of an aircraft status sheet (see AC 105-2E, Figure 1, FAA Aircraft Status Inspection List Example).

8. **PILOT RESPONSIBILITIES.** The pilot in command (PIC) must adhere to all regulations applicable to the operation conducted. This includes, but is not limited to, the following:

a. **Pilot Certification, Experience, and Operating Requirements.** The PIC is responsible for meeting the certification, proficiency, operating, and experience requirements of, but not limited to, 14 CFR parts 61, 91, and 105. Pilots conducting flight operations for compensation or hire are required to possess a Commercial Pilot Certificate with the appropriate ratings for the aircraft being flown and must have a current Class 2 medical certificate or equivalent.

b. **Jump Pilot Training.** For those DZOs and parachuting operations that do not have a nationally recommended jump pilot training program, the FAA recommends that pilots flying aircraft for the purpose of sport parachuting have appropriate initial and recurrent training. The training program should

FIGURE 1. FAA AIRCRAFT STATUS INSPECTION LIST EXAMPLE

N _____ S/N _____ A/C Make and Model (M/M) _____

Name of Airframe and Powerplant (A&P), Inspection Authorization (IA) or FAA Repair Station responsible for the inspection of the aircraft:

_____

A&P or IA Certificate No. or Repair Station No.: _____

Inspection/Item Pending	Hours/Date	Next Due
Annual or Progressive Inspection		
100-Hour Inspection		
Static System Check		
Altimeter Check		
Transponder Check		
Emergency Locator Transmitter (ELT) Battery		

Airworthiness Directive (AD) Number	Description	Hours/Date Completed	Next Due

9-2 ADVISORY CIRCULARS

include testing to ensure a high level of competence in the jump aircraft being flown. The training should include at least the following:

(1) Ground Training.

   (a) Preflight inspection specific to jump aircraft and modifications.

   (b) Aircraft limitations.

   (c) Weight and Balance (W&B).

   1. Takeoff computations.
   2. Weight shift in flight procedures for exiting jumpers.
   3. Landing configuration.

   (d) Low-speed operations for jump runs.

   1. Maneuvering at minimum speed.
   2. Opening and closing jump door, if applicable.
   3. Stall recognition and recovery.

   (e) Emergency procedures.

   1. Standard aircraft emergencies.
   2. Emergencies caused by jump activities.
   3. Bailout procedures.

   (f) Aircraft airworthiness determination.

   1. Maintenance requirements and procedures.
   2. Aircraft Status Inspection List (Figure 1).
   3. Minimum equipment list (MEL), if applicable.
   4. Logging maintenance discrepancies.

   (g) Parachute packing in compliance with § 105.43.

   (h) Drop zone surface and airspace familiarization.

   (i) Descent Procedures.

   1. Aircraft best-glide speed for engine failure.
   2. AAD activation considerations with skydivers onboard.

(2) Flight Training.

   (a) Takeoffs and landings with representative loads.

   (b) Center of gravity (CG) shift with jumper exit.

   (c) Stall-spin prevention and recovery.

   (d) Configuration for jump run and jumper exit including procedures for tail strike avoidance

   (e) Skydive aircraft formation flying (if applicable), in accordance with USPA Formation Flying 101 guidance.

c. W&B Procedures. The PIC is solely responsible for assuring that the aircraft being flown is properly loaded and operated so that it stays within gross weight and CG limitations. The PIC should obtain additional aircraft station position information (loading schedule) for future W&B computations. The PIC is also responsible for reviewing these records and the flight manual to gain familiarity with an aircraft's W&B procedures and flight characteristics.

d. Computing W&B. The PIC must include the following factors:

   (1) The maximum allowable gross weight and the CG limitations.

   (2) The currently configured empty weight and CG location.

   (3) The weight and CG location prior to each flight.

   (4) The weight and location of jumpers during each phase of the flight in order to ensure that the aircraft stays within CG limits. The PIC must remain aware of CG shifts and their effects on aircraft controllability and stability as jumpers move into position for exiting the aircraft and as they exit.

e. Operational Requirements. The PIC is solely responsible for the operational requirements of parts 91 and 105, including compliance with the special operating limitations and placards required for flight with the door open or removed. The PIC is also responsible for ensuring that each occupant has been briefed on operation of his or her restraint system, procedures for ensuring aircraft W&B stays within limits while jumpers exit, and procedures to avoid tail strikes.

f. Suitable Placards. Placards should be located in the aircraft to help the pilot inform jumpers of the maximum approved loading and weight distribution. These placards should be located where anyone boarding the aircraft can see them. They should also clearly show the maximum approved seating capacity and the load distribution.

g. Seatbelts and Approved Loading. Section 91.107(a)(3)(ii) permits persons aboard an aircraft for the purpose of participating in sport parachuting activities to use the floor of the aircraft for a seat. However, among jump aircraft there are a wide variety of seats, benches, troop seats, and floor seating arrangements. In all cases, each person must have access to an installation-approved seatbelt. See Appendix 3, Seats and Restart Systems, for additional information describing seat and restraint system configurations. The maximum number of skydivers is determined by that aircraft's W&B limitations, as long as there is a seatbelt or restraint for each skydiver. The approved number of skydivers that each aircraft can carry for parachute operations will most commonly be found on FAA Form 337, Major Repair and Alteration (Airframe, Powerplant, Propeller, or Appliance), used for field approvals, or an aircraft Supplemental Type Certificate (STC).

h. Oxygen. Pilots must use oxygen when flying above 14,000 feet mean sea level (MSL). Operators must provide oxygen to occupants when the jump plane is above 15,000 feet MSL. Above 25,000 feet MSL, occupants should use pressure-demand oxygen systems. High-altitude jumps should be made only after becoming familiar with the problems and hazards created by low temperatures, lack of oxygen, and the various types of oxygen equipment. Jumpers should not attempt high-altitude jumps without an adequate supply of breathing oxygen (refer to § 91.211). Also, pilots must use oxygen while flying between 12,500 to 14,000 feet MSL for a duration of over 30 minutes.

i. **Altitude Reporting.** Pilots report altitudes in feet above MSL.

9. **PARACHUTE OPERATIONS IN DESIGNATED AIRSPACE.** Section 105.25 contains information on the ATC authorization and notification process (see Appendix 1, Table of Location of Jump Authorization or Notification).

    a. **Parachute Operations Restrictions.** No person may conduct a parachute operation, and no PIC of an aircraft may allow a parachute operation to be conducted from that aircraft:

       (1) Over or within a restricted or prohibited area, unless the controlling agency of the area concerned has authorized that parachute operation;

       (2) Within or into a Class A, B, C, or D airspace area without, or in violation of the requirements of, an ATC authorization issued under § 105.25; or

       (3) Within or into a Class E or G airspace area (except as provided in subparagraphs 9c and 9d), unless the ATC facility that has jurisdiction over the airspace at the first intended exit altitude receives notification of the parachute operation no earlier than 24 hours before and no later than 1 hour before the parachute operation begins.

    b. **Request for a Parachute Operation Authorization or Notification.** Submit each request for a parachute operation authorization or notification required under this section to the ATC facility that has jurisdiction over the airspace at the first intended exit altitude and include the information prescribed by § 105.15(a).

    c. **Notification of Parachute Operations.** For the purposes of subparagraph 9a(3), ATC facilities may accept a written notification from an organization that conducts parachute operations and lists the scheduled series of parachute operations over a period of time not longer than 12 calendar-months. The notification must contain the information prescribed by § 105.15(a) (see Appendix 1).

    d. **Armed Force.** Subparagraph 9a(3) does not apply to a parachute operation conducted by a member of a Department of Defense (DOD) armed force within a restricted area that extends upward from the surface when that area is under the control of the DOD armed force.

10. **JUMPS OVER AND INTO CONGESTED AREAS AND OPEN-AIR ASSEMBLIES OF PERSONS**

    a. **Off-Airport Jumps.** A skydiver may make parachute jumps away from the usual on-airport parachute school, club, or center location, as long as landowner permission is obtained for the off-airport location.

    b. **Certificate of Authorization (COA).** Section 105.21(a) requires an FAA COA in order to conduct a parachute operation over or into a congested area of a city, town, or settlement, or an open-air assembly of persons. The responsible person of the proposed jump must obtain this COA from the FAA FSDO that has jurisdiction over the site where the jump is proposed by submitting an application, FAA Form 7711-2, Certificate of Waiver or Authorization Application. A copy of FAA Form 7711-2 and information on filling out this form can be obtained from the local FSDO or downloaded from http://www.faa.gov. An application for a COA should be submitted at least 10 working days in advance of the intended jump date to allow time for processing. Approval or denial of the application must be completed within 5 working days of receipt by the FSDO.

11. **AUTHORIZATION AND NOTIFICATIONREQUIREMENTS FOR PARACHUTE OPERATIONS.** Whether regulations require verbal or written authorization or a COA (FAA Form 7711-1, Certificate of Waiver or Authorization) for a parachute operation depends upon the type of airspace involved and the area where the parachutist intends to land. The airspace and landing area will determine the requirements. Parachutists and pilots can use Appendix 1 to determine what authorization or notification requirements are necessary for various types of jumps. The FAA recommends that anyone establishing a permanent drop zone or a temporary jump site contact the ATC facilities nearest the site as early as possible. ATC personnel are in the best position to provide information on arrival and departure routes, airspace classifications, and other airspace operations that may affect the safe and efficient flow of a parachuting operation. If you are uncertain of the requirements after looking at Appendix 1, contact your local FSDO and/or ATC facility for additional information.

12. **EXHIBITION JUMPS AT OFF-AIRPORT LOCATIONS**

    a. **Parachute Landing Areas.** The FAA requires the following size areas when issuing a COA for parachuting operations conducted over or into a congested area or an open air assembly of persons.

       (1) **Open Field.** An open area, no less than 500,000 square feet (e.g., approximately 710 feet by 710 feet, or dimensions with a sum total that equals or exceeds 500,000 square feet) that will accommodate landing no closer than 100 feet from spectators. Allows a jumper to drift over the spectators with sufficient altitude (250 feet) so as to not create a hazard to persons or property on the ground.

       (2) **Level I.** An open area that will accommodate a landing area no smaller than 250,000 square feet (e.g., approximately 500 feet by 500 feet, or dimensions with a sum total that equals or exceeds 250,000 square feet) and which will accommodate landing no closer than 50 feet from spectators. Allows a jumper to pass over the spectators no lower than 250 feet, including the canopy and all external paraphernalia. Many open field athletic areas and airport operational areas constitute Level I landing areas.

       (3) **Level II.** An open area that will accommodate a rectangular, square, oval, or round-shaped landing area of approximately 5,000 square feet for no more than four jumpers, with at least 50 feet in width. Also accommodates an additional 800 square feet minimum for each additional jumper over four for any jumper landing within 30 seconds of the last of any four jumpers. This permits jumpers to land no closer than 15 feet from spectators and to pass over the spectators no lower than 50 feet

9-2 ADVISORY CIRCULARS

including the canopy and all external paraphernalia.

(4) **Stadium.** A level II landing area smaller than 450 feet in length by 240 feet in width and bounded on two sides or more by bleachers, walls, or buildings in excess of 50 feet high.

(5) **Other Landing Area Considerations.**

   (a) A landing area that exceeds the maximum dimensions of a Level I landing area, that permits a parachutist to drift over a congested area or open air assembly with a fully deployed and properly functioning parachute (if the parachutist is at sufficient altitude to avoid creating a hazard to persons and property on the ground) and that has no other safety concerns would likely not require a COA as required by § 105.21.

   (b) Any parachute jumping demonstration planned in conjunction with a public aviation event will require a COA with appropriate special provisions as required by § 105.21, even if the landing area exceeds the maximum dimensions for a Level I area. A parachute jumping demonstration planned in conjunction with a public aviation event is one that takes place any time after the first spectator arrives for the event that day.

(6) **Tandem Jump Demonstrations.** Only tandem instructors, rated by the USPA or authorized by the FAA General Aviation and Commercial Division (AFS-800), Federal Aviation Administration, Flight Standards Service, 800 Independence Avenue, SW, Washington, DC 20591 may conduct tandem demonstrations. Tandem jumps may be authorized as follows:

   (a) Tandem jumps into open field and Level I landing areas do not require any previous jump experience for the passenger.

   (b) Tandem jumps into Level II areas require the passenger to have a USPA category D license with a Professional Exhibition Rating (PRO)

(7) **Alternate Landings Areas.** Regardless of the parachutists' experience, "runoffs" or escape areas must be identified.

(8) **Intentional Cutaway.** Cutaways may not be performed if the cutaway equipment will drift into the spectator area.

b. **Qualification and Currency Requirements.** In addition to landing area size requirements, the FAA also imposes qualification and currency requirements. The FAA recognizes and accepts USPA licenses and ratings found in the parachutist's license and recent experience requirements that are established in the current edition of FAA Order 8900.1, Flight Standards Information Management System (FSIMS), Volume 3, Chapter 6, Section 1, Issue a Certificate of Waiver or Authorization for an Aviation Event, located at http://fsims.faa.gov. In accordance with Order 8900.1, parachutists and instructors who are not members of the USPA and who wish to participate in a demonstration or exhibition jump over or into a congested area must present satisfactory evidence of the experience, knowledge, and skill equivalent to that required by the USPA and must have a letter of approval from AFS-800.

13. PARACHUTE EQUIPMENT RULES

a. **Parachute.** Title 14 CFR part 1, § 1.1 defines a parachute as a device used, or intended to be used, to retard the fall of a body or object through the air. For the purposes of this AC, a parachute assembly normally, but not exclusively, consists of the following major components: a canopy, a deployment device, a pilot chute and/or drogue, risers, a stowage container, a harness, and an actuation device (ripcord). There are, of course, some lesser parts associated with these major components such as connector links, bridles, and hardware. The term "pack," when used in this AC, refers to the complete harness-container system, including the main parachute container, plus the reserve parachute and associated components. Except for an RSL (if installed), it does not include the main canopy, main risers, or components that depart with the main canopy if it is jettisoned. If a container is designed to be easily disconnected from its harness (for storage or transport, for example), the term "pack" refers to the container/canopy assembly by itself, without the harness.

b. **Parachute Harness.** Section 105.43 requires a solo parachutist making an intentional jump wearing a single-harness dual-pack parachute to have at least one main parachute and one approved reserve parachute. For tandem jumps, the parachute system defined in § 105.3 includes a main parachute, a reserve parachute, a harness and dual parachute container, an AAD, and a forward harness for a passenger parachutist. For both solo and tandem parachutists, the harnesses (including the forward harness of a tandem system) and reserve parachute packs must be approved types, but the main parachutes do not need approval. The following are examples of approved parachutes as defined in § 105.3:

   (1) **Parachutes Manufactured under TSO-C23.** This TSO prescribes the minimum performance and QA standards for personnel parachutes that are carried aboard civil aircraft or by skydivers for emergency use, including reserve parachutes used for intentional jumps. The manufacturer must meet these standards before labeling its parachute or components as complying with the TSO.

   (2) **Demilitarized or Military Surplus Parachutes.** Military personnel-carrying parachutes (other than high-altitude, high-speed, or ejection kinds) identified by military drawing number, military order number, or any other military designation or specification. These parachutes are often referred to as demilitarized or military surplus parachutes.

c. **Assembly of Major Components.** The assembly or mating of approved parachute components from different manufacturers may be made by a certificated, appropriately rated parachute rigger in accordance with the parachute manufacturer's instructions and without further authorization by the manufacturer or the FAA. Specifically, when various parachute components are interchanged, the parachute rigger should follow the canopy manufacturer's instructions as well as the parachute container manufacturer's instructions. However, the container manufacturer's instructions take precedence when there is a conflict between the two.

(1) Assembled parachute components must be compatible. Each component of the resulting assembly must function properly and may not interfere with the operation of the other components. For example:

   (a) Do not install a canopy of lesser or greater pack volume than the intended design criteria for the specific size of container, since it could adversely affect the proper functioning of the entire parachute assembly.

   (b) A TSO'd canopy may be assembled with a demilitarized harness, or vice versa, as long as the assembled components comply with the safety standard of the original design.

   (c) In cases where a main canopy that is already mounted on risers is assembled to an existing harness/container system, ensure that the completed assembly functions correctly. Refer to the manufacturer's instructions to see if and how the RSL (if installed) may be deactivated when equipment configuration does not permit its use.

(2) Any questions about the operation of the assembly should be resolved by actual tests by the rigger to make certain the parachute is safe for emergency use.

(3) For a single-harness parachute system, the strength of the harness must always be equal to or greater than the maximum force generated by the canopy during certification tests. The rigger who assembles the system should record these limits in a place accessible to the user when he or she dons the assembly. Some manufacturers may also specify minimum weights or speeds for safe operation.

   (a) The maximum operating weight and maximum pack opening speed of components manufactured under TSO-C23c, TSO-C23d, and TSO-C23f are marked on the components themselves.

   (b) In the case where either the harness or canopy of a single-harness system is certified under TSO-C23b and the manufacturer has not specified operating limits, derive the maximum pack opening speed for that component from the strength test table in the National Aerospace Standards Specification (NAS)-804, Parachutes.

      1. For the maximum operating weight of the TSO-C23b component, use the highest weight in the table less than or equal to the maximum operating weight of the other component and use the corresponding speed in the table as the maximum pack opening speed of the TSO-C23b component.

      2. For the maximum pack opening speed of the TSO-C23b component, use the highest speed in the table less than or equal to the maximum pack opening speed of the other component and use the corresponding weight in the table as the maximum operating weight of the TSO-C23b component.

(4) For tandem systems, there may be additional limits for each harness.

d. **AAD Installation.** The FAA accepts the installation (addition of pockets, channels, guides, etc., required for the AAD assemblage in the parachute container) of each make/model AAD as part of the paperwork that is submitted by the parachute manufacturer during the TSO approval for parachute harness/container systems. The TSO approval by the FAA and the AAD approval by the manufacturer (mentioned, for example, in § 105.43(b)) are for the installation only, and are based on AAD operation not interfering with normal function of the parachute. A retrofit installation, or installation of a make or model AAD other than those specifically authorized for use by the parachute manufacturer for a particular TSO or Military Specifications (MIL-SPEC)-approved parachute, constitutes an alteration to that parachute (see paragraph 16). Manufacturer and retrofit installation are done in consultation and agreement with the AAD manufacturer, and in accordance with established test procedures such as PIA Technical Standard (TS)-112, Harness/Container - AAD Installation Test Protocol.

e. **Instructions for Maintenance, Repair, or Alteration of Specific Parachutes.** These instructions may be available by contacting manufacturers. Many manufacturers provide their manuals online through their websites. The PIA website, http://www.pia.com, provides a good starting point for searches. When such instructions are not available, The Parachute Manual, Volumes I and II (Dan Poynter, 1991) and FAA-H-8083-17, Parachute Rigger Handbook, set out commonly accepted repair practices. The Parachute Manual and The Parachute Rigger Handbook can be purchased from commercial booksellers; The Parachute Rigger Handbook is also available for download at: faa.gov/regulations_policies/handbooks_manuals/aviation/.

f. **Parachutist's Handling of Equipment.** The user of a parachute system may perform simple assembly and disassembly operations necessary for transportation, handling, or storage between periods of use if the parachute's design simplifies such assembly and disassembly without the use of complex operations.

g. **Removal of Pilot Chute.** A certificated senior or master parachute rigger may remove the pilot chute from a front-mounted (e.g., chest-type) reserve parachute if the canopy does not use a diaper, bag, or other deployment device. When complete, the parachute must have the plain marking, "PILOT CHUTE REMOVED." This kind of parachute can be used for intentional jumping only.

h. **Extra Equipment.** The FAA does not consider the attachment of an instrument panel, knife sheath, or other material to the exterior of the parachute assembly an alteration. If attaching any extra equipment, take care not to impair the functional design of the system.

14. PARACHUTE PACKING

a. **Reserve Parachutes.**

(1) A certificated and appropriately rated parachute rigger must pack the reserve parachute.

(2) Visiting foreign parachutists jumping parachute systems that the FAA has not approved must have their reserve parachutes packed by someone acceptable to the foreign parachutist's Civil Aviation Authority (CAA) or by a FAA-certificated rigger.

(3) The certificated and appropriately rated parachute rigger must pack the reserve parachute within 180 days before the date of use if the parachute system is made of materials substantially resistant to mold, mildew, or other rotting agents, or within 60 days of the date of use otherwise.

(4) A parachute user must ensure that an AAD is maintained in accordance with the AAD manufacturer's instructions and service requirements. When a rigger packs a reserve parachute, the rigger is only certifying that it meets all safety requirements on the day it is packed; therefore, riggers should note any maintenance or battery replacement due date(s) on the packing data card so that users are able to determine AAD airworthiness and ensure conformance to the regulations. AADs are to be installed in accordance with the harness/container manufacturer's instructions.

(5) Only the rigger who did the packing, and whose seal is removed to permit scheduled or unscheduled maintenance or repairs to the reserve container, may open, reclose, and reseal it (e.g., AAD service or closing loop adjustment) within the 180-day or 60-day period in subparagraph 14a(3).

b. **Main Parachutes.** Main parachutes must be packed within 180 days before the date of use and be packed by any certificated parachute rigger or a person working under the direct supervision of a certificated parachute rigger. The person making the next jump (including a tandem parachutist in command, but not the passenger parachutist) may also pack the main parachute.

15. PARACHUTE REPAIRS

a. **Major Repair.** A major repair, as defined in § 1.1, is a repair that, if improperly done, might appreciably affect airworthiness.

b. **Minor Repair.** A minor repair is a repair other than a major repair.

c. **Major or Minor Repair Determination.** When there is a question about whether a particular repair is major or minor, follow the manufacturer's instructions. In the absence of the manufacturer's instructions, riggers should use the FAA's Parachute Rigger Handbook (FAA-H-8083-17) and Poynter's Parachute Manual Volume I and II as guides. If the procedure calls for a master rigger, it should be considered a major repair. If the procedure allows for a senior rigger, it should be considered a minor repair.

(1) The same kind of repair may be classed as major or minor depending on size or proximity to key structural components. For example, a basic patch may be a minor repair if it is small and away from seams, but may be a major repair if it is large or adjacent to a seam.

(2) The same kind of repair may be classed as major or minor depending on whether it is done to an approved or unapproved component. For example, replacement of a suspension line on a reserve canopy is usually a major repair, while replacement of a suspension line on a main canopy is generally considered a minor repair (even if the identical technique is required for both replacements).

(3) If an operation results in an approved configuration, the operation is considered a repair. For example, if a parachute system is approved with and without an RSL, then removing or replacing RSL components is a repair that may be major or minor depending on whether, if improperly done, it might appreciably affect airworthiness. Similarly, resizing a harness, when the original design permits a range of sizes, is a repair when the resized harness remains within the permitted range.

(4) Only an appropriately rated master rigger or a manufacturer of approved parachute components may make major repairs. The manufacturer may designate certain repairs to be done only by the manufacturer or the manufacturer's designee.

16. PARACHUTE ALTERATIONS

a. **Configuration.** Alterations are changes to a parachute system configuration that the manufacturer or the manufacturer's supervising FAA Aircraft Certification Office (ACO) has not approved. Examples include removing a deployment device from a reserve canopy, adding harness fittings to permit attaching an additional canopy, using nonstandard repair materials or techniques, or installation of a specific make/model AAD when the manufacturer has not authorized such changes. Changes that result in an approved configuration are considered repairs (see paragraph 15).

b. **Approval.** An alteration to an approved parachute system must be done in accordance with approved manuals and specifications and only by those with specific authorization to perform that alteration. Specific approval is not needed for the method of altering a non-TSO'd main parachute canopy. A person seeking authorization to alter an approved parachute system should proceed as follows:

(1) A person qualified to alter a parachute (as listed below) should contact his or her local FAA FSDO inspector to discuss the proposed alteration. The applicant should be prepared to show the inspector the nature of the alteration by using a sample assembly, sketch, or drawing and be prepared to discuss the nature of the tests necessary for showing that the altered parachute meets all applicable requirements.

(2) The inspector will review the proposal with the applicant and a plan of action will be agreed upon.

(3) The applicant will then prepare an application, in the format of a letter, addressed to the local FSDO. Attach all pertinent data. The data should include:

- A clear description of the alteration;
- Drawings, sketches, or photographs, if necessary;
- Information such as thread size, stitch, pattern, materials used, and location of altered components; and
- Some means of identifying the altered parachute (model and serial number).

(4) The FSDO aviation safety inspector (ASI) may send an alteration to the ACO for review if the ASI is not experienced in parachute alterations. When satisfied, the inspector will indicate approval by date stamping, signing, and placing the FSDO identification stamp on the letter of application.

(5) Only a certificated and appropriately rated master parachute rigger, a current manufacturer of approved parachute systems or components, or any other manufacturer the Administrator considers competent may perform alterations to approved parachutes.

17. MATERIALS USED FOR REPAIRS TO TSO-APPROVED COMPONENTS

a. **Material Quality.** Materials used for repairs to TSO-approved components including, but not limited to, fabric, suspension line, tape, webbing, thread, and hardware, must meet the same specifications, requirements, and certifications of the original materials used by the manufacturer.

b. **Parachute Fittings.** Hardware may be reconditioned and reused, as long as it complies with subparagraph 17a. However, the plating or replating of load-carrying parachute fittings may cause hydrogen embrittlement and subsequent failure under stress unless the plating is done properly. Chrome- or nickel-plated harness adjustment hardware may also have a smoother finish than the original and may permit slippage.

John Barbagallo
Director, Flight Standards Service

APPENDIX 2. OPERATION OF AIRCRAFT WITH DOOR REMOVED OR MODIFIED FOR PARACHUTING OPERATIONS

1. **OPERATING LIMITATIONS REVISION.** The previous revision, Advisory Circular (AC) 105-2D, Sport Parachuting, Appendix 2, provided a list of aircraft that have Federal Aviation Administration (FAA)-approved door open or removal procedure authorization with operating limitations. That list did not include all the aircraft currently used in skydiving operations. Instead of continuing with the use of that list, contact your local Flight Standards District Office (FSDO) for information on getting an authorization to operate your aircraft with the door removed and/or a door modified to open/close in flight. Aircraft that have approved procedure and operating limitations in their FAA-approved Aircraft Flight Manual (AFM) or a FAA-approved Supplemental Type Certificate (STC) may operate in accordance with those documents.

2. **OPERATION WITH MODIFIED OR REMOVED DOOR.** Any aircraft type, utility/normal category model that has had FAA-approved data used for skydiving operations or door removal can be considered.

APPENDIX 1. TABLE OF LOCATION OF JUMP AUTHORIZATION OR NOTIFICATION

Location of Jump	Kind of Authorization Required	When to Apply or Notify	Where to Apply or Notify	Title 14 CFR Section Reference
Over or onto any airport	Prior approval	Prior to jump	Airport management	§ 105.23
In or into Class E or G airspace	Air Traffic Control (ATC) notification	Between 24 hours and 1 hour prior to jump	ATC facility having jurisdiction	§ 105.25
In or into Class A, B, C, or D airspace	ATC authorization (see Note)	Prior to jump	ATC facility having jurisdiction	§ 105.25
Over or within a restricted or prohibited area	Prior authorization	Prior to jump	Controlling agency, as noted on sectional chart	§ 105.25
Over or into a congested area or open air assembly of persons	FAA Form 7711-1, Certificate of Authorization	10 working days prior to jump	Flight Standards District Office (FSDO) having jurisdiction over the area where jump is to be made	§ 105.21

Note: Verbal authorization normally issued.

a. **Required Data.** It is the responsibility of the applicant to supply the FAA aviation safety inspector (ASI) with any data necessary to have his or her aircraft approved to operate with a door removed or a door modified to open/close in flight during jump operations. If the aircraft is altered and operated in accordance with an STC, no other limitations are required.

b. **Approved Data.** Many aircraft have jump door and/or restraint systems approved by type certificate (TC), STC, or field approval. Aircraft that have not been FAA-approved by TC, STC, or field approval must have the required data to address the alteration from a Designated Engineering Representative (DER), Organization Designation Authority (ODA), or other FAA-approved data. This data will allow the owner/operator the ability to apply for a field approval or one-time STC for that aircraft.

3. **PREVIOUSLY APPROVED FIELD APPROVALS.** Applicants can present a previously FAA-approved field approval for jump door, handles, step, and skydiver restraint systems as data for the field approval process if the FAA-approved data are for the same aircraft make, model, and series (M/M/S).

4. **FIELD APPROVAL PROCESS.** Applicants need to follow the latest guidance found in FAA Order 8900.1, Flight Standards Information Management System (FSIMS), Volume 4, Chapter 9, Selected Field Approvals, for a field approval process. This guidance can be found at http://fsims.faa.gov. Any changes to the flight manual require FAA and Aircraft Certification Office (ACO) approval. Applicants must include placards and skydiver restraint systems in the continued airworthiness instructions covering the repair of placards, restraint system components, steps, handles, jump doors, etc. Installation, removal, and inspection of installed equipment will be entered in the aircraft maintenance records, including the inspection checklist for the installation and operational check of restraint systems.

APPENDIX 3. SEATS AND RESTRAINT SYSTEMS

1. **SEATING CONFIGURATION AND RESTRAINT SYSTEM SAFETY.** Not all seating and restraint system configurations used in jump aircraft provide the same level of safety in the event of an emergency landing. This appendix provides general information concerning the relative safety of commonly used seating configurations and restraint systems. These safety assessments are based on available research data and in-service experience.

2. **GENERAL INFORMATION**

   a. **Quick Release Track Fittings.** Single stud quick release track fittings have been shown to release from the track at dynamic loads much lower than their rated strength. Dual stud quick release fittings did not exhibit this behavior in dynamic tests. Therefore, dual stud quick release fittings of the type shown in Figure 2, Dual Stud Quick Release Track Fitting, provide a much more reliable restraint anchorage than single stud fittings.

   b. **Lap Belts.** Lap belts are only effective if there is a solid support surface behind the occupant, such as a seat back, aircraft sidewall, or bulkhead. Otherwise, a tether restraint that attaches to the parachute harness provides more effective restraint.

   c. **Restraint for Aft-Facing Parachutists.** Research has shown that to restrain aft-facing parachutists, the most effective point to attach a tether restraint to a parachute harness is at the junction of the leg straps, main lift web, and the horizontal back strap. Figure 3, Tether Restraint Usage, illustrates this attachment method, in which the tether loop encircles the junction by passing between the main lift web and the horizontal back strap, and between the upper leg strap and the lower leg strap. One way to achieve this is to route the tether loop under the upper leg strap, then under the main lift web before latching the loop, as depicted in Figure 4, Pass Tether Loop Under Upper Leg Strap, Figure 5, Pass Tether Loop Under Main Lift Web, and Figure 6, Latch Tether Loop Around Parachute Harness. Since these two components of the harness are easily accessible by the wearer, this attachment method should not be prone to misuse. It also provides more effective restraint than attaching at other points on the parachute harness since the restraining force is applied near the seated occupant's center of gravity (CG).

   d. **Restraint Belts or Tethers.** Past experience and testing have shown the validity of attaching a restraint belt(s) or tether(s) to the parachute harness as part of the overall integrated restraint system. However, most manufactures have not tested their parachute harness configurations to see if they can accept the load vectors that would be experienced during the actual use of this type of restraint configuration. Because of this, any parachute harness that has been subjected to actual use as part of an integrated restraint system must be removed from service and inspected by the manufacturer or a parachute rigger designated by the manufacturer to determine the continued airworthiness of the parachute harness. If the inspection shows that the harness is Airworthy, it may be returned to service.

3. **SPECIFIC SEATING/RESTRAINT CONFIGURATIONS**

   a. **Side-Facing.** Conventional side-facing bench seats employing dual point lap belts are a superior means of carrying parachutists in aircraft large enough to accommodate them. They offer the advantages of being simple to use and can be designed to provide significant vertical energy absorption.

   b. **Rear-Facing Floor Seating.**

   (1) Restraints are more effective if attached to the floor instead of the sidewall. Only use sidewall attachments if floor attach points are not available.

   (2) Effectiveness is increased if overall tether length is kept as short as possible and the tether attachment to the aircraft is aft of the harness attachment point.

   (3) Single point, single tether restraints are not recommended.

   (4) Dual point, dual tether restraints offer superior restraint compared to single point, single tether restraints. This restraint method consists of two straps, each connecting the parachute harness to the aircraft floor on

both sides of the parachutist as shown in Figures 7, Tether Restraint Attachment To Floor For Rear-Facing Floor Seats, Figure 8, Dual Point, Dual Tether Restraint Configuration For Rear-Facing Floor Seats, and Figure 9, Dual Point, Dual Tether Restraint Attachment To Floor For Rear-Facing Straddle.

c. **Rear-Facing on Straddle Bench.**

(1) Straddle benches can offer more occupant crash protection than floor seating since they can be designed to provide significant vertical energy absorption.

(2) As with floor seating, restraints are more effective if attached to the floor instead of the sidewall.

(3) Restraint effectiveness is improved if the tether strap is attached to the floor such that it is at an approximately 45 degree angle, as shown in Figure 9.

(4) Single point, single tether restraints are not very effective.

(5) Dual point, dual tether restraints offer superior restraint compared to single point, single tether restraints.

Figure 2. Dual Stud Quick Release Track Fitting

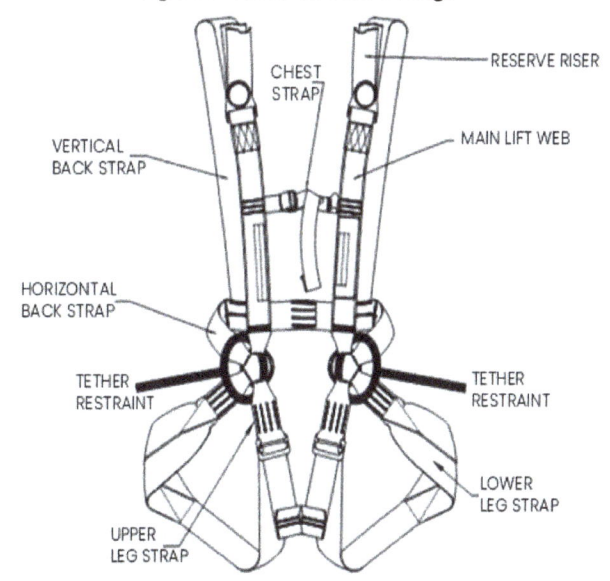

Figure 3. Tether Restraint Usage

Figure 4. Pass Tether Loop Under Upper Leg Strap

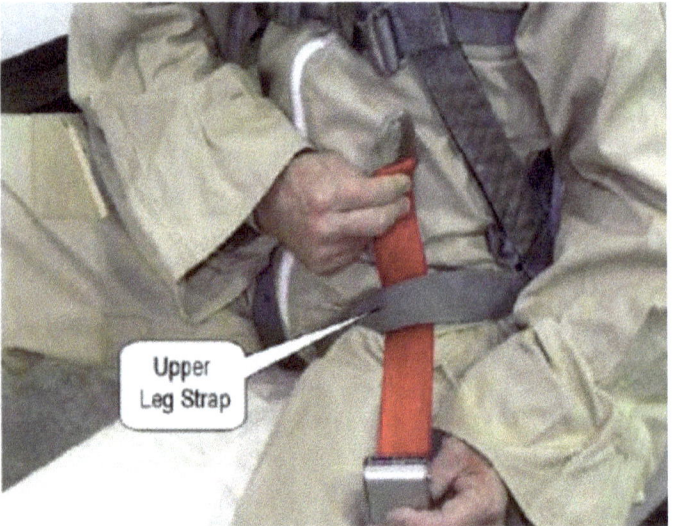

Figure 7. Tether Restraint Attachment To Floor For Rear-Facing Floor Seats

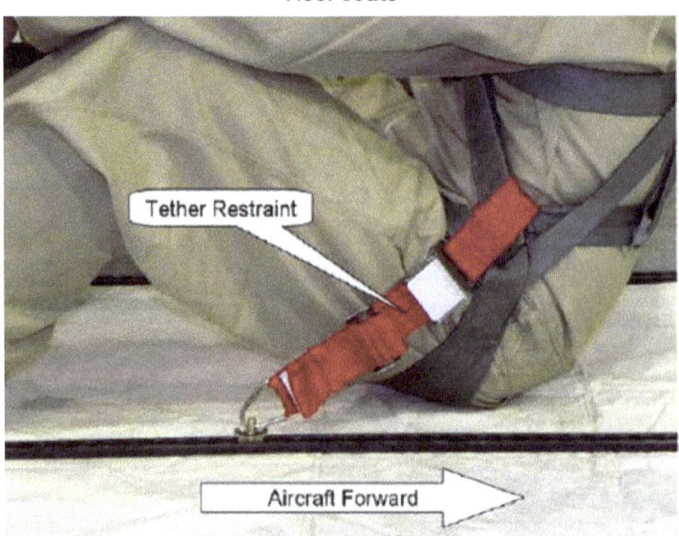

Figure 5. Pass Tether Loop Under Main Lift Web

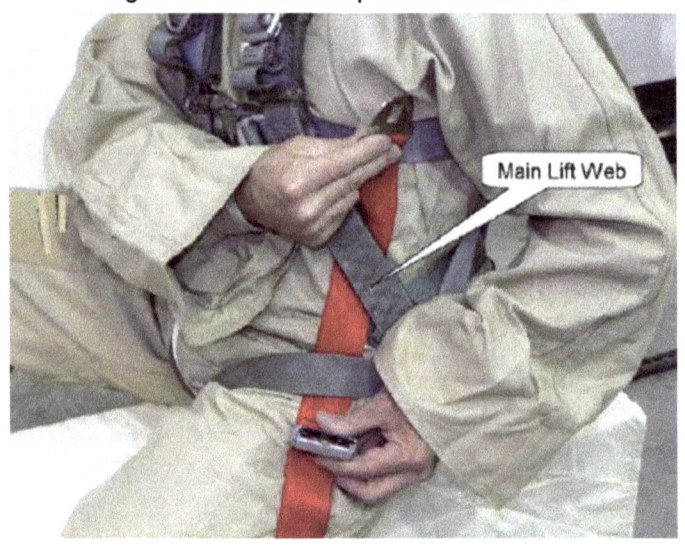

Figure 8. Dual Point, Dual Tether Restraint Configuration For Rear-Facing Floor Seats

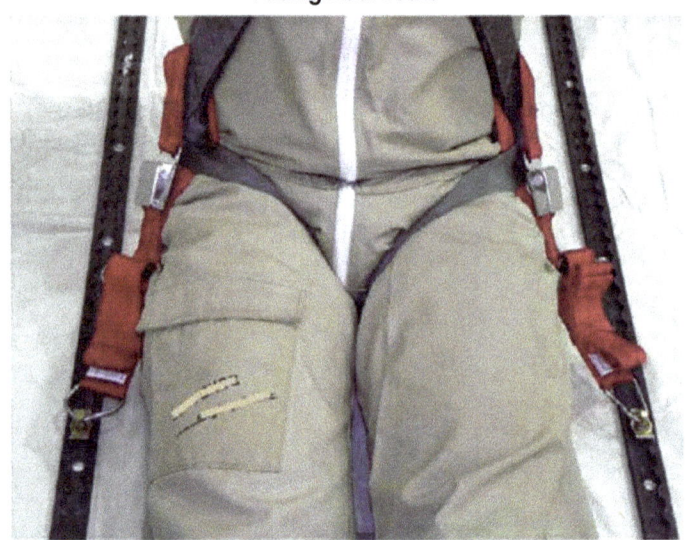

Figure 6. Latch Tetcher Loop Around Parachute Harness

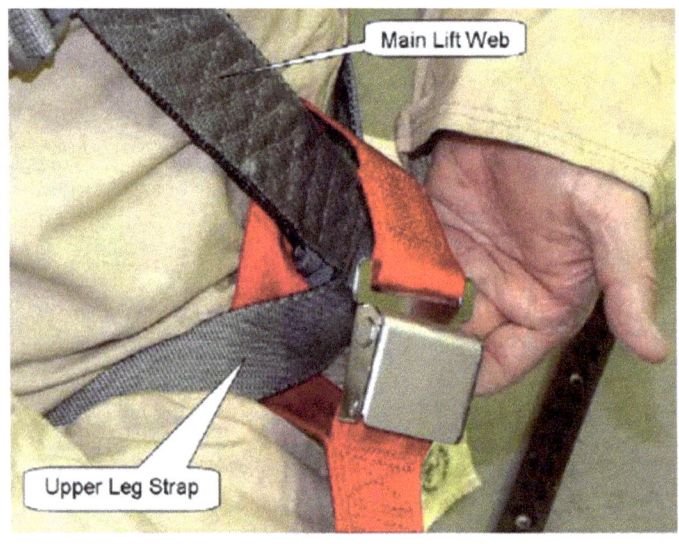

Figure 9. Dual Point, Dual Tether Restraint Attachment To Floor For Rear-Facing Straddle

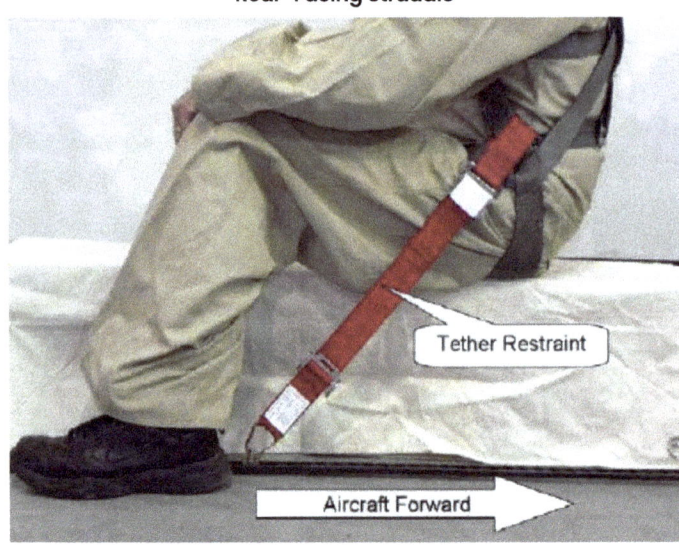

9-3: FAA AIR TRAFFIC BULLETINS

Air Traffic Bulletins are published by FAA Headquarters quarterly or as needed to brief air traffic controllers on specific issues. These two bulletins addressed skydiving issues.

Parachute Jumping

/*TEF/ Portions of this article have been used with the permission of the National Aeronautics and Space Administration, Ames Research Center, which has been involved in data collection of parachute jumping incidents through the Aviation Safety Reporting System. We gratefully acknowledge its efforts in increasing the aviation community's awareness of this subject.

As spring approaches and temperatures moderate we can count on the annual increase of parachute jumping activities. We would like to take this time to remind facilities and controllers of their responsibilities when it comes to parachute jumping operations.

Order 7110.65, Chapter 9, Parachute Jumping, details the specific responsibilities of controllers, and we encourage you to review this section. Experience has shown that most of the questions concerning a controller's responsibility for parachute jumping activities relate to Class E airspace. Coincidentally, most parachute jumping activity occurs in Class E airspace, and that is where we would like to address these operations.

Class E airspace is that airspace which "flows" around and over Classes B, C, D, and G airspace and has a ceiling of 18,000 feet MSL. Because most jump activities take place in Class E airspace, the majority of problems occurring with these operations are taking place there. Several additional clarifications on Air Traffic Control responsibilities in Class E airspace are important.

Controllers are not authorized to impose restrictions (for example, to deny or approve a jump) on parachute operations in Class E airspace, as they are authorized to do in Class A, B, C, or D airspace.

Controllers are required to give traffic advisories to jump aircraft before the jump, and to issue advisories to all known aircraft that will transit the Class E airspace within which the jump operations will occur. When time or the number of aircraft make individual transmissions impractical, advisories to nonparticipating aircraft may be broadcast on appropriate frequencies.

The point of these clarifications is to emphasize the special need in Class E airspace jump operations for both pilots and controllers to plan ahead, communicate clearly, and utilize extra vigilance in areas where jump zones are close to airways or approach corridors.

—December 1995

Parachute Operations

/*TERF/ It has come to our attention that there may be some confusion among controllers regarding the regulations and procedures for the conduct of parachute operations. In 2001, title 14, Code of Federal Regulations (14 CFR), part 105, was amended and may be the cause of some of the confusion. Therefore, we would like to provide the following information and remind controllers of their responsibilities to aircraft conducting parachute operations.

Regulations addressing parachute operations are contained in, 14 CFR, part 105. Additional procedures and guidance can be found in Federal Aviation Administration Order (FAAO) 7110.65, Air Traffic Control, chapter 9, and FAAO 7210.3, Facility Operation and Administration, chapter 18.

1. *Why is a letter of notification received by air traffic facilities on a yearly basis from local parachute operators?*

In accordance with 14 CFR, section 105.25(a)(3), prior to conducting parachute operations within Class E or Class G airspace, persons must notify the air traffic control (ATC) facility having jurisdiction over the airspace at the first intended exit altitude. Notice may be provided via telephone and must be given no earlier than 24 hours before and no later than 1 hour before the parachute operation begins. However, 14 CFR, section 105.25(c), provides for air traffic facilities to accept written notification from skydiving centers and clubs on an ongoing basis, over a stated period of time, not to exceed 12 calendar months. Written notification of parachute jump operations is not required within Class E and Class G airspace areas. However, in areas where jumps take place on a regular basis, a letter that contains information about the parachute operations is helpful and is preferred over a phone call. Please note that this is not a change from the prior rule. However, more facilities have received letters recently as the United States Parachute Association has encouraged its members to write. Providing air traffic facilities with information regarding the drop zones, dates, times of jumps, aircraft registration number, and pilot names helps reduce phone calls and frequency congestion and contributes to the safety of aircraft operating when parachute operations are being conducted.

2. *In Class A, B, C and D airspace areas, what authorization do parachute operators need and who issues the authorization?*

In accordance with 14 CFR, section 105.25(a)(1) and (2), no person may conduct a parachute operation and no pilot in command of an aircraft may allow a parachute operation to be conducted from that aircraft unless an air traffic control authorization has been issued. The parachute operator must provide the information specified in 14 CFR, section 105.15(a), that includes drop zone location, times of jumps, aircraft registration number, name and address of pilot, and intended exit altitude. The ATC facility (terminal or en route center) having jurisdiction over the airspace containing the first intended exit altitude is responsible for issuing the authorization. In most cases, since parachute operations descend through numerous altitudes, as well as air traffic facility boundaries and sectors, it is incumbent on the ATC facility that issues the authorization to coordinate with other facilities that may be impacted by this operation.

3. *How has the role of flight service stations (FSS) changed since 14 CFR, part 105, was amended?*

The FSS's vital role of providing weather briefings and issuing Notices to Airmen of parachute operations remains current. Prior to the automation of FSSs, most FSS facilities were located at airports and had an active role in providing airport advisories. Previously, 14 CFR, part 105, contained a provision that required parachute operators to contact the nearest ATC facility or FSS at least 5 minutes prior to the jump for the sole purpose of obtaining traffic advisories. Since most FSSs are no longer located at airports, the rule has been amended. 14 CFR, section 105.13(a)(1)(ii), now states that communications must be established between the jump aircraft and the ATC facility having jurisdiction over the affected

9-3 AIR TRAFFIC BULLETINS

airspace of the intended exit altitude. In other words, the pilot of the jump aircraft will be in communication with and receive traffic advisories from the ATC facility that is responsible for and has real-time information about other air traffic in the area.

4. *When is a certificate of authorization required and who issues it?*

In accordance with 14 CFR, section 105.21(a), a certificate of authorization is required when conducting parachute operations over or into a congested area of a city, town, or settlement, or an open-air assembly of persons. The person conducting the parachute operation must apply to the local Flight Standards District Office for the certificate of authorization. This certificate addresses the safety aspects of the operation for persons and property on the ground and does not replace the ATC clearance or authorization needed for operations within Class A, B, C, or D airspace.

5. *Are air traffic controllers required to issue traffic advisories to jump aircraft?*

Yes. FAAO 7110.65, Air Traffic Control, paragraph 9-8-4, requires that controllers issue traffic advisories to the jump aircraft before the jump. Controllers must issue advisories to all known aircraft that will transit the airspace when the jump operations will be conducted.

6. *Are air traffic controllers required to separate jump aircraft that operate within a Class E airspace area?*

No. Traffic advisories shall be provided, but ATC is not required to separate visual flight rules aircraft within Class E airspace. However, in accordance with FAAO 7110.65, Air Traffic Control, paragraph 9-8-4, ATC may assist pilots of non-participating aircraft that request help in avoiding the jump airspace. In addition, if there is other traffic in the jump area, ATC does not authorize or deny jump operations due to traffic. The jump pilot shall be issued traffic advisories. The jump pilot and jumpers will make a decision on whether or not to allow the jumpers to leave the aircraft. 14 CFR, section 105.5, clearly places the burden on the jump pilot and parachutist by stating that no person may conduct a parachute operation and no pilot in command of an aircraft may allow a parachute operation to be conducted from an aircraft, if that operation creates a hazard to air traffic or to persons or property on the ground. (ATO-R System Ops)

—July 2004

Glossary

A

A&P: Acronym. 1. Assemble and Pack, Used on reserve parachute packing record cards. 2. Airframe and Powerplant Mechanic.

A LICENSE: The first level license which signifies that a skydiver has advanced beyond the student phase. Persons holding a USPA A License are able to jumpmaster themselves, perform basic group freefall jumps and water jumps, participate in certain USPA collegiate competition events, and pack their own main parachute.

AAD: (see AUTOMATIC ACTIVATION DEVICE)

ACCELERATED FREEFALL (AFF), USPA: Harness-hold freefall skydiving student training discipline developed under Ken Coleman and adopted by USPA. AFF-rated USPA Instructors accompany the student in freefall during the initial training jumps.

AGL: Above ground level. Refers to altitude, e.g., 5,000 feet AGL.

AIR SPEED: The speed of an airborne aircraft or parachute, relative to the air.

AIRCRAFT: Any machine or device, including airplanes, helicopters, gliders, balloons, etc., capable of atmospheric flight. For the purposes of regulation, parachutes are not considered aircraft.

ALTERATIONS: Any change or modification to any part of the parachute assembly from its original manufacturer's specifications. (see also MAJOR ALTERATION and MINOR ALTERATION)

ALTIMETER: A device that measures height above the surface (altitude); for skydivers, typically above the intended skydiving landing area. (see also AUDIBLE ALTIMETER)

ANGLE FLYING: A degree of back/belly flying that has a steeper angle than tracking used at breakoff. (achieving maximum horizontal separation or lift). This angle is much steeper but not fully vertical (straight up and down).

ANGLE OF ATTACK: The relative pitch (leading edge up or down) angle of a wing measured between the chord line and the relative wind.

ANGLE OF INCIDENCE: The relative pitch (leading edge up or down) angle of a wing measured between the chord line and the horizon.

APPROACH ANGLE: (see GLIDE PATH)

APPROPRIATELY RATED: adj. Refers to a USPA Instructor or Examiner rated in the method-specific instructional discipline necessary to perform a particular task in accordance with the BSRs.

ARCH: n. Position skydivers use to orient the front of their torso to the relative wind. Described, it is hips forward with back arched; legs extended to 45 degrees, toes pointed; knees at shoulder width; arms bent 90-120 degrees at the shoulders and elbows and relaxed; head up.

ARTISTIC EVENTS: Skydiving competition events that include freeflying, freestyle skydiving, and skysurfing.

AS 8015 (AEROSPACE STANDARD 8015): Standard of tests and minimum safety and performance requirements which must be met to receive approval under technical standard order (TSO) certification. AS 8015A, the standard for TSO C-23c was adopted in 1984 to supersede NAS 804, the standard for TSO C-23b. In June, 1994, AS 8015B became the standard for TSO C-23d.

ASPECT RATIO: The aspect ratio of a ram-air parachute canopy is the ratio of its length (span) to its breadth (chord).

ASSISTED DEPLOYMENT: Refers to a pull sequence prompted or cued by the instructor where the student begins the sequence and is completed by the student but may be assisted by the instructor.

AUDIBLE ALTIMETER: An alarm used by skydivers to alert them about reaching one or more pre-set altitudes.

AUTOMATIC ACTIVATION DEVICE (AAD): A self-contained mechanical or electro-mechanical device that is attached to the interior of the reserve parachute container, which automatically initiates parachute deployment of the reserve parachute at a pre-set altitude, time, percentage of terminal velocity, or combination thereof. (FAR 105 definition)

AUXILIARY PARACHUTE: (See RESERVE PARACHUTE)

B

B LICENSE: The second level USPA license. Persons holding a USPA B License are authorized to participate in the USPA collegiate 4-way formation skydiving event, perform night jumps, and when qualified, apply for a USPA Coach rating.

BARREL ROLL: A maneuver in which a skydiver rolls about their longitudinal axis.

B.A.S.E. JUMPING: An activity involving the use of a parachute for descent from fixed objects. The acronym derives from the first initials of four possible launch categories: buildings, antennae, spans (bridges), and earth (cliffs). Because BASE jumping does not meet the FAA's definition of "the descent of an object to the surface from an aircraft in flight," it is not regulated by the FAA or addressed by USPA.

B-12S: (jar.) Clip hardware sometimes used for leg-strap attachment on a parachute harness. Refers generally to the MS 22044 hardware originally used on the U.S. Army B-12 parachute assembly. (see THREAD-THROUGH)

BAG: n. (see DEPLOYMENT DEVICE)

BAG LOCK: n. A malfunction of a deployed parachute where the canopy remains in the deployment bag.

BASE: n. 1. When building a freefall or canopy formation, the initial target individual or group of people to which the others fly. 2. Base (leg): n. The portion of the three-legged landing pattern where the jumper flies across the direction of the wind downwind of the landing area before turning for final approach into the wind toward the target.

BASIC SAFETY REQUIREMENTS (BSRS), USPA: Minimum standards overseen and published by USPA and generally agreed upon as the acceptable standard for safe skydiving activities. The BSRs form the foundation of self-governing by skydivers. USPA oversees the BSRs.

BELLY FLYING: (see FLAT FLYING)

BOARD OF DIRECTORS (BOD). USPA: Those representatives elected by the general members of USPA every three years as set forth in the USPA By-Laws; authorized by the by-laws to have general charge and control of the affairs, funds, and property of the organization and to carry out the objectives of the organization and its by-laws; elects officers from among current USPA Board members. The USPA Board of Directors consists of: 1. National Directors—those directors elected at large by the general membership; 2. Regional Directors—those Directors of a specified geographical area, elected by and responsible for representing the interests of the skydivers in a USPA Region; and 3. An ex officio member representing the National Aeronautical Association.

BRAKED TURN: A turn under an open parachute canopy made by using the steering toggles to slow the forward speed of the canopy and then allow one side to fly slightly faster to change heading. Used to reduce altitude loss in a turn.

GLOSSARY

BRAKE FIRE: A premature brake release during the canopy deployment.

BRAKES: n. 1. The steering controls of a ram-air parachute. (see also TOGGLES) 2. n. The position of the parachute steering controls, measured in relative increments (quarter brakes, deep brakes, etc.), to control speed and descent in a stable state of flight.

BREAK OFF: v. Act of a group of jumpers separating from a freefall or canopy group.

BREAKOFF: n. Procedure in group skydiving where jumpers cease group activity and separate. In freefall, jumpers begin to track at a predetermined altitude for a clear area to open safely; jumpers building canopy formations break off at a predetermined altitude to gain safe separation and allow jumpers to prepare for a landing approach.

BREAKOFF ALTITUDE: Planned altitude for initiating separation of jumpers during a group jump.

BRIDLE: n. The device, usually made of webbing or tape, connecting the pilot chute to the deployment bag or the canopy.

BSRS: (see BASIC SAFETY REQUIREMENTS, USPA)

C

C LICENSE: The third level license issued by USPA. USPA C-license holders may apply when qualified for the USPA AFF, IAD, and Static-Line Instructor ratings, ride as passenger on USPA Tandem Instructor training and rating renewal jumps, and participate in intermediate-altitude jumps and open field and level 1 exhibition jumps.

CANOPY: The major component of the parachute system comprised of fabric membranes that connect to the parachute harness by suspension lines and provide the means for the jumper to descend safely.

CANOPY FORMATION (CF); CANOPY RELATIVE WORK; (CRW): n. 1. The intentional maneuvering of two or more open parachute canopies in proximity to or in contact with one another during descent. 2. The FAI competition discipline involving the building of canopy formations.

CANOPY RELEASE: A device which allows immediate separation of the parachute canopy and risers from the harness.

CANOPY WRAP: The canopy of one jumper is wrapped around another jumper.

CASCADE: The point where two or more lines of a canopy join into one.

CELL: n. Chordwise section of a parachute canopy between the load-bearing ribs. Sometimes, any portion of a canopy separated by vertical ribs.

CERTIFICATED: adj. Refers to FAA-approval status of parachute components, technicians (riggers), and aircraft pilots.

CHECK OF THREES: Pre-jump equipment self-check performed in the aircraft: check three-ring release system (and RSL) for correct assembly; check three points of harness attachment for snap assembly or correct routing and adjustment; check three operation handles—main activation, cutaway, reserve—in place.

CHORD: n. The longest dimension from the front to the back of a wing at any given point along the span.

CHUTE ASSIS: n. French for "falling seated," a freeflying orientation credited to that country. (see also SIT FLYING)

CLEARED: adj. Refers to a student who has received a signature from a USPA Instructor to advance.

CLIMBOUT: n. The act of a jumper positioning himself or herself in or near the door or on protuberances or structures outside the aircraft to prepare for launch, usually with a group.

CLOSING LOOP: A lace that when threaded through eyelets in the parachute container flaps and locked with a closing pin, keeps the parachute contained until activation.

COACH: n. A non-rated operative who provides advanced skydiving training. (see also COACH, USPA)

COACH, USPA: n. The entry-level USPA instructional rating whose holder may teach the general (non-method-specific sections of the first-jump course) and conduct group freefall skills training and jumps with students, all under the supervision of a USPA Instructor.

COACH JUMP: n. A Coach jump is any jump where a USPA Coach jumps with any person and provides instruction and/or critique to that person.

COLLAPSIBLE PILOT CHUTE: A hand-deployed pilot chute that automatically collapses after deployment.

COLLAPSIBLE SLIDER: A slider rigged so the jumper can compress or wrap it to reduce drag (see also SLIDER).

COLLINS LANYARD: A lanyard attached to the Reserve Static Line which is designed to release the non-RSL side riser in the event the RSL side riser breaks.

CONTAINER: The portion of the parachute system that closes around and stores the folded parachute canopy and deployment device until deployment.

CORK: v. (jar.) During high-speed group freefall maneuvers, to lose control and decelerate rapidly.

CREW: (see CANOPY FORMATION)

CROSS BRACED: (adj.) Refers to a canopy designed with longitudinal trussing between the vertical ribs to flatten and stiffen the wing in flight.

CROSS CONNECTORS: Straps attached between the risers. Used for canopy formation, they should be from front to rear only to prevent the docked jumper from sliding back up the lines. Especially important for plane formations. Also used with some reserve static-line systems and attached from side to side to prevent premature reserve deployment if only one riser is released.

CROSSPORT: n. A vent cut into the structural rib of a parachute canopy to equalize air pressure between two cells.

CROSSWIND: Perpendicular to the direction of the wind.

CUTAWAY (N): Procedure where the jumper releases from the main parachute prior to activating the reserve parachute. Used in the event of a main parachute malfunction to prevent an entanglement with the deploying reserve; in the event of a canopy entanglement with another jumper; and also in case the wind causes the canopy to drag a jumper after landing.

CUTAWAY HANDLE: Pillow or loop handle of a two-handled system, normally located on the jumpers right-side chest, used to initiate a cutaway. Sometimes referred to as a three-ring release handle.

D

D LICENSE: The fourth and highest level or license issued by USPA. USPA D-license holders may participate in all competitions at the national level, apply when qualified for all USPA instructional and proficiency ratings, and participate in high-altitude jumps.

DECISION ALTITUDE: A predetermined altitude at which you must decide and act during an emergency.

DELTA: Freefall position with legs extended and arms back to initiate a forward dive.

DEMONSTRATION JUMP (DEMO): (see EXHIBITION JUMP)

DENSITY ALTITUDE: An expression of air density relative to standard atmospheric pressure at sea level. The pilot calculates pressure altitude and temperature and compares the result with an equivalent altitude MSL at standard temperature.

DEPLOYMENT: After activation, extraction of the parachute from the container and full extension of the system prior to inflation.

DEPLOYMENT DEVICE: Intermediate container, usually a bag (D-bag), that contains or constricts the folded parachute through complete line deployment.

DESCENT RATE: The downward horizontal speed of an aircraft or parachute, usually measured in feet per minute.

GLOSSARY | G

DIAPER: A type of deployment device consisting of a fabric panel attached near the lower part of a canopy which prevents canopy inflation until full line stretch. Used frequently with round parachutes to reduce opening shock and malfunctions.

DIRECT SUPERVISION: 1. The attentive oversight of an activity taking place in the immediate presence of the supervisor, who is personally responsible for the proper conduct of the activity. (USPA definition) 2. A certificated rigger personally observes a non-certificated person packing a main parachute to the extent necessary to ensure that it is being done properly, and takes responsibility for that packing. (FAR 105 definition) (see also Supervision)

DIVE BLOCKS: Hand grips (not loops) on the front risers to facilitate diving the canopy.

DIVE LOOPS: Handles on the front risers to facilitate diving the canopy.

DIVER EXIT: Leaving an aircraft by diving out of the aircraft door; made without positioning or bracing to achieve a stable entry into the airstream.

DIVING (FREEFALL): To rapidly descend toward and then make a controlled approach relative to a target.

DOCK: v. To make physical controlled contact with another skydiver while in freefall; or, when building canopy formations, with another jumper's canopy.

DOOR EXIT: (see DIVER EXIT)

DOWNWIND: 1. adj. The direction toward which the air is moving. 2. adv. or adj. positioned farther along the wind's path. 3. n. (jar.) a downwind-facing landing.

DOWNWIND LEG: The portion of the landing approach flown with the wind blowing from behind the jumper.

DROGUE: A trailing drag device used to retard the movement of an object through the air, used in skydiving to regulate the fall rate of tandem skydivers.

DROGUEFALL: In tandem skydiving, the portion of the descent where a drogue has been deployed between freefall and main parachute deployment.

DROP ZONE: n. 1. Skydiving establishment or intended parachute landing area. (USPA definition) 2. Any pre-determined area upon which parachutists or objects land after making an intentional parachute jump or drop. The center-point target of a drop zone is expressed in nautical miles from the nearest VOR facility when 30 nautical miles or less; or from the nearest airport, town, or city depicted on the appropriate Coast and Geodetic Survey World Aeronautical Chart or Sectional Aeronautical Chart, when the nearest VOR facility is more than 30 nautical miles from the drop zone. (FAR 105 definition) (see also Sanctioned Drop Zone)

DUAL ASSEMBLY: Refers to a two-canopy parachute system. Includes the main and reserve canopies, harness and container system, and all other components.

DUMMY RIPCORD PULL (DRCP): (see PRACTICE DEPLOYMENT)

DYNAMIC STALL: n. An action that occurs following the flare of a ram-air canopy, where the load (jumper) has swung forward under the canopy from the braking action and begins to swing back. (see also REVERSE FLIGHT and STALL)

E

ELLIPTICAL: n., adj. (jar.) Refers to a class of canopies with a tapered or approximately elliptical planform.

EMERGENCY PARACHUTE: A certificated parachute which is intended for emergency use; typically, the parachute a pilot wears.

END CELL: The last chordwise section of a parachute canopy on either end.

END-CELL CLOSURE: Deflated end cell. Routine opening problem, usually correctable.

ENDORSEMENT: An act of giving one's public approval or support to someone or something.

EXAMINER, USPA: The highest level of the instructional rating program. An Examiner is an experienced USPA Instructor who has met additional proficiency requirements and passed a series of written examinations on a wide variety of skydiving related subjects. An Examiner has all of the privileges of a USPA Safety and Training Advisor.

EXHIBITION JUMP: An exhibition jump, also called a display or demonstration jump, is a jump at a location other than an existing drop zone done for the purpose of reward, remuneration, or promotion and principally for the benefit of spectators.

EXIT POINT: The point on the ground over which skydivers leave the aircraft.

EXIT WEIGHT: The combined weight of the jumper and all his or her equipment for that jump.

EXTRAORDINARY SKYDIVE: n. Night jump, water jump, jump from above 15,000 feet MSL, exhibition jump, pre-planned cutaway jump, and other jumps requiring special equipment and procedures that might be unfamiliar to most jumpers.

F

FAA: (see FEDERAL AVIATION ADMINISTRATION)

FAI: (see FEDERATION AERONAUTIQUE INTERNATIONALE)

FARMER MCNASTY: (jar.) Unenlightened term for a disenchanted drop zone neighbor with whom communications with jumpers are strained or have broken down.

FEDERAL AVIATION ADMINISTRATION (FAA): An agency of the U.S. Department of Transportation whose primary function and responsibility is to control the nation's air traffic, including the certification of all civil aircraft and accessories, licensing of all civil pilots, mechanics, and riggers, and administration of the Federal Aid to Airports Program.

FEDERAL AVIATION REGULATIONS (FARS): The parts of the Code of Federal Regulations that apply to aviation.

FEDERATION AERONAUTIQUE INTERNATIONALE (FAI): An international organization which governs all aviation sports, certifies all official aviation and space records, and governs official international competitions. Operates through a non-profit National Aero Club in each country.

FINAL APPROACH: The final portion of flight before a jumper or aircraft lands.

FLARE: 1. v. Under canopy: To convert the downward speed of a parachute momentarily into lift. 2. v. In freefall: To decelerate prior to approaching a formation. 3. n. The act of flaring. 4. n. A membrane used to distribute the load of a parachute at the line attachment points of some canopies.

FLAT DELTA: Freefall position with the body on one plane, legs extended and arms swept back, used as a starting or intermediate position when developing a track.

FLAT FLYING: Freefall orientation primarily belly to earth.

FLAT TURN: A canopy turn performed at braked flight that conserves altitude.

FLOATER: A jumper positioned outside the aircraft to leave slightly prior to the person or group designated as the target for the initial freefall formation (see also BASE). A floater maneuvers from a position below the base relative to the horizon.

FOREIGN PARACHUTIST: A parachutist who is neither a U.S. citizen nor a resident alien and is participating in parachute operations within the United States using parachute equipment not manufactured in the United States. (FAR 105 definition)

FORMATION SKYDIVING (RELATIVE WORK): 1. Aerial maneuvers by two or more freefalling skydivers with each other, usually to form geometric formations. 2. Competition discipline of flat-flying.

FREE BAG: Intermediate container that contains or constricts the folded parachute through complete line deployment that is not attached to the deploying parachute.

FREE FLY: v. To exit unlinked with other jumpers.

GLOSSARY

FREEFALL: The portion of a parachute jump or drop between aircraft exit and parachute deployment in which the parachute is activated manually by the parachutist at the parachutist's discretion or automatically, or, in the case of an object, is activated automatically. (FAR 105 definition)

FREEFLYING: n. 1. An unrestricted freefall discipline characterized by varied presentations to the relative wind. (see also SIT FLYING and HEAD DOWN) 2. n. The competition event of freeflying.

FREESTYLE: 1. A solo freefall discipline that involves choreographed multi-orientation static and dynamic maneuvers. 2. The competition event of freestyle performed as part of a team with a camera flyer (freestyle skydiving).

FULL FLIGHT: The stabilized state of hands-off canopy flight under an open and fully functioning parachute.

FUNNEL: n., v. A freefall skydiving formation which has become unstable, usually due to one or more jumpers flying out of position, causing the participants to collapse the formation and land on top of each other.

G

GLIDE: n., v. The combined horizontal and vertical movement of a descending canopy.

GLIDE ANGLE: (see GLIDE PATH)

GLIDE PATH: The trajectory of a parachute as it descends in flight towards a landing point on the ground.

GO-AROUND: n. (jar.) An in-flight operation where the aircraft circles at jump altitude.

GOVERNANCE MANUAL, USPA: The official bound collection of the USPA Constitution and By-Laws.

GROUND SPEED: The speed of an airborne aircraft or parachute relative to the ground it traverses in a given period of time.

GROUP MEMBER: Skydiving centers that have pledged to follow USPA Basic Safety Requirements, including providing USPA-developed first-jump courses, using current USPA-rated instructors and providing USPA-required skydiving equipment. At USPA Group Member skydiving centers, all skydivers cleared for self-supervision must be current USPA members.

H

HAND-DEPLOYED PILOT CHUTE: A small parachute thrown by hand in freefall to extract the main parachute from its container. (see also PULL OUT and THROW OUT)

HARD DECK: A predetermined altitude above which an action must occur or below which an action must not occur. In rating courses, it indicates a minimum altitude by which a certain maneuver must be performed in order to get credit for the action.

HARNESS: n. The webbing of a parachute system that surrounds and retains a jumper.

HARNESS AND CONTAINER SYSTEM: The major component of a parachute system, usually unitized, which the jumper dons for the jump. It contains the canopies and certain accessory devices.

HARNESS HOLD: A skydiving training discipline where a student is trained for independent, solo freefall but is accompanied by at least one USPA AFF Instructor until meeting the requirements in the BSRs for self-supervision in freefall. On the initial jumps, the AFF Instructor(s) assist the student on exit via a harness grip.

HEAD DOWN: adj., adv. Inverted vertical or nearly vertical freeflying orientation.

HIGH-PERFORMANCE LANDING AREA: An area at a drop zone that DZ management has designated as separate from the normal landing area for canopy pilots to perform high-performance landings.

HOOK KNIFE: A hook-shaped knife with an inside cutting edge. Used in certain emergencies to sever problem lines or components of a parachute system.

HOOK TURN: (jar.) A canopy maneuver that results in a steep dive.

HOOKER HARNESS: A single-point aircraft passenger restraint system that integrates with a parachute harness. Designed by Jack Hooker.

HORSESHOE: n. A partial parachute malfunction where part of the deployed parachute is entangled with the jumper or his or her equipment.

I

I&R: (see INSPECT AND REPACK)

IAD: (see INSTRUCTOR-ASSISTED DEPLOYMENT)

INITIATED DEPLOYMENT: Refers to a pull sequence prompted or cued by the instructor where the student begins the sequence but may be completed by the instructor.

INSPECT AND REPACK: Rigging term used on reserve parachute packing data cards.

INSTRUCTIONAL RATING MANUAL (IRM), USPA: The manual containing the collected documents and references required to conduct any course for USPA Coach or USPA Instructor ratings.

INSTRUCTOR RATING COURSE, USPA: A course registered with USPA Headquarters to train, qualify, and test applicants for the USPA Instructor rating.

INSTRUCTOR, USPA: The holder of a USPA Instructor rating qualified in one or more of four methods of instruction: USPA Accelerated Freefall, instructor-assisted deployment, static line, or tandem. The mid level of the USPA instructional rating hierarchy. A USPA Instructor may train and certify a student for the USPA A License, supervise USPA Coaches, and is eligible for appointment as USPA Safety and Training Advisor.

INSTRUCTOR-ASSISTED DEPLOYMENT (IAD): A method of passive deployment used for training skydiving students making their initial jumps. A USPA IAD Instructor controls a hand-deployed pilot chute while a student moves into position and jumps, at which point the instructor releases the pilot chute.

J

JUDGE: The official who evaluates a competitor's performance. USPA issues judge ratings at both the Regional and National levels. The FAI issues a rating for internationally recognized judges.

JUMP ALTITUDE: Actual altitude of an aircraft above the ground at the time a skydiver exits.

JUMP: (see SKYDIVE)

JUMP RUN: The flight of the aircraft prior to exit, generally following a predetermined path.

JUMPER: (see SKYDIVER)

JUMPMASTER: n. 1. A skydiver, typically a senior jumper or instructional rating holder, who coordinates boarding and exit order, jump flight procedures, spotting, and emergency operations with the pilot. 2. v. To dispatch jumpers. 3. n. Prior to 2002, a USPA instructional rating for supervising student jumps.

JUMPSUIT: A garment used for protection or alter performance.

L

LANDING PATTERN: n. The deliberate flight path, usually rectangular, that a jumper uses in the final phase of descent under canopy.

LICENSE: Certificate of proficiency recognizing that a skydiver has met a specified level of experience, skill, and knowledge. There are four classes of USPA licenses: A, B, C and D. USPA licenses are recognized internationally through the FAI.

LINE DOCK: The docking of two canopies with the docker's canopy above the head of the person receiving the dock.

LINE TWIST: n. A condition of parachute opening where the canopy has attained full or nearly full inflation but one or more complete twists have developed in the lines and/or risers. Can be dangerous when associated with a spin.

LINEOVER: n. A partial malfunction of a deployed parachute resulting in lines going over the top of the canopy. Also refers loosely to the partial inversion of a round canopy. (see also Partial Inversion)

M

MAE WEST: n. (jar., archaic) WWII term for partial inversion. (see also PARTIAL INVERSION)

MAIN-ASSISTED RESERVE DEPLOYMENT (MARD): A device which uses the drag from the cutaway main canopy to assist in extracting the reserve canopy.

MAIN PARACHUTE: A parachute worn as the primary parachute used or intended to be used in conjunction with a reserve parachute. (FAR 105 definition)

MAINTENANCE: Inspection, overhaul, repair, preservation, and replacement of parts.

MAJOR ALTERATION: An alteration not listed in the manufacturer's specifications that might appreciably affect weight, structural strength, performance, flight characteristics, or other qualities affecting airworthiness or that cannot be done by elementary operations. (see also Alteration)

MAJOR REPAIR: A repair that if improperly accomplished may affect weight, structural strength, performance, flight characteristics, or other qualities which determine airworthiness.

MALFUNCTION: The complete or partial failure of a parachute canopy to accomplish proper opening, descent, or flight characteristics.

MARD: (see MAIN-ASSISTED RESERVE DEPLOYMENT)

MASTER RIGGER: The higher of two certification levels for FAA riggers. May perform more complex repair tasks and approved alterations. (see also SENIOR RIGGER)

MENTOR (SKYDIVING): An experienced skydiver, usually D-licensed, who can offer advice and guidance on skydiving related matters to jumpers with less experience.

MINI THREE-RING: Refers to a scaled-down version of the original three-ring release system. (see also three-ring release)

MINOR ALTERATION: An alteration other than a major alteration. (see also ALTERATION and MAJOR ALTERATION)

MINOR REPAIR: A repair other than a major repair. (see also MAJOR REPAIR)

MSL: Altitude measured from sea level.

N

NAA: (see NATIONAL AERONAUTIC ASSOCIATION)

NAS 804: (National Aircraft Standard 804) defines the tests and minimum performance and safety standards which must be met for a parachute to receive approval under TSO C-23b. Adopted in 1949 and superseded in 1984 by AS 8015A.

NASSER TOGGLES: Control loops on the front risers attached to one or more A or A-B lines to facilitate diving the canopy toward a canopy formation. Designed by Nasser Basir.

NATIONAL AERONAUTIC ASSOCIATION (NAA): The National Aero Club of the USA that represents the FAI. USPA is a division of the NAA.

NATIONAL DIRECTOR: (see BOARD OF DIRECTORS).

NIGHT JUMP: A skydive made from one hour after official sunset to one hour before official sunrise. The FAA considers any jump made after sunset and before sunrise a night jump requiring equipment specified in FAR 105.

NORMAL LANDING AREA: A landing area at a drop zone that DZ management has designated as separate from the high-performance landing area.

NOTAM (NOTICE TO AIRMEN): An air traffic advisory or notice filed with an FAA Flight Service Station by an airspace user.

O

OBJECT: Any item other than a person that descends to the surface from an aircraft in flight when a parachute is used or is intended to be used during all or part of the descent. (FAR 105 definition)

OPEN BODY OF WATER: A body of water in which a skydiver could drown.

OPENING POINT: The ground point of reference over which the skydiver opens the parachute.

OPENING SHOCK: (jar.) The decelerating force exerted on the load as the parachute deploys and inflates. Caused by the resistance of the canopy and items associated with it.

OSCILLATION: 1. The swinging or pendulum motion of the suspended load under a canopy. 2. In canopy formation, the swaying or swinging of a formation caused by poor docking, turbulent air, or too much movement of the people in the formation.

OUTBOARD: Facing to the outside, such as a ripcord facing to the side of the jumper rather than toward the breast bone.

P

PACK: v. To fold and close a parachute system in preparation for jumping.

PACKING DATA CARD: A card kept with a parachute system which records the maintenance on that system.

PARACHUTE: A fabric device that slows the descent of a falling object; derived from the French words "para," to shield, and "chute," to fall. Thus, parachute literally means "to shield from a fall."

PARACHUTE DROP: The descent of an object to the surface from an aircraft in flight when a parachute is used or intended to be used during all or part of that descent. (FAR 105 definition)

PARACHUTE JUMP: A parachute operation that involves the descent of one or more persons to the surface from an aircraft in flight when a parachute is used or intended to be used during all or part of that descent. (FAR 105 definition)

PARACHUTE LANDING FALL (PLF): n. A method developed by the U.S. military to minimize the chance of injury from a hard landing under parachute. The jumper distributes the force of the landing in an orderly manner over the most robust areas of the body.

PARACHUTE OPERATION: The performance of all activity for the purpose of, or in support of, a parachute jump or a parachute drop. This parachute operation can involve, but is not limited to, the following persons: parachutist, parachutist in command and passenger in tandem parachute operations, drop zone or owner or operator, jump master, certificated parachute rigger, or pilot. (FAR 105 definition)

PARACHUTIST: A person who intends to exit an aircraft while in flight using a single-harness, dual parachute system to descend to the surface. (FAR 105 definition) (see also SKYDIVER)

PARACHUTIST IN COMMAND: The person responsible for the operation and safety of a tandem parachute operation. (FAR 105 definition) Not necessarily a USPA instructional rating holder.

PARAGLIDING: n. (also Parapente): An activity involving the use of a ram-air inflated wing, resembling a parachute, for gliding. Flights typically initiate by foot-launching from a hill or from a ground-based tow. Because paragliding jumping does not meet the FAA's definition of "the descent of an object to the surface from an aircraft in flight," it is not regulated by the FAA or addressed by USPA.

PARTIAL INVERSION: Inflation malfunction of a round canopy where one side passes through and inflates between two lines of the other side, resulting in two inflated lobes. (see also LINEOVER)

GLOSSARY

PASSENGER PARACHUTIST: A person who boards an aircraft, acting as other than the parachutist in command of a tandem parachute operation, with the intent of exiting the aircraft while in flight using the forward harness of a dual harness tandem parachute system to descend to the surface. (FAR 105 definition) USPA further defines a passenger parachutist as either a licensed skydiver or a tandem student.

PERMEABILITY: The amount or volume of air which can pass through a fabric assembly.

PILOT CHUTE: A small parachute used to initiate and/or accelerate deployment of a main or reserve parachute. (FAR 105 definition)

PILOT CHUTE ASSIST: A method of rigging a static line to a parachute where the static line opens the container and positively extracts the pilot chute before separating from the system. Typically a velcro strip or break cord of known strength is used.

PIN: 1. v. To fly to another jumper and take grips on the jumper (freefall) or canopy (canopy formation). 2. n. The first jumper to make contact with the base, or target jumper, to begin a formation. 3. n. Retaining device that when passed through a closing loop, locks the parachute system closed until activation.

PIN CHECK: n. (jar.) Pre-jump inspection of the parachute.

PLF: (see PARACHUTE LANDING FALL)

PLANE: n. A compressed vertical canopy formation.

PLANFORM: The shape or footprint of a wing surface.

PLANING: v. The act of compressing a parachute stack.

POISED EXIT: A departure from an aircraft wherein the jumper uses an external structure as a brace to assist in gaining a stable position immediately upon leaving the aircraft.

POROSITY: The ratio of open area to closed area in a fabric. Graded as high, low, or zero. Tightly woven and treated material has a lower porosity than loosely woven material.

PRACTICE DEPLOYMENT: An in-air exercise used to learn how to locate and operate a parachute deployment handle prior to opening. It may consist of pulling or throwing a practice or dummy handle (instructor-assisted deployment or static-line jumps) or touching the actual deployment handle in freefall or tandem droguefall.

PREMATURE OPENING: Unintentional opening of a parachute.

PROJECTED LANDING POINT: The expected landing spot on the ground, based on the glide path of the parachute.

PROP BLAST: 1. n. The airflow created by a propeller that is developing thrust. 2. n. (jar.) relative wind on exit

PUD: n. (jar.) An aerodynamically low-profile, soft handle that is ergonomically designed to fit into a clenched fist. Used for various parachute operation handles.

PULL OUT: n. A type of hand-deployed parachute activation system. The jumper pulls a handle connected to the container closing pin and the internally packed pilot chute. (see also HAND DEPLOYED PILOT CHUTE)

PULL-UP CORD: A packing aid used to thread the closing loop through eyelets in the container and removed once the closing pin is inserted.

R

RAM-AIR PARACHUTE: A parachute with a canopy consisting of an upper and lower surface that is inflated by ram air entering through specially designed openings in the front of the canopy to form a gliding airfoil. (FAR 105 definition)

RATING RENEWAL SEMINAR, USPA: A meeting of USPA instructional rating holders to exchange information, introduce and discuss new ideas, and to develop, improve, or assure the quality of skydiving instruction.

RECOMMENDATIONS, USPA: Principles, policies, and concepts applicable to skydiving or a related subject which are derived from experience or theory, compiled by USPA, and offered for guidance.

REGIONAL DIRECTOR, USPA: Members of the USPA Board elected from a specified geographical area and responsible for representing the interests of the skydivers in that USPA Region.

RELATIVE WIND: The relative airflow opposite a body's trajectory, irrespective of the horizon.

RELATIVE WORK (RW): (see FORMATION SKYDIVING)

REMOVABLE DEPLOYMENT SYSTEM (RDS): Primarily used by high performance canopy pilots it is a system that allows the slider and in some cases the deployment bag and pilot chute to be removed after opening and helps decrease drag.

RESERVE PARACHUTE: An approved parachute worn for emergency use to be activated only upon failure of the main parachute or in any other emergency where use of the main parachute is impractical or use of the main parachute would increase risk. (FAR 105 definition)

RESERVE STATIC LINE (RSL): A connection between the main risers and the reserve activation system intended to initiate reserve activation following the release of a deployed main parachute.

REVERSE FLIGHT (FULL STALL): A non-flying canopy maneuver that collapses the canopy and may cause it to spin. Results from depressing the toggles until the trailing edge is lower than the leading edge. May result in an unrecoverable malfunction. (see also STALL and DYNAMIC STALL)

RIB: A vertical and longitudinal fabric membrane that forms the airfoil shape and primary structure of a ram-air canopy.

RIG: (jar.) 1. n. The complete parachute system used for skydiving. 2. v. The act of maintaining, repairing, or modifying a parachute system. 3. v. To don a parachute (Rigging Up).

RIGGER: An FAA-certificated parachute technician. (see also MASTER RIGGER and SENIOR RIGGER)

RIPCORD: An assembly, usually constructed with a metal cable that, when pulled, activates an operation on a parachute system.

RISER DOCK: In canopy formation, a momentum dock that puts the risers into the hands of the receiver. A very advanced technique.

RISER LOOPS; RISER BLOCKS: Gripping loops or devices on a riser that make it easier to grasp.

RISER(S): Webbing straps that connect the main lift webs of the parachute harness to the lines of the canopy.

RSL: (see RESERVE STATIC LINE)

S

SAFETY AND TRAINING ADVISOR (S&TA), USPA: A local person appointed by the USPA Regional Director as his or her representative and who is available to provide advice and administrative assistance as the USPA representative at an individual drop zone or specified area.

SANCTIONED DROP ZONE: A drop zone which has been verified by a USPA Safety and Training Advisor or a USPA Regional Director as complying with the minimum drop zone requirements as stated in the USPA Basic Safety Requirements section of the USPA Skydiver's Information Manual. (see also Drop Zone)

SELF-SUPERVISION: The point within a student's training when he has been cleared by a USPA Instructor to jump without instructor supervision in freefall but has not yet completed all of the requirements for the USPA A license. At USPA Group Member skydiving centers, all skydivers cleared for self-supervision must be current USPA members. See Category E: Introduction of the Integrated Student Program.

SENIOR RIGGER: The initial certification level for FAA riggers that allows its holder to pack and maintain a parachute system and perform simple repairs. (see MASTER RIGGER)

SIM: Abbreviation for Skydiver's Information Manual (this book). (see SKYDIVER'S INFORMATION MANUAL)

SINGLE OPERATION SYSTEM (SOS): Refers to a parachute harness and container operation system with a combined single-point riser release and reserve ripcord handle. Pulling one handle will both release the risers and pull the reserve. (See also TWO-HANDLED SYSTEM)

SINGLE-HARNESS, DUAL-PARACHUTE SYSTEM: The combination of a main parachute, approved reserve parachute, and approved single-person harness and dual-parachute container. This parachute system may have an operational automatic activation device installed. (FAR 105 definition)

SIT FLYING: Upright vertical freefly orientation based on a seated position. (see also CHUTE ASSIS)

SKYBOARD: (see SURFBOARD)

SKYDIVE: 1. n. The descent of a person to the surface from an aircraft in flight when he or she uses or intends to use a parachute during all or part of that descent. 2. v. To jump from an aircraft with a parachute.

SKYDIVER: A person who engages in skydiving.

SKYDIVER'S INFORMATION MANUAL (SIM), USPA (THIS BOOK): The official bound collection of the USPA Basic Safety Requirements, USPA recommendations, relevant FAA references, and other USPA policies and programs that affect the majority of skydivers.

SKYSURFER: A skydiver who jumps with a surfboard (skyboard).

SKYSURFING: 1. A freefall skydiving discipline using a specially rigged surfboard (skyboard). 2. The competition event by that name.

SLIDER: A device which controls a canopy's inflation by progressively sliding down the suspension lines during inflation. Found on most ram-air canopies.

SLINKS: A type of Spectra fabric connector link developed by Performance Designs, Inc., for attaching the lines of the parachute to the risers.

SOLO DEPLOYMENT: Refers to a pull sequence not prompted or cued by the instructor where the student starts and finishes their pull sequence without instructor contact.

SOLO JUMP: A jump where a skydiver is not engaged in formation skydiving.

SOLO JUMPER: A skydiver who is not engaged in formation skydiving.

SOLO SKYDIVER: See solo jumper.

SOLO STUDENT: A skydiving student who uses a single-harness, dual-parachute system.

SOS: (see SINGLE OPERATION SYSTEM)

SPAN: The dimension of a wing measured from tip to tip.

SPEED SKYDIVING: Skydiving discipline in which the goal is to achieve and maintain the highest possible speed for a predetermined amount of time.

SPOTTING: Selecting the correct ground reference point over which to leave the aircraft, selecting the course for the aircraft to fly, and directing the pilot on jump run to that point.

STABILITY: That property of a body which causes it, when its equilibrium is disturbed, to develop forces or movements tending to restore the original condition. In skydiving, control of body position during freefall.

STABLE FREEFALL POSITION: A position attained by a freefalling skydiver in which only controlled, planned movements are made.

STACK: A vertical canopy formation with the jumpers gripping the canopy or lines just below the canopy.

STALL: n. The state of canopy flight control characterized by decreased glide and increased rate of descent. (see DYNAMIC STALL and REVERSE FLIGHT)

STATIC LINE: A line of cable or webbing, one end of which is fastened to the parachute, the other to some part of the aircraft, used to activate and deploy or partially deploy the parachute as the load falls away from the aircraft.

STATIC-LINE JUMP: A parachute jump during which a static line is used to deploy or partially deploy the parachute. Used for training student skydivers.

STEP-THROUGH: (see THREAD-THROUGH)

STUDENT: A skydiver trainee who has not been issued a USPA A license.

SUPERVISION: The general oversight of an activity taking place where the supervisor is readily available for counsel and direction and who is responsible that the activity is satisfactorily completed. (see DIRECT SUPERVISION)

SURFBOARD (SKYBOARD): n. A rigid panel, similar to a snowboard, attached to a jumper's feet.

SUSPENSION LINES: Cords, attached from the bottom of the parachute canopy to the risers, that distribute and suspend the weight of a skydiver under the inflated canopy.

SWOOP: The controlled flight from above of one body to meet or fly close to another body, a stationary object, or the ground.

SWOOP POND; SWOOP DITCH: A water obstacle used as a high-performance landing area.

T

TANDEM JUMP OR TANDEM SKYDIVE: Any skydive made using a tandem parachute system with a tandem student or licensed skydiver attached.

TANDEM JUMPING: A method of skydiving, typically used for training student skydivers where one skydiver shares a tandem parachute system with another.

TANDEM PARACHUTE OPERATION: A parachute operation in which more than one person simultaneously uses the same tandem parachute system while descending to the surface from an aircraft in flight. (FAR 105 definition)

TANDEM PARACHUTE SYSTEM: The combination of a main parachute, approved reserve parachute, and approved harness and dual parachute container, and a separate approved forward harness for a passenger parachutist. This parachute system must have an operational automatic activation device installed. (FAR 105 definition)

TANDEM STUDENT: Any person making a tandem skydive who has not been issued a USPA license.

TARGET: The landing area on a drop zone. For officially sanctioned competition, a three-centimeter disk.

TECHNICAL STANDARD ORDER (TSO): Issued by the FAA, requires compliance with minimum performance standards and specifications for material and products. Parachute specifications are referenced in TSO-C23.

TERMINAL VELOCITY: The equilibrium velocity that a freefalling body can attain against the resistance of the air. The greatest speed at which a body falls through the atmosphere.

THREAD-THROUGH (STEP-THROUGH): (jar.) n. A leg strap configuration on a parachute harness that uses a single piece of adjustable hardware. The leg strap must be un-threaded to be disconnected, or the jumper simply steps into the connected leg straps when donning the rig. (see B-12s)

THREE-RING RELEASE: A type of single point release invented by Bill Booth. The system is based on three interlocking rings on each riser held in place by a small loop that is retained by a cable. Pulling one handle releases both main risers simultaneously or nearly simultaneously.

THROW OUT: 1. n., adj. A type of hand-deployed parachute activation system. The pilot chute is folded into an external pouch, extracted and thrown. A curved closing pin or equivalent locking device on the bridle is extracted as jumper falls away from the pilot chute and bridle, allowing the container to open. (see Hand Deployed pilot chute) 2. v. (jar.) To initiate deployment.

TOGGLES: n. Handles attached to the ends of the steering lines of a parachute canopy. (see also BRAKES)

TRACK: 1. n. A freefall position with the legs fully extended, knees locked, arms swept back, elbows locked, and torso fully extended and slightly bowed forward to achieve the maximum horizontal speed. 2. v. To move at maximum horizontal speed in freefall.

TRACKING SUIT: A 2-piece inflating suit that transforms the body into a human airfoil.

TRIM TABS: A front riser pulley system for adjusting a canopy's angle of incidence or flight attitude.

TSO-C23: (see TECHNICAL STANDARD ORDER)

TURBULENCE: Disturbed air that can affect canopy flight and integrity.

TWO-HANDLED SYSTEM: Refers to a parachute harness and container operation system that uses separate handles for the canopy release and for reserve activation. (see SINGLE OPERATION SYSTEM)

U

UNITED STATES PARACHUTE ASSOCIATION (USPA): A not-for-profit, voluntary membership association of skydivers whose purpose is promoting and representing skydiving. As a division of the NAA, it is the official representative of the FAI for skydiving in the U.S.

UPWIND: The direction from which the wind is blowing.

W

WAIVER: n. 1. Exception to the BSRs filed by a USPA official indicated in SIM Section 2-2. 2. (jar.) A liability release.

WATER JUMP: n. A skydive which includes intentionally landing in an open body of water.

WHUFFO: n. (jar.) Term for a non-skydiver ("Whuffo you jump out of airplanes?") Considered insensitive.

WIND DRIFT INDICATOR (WDI): n. A device used to determine the wind drift which a descending parachute will experience, so constructed as to descend at a rate comparable to a skydiver of average weight descending under a fully deployed main canopy of average specifications. Usually a weighted strip of crepe paper 10 inches wide and 20 feet long.

WING LOADING: n. The jumper's exit weight divided by the area of the parachute canopy, expressed in the United States in pounds per square foot.

WING SUIT: n. A gliding jumpsuit designed with fabric membranes between the legs of the jumper and from each arm to the torso.

Z

ZOO DIVE: A skydive that becomes chaotically disorganized with many jumpers out of position both vertically and horizontally.

Appendix A

FREEFALL HAND SIGNALS

pelvis forward (arch)

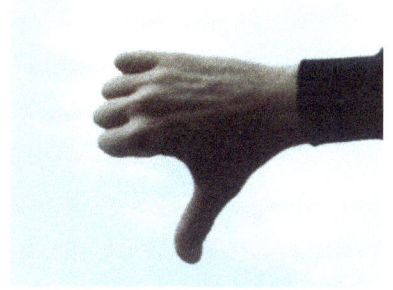

circle of awareness (altitude check)

OK

arch

deploy the parachute (pull)

legs in (retract legs slightly)

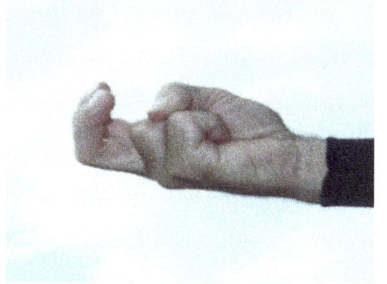

extend legs six inches and hold

open hand (release pilot chute)

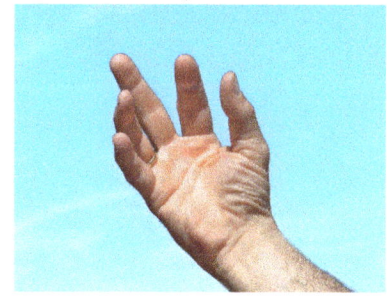

check arm position

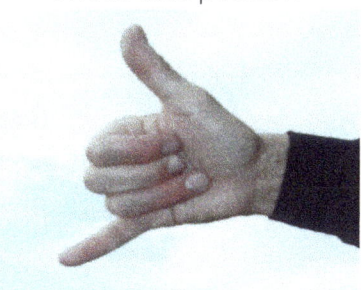

knees together slightly —or— toe taps

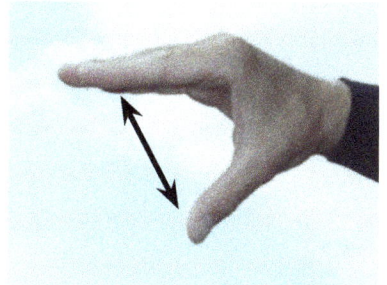

perform the practice deployment sequence

relax (breathe)

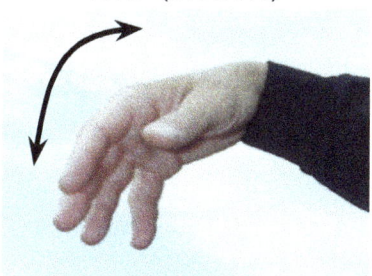

Appendix B

USPA CATEGORY QUIZ ANSWERS

CATEGORY A

1. Approach fixed-wing aircraft from the rear.
   (first-jump course outline)

2. pilot and jumper
   (FAR 91.107.A.1 through .3)

3. movement on the surface (taxi), takeoff, and landing
   (FAR 91.107.A.2)

4. my instructor
   (first-jump course outline)

5. AFF and tandem students: helps student and instructors to leave at the same time all students: to leave at the right place over the ground
   (first-jump course outline)

6. ahead
   (first-jump course outline)

7. best position for deployment
   (first-jump course outline)

8. dives
   (first-jump course outline)

9. a. Land with the wing level and flying in a straight line.

   b. Land in a clear and open area, avoiding obstacles.

   c. Flare to at least the half-brake position. d. Perform a parachute landing fall
   (first-jump course outline)

10. convert forward speed to lift
    (first-jump course outline)

11. Student should demonstrate: feet and knees together, hands and elbows in, roll on landing.
    (first-jump course outline)

12. Note to tandem students: Your instructor may teach you a modified PLF that is more appropriate for tandem equipment.

CATEGORY B

1. USPA Instructor rated for my discipline
   (BSRs 2-1.F.2.b)

2. altitude awareness to recognize and act at the assigned pull altitude
   (Category B outline)

3. ten mph for a round reserve canopy; 14 mph for a ram-air reserve, waiverable by an S&TA
   (BSR 2-1.G.1)

4. Change body position to modify the air flow over my back
   (Category A and B outline)

5. 2,500 feet
   (SIM 5-1.E)

6. a. Before releasing the brakes, spread risers or twist risers to transfer line twist to risers, kick in opposite direction, watch altitude to 2,500 feet.

   b. Pump rear risers or steering controls at the bottom of the stroke while watching altitude to 2,500 feet.

   c. Pull toggles to flare position and hold (or pull down rear risers and hold) and watch altitude. If stubborn, determine controllability with turn and flare by 2,500 feet.

7. Immediately deploy the reserve parachute, but not below 1,000 feet with an SOS system.
   (Category A and B outline)

8. If the canopy flares and turns correctly, it is probably safe to land
   (Category A and B outline)

9. no more than two tries or two seconds to locate and deploy the main pilot chute; if no success, cut away and deploy the reserve
   (SIM Section 5-1.E)

10. Cut away and deploy the reserve.
    (Category A and B outline)

11. Cut away and deploy the reserve.
    (Category A and B outline)

12. local runway headings
    (Instructor)

13. cardinal directions of the reference runway
    (Instructor)

14. local runway length
    (Instructor)

15. downwind (with the wind), base (across the wind but downwind of the target), and final (into the wind)
    (Category A and B outline)

16. local pattern entry altitude
    (Instructor)

17. approaching and departing aircraft
    (Category B outline)

CATEGORY C

1. 5.5 seconds
   (Category C syllabus)

2. altitude, arch, legs, relax
   (Category C syllabus)

3. Pull at the planned altitude, regardless of stability.
   (Category C syllabus)

4. to signal other jumpers
   (Category C syllabus)

5. It protects against hard landings, and all skydivers have hard landings
   (Category C syllabus)

6. the intersection of the base and final approach legs
   (Category C syllabus)

7. shortens the final approach, shortens the base leg, lengthens the downwind leg, and places the planned pattern entry point farther upwind
   (Category C syllabus)

8. 10-20 times the height of the obstacle
   (Category C syllabus)

X-B USPA CATEGORY QUIZ ANSWERS

9. Keep the canopy flying in a straight line at full flight (or as directed by the owner's manual).
   (Category C syllabus or owner's manual)

10. according to the local landing area and obstacles
    (Instructor)

11. keeps them in place and prevents accidental or premature deployment
    (Category C syllabus)

12. top to bottom, back to front
    (Category C syllabus)

13. Pull the cables to release the cloth loop.
    (closed parachute system briefing)

14. information found on the reserve packing data card
    (closed parachute system briefing)

15. rigger's packing seal on the reserve ripcord
    (closed parachute system briefing)

16. east
    (Category C syllabus)

17. Divide the exit weight by the square footage.
    (Instructor)

18. 170 square feet/170 pounds
    (Category C syllabus)

19. when the jumper has control of all the variables and has executed a good flare at the appropriate altitude
    (Category C syllabus)

CATEGORY D

1. 15 seconds
   (Category D outline)

2. altitude, arch, legs, relax
   (Category D outline)

3. Look first in the direction of the turn.
   (Category D outline)

4. rear riser turn with the brakes still set
   (Category D outline)

5. use the rear risers
   (Category D outline)

6. practice with rear-riser flares at altitude with that canopy during a routine jump
   (Category D outline)

7. Disconnect the RSL (if time), contact the building feet first, PLF, cut away after landing on top of a building, wait for competent help.
   (SIM Section 5-1.F)

8. to back up the jumper's emergency procedures
   (SIM Section 5-3.G)

9. Check three-ring release system for correct assembly and RSL; three points of harness attachment for snap assembly or correct routing and adjustment; three operation handles—main activation, cutaway, reserve.
   (Category D outline)

10. place head completely outside the aircraft and look straight down
    (Category D outline)

11. a. below 10,000 feet MSL? 2,000 feet; b. 10,000 feet MSL and above? one mile
    (FAR 105.17)

12. a. below 10,000 feet MSL? three miles
    b. 10,000 feet MSL and above? five miles
    (FAR 105.17)

13. jumper and pilot
    (FAR 105.17)

14. All student jumps must be completed by sunset.
    (SIM Section 2-1.F.9)

15. Determine two lines from the horizon, one ahead and one abreast, and find the intersection of those two lines.
    (Category D outline)

16. clouds and other aircraft
    (Category D outline)

CATEGORY E

1. increases
   (Category E outline)

2. reads unreliably
   (SIM 5-3.J.6.f)

3. Smoothly raise the controls.
   (Category E outline)

4. stable state of decreased glide and increased rate of descent
   (Category E outline)

5. at the end of a flare when the jumper begins to rock back under the canopy
   (Category E outline)

6. full stall
   (Category E outline)

7. Practice different rates of flare entry at different depths of flare
   (Category E outline)

8. Stay well downwind of any obstacle, face into the wind early, disconnect the RSL, land with a PLF, pull one toggle down completely, and after landing, cut away if necessary.
   (Category E outline)

9. ten
   (Category E Open Canopy Orientation)

10. tail or trailing edge
    (Category E Open Canopy Orientation)

11. C, D, and brakes
    (Category E Open Canopy Orientation)

12. top center
    (Category E Open Canopy Orientation)

13. FAA rigger, person jumping the parachute, person under rigger's supervision
    (FAR 105.43)

14. every 180 days
    (FAR 105.43)

15. pilot
    (FAR 91.3.A)

16. to maintain the correct balance; protection in a crash
    (Category E Aircraft briefing)

17. pilot
    (FAR 91.7.B)

18. 14,000 feet
    (FAR 91.211.A.2)

19. 15,000 feet
    (SIM 2-1.M; FAR 91.211.A.3)

20. remain forward until it is time for their group to exit
    (Category E Aircraft Briefing)

21. other canopies
    (Category E outline)

22. see and remain clear of other jumpers.
    (Category E outline)

23. forms a separable link between the main riser and reserve ripcord so that cutting away the main activates the reserve, if the RSL is hooked up
    (SIM Section 5-3.F)

USPA CATEGORY QUIZ ANSWERS X-B

24. The reserve deploys with the main still attached by the other riser.
    (SIM Section 5-3.F.)

25. inspection and maintenance; correct packing, tight line stowage, and stable deployment, all to prevent hard openings
    (SIM Section 5-3.F)

26. Any of the following:
    a. Deploy the main parachute at the correct altitude to avoid AAD activation.

    b. Initiate malfunction procedures high enough to cut away safely and avoid AAD activation

    c. Maintain and correctly operate hand-deployed pilot chutes, especially collapsibles.

    d. Protect equipment before exit to prevent pins or handles from being knocked loose.

    e. Maneuver gently below the AAD's firing range
    (Category E outline)

27. a. Biplane
    Release the brakes on the front canopy only and steer that canopy gently; PLF.

    b. Side by side
    Release the brakes on the dominant canopy only and steer that canopy gently; or release the RSL (if time) and cut away; PLF.

    c. Downplane
    Release the RSL (if time) and cut away.
    (SIM 5-1.E)

CATEGORY F

1. braked turns
   (Category F outline)

2. stalls
   (Category F outline)

3. Flaring from half brakes requires a quicker stroke, the stroke is shorter, and stalls occur sooner.
   (Category F outline)

4. slows descent, changes glide
   (Category F outline)

5. The angle at which the parachute descends towards its projected landing point.
   (Category F outline)

6. Look ahead to find the point on the ground that appears not to rise or sink.
   (Category F outline)

7. The glide path will become steeper as the wind decreases when flying with the wind. The glide path will become steeper as the wind speed increases when flying into the wind.
   (Category F outline)

8. Dip one shoulder slightly in the direction of the turn.
   (Category F outline)

9. to avoid other groups ahead and behind
   (Category F outline)

10. 40 knots
    (pre-flight planning)

11. gauge separation according to position over the ground
    (SIM Section 5-7)

12. lines straight and in place in the center, slider up, tight line stows
    (Category F outline)

13. clear path from snap shackle to guide ring
    (Category F outline)

14. What is the make and model of parachute system you are jumping?
    a. Main canopy?

    b. Harness and container system?

    c. Automatic activation device?
    (equipment data)
    (Instructor)

15. 3,000 feet
    (SIM 2-1.H)

16. 14 mph
    (SIM 2-1.G)

17. a. 1/2 mile

    b. east
    (Category F outline)

18. Avoid the area early during the descent, minimum braked turn necessary to avoid lines, land parallel to the wires, braked landing, prepare for PLF, try to touch only one line at a time, wait for help and confirmation that the power has been turned off and will remain off until recovery operations are complete.
    (SIM 5-1.F)

19. jumpmaster, or spotter
    (Category F outline)

20. DZ policy
    (Instructor)

21. school policy
    (Instructor or pilot)

22. 25
    (SIM 3-1.E, A license)

23. jump without supervision, pack his or her own main parachute, engage in basic group jumps, and perform water jumps
    (SIM 3-1.E, A license)

24. make at least one jump under the supervision of a USPA instructional rating holder
    (SIM Section 5-2, Currency Training)

25. make at least one jump beginning in Category D with a USPA AFF Instructor or in Category B with a USPA IAD Static-Line, or Tandem Instructor before proceeding to unsupervised freefall
    (SIM Section 5-2, Currency Training)

CATEGORY G

1. legs
   (Category G outline)

2. 1,500 feet above planned deployment altitude
   (SIM Section 6-1.C)

3. line twist
   (Category G outline)

4. dives
   (Category G outline)

5. line twist, collision with jumpers, collision with the ground
   (Category G outline)

6. check altitude, establish communication
   (SIM 5-1.H)

7. bridle routing and placement
   (packing lesson)

8. unnecessary wear on the three-ring release webbing and loops
   (Category G outline)

9. covers the hook velcro, which can damage other components, prevents tangles
   (Category G outline)

X-B | USPA CATEGORY QUIZ ANSWERS

10. FAA rigger
    (FAR 65.125.a.1)

11. Ultraviolet rays degrade nylon.
    (Category G outline)

12. shorter life for AAD batteries, stow band degradation
    (Category G outline)

13. loses tackiness
    (Category G outline)

14. distortion
    (Category G outline)

15. FAA
    (rigger briefing)

16. collision with formation, funnel
    (Category G outline)

17. AAD activation near the open door of an aircraft presents a dangerous situation.
    (Category G outline)

18. possibility of AAD activation or other accidental or unplanned pack opening
    (Category G outline)

19. to improve their chances for correct operation, to help prevent premature AAD activations, to comply with the law
    (Category G outline)

20. Deploy the reserve (may not be a safe option with an SOS system).
    (SIM Section 5-1.H)

21. Face into the wind, prepare for PLF, flare to half brakes, protect face and under arms, wait for help.
    (SIM 5-1.F)

22. thunderstorms in the area
    (SIM Section 5-5)

23. thunderstorms in the gust front; rapid and significant changes in winds
    (SIM Section 5-5)

24. each will increase
    (SIM Section 5-5)

CATEGORY H

1. to see others and avoid a collision
   (Category H outline)

2. slow fall position with arms forward and knees down
   (Category H outline)

3. premature deployment
   (Category H outline)

4. Sludge-like dirt and oil deposits cause them to bind.
   (Category H outline)

5. Neutralize the turn and get the canopy overhead.
   (SIM Section 5-1.I)

6. dramatic increase in rate of descent
   (jump experience)

7. Keep them in your hands.
   (Category H outline)

8. collisions with other jumpers, collision with the ground
   (Category H outline)

9. serious injury or death
   (SIM Section 5-1.I)

10. Inflate flotation device, disconnect chest strap and RSL, prepare for PLF, face into wind, flare, hold breath, cut away once feet are wet, remove leg straps, swim upwind; if under the canopy, dive deep and swim away or follow one seam until out from underneath.
    (SIM Section 5-1.F)

11. ten percent
    (Category H outline)

12. no
    (FAR 105.13.a.1)

13. one hour
    (FAR 105.25.a.3)

14. AC 105.2, Appendix 2, or aircraft owner's manual
    (Category H outline)

15. person giving notice
    (FAR 105.15.a.6)

Appendix C

USPA LICENSE STUDY GUIDE | X-C

USPA LICENSE STUDY GUIDE

A. EXAM STUDY INSTRUCTIONS

1. Use this guide to find the correct areas of the Skydiver's Information Manual to study for USPA license written exams.
2. Study guide information for the USPA A license exam is listed in the "Book Stuff" at the beginning of each Category of the Integrated Student Program in SIM Section 4.
3. Look in SIM Section 3 for more information on licenses and all license exams.
4. Refer to the USPA B, C, and D license application and written exam answer sheet available online at uspa.org/downloads.

B. PASSAGES TO STUDY

A LICENSE
SIM Sections:
2-1 (all)
4, all categories
5-1
5-2
6-2
6-8
9, FAR 105

B LICENSE
SIM Sections:
2-1 (all)
4, Category D
4, Category F
4, Category G
4, Category H
5-1
5-2
5-3
6-2
6-4
6-6
9-1 FAR 91.17
9-1 FAR 91.211
9-1 FAR 119.1

C LICENSE
SIM Sections:
2-1 (all)
4, Category C
5-1
5-2
5-6
6-2
6-7
6-8
6-9
6-10
7-1
9-1 FAR 91.15
9-1 FAR 91.151
9-1 FAR 91.409
9-1 FAR 105.17

D LICENSE
SIM Sections:
2-1
4, Category F
4, Category G
4, Category H
5-1
5-2
5-3
5-4
5-5
5-6
6-1
6-2
6-4
6-6
6-7
6-8
6-9
6-10
7-1
9-1 FAR 91.151
9-1 FAR 91.211
9-1 FAR 105.17
9-1 FAR 105.43